Black, White, and *Brown*

The Landmark School Desegregation Case in Retrospect

Editors Clare Cushman and Melvin I. Urofsky
Foreword by Chief Justice William H. Rehnquist

Supreme Court Historical Society
CQ Press
2004

CQ Press
1255 22nd Street, N.W., Suite 400
Washington, D.C. 20037

202-729-1900; toll-free, 1-866-4CQ-PRESS (1-866-427-7737)

www.cqpress.com

Printed and bound in the United States of America
08   07   06   05   04   5   4   3   2   1

⊗The paper used in this publication exceeds the requirements of the American National Standard for Information Sciences—Permanence of Paper for Printed Library Materials, ANSI Z39.48-1992.

Cover photo: Spectators waiting to attend reargument for the *School Segregation Cases* at the Supreme Court on December 7, 1953.

LIBRARY OF CONGRESS CATALOGING-IN-PUBLICATION DATA

Black, white, and Brown : the landmark school desegregation case in retrospect / editors,
   Clare Cushman and Melvin I. Urofsky ; foreword by William H. Rehnquist.
      p. cm.
   Includes bibliographical references and index.
   ISBN: 1-56802-911-X (hardcover : alk. paper)
      1. Brown, Oliver, 1918—Trials, litigation, etc. 2. Discrimination in education—Law and
   legislation—United States—History. 3. Segregation in education—Law and
   legislation—United States—History. 4. African Americans—Civil rights—History. I.
   Cushman, Clare. II. Urofsky, Melvin I. III. Supreme Court Historical Society.

   KF228.B76B58 2004
   344.73'0798–dc22

                                                                        2004045714

Contents

Foreword
CHIEF JUSTICE WILLIAM H. REHNQUIST ...v

MELVIN I. UROFSKY 1
  *"Among the Most Humane Moments
  in All Our History"*
    Brown v. Board of Education
    in Historical Perspective

ANDREW KULL 47
  Post-Plessy, Pre-Brown
    "Logical Exactness" in Enforcing Equal Rights

DAVID W. LEVY...............................67
  Before Brown:
    The Racial Integration
    of American Higher Education

JEFFREY D. HOCKETT 89
  Justice Robert H. Jackson and Segregation
    A Study of the Limitations and Proper Basis
    of Judicial Action

JOHN D. FASSETT 117
  A Plea for the Demise of a Stubborn Myth

BRADLEY D. HAYES 151
  Linda Brown and the Fight for Educational Equality

PAUL E. WILSON 157
  A Time to Lose

  Brown v. Board of Education of Topeka (1954), (1955)............ 171

  ILLUSTRATIONS 184

HERBERT BROWNELL 193
  Brown v. Board of Education Revisited

GERALD N. ROSENBERG 203
  African-American Rights After Brown

JEFFREY D. HOCKETT 241
  The Battle Over Brown's Legitimacy

DIANA E. HESS 275
  Brown as a Classroom Icon

JAMES T. PATTERSON 297
  Legacies and Lessons

MELVIN I. UROFSKY 319
  Selected Bibliography

  Contributors... 325

  Index.. 327

Foreword

Chief Justice William H. Rehnquist

Almost fifty years ago, on May 17, 1954, the Supreme Court issued its unanimous decision in *Brown v. Board of Education*. *Brown* held that legally enforced racial segregation in public schools violated the Equal Protection Clause of the United States Constitution, and struck down the "separate-but-equal" doctrine of *Plessy v. Ferguson*. I had the privilege of serving on the Supreme Court for almost twenty years with Justice Thurgood Marshall, who successfully argued the *Brown* case as a lawyer.

Earl Warren was Chief Justice at that time. When Warren joined the Court, it was sharply divided over the issue of racial segregation in schools. He understood the magnitude of the issue and worked hard and patiently to ensure that the Court's opinion was unanimous. To commemorate the 50th anniversary of this signal decision, the Supreme Court Historical Society has assembled the following collection of essays about the *Brown* decision and its legacy.

❧ M E L V I N I . U R O F S K Y

"*Among the Most Humane Moments in All Our History*"

Brown v. Board of Education in Historical Perspective

On May 17, 1954, before a crowded yet hushed Supreme Court chamber, Chief Justice Earl Warren announced "that in the field of public education the doctrine of 'separate but equal' has no place. Separate educational facilities are inherently unequal."[1] With that one sentence, the Supreme Court of the United States set in motion a social, economic and constitutional revolution that, fifty years after the decision, has not yet been fully played out.

No Supreme Court decision stands in isolation. Cases often reach the nation's highest tribunal because the facts underlying it, many with roots and traditions going back many years, now are at odds with other developments in the larger society. *Brown v. Board of Education* (1954), however, is unique in that its roots go back practically to the settling of the eastern seaboard by Europeans in the early seventeenth century, and its effects are still being debated and analyzed a half-century later. The story of the case is both simple and complex. Simple because at heart it represents the yearning of people of color to be able to live as free and equal citizens, a promise made to them in the Equal Protection Clause of the Fourteenth Amendment in 1868. Complex because in the nine decades following ratification of the Fourteenth Amendment not only had the Equal Protection Clause been ignored, but an intricate legal system of segregation had developed in the southern states, one that many whites took not only for granted but considered morally right as well.

In retrospect we can see that many factors contributed to the Court hearing and deciding *Brown* when it did. Sorting out these strands is the first step in understanding how *Brown* came to the Court, and the impact of what many people consider the most important decision the Court handed down in the twentieth century.

ॐ

After the Civil War, one might have expected the southern states to immediately create some system to segregate the races, but this did not happen. Instead the confusion of Reconstruction led to a number of patterns, any one of which might have emerged as dominant in the end. In some states, the new black codes established fairly rigid separation in certain areas; Texas, for example, required that passenger trains carry one car in which all freedmen had to sit. Segregation in southern schools seemed fairly widespread, although New Orleans had fully integrated public schools until 1877. In North Carolina, Negroes sat on juries with little protest from whites, and shortly after the Civil War the *Raleigh Standard* complained that "the two races now eat together at the same table . . . work together, visit and hold debating societies together."[2] The Reconstruction Act of March 1867[3] encouraged freedmen in all parts of the South to protest, often successfully, against the incipient Jim Crow rules, and following the Civil Rights Act of 1875,[4] blacks could be found riding railroad and steamer lines beside whites.

Inconsistent segregation practices dominated the North and South well into the 1880s. One white proponent of civil rights noted that in Virginia in 1885, blacks "may ride exactly as white people do and in the same cars." That same year, a black man took trains from Boston to South Carolina with the intent of discovering if any restrictions existed; although he was ready to find the worst, he admitted at the end of his journey that he had been treated far better in the South than in the North.[5] Yet one must also note evidence of racial violence in the South, especially lynching, which reached an all-time high in the early 1890s.[6]

But if legally established and enforced segregation did not emerge immediately after the war, the evidence points to a widespread *de facto* separation of the races. There is a great deal of scholarly debate both over the extent of this *de facto* segregation, and also whether blacks as well as whites wanted separation. Howard Rabinowitz has suggested that the real option for blacks vis-à-vis public institutions such as schools and transportation in the 1870s and 1880s was not between segregation and integration (which occurred rarely), but between segregated facilities and total exclusion. Having a black school or a black railroad car would be preferable to having no school or any means of public transportation.[7]

The proponents of overt segregation began to get the upper hand in the 1880s and early 1890s, when one southern state after another adopted Jim Crow regulations that eventually reached into all aspects of life.[8] Initially, segregation laws applied only to schools, passenger trains, steamboats and other forms of transportation, and some states did not enact restrictions until the turn of the century. By then, however, not only had northern liberals abandoned southern blacks, but the Supreme Court had given the process a green light through its rulings in several civil rights cases.

In the last of the great Reconstruction statutes, the Civil Rights Act of 1875, the Republican majority in Congress tried to secure by law some semblance of racial equality that could be protected by the government and the courts. It is doubtful that the country as a whole endorsed this idea, for most white Americans, North and South, believed in white supremacy. Secretary of the Navy Gideon Welles captured the prevailing sentiment when he wrote: "Thank God slavery is abolished, but the Negro is not, and never can be the equal of the White. He is of an inferior race and must always remain so."[9] No one, therefore, expected that civil rights legislation would change white attitudes or compensate for what many took as the natural inferiority of blacks; rather, the law aimed to protect the freedmen from deprivation of the minimal rights of citizenship.

A crucial feature of the law was a prohibition of racial discrimination in public places, what would later be called "public accommodations," which rested on Section 5. of the Enforcement Clause, of the Fourteenth Amendment. Five cases testing the application of this section arose in both the North and the South, and the Court combined them for a single hearing in the *Civil Rights Cases* (1883).[10] The government argued that the Thirteenth Amendment had not only abolished slavery, but had conferred all the rights of free citizens on the former slaves, while the Fourteenth Amendment had given Congress the power to legislate in order to protect those rights.

In his opinion for the Court, Justice Joseph P. Bradley denied both of the government's contentions and in doing so robbed the Amendments of much of their meaning. Bradley stood on fairly firm ground when he claimed that not every example of discrimination against Negroes could be interpreted as a renewal of slavery and therefore that the Thirteenth Amendment could not be invoked as a ban on racial prejudice.

Although the Fourteenth Amendment, on the other hand, had been drafted specifically to ensure freedmen's rights, Bradley denied that Congress had any affirmative powers under the amendment. Congress could act only in a remedial manner; that is, if a state enacted a law that restricted black rights, Congress could act to correct the injustice. In the absence of positive state action, Congress could not initiate legislation in this area. Bradley also indicated that if a state failed to act itself, but by inaction tolerated private discrimination—such as exclusion from hotels, restaurants, and clubs—Congress could still not legislate. This essentially put so-called "private" discrimination beyond the reach of legislation. By this decision, the Court in one stroke severely restricted congressional power under the Fourteenth Amendment to protect the freedmen and left their fate to the states and the courts.

Justice John Marshall Harlan entered a lone dissent, pointing out correctly that the Court had deprived the Fourteenth Amendment of most of its meaning. He also noted the inherent bias in the Court's judgment, since before the war the Court had accorded Congress comparable powers in upholding the various fugitive slave laws.[11] But although he wrote in dissent, Harlan sketched out a theory of "state action" that would become the basis of civil rights jurisprudence six decades later.[12] He utilized the idea of "affected with a public interest," which the Court had expressed in *Munn v. Illinois* (1877),[13] and argued that facilities such as railroads, hotels, restaurants, and theaters filled a public function, which is why they had long been regulated. If such businesses discriminated, then they did so with the consent of the state;

this constituted state action, and could be reached under the Fourteenth Amendment, even using Bradley's limited view of Section 5 power.

The *Civil Rights Cases* effectively barred Congress from both taking affirmative steps against racial discrimination and legislating against private discrimination. But what if the states took positive steps to impose racial segregation? Theoretically, Congress still had the power to reach this type of state action; but if Congress did not choose to act, would the courts find a violation of the Fourteenth Amendment?

In *Hall v. DeCuir* (1878), the Court ruled that states could not prohibit segregation on common carriers, such as railroads, streetcars, or river boats.[14] Chief Justice Morrison R. Waite considered it important that there be uniformity of practice. "No carrier of passengers," he wrote, "can conduct his business with satisfaction to himself, or comfort to those employing him, if on one side of a State line his passengers, both white and colored, must be permitted to occupy the same cabin, and on the other be kept separate."[15] Only Congress, declared Waite, could regulate interstate commerce. A dozen years later the Court approved a Mississippi statute requiring segregation on intrastate carriers in *Louisville, New Orleans & Texas Railway v. Mississippi* (1890);[16] in doing so it acquiesced in the South's solution to the problems of race relations. Only Justices Harlan and Bradley dissented, on the ground that such laws, even if confined to intrastate lines, had an inhibitive effect on interstate commerce.

In the best known of the early segregation cases, *Plessy v. Ferguson* (1896), Justice Henry Billings Brown asserted that distinctions based on race ran afoul of neither the Thirteenth nor the Fourteenth Amendments.[17] Although the Fourteenth had been intended to establish an absolute equality of the races before the law, Brown noted that "in the nature of things it could not have been intended to abolish distinctions based upon color, or to enforce social, as distinguished from political, equality, or a commingling of the two races unsatisfactory to either."[18] Although nowhere in the opinion can the phrase "separate but equal" be found, the Court's ruling approved legally enforced segregation so long as the law did not make facilities for blacks inferior to those for whites.

In a famous and eloquent dissent, Justice Harlan protested that states could now impose criminal penalties on a citizen simply because he or she wished to use public highways and common carriers. Such legislation is "inconsistent not only with equality of rights which pertains to citizenship, National and State, but with the personal liberty enjoyed by everyone within the United States." As for the majority's disingenuous contention that segregation did not in itself constitute discrimination, the Kentucky-born Justice condemned segregation statutes as "conceived in hostility to, and enacted for the purpose of humiliating citizens of the United States of a particular race." Such laws defeated the entire purpose of the Civil War Amendments and made any real peace between the races impossible. "The destinies of the two races . . . are indissolubly linked together, and the interests of both require that the common government of all shall not permit the seeds of race hate to be planted under the sanction of law."[19] Harlan's plea that the "Constitution is color-blind" fell on deaf ears, not only within the Court, but in the country as well. The surest sign of the changing temper of the nation was that where there had been a vociferous protest in the North over the *Civil Rights Cases* thirteen years earlier, the *Plessy* decision caused hardly a ripple.

Between 1900 and 1920, Jim Crow—the legal and systematic segregation of the races—triumphed throughout the former slave states. Signs marked "Whites Only" and "Colored" showed up everywhere—in theaters, restaurants, railroad cars, boarding houses, and even water fountains. South Carolina prohibited blacks and whites from working together in the same room in textile plants, and from using the same entryways, exits, or lavatories, as well. Mississippi statutes required segregation in hospitals, a practice soon adopted by other states. The state even forbade white nurses from attending black patients. Hundreds of Jim Crow laws existed on the books, but the laws by themselves did not provide an adequate gauge of the extent of segregation and its accompanying discrimination in southern life at the turn of the century.[20] The laws established minimal requirements; in practice, segregation normally went well beyond what the statutes required. Institutionalized segregation bred hatred and distrust among both whites and blacks, attitudes that would not be easily broken down even after the Supreme Court reversed itself and declared segregation unconstitutional in 1954.

But in sustaining racial segregation in the early 1900s, the Court certainly reflected popular opinion, not only in the South but in the North as well. When the Court in 1908, again over a strenuous objection from Justice Harlan, upheld a state statute requiring segregation in private schools,[21] editorial opinion proved as favorable above the Mason-Dixon line as below. President Theodore Roosevelt looked down on blacks "as a race and as a man . . . altogether inferior to the whites," despite making a few token black appointments and inviting educator Booker T. Washington to the White House.[22] President Taft had no better opinion, and Woodrow Wilson's was even worse. As the first southerner elected president since the Civil War, Wilson and his lieutenants approved the segregation of all federal facilities. Indeed, racist thought permeated much of the Progressive movement.[23]

ॐ

In the 1930s the National Association for the Advancement of Colored People (NAACP) began its campaign to eliminate segregation, and made a deliberate decision that the only way it could be successful would be by attacking racial prejudice through the courts.[24] In the first major case to reach the Court, Chief Justice Charles Evans Hughes had startled the South by insisting that if it wanted to keep segregated schools, then it would have to make them equal as well.[25] World War II temporarily prevented the NAACP from aggressively pursuing its goals, but the *Gaines* decision had given the organization its first real tactical victory.

During the war, the nation's declared goal of fighting intolerance abroad led black Americans to a greater determination to end racial injustice at home. The NAACP membership grew ten-fold during the war years, to some half-million members. Under pressure from A. Philip Randolph and other black leaders, President Franklin D. Roosevelt took the first step in an executive order on June 25, 1941, directing that Negroes be accepted into job-training programs in defense plants. The order also forbade discrimination by employers holding defense contracts, and set up a Fair Employment Practices Commission (FEPC) to investigate charges of racial discrimination. But aside from this one step, civil rights remained a low priority during the Roosevelt Administration.

Harry S. Truman, overwhelmed at the multiplicity of problems facing him when he suddenly inherited the presidency in April 1945, put up no protest when Congress killed the wartime FEPC. But although Truman came from a segregated border state, he believed discriminating on the basis of race to be wrong. He asked Congress to create a permanent

FEPC, and in December 1946 Truman appointed a distinguished panel to serve as the President's Committee on Civil Rights to recommend "more adequate and effective means and procedures for the protection of the civil rights of the people of the United States."[26] The commission issued its report, "To Secure These Rights," in October 1947, and defined the nation's civil rights agenda for the next generation. The commission noted the many restrictions on African Americans and urged that every American, regardless of race, color, creed or national origin, should have access to equal opportunity in securing education, decent housing, and jobs. Among its proposals, the commission suggested anti-lynching laws, abolishing poll taxes, a permanent FEPC, and strengthening the civil rights division of the Justice Department.[27]

In a courageous act, the President sent a special message to Congress on February 2, 1948, calling for prompt implementation of the commission's recommendations. The southern delegations promptly blocked any action by threatening to filibuster. Unable to secure civil rights legislation from Congress, Truman moved ahead by using his executive authority. He bolstered the Justice Department's civil rights section and ordered it to assist private litigants in civil rights cases. He appointed the first black judge, William H. Hastie, to a U.S. Court of Appeals and named several blacks to high-ranking positions in the administration. Most important, by Executive Order 9981, the president abolished segregation in the armed forces and ordered full racial integration of the nation's military.[28]

While Congress refused to create a federal FEPC, a number of states set up agencies to enforce civil rights. New York acted first in 1945, establishing a State Commission Against Discrimination to investigate and stop prejudice in employment. In the next decade other northern states passed similar laws, so that nearly two-thirds of the entire population of the country came under some form of governmental protection against discrimination in the labor market.

In addition, the Cold War provided a further impetus to the Truman Administration to move forward in the area of civil rights. It was awkward for the United States to court the new third-world countries, consisting of and led by people of color, when it treated its own black citizens so shamefully. Diplomats from Africa could not travel outside of Washington without being treated as pariahs. All this led Secretary of

State Dean Acheson to conclude that race discrimination "remains a source of constant embarrassment to this Government in the day-to-day conduct of its foreign relations; and it jeopardizes the effective maintenance of our moral leadership of the free and democratic nations of the world."[29]

⤳

Against this backdrop the NAACP resumed its campaign, or to be more accurate, intensified its efforts, because even during the war it had not been quiescent, and one of its suits had led the Court to strike down the all-white primary in *Smith v. Allwright.*[30] The NAACP always had as its ultimate goal the elimination of the "separate-but-equal" doctrine, but its leaders, especially Thurgood Marshall, realized that in terms of tactics it would initially have to attack the South's failure to provide equal facilities. In a wide range of cases, decided primarily in lower courts on the basis of *Gaines,* Marshall and his colleagues forced southern states to improve the physical facilities of all-black schools and to pay black teachers on a par with white teachers.[31]

The tide had begun to change in 1941, when the Court for the first time since 1873 upheld a black plaintiff's challenge to segregated transportation. Arthur W. Mitchell, a congressman from Illinois, had bought Pullman accommodations, and he and some white passengers had enjoyed the luxury coach until the train crossed the Arkansas border. There the conductor ejected him from the Pullman car because Arkansas law required segregation. Mitchell filed a complaint, not in court, but with the Interstate Commerce Commission, claiming that he had been discriminated against in violation of the 1887 Interstate Commerce Act. The ICC ruled that the railroad's failure to provide anything except second-class cars for blacks did not constitute an "unjust or undue" discrimination, but on appeal, the Supreme Court upheld Mitchell's complaint.[32] The ruling did not directly affect the *Plessy* doctrine, but following the Hughes dictum in *Gaines,* the Court again warned southern states that if they wished to sustain segregation, truly equal facilities would have to be provided by public carriers for their non-white customers.[33]

In the spring of 1946 Thurgood Marshall and William Hastie came before the Supreme Court to argue another transportation case. Irene

Morgan, a black woman, had boarded a Greyhound bus in Virginia to go to Baltimore, and had been ordered to go to the back of the bus as Virginia state law required. Morgan refused and claimed that since she was an interstate passenger Virginia's law did not apply to her. The bus driver had her arrested, the court fined her ten dollars, and the NAACP took the case on appeal.

By the time the Morgan case reached the Vinson Court it appeared that the Justices had decided to take a closer look at racial classification. Justice Stanley F. Reed, writing for a 7-1 majority, declared that he was merely following the rule of *DeCuir,* and that "seating arrangements for the different races in interstate motor travel require a single, uniform rule to promote and protect national travel."[34] The careful wording of the decision applied only to passengers on interstate buses, and did not affect intrastate Jim Crow laws. But it can hardly be doubted that the Justices had paid close attention to the NAACP brief, which concluded:[35]

> Today we are just emerging from a war in which all of the people of the United States were joined in a death struggle against the apostles of racism. . . . How much clearer, therefore, must it be today than it was in 1877, that the national business of interstate commerce is not to be disfigured by disruptive local practices bred of racial notions alien to our national ideals, and to the solemn undertakings of the community of civilized nations as well.

Only Justice Harold H. Burton dissented, but he did so not to defend segregation[36] as much as to uphold a notion of federalism in which state laws had to be given due respect. He attacked the lack of evidence to support the claim of an undue burden on interstate commerce, and he reviewed various state practices to show how divergent they were: eighteen states prohibited segregation by public motor carriers, twenty made no provision, ten contiguous states required segregation. He disputed the need for a court-ordered uniformity; the fact that eighteen states had already prohibited segregation marked "important progress in the direction of uniformity."[37] Moreover, he warned, the Commerce Clause used here to strike down discrimination might well have to be used in other circumstances to protect such bias.

Burton's warning almost materialized two years later in *Bob-Lo Excursion Co. v. Michigan.*[38] A Detroit amusement park company operated a steamboat to Bois-Blanc Island on the Canadian side of the

Detroit River, a location, as was noted during oral argument of the case, that had once been the end of an underground railroad line for escaping slaves prior to the Civil War. The company had refused to allow a young black woman, Sarah Elizabeth Ray, in a group outing with a number of white classmates, to accompany them on the ride. The assistant general manager later testified that company policy excluded "so-called 'Zoot suiters,' the rowdyish, the rough and the boisterous, and it also adopted the policy of excluding colored."[39] The company claimed that the Michigan Civil Rights Act had no applicability since the steamboat ran in foreign commerce.

Under its prior decisions, the Court should have upheld the company's claim, but instead a majority led by Justice Wiley Rutledge evaded the precedents by ruling that the commerce, although technically foreign, was actually "highly local" with the island "economically and socially, though not politically, an amusement adjunct of the city of Detroit." The Court thus distinguished the earlier cases because they supposedly did not involve "locally insulated" situations; moreover, in neither of the earlier cases had anyone tried to exclude blacks totally as Bob-Lo had done here. Rutledge evidently had wanted to make his opinion much more of an attack on segregation in general, but Felix Frankfurter convinced him that this was not the case and the time not yet ripe.[40] Justice Robert H. Jackson and the Chief Justice dissented, not to support discrimination, but because the majority opinion allowed state power to control interstate commerce. "The Court admits," wrote Jackson, "that the commerce involved in this case is foreign commerce, but subjects it to the state police power on the ground that it is not very foreign."[41]

As Herman Pritchett noted, *Bob-Lo* "highlighted the Court's problem in attempting to achieve equalitarian goals through the cold-blooded and clumsy constitutional concept of commerce."[42] Justice William O. Douglas picked up on this theme in his concurrence, in which he suggested that a revived Equal Protection Clause would be a far better ground on which to base a decision, since in essence what the young woman wanted was the opportunity to ride on the boat. "If a sister State undertook to bar Negroes from passage on public carriers, that law would not only contravene the federal rule but also invade a 'fundamental individual right which is guaranteed against state action by the Fourteenth Amendment.' Nothing short of at least 'equality of legal right' in obtaining transportation can satisfy the Equal Protection Clause."[43]

⌇

African Americans had been discriminated against in housing as well as in other areas of private life, and in confronting this issue the Justices struck a blow against racial bias that would have far-reaching effects later on. In 1917 the Court had voided local residence ordinances enforcing racial segregation as a deprivation of property rights in violation of the Fourteenth Amendment.[44] To get around this ruling, white property owners turned to restrictive covenants which, as private agreements between buyers and sellers, presumably did not come within the reach of the Due Process or Equal Protection Clauses.

Immediately after the war some commentators predicted that if a case reached the Supreme Court, the Justices would find enforcement of the restrictions unconstitutional.[45] By the time a case did reach the Court, the Cold War had erupted, and at an NAACP lawyers conference on January 26, 1947, Francis Dent predicted that given the current state of international relations, the Court "would be most loath to uphold and enforce restrictive covenants since it would be embarrassing to the American position in foreign policy in which we propose to be the leader of the democratic forces."[46]

In *Shelley v. Kraemer* (1948),[47] Chief Justice Fred Vinson ruled for all six sitting Justices that so long as the discriminatory intent of the covenants had to be enforced in state courts, then the states were sanctioning racial discrimination in violation of the Fourteenth Amendment. The Justices did not rule the covenants themselves illegal, since private discrimination remained constitutionally permissible, but it did make them unenforceable. In a companion case the Court also voided enforcement of restrictive covenants in the District of Columbia. Although the Fourteenth Amendment did not apply to the national government, the Chief Justice held that such agreements violated the 1866 Civil Rights Act, and that it went against public policy to allow a federal court to enforce an agreement that was unenforceable in state courts.[48]

The importance of the case lay not just in its immediate results, or even in the fact that this was the strongest statement yet made by the

Court against segregation. By expanding the notion of state action to include enforcement of a contract by state courts, the decision greatly expanded the meaning of state action. In the future, the Warren Court would use the nexus of state action to strike down any form of segregation that had even a remote connection to state government.[49] The state action doctrine would prove a potent tool against discrimination, putting teeth into the Fourteenth Amendment's Equal Protection Clause.

Following *Shelley,* the Court began to hear more and more cases involving claims of racial segregation. Some cases involved restrictive covenants,[50] some involved labor unions,[51] but everyone recognized that the most explosive issue would be segregation in public schools.

~

In 1948, a few months before *Shelley,* the Court heard and decided the case of Ada Lois Sipuel, a black woman who had been excluded from the University of Oklahoma Law School.[52] State law prohibited the university from accepting African Americans; in fact, the legislature was so vehement in its opposition to racially integrated education that it enacted a variety of statutes calling for fines of $100 to $500 a day against any institution that taught whites and blacks together, and any student—white or black—attending such a school could be fined five to twenty dollars a day.

The NAACP immediately sued in state court for admission, knowing it would lose, but after Oklahoma's highest court upheld the segregation statutes, the NAACP sought review in Washington. The Supreme Court granted certiorari, and heard oral argument on the case in the first week of 1948. Only four days later, the Justices handed down a *per curiam* opinion ordering Oklahoma to provide Sipuel with a legal education "in conformity with the equal protection clause of the Fourteenth Amendment and provide it as soon as it does for applicants of any other group."[53] It sent the case back to the Oklahoma Supreme Court, which now had no choice but to order the university to admit Sipuel to the existing all-white law school, open a separate one for her, or close the existing law school until such time as there would be one for Negroes.

The state Board of Regents angrily created a law school overnight, roping off a small section of the state capitol in Oklahoma City and assigning three teachers to attend to the instruction of Sipuel and "others similarly situated." Sipuel would have nothing to do with this farce, and more than a thousand white students on the University of Oklahoma campus held a protest rally against the Regents' decision. Addressing the rally, one law school professor decried the action as "a fake, a fraud, and . . . I think it is indecent." When the NAACP appealed back to the Supreme Court, a majority of the Justices refused to consider whether the state had in fact established an equal facility. The Chief Justice worked hard to keep the brethren from going beyond what he termed "the only question before us," namely, "whether or not our mandate has been followed." According to Vinson, "it is clear that it has been followed."[54] In a 7-2 opinion, from which Murphy and Rutledge dissented, the Court held that the original *Sipuel* case had not presented the issue of whether the Equal Protection Clause prevented a state from establishing a separate law school for blacks.[55] To a friend Rutledge wrote: "I was not greatly surprised at the outcome. . . . It is not for me to criticize the action of my brethren, at any rate in any public way other than by speaking in dissent, but I can say to you in confidence that this is not the only time this term when I have felt great discouragement resulting from action taken by the Court."[56]

The NAACP could not claim any real victory in the *Sipuel* case, mainly because the Court still refused to face the central issue of whether separate education could be truly equal under the Constitution. The strategy that the organization had been relying on for more than a decade had been to force the southern states to pay so much to make black facilities equal to that of whites that in the end the states would finally agree to integration because of the costs involved. One of the NAACP expert witnesses in the state trial of Sipuel's suit was Walter Gellhorn of Columbia. During a recess he spoke with Mac Q. Williamson, the attorney general of Oklahoma, who was defending the state's Jim Crow law. "I was saying to him how I thought that even if they were eventually able to persuade the Supreme Court that the facilities of the Negro law school were equal," Gellhorn recalled, "what was the state going to do when a Negro applied for a medical education—build him a whole medical school? He suddenly saw a flash of light, I guess, and struck his forehead with his palm as the revelation hit. 'Oh, my God,' he said, 'suppose one of them wanted to be a petroleum engineer! Why, we've got the biggest petroleum-cracking laboratory in the country here.' And I think the fire went out of his case after that."[57]

Perhaps some southerners like Williamson saw the economic problems of continued segregation as potentially ruinous, but as long as *Plessy* remained unchallenged, the NAACP saw no way to force the issue. Thurgood Marshall and his staff, while dropping hints in their legal briefs that separate could never be truly equal, had so far seen no indication that the Justices had an inclination to overrule *Plessy*, much less even open up that avenue.

Then on June 5, 1950 the Court handed the NAACP three major victories. In *Henderson v. United States*,[58] the Court struck down the practice of segregated dining cars on interstate carriers. The Court still did not address the core issue of separate but equal, but it was making it more difficult and expensive for interstate carriers to meet the standard.

Then it once again slapped down the University of Oklahoma. Following the *Sipuel* decision, the University had grudgingly admitted 68-year-old George W. McLaurin to its graduate school, where he hoped to earn a doctorate in education. But McLaurin had to sit in the corridor outside the regular classroom, use a separate desk on the mezzanine of the library, and eat alone in a dingy alcove in the cafeteria and at a different time than did the white students. McLaurin, who had a masters degree and had long been a teacher in an all-black college, came before a special three-judge federal district court and declared that it was "quite strange and humiliating to be placed in that position." The district court nonetheless turned McLaurin down,[59] and Thurgood Marshall appealed the case directly to the Supreme Court.

When the Court accepted the appeal, university officials allowed McLaurin inside the classroom but surrounded his seat with a railing marked "Reserved for Colored." White students tore the sign down and protested until the university relented and permitted McLaurin to sit in an unmarked row set aside for him. They also let him onto the main floor of the library, and let him eat at the same time as white students, but still in a separate place. In its brief to the Court, Oklahoma described these restrictions as merely nominal, and necessary for the university to obey the state's separate-but-equal laws. The state, however, portrayed a dark picture of the social turmoil that would result should McLaurin be allowed to intermingle freely with the white students.

The Court now had to begin facing up to the core issue of segregation. Unlike the situation in *Sipuel,* the state had not attempted to shuttle McLaurin off to a completely separate school; he received the same education as white students in objective terms—same courses, same buildings, same faculty, same state outlay of funds per pupil. But he had been forced to sit by himself, eat by himself, and study by himself; in short, he had been segregated. Did this in any way make his education inferior?

At the same time it heard the Oklahoma case, the Court also heard the NAACP argue the case of Heman Marion Sweatt, a black mailman who sought admission to the University of Texas Law School. Sweatt had first applied for admission in 1946, about the same time that Ada Sipuel tried to get into Oklahoma, and a trial court in Travis County gave the state six months to establish a law school at the all-black Prairie View University. Prairie View represented all that was wrong with segregated higher education; it had a ramshackle physical plant and gave college credit for broom-making and other vocational skills. If the state did not establish a law school, then Sweatt would have to be admitted to the University of Texas in Austin.

The president of the University of Texas, Homer Rainey, also believed that segregation should end, and his remarks about providing better education opportunities for blacks so displeased the trustees that they fired him and replaced him with an arch-segregationist, Theophilus Schickel Painter. Texas fought the case at every step of the way, and when the original *Sipuel* decision came down, even went so far as to appropriate three million dollars to create a new Texas State University for Negroes, of which $100,000 would be earmarked for the establishment and maintenance of a law school. In the meantime the state abandoned the Prairie View travesty, and for the period until the new Texas State University for Negroes would be in operation, opened a law school in downtown Austin, just blocks away from the state capital and the University of Texas. The school consisted of three small rooms in a basement, three part-time faculty members who were first-year instructors across town at the regular law school, a library of 10,000 volumes and access to the state law library in the capital. It would open on March 10, 1947 if Sweatt chose to attend. He did not and went back to court.

The Court that heard the McLaurin and Sweatt cases had lost two of its most liberal members, Frank Murphy and Wiley Rutledge, who had been replaced by Tom Clark and Sherman Minton, neither of whose record gave civil libertarians much comfort. But Clark, in a memorandum to the brethren, said he believed that both cases had to be reversed. The restrictions applied to McLaurin appalled him, and directly implicated the *Plessy* doctrine. While he was not willing at the time to overrule *Plessy,* he laid out a number of reasons why the precedent should not apply to graduate schools.[60]

The Justices discussed the two cases at their conference on April 8, 1950. It is one sign of the changing attitude within the Court, and one may venture in the country as well, that in both cases they unanimously agreed to uphold the challenges of the black plaintiffs.[61] The Court did not go as far as Thurgood Marshall would have liked, but it opened the door at least a crack, large enough for the NAACP to take hope and move ahead. Moreover, in a move no one had anticipated, the Justice Department filed *amicus* briefs in both cases bluntly urging the Court to abandon *Plessy.* The Justices were still not ready. In a memo to Vinson, Frankfurter urged that the Court "now not go a jot or tittle beyond the *Gaines* test. The shorter the opinion, the more there is an appearance of unexcitement and inevitability about it."[62]

Vinson did in fact draft narrow opinions in both cases and, as he had hoped, managed to get a unanimous Court in both cases. He announced the two cases together, along with the *Henderson* opinion. In the case of George McLaurin, Vinson made no bones about the Court's view that Oklahoma had treated him shamefully, and these "inequalities" (the Court chose not to use the word "segregation") had to be ended. Such indignities would, in fact, harm McLaurin's education. McLaurin, Vinson declared:[63]

> is attempting to obtain an advanced degree in education, to become, by definition, a leader and trainer of others. Those who will come under his guidance and influence must be directly affected by the education he receives. Their own education and development will necessarily suffer to the extent that his training is unequal to that of his classmates. State-imposed restrictions which produce such inequalities cannot be sustained.

As to the state's argument that lifting the restrictions would not make any difference in how other students treated McLaurin, Vinson responded:[64]

> There is a vast difference—a Constitutional difference—between restrictions imposed by the state which prohibit the intellectual commingling of students, and the refusal of individuals to commingle where the state presents no such bar. . . . The removal of the state restrictions will not necessarily abate individual and group predilections prejudices and choices. But at the very least, the state will not be depriving appellant of the opportunity to secure acceptance by his fellow students on his own merits.

In the Texas case, the state had contended that it had in fact created an equal law school, and the fact that Sweatt chose not to go there did not mean that he had to be admitted to the University of Texas. But if nothing else, the Justices knew what made a good law school, and unanimously rejected the state's claim that its separate law school for blacks was equal to that at Austin. According to the Chief Justice:[65]

> [T]he University of Texas Law School possesses to a far greater degree those qualities which are incapable of objective measurement but which make for greatness in a law school. Such qualities, to name but a few, include reputation of the faculty, experience of the administration, position and influence of the alumni, standing in the community, traditions and prestige. It is difficult to believe that one who had a free choice between these law schools would consider the question close.

The Court ordered Sweatt admitted to the University of Texas Law School, the first time it had ever ordered a black student admitted to a previously all-white institution.

Some southern states promptly responded to the *Sweatt* decision. South Carolina, after *Sipuel,* had established a black law school at South Carolina State College, but after *McLaurin* and *Sweatt,* the state closed down the State College law school and gradually began to accept blacks into the previously all-white University of South Carolina Law School.

Although the NAACP and the Justice Department had invited the Court to reexamine the *Plessy* doctrine, the Justices had declined. But in detailing how the inequalities afflicting George McLaurin detracted from the quality of his education and how the separate law school in Texas lacked the intangible aspects of a great law school, the opinions in the two cases did in fact indicate that the Court, willingly or not, now stood ready to reconsider the separate-but-equal doctrine. For

Thurgood Marshall, the Texas opinion was "replete with road markings telling us where to go next."[66] The NAACP would now attack the *Plessy* doctrine frontally, by massing overwhelming evidence to show that separate education could never be truly equal.

⤳

Some members of the Court had anticipated that a direct attack against separate but equal would soon be on their doorstep. Seventeen southern and border states, as well as the nation's capital, legally required racial segregation in public schools; another four states permitted it. The attack on segregation *per se* and not just on the lack of equal facilities had been the goal of the NAACP for years, but in deciding to take on these cases Thurgood Marshall and his legal team knew they would face formidable obstacles. On June 7, 1952, the Court announced it would hear arguments the following December in cases challenging the school segregation laws of Delaware, Virginia, South Carolina and Kansas, as well as the District of Columbia. The Court consolidated the cases with the Kansas appeal as the lead case, according to Justice Clark, so that "the whole question would not smack of being a purely Southern one."

In the same Term as the brethren wrestled with the school cases they also heard a challenge to the South's white primary system. For more than fifty years the Jaybird Democratic Association of Fort Bend County in Texas, just southwest of Houston, had been holding a May primary, separate from the official one run by the county the following month. The criteria for voting in the Jaybird election were almost identical to those of the county, except that blacks could not participate (as they did in the county primary thanks to *Smith v. Allwright*[67]), and in court the Jaybird officials acknowledged that their intent had been to exclude Negroes. Whoever won the Jaybird primary always won in the county primary and in the general election. The Jaybirds argued that they ran a private canvass without money from or regulation by the state, and therefore their exclusion of blacks did not qualify as state action.

Writing for the Court in *Terry v. Adams*, however, Justice Hugo L. Black saw the Jaybird primary as a subterfuge, one tolerated by the state to defeat the purpose of the Fifteenth Amendment. "The only election that has counted in this Texas county for more than fifty years has been that held by the Jaybirds. . . . [It] has become an integral part, indeed the only effective part, of the elective process that determines who shall rule and govern in the county."[68] Only Sherman Minton accepted the Jaybird's claim of being a private group, and he noted in his dissent that the record "will be searched in vain for one iota of state action sufficient to support an anemic inference" that the official government had been involved in the plan.[69]

The major civil rights issue that Term, of course, remained the school cases. The Justices had assigned an unusual three days to hear oral arguments, December 9, 10 and 11, and then met for the first time in conference to discuss the matter on the 13th. Not surprisingly, they could not reach agreement, and there has been some disagreement over exactly who on the Court was ready to strike down *Plessy.* For a number of years, scholars followed the version put forward in what is undoubtedly the classic study of the case, Richard Kluger's **Simple Justice.**[70] By this account, the Justices stood deeply divided after the initial arguments. Frankfurter later wrote to Reed that he had no doubt that if the segregation cases had been decided earlier, there would have been at least four dissents, by Vinson, Reed, Jackson and Clark, and multiple majority opinions. Law clerks at the time believed that a majority of the Justices would not have voted to overrule *Plessy,* and John W. Davis, who argued on behalf of South Carolina, commented after the oral argument that "I think we've got it won, five-to-four—or maybe six-to-three."[71]

By this accounting, Black and Douglas had been prepared to overturn segregation from the start, and had the support of Burton and Minton. Frankfurter and Jackson, although personally opposed to segregation, had reservations about the Court's power in this area as well as how such a reversal of *Plessy* would be received in the South, and Frankfurter in particular urged caution and delay. Vinson and Reed, both from Kentucky, saw nothing wrong with segregation so long as the southern states provided equal facilities, and Clark leaned in their direction.

Much of this account relies on notes and statements made after the Court finally decided the segregation cases in May 1954. In a memorandum to the files written on the day Earl Warren announced the *Brown* decision, Justice Douglas declared that:[72]

> In the original conference there were only four who voted that segregation in the public schools was unconstitutional. Those four were Black, Burton, Minton and myself. Vinson was of the opinion that the *Plessy* case was right and that segregation was constitutional. Reed followed the view of Vinson and Clark was inclined that way. In the 1952 conference Frankfurter and Jackson viewed the problem with great alarm and thought that the Court should not decide the question if it was possible to avoid it. Both of them expressed the view that segregation in the public schools was probably constitutional. Frankfurter drew a distinction between segregation in the public schools in the States. He thought that segregation in the public schools of the District of Columbia violated due process but he thought that history was against the claim of unconstitutionality as applied to the public schools of the States.

The problem is that Douglas's memo is not completely reliable, given the bad blood between himself and Frankfurter, and he wrote these memos to the file with a distinct eye to making sure that historians would appreciate his view of what happened.[73] At the same time, Frankfurter also left a considerable paper trail, and told many people that he had delayed the decision in *Brown* in order to help the Court reach the right judgment.[74]

Recent scholarship, as well as common sense, tells us that the supposed divisions on the bench in 1952 could not have been that concrete, since with the exception of one person, the Court that handed down the unanimous decision in *Brown* in 1954 was the same Court that first heard it in 1952. In an exhaustive survey of manuscript records that had been unavailable to earlier scholars, Mark Tushnet and Katya Lezin have suggested that there was less division on the Court than had been supposed, and that while Frankfurter supplied a format on which the Warren Court could agree, the key person in shaping the Warren Court's mind may well have been Justice Jackson.[75]

In the last year of the Vinson Court, the segregation cases worried all of the Justices. The Court, in granting review, could no longer avoid the question of whether segregation, even in equal facilities, violated the Constitution; they would either have to overrule *Plessy* or reaffirm it. Frankfurter's caution on segregation has occasionally been misinterpreted as hostility to civil rights or support for the separate–but–equal doctrine. In the late forties Frankfurter began a file on school segregation for his personal use, and understood how sensitive and volatile a departure from separate but equal would be. This added to his already cautious approach to decision-making, and he kept warning his colleagues in the pre-*Brown* cases to write as narrowly as possible. Instead of charging up to the central—and to Frankfurter the inescapable—question of whether segregation violated the Constitution, he preferred a more conservative approach, taking cases as they came and deciding them on the narrowest possible grounds. The Court did not have to "go out and meet problems," he told his colleagues.[76]

But Frankfurter's commitment to civil rights should not be doubted. He had been an early supporter of the NAACP, and in every case involving civil rights for African Americans that came before the Court in his twenty-three year tenure, he voted to support the claims of black Americans. It was Frankfurter who hired the first black clerk on the high court and, as he told Paul Freund, "I don't care what color a man has, any more than I care what religion he professes or doesn't."[77] William T. Coleman, Jr., who broke the color barrier in clerking for Frankfurter in the October 1948 Term, always considered Frankfurter a champion of civil rights, but one who felt constrained by the limits of judicial restraint.[78]

Frankfurter and Jackson, the Court's two leading advocates of judicial restraint, did not know whether the Court could reach out and summarily overturn a half-century of precedent to invalidate segregation. Frankfurter hoped that history might shed some light on what the framers of the Fourteenth Amendment had intended, and he set his law clerk, Alexander Bickel, to work researching that topic. Bickel's labors yielded a lengthy memorandum that, at best, indicated an ambiguity on the part of those who drafted and then voted to ratify the amendment. While it certainly did not provide the support Frankfurter wanted, to his credit he circulated the memorandum so that his colleagues, whatever their views, might be able to consult it.[79]

Frankfurter correctly understood that if the Court decided to reverse *Plessy*, it could not do so by a 5-4 or even a 6-3 vote; it would have to be unanimous. According to Bickel, the Justice worried that a decision striking down segregation would be disobeyed, "which would be the beginning rather than the end of a controversy."[80] So with the exception of Douglas and Black, all the other Justices had good reason to want the cases delayed. Some merely wanted to avoid a hard decision; for

Frankfurter procrastination might be the only way eventually to bring the Court around to a position acceptable to all of its members. During that spring of 1953, Frankfurter described himself as a *Kochleffel,* a cooking spoon, stirring things up and keeping them simmering until the right time would come for the Court to act.[81]

As the Term came to an end, Frankfurter circulated a series of questions that he suggested should be addressed by counsel when they re-argued the case. For once the brethren agreed with him, and at the last conference of the Term on May 29, 1953, the Court set down the segregation cases for re-argument the following fall. The Court asked all sides to address the issues of (1) congressional intent in the drafting of the Civil War Amendments; (2) what the framers of these amendments understood regarding segregation in public schools; (3) whether federal courts could abolish public school segregation; and (4) what kinds of remedies the Court should adopt if it found *Plessy* inconsistent with the Fourteenth Amendment.[82]

Frankfurter's demand for caution and delay found a ready response with the Chief Justice. But as recent scholarship has shown, Vinson, while he may have been uncomfortable at the idea of directly overruling *Plessy,* had nonetheless been moving steadily in that direction. The 1950 trilogy of civil rights cases put a "hydraulic pressure" on all the Justices, but especially on those most wary of a broad-based challenge to segregation.[83] It would appear that the Chief Justice's real concerns lay primarily in matters of timing and the scope of the remedy.[84] Had he overcome these considerations earlier, it might well have been, as Philip Kurland has suggested, that Vinson and not his successor could have written the unanimous opinion in *Brown.*[85]

Then on September 8, 1953, Fred Vinson unexpectedly died of a heart attack in his Washington hotel apartment at the age of sixty-three. All the members of the Court came to his funeral in Louisa, Kentucky, and at the graveside at least one of them quietly rejoiced in his passing. Felix Frankfurter wrongly viewed Vinson, despite his opinions in *Sipuel, Shelley* and *Sweatt,* as having been the chief obstacle to the Court reaching a workable and a judicially defensible settlement of the segregation cases. With the five consolidated cases due for reargument that fall, Frankfurter viewed Vinson's death as almost providential. "This is the first indication I have ever had," he somewhat maliciously told a former clerk, "that there is a God."[86] Three weeks later, Dwight Eisenhower named Earl Warren as Chief Justice of the United States, and a new era in American constitutional history began.

᠅

The Court, with Earl Warren presiding, heard reargument in the cases beginning December 7, 1953. Instead of the usual hour permitted for oral presentation, the Justices sat through an unprecedented ten hours spread over three days. The redoubtable John W. Davis, a former solicitor general of the United States, represented South Carolina, and he defended racial segregation in an emotional coda to a long and distinguished career. He denied that the Court had any authority to intrude in an area reserved for the states alone, or interfere with practices hallowed by the usages of time. "To every principle," he intoned, "comes a moment of repose when it has been so often announced, so confidently relied upon, so long continued, that it passes the limits of judicial discretion and disturbance."[87] T. Justin Moore, the attorney for the Commonwealth of Virginia, asked the Court to understand that "We recognize that there are a great many people of the highest character and position who disapprove of segregation as a matter of principle or as ethics. We think that most of them really do not know the conditions, particularly in the South, that brought about that situation."[88]

For Thurgood Marshall, leader of the NAACP legal team, the moment was equally dramatic; his very presence in the courtroom symbolized what he demanded of the Court and of the nation—equality for all people regardless of the color of their skin. He condemned school segregation laws as nothing but Black Codes, which could only be sustained if the Court found "that for some reason Negroes are inferior to all other human beings." Marshall directly answered the arguments of the southern lawyers when he told the Court:[89]

> I got the feeling on hearing the discussion yesterday that when you put a white child in a school with a whole lot of colored children, the child would fall apart or something. Everybody knows that is not true.
>
> Those same kids in Virginia and South Carolina—and I have seen them do it—they play in the streets together, they play on their farms together, they go down the road together, they separate to go to school, they come out of school and play ball together. They have to be separated in school.

> There is some magic to it. You can have them voting together, you can
> have them not restricted because of law in the houses they live in. You can
> have them going to the same state university and the same college, but if
> they go to elementary and high school, the world will fall apart.

To buttress his case, Marshall argued that segregation not only violated
the Constitution, but had adverse and lasting psychological effects on
black children who were consigned to an obviously inferior position.
The NAACP submitted a "Brandeis brief," citing the latest social science research to support this contention.[90]

The decision on segregation in education did not come down until
the following spring. Part of the delay may be attributed to the fact
that Warren, who held only an interim appointment, did not receive
Senate confirmation until March. But the Chief Justice used that time
to "mass the Court," so that when he began reading the opinion in
Brown v. Board of Education at 12:52 P.M. on May 17, 1954, he spoke
for a unanimous bench.[91]

Considering its epochal significance, the *Brown* decision was decep-
tively simple, running only eleven pages;[92] Warren intended it to be short
enough so that the nation's newspapers could run it in its entirety. The
history of the Fourteenth Amendment and its relation to education, which
the Court had asked both sides to argue, had been "inconclusive"—in part
because public education in the South in 1868 had been so primitive that
no one had bothered to think about it. Warren then briefly examined the
Plessy doctrine and noted the extent of segregation in northern as well as
southern states. Times had changed, Warren declared, and "[i]n approaching this problem, we cannot turn the clock back to 1868 when the
Amendment was adopted, or even to 1896 when *Plessy v. Ferguson* was
written. We must consider public education in the light of its full development and its present place in American life throughout the Nation."[93]
Education played a crucial role in training people to become produc-
tive members of society; even more important, it prepared them to be
citizens and to participate in the critical political choices facing the country. When the state undertook to provide education, it had to do so on
equal terms to all.

By now Warren had read through two-thirds of the opinion, and he
finally reached the crucial question: "Does segregation of children in public schools solely on the basis of race . . . deprive the children of the

minority group of equal educational opportunities?" Pausing for a moment, Warren said "We unanimously believe it does." Reaffirming the eloquent dissent of the first Justice Harlan in *Plessy*, that separate could never be equal, Warren declared that to segregate black schoolchildren[94]

> from others of similar age and qualifications solely because of their race generates a feeling of inferiority as to their status in the community that may affect their hearts and minds in a way unlikely ever to be undone. . . . Segregation with the sanction of law, therefore, has a tendency to retard the educational and mental development of Negro children.

As a result, the Court concluded "that in the field of public education the doctrine of 'separate-but-equal' has no place. Separate educational facilities are inherently unequal."[95] When Warren announced that the decision was unanimous, he later recalled, "a wave of emotion swept the room."[96]

Each member of the Court understood the importance of the decision, and knew that the opinion would be widely and closely read. They knew they did not have to convince black Americans and the many northern whites who already believed the Fourteenth Amendment prohibited official racism, and they also recognized that unregenerate racists would disagree no matter what the Court said. But the Court hoped to reach those who could be persuaded, and who could be brought to understand the need to do away with state-sanctioned segregation. In a memorandum accompanying a draft of the *Brown* opinion, Earl Warren explained that he had operated on the theory that the opinions should be short, readable by the lay public, "non-rhetorical, unemotional and, above all, nonaccusatory." He saw this as the one chance to bring as many southern whites as possible to understand and support the decision.[97]

The last paragraph of the *Brown* opinion showed Warren's famed political astuteness. Noting the wide applicability of the decisions and the complexity of devising an appropriate solution, he invited the parties to assist the Court in fashioning a proper remedy and declared that arguments would be heard that fall. The "wide applicability" phrase broadcast the intention of the Court to order desegregation in all school districts, North and South, urban and rural. The reference to the complexity of the problem and the delay in issuing implementing orders signaled to the South that the Justices recognized the emotional crisis that the decision would cause, and that they would allow time for the states to accustom themselves to the idea. By inviting the different parties to join in fashioning a remedy, the Court hoped that the Jim Crow states would cooperate and thus avoid the imposition of harsher solutions should they refuse. Finally, Warren carefully framed the opinion to apply to only one area, the legal segregation of children by race in primary and secondary public schools, the group most likely to win public sympathy as victims of racism. The decision did not strike down all Jim Crow laws, nor declare all discriminatory statutes unconstitutional. Critics might predict that such would be the logical extension of *Brown,* but for the moment the Court concerned itself only with education.

Within an hour of the opinion, the Voice of America beamed news of the decision around the world in over thirty languages. Northern newspapers for the most part hailed the decision as "momentous." What the Justices have done, declared the *Cincinnati Enquirer,* "is simply to act as the conscience of the American nation." Within the black community, reaction was mixed, as leaders waited to see how the lofty words would be translated into action. The *Chicago Defender,* a leading black newspaper, called the decision a "second emancipation proclamation . . . more important to our democracy than the atomic bomb or the hydrogen bomb." Local black columnist Nat Williams, writing in Memphis, said "there was no general 'hallelujah, 'tis done' hullaballoo . . . Beale Streeters are sorta skeptical about giving out with cheers yet." Such skepticism, unfortunately, proved well founded.[98]

Initially, the South heard voices of moderation, more so than one might have expected. The governor of Virginia, Thomas Stanley, called for "cool heads, calm study, and sound judgment." Governor "Big Jim" Folsom of Alabama declared that "When the Supreme Court speaks, that's the law." The governor of Arkansas promised that "Arkansas will obey the law. It always has." The respected *Louisville Courier-Journal* assured its readers that "the end of the world has not come for the South or for the nation. The Supreme Court's ruling is not itself a revolution. It is rather acceptance of a process that has been going on for a long time." The editors urged Southerners to follow the Court's example of moderation, advice akin to that of the *Atlanta Constitution,* which called on Georgians "to think clearly."[99] All in all, as Dewey Grantham has noted, "the Southern response was surprisingly mild, in part, no doubt, because the court had decided not to order immediate desegregation of the schools."[100]

༄

The Court had expected criticism of the decision not only from the South, which would naturally defend its way of life, but few of the Justices expected that the scholarly community would be critical as well. The Chief Justice's insistence that the opinion be "short, readable by the lay public, non-rhetorical, unemotional and, above all, non-accusatory," had been a brilliant political stroke, papering over theoretical differences among the Justices, but it robbed the decision of intellectual force and authority. The Court's dismissal of the background and relevance of the Fourteenth Amendment as "inconclusive," for example, led to charges that the Court had misunderstood history. One can legitimately argue that the Amendment had been designed to ensure black equality, and therefore that the framers had intended it to prevent segregation in the schools and elsewhere. One can also argue, with equally plausible evidence, that the "original understanding" of those responsible for the Fourteenth Amendment did not encompass regulation of race relations.[101]

The most intense criticism, from both southerners opposed to the ruling as well as from academics who supported it, focused on footnote eleven. In its "Brandeis brief," the NAACP had cited whatever material it could find to support the claim that segregation hurt black children. The Chief Justice, to buttress his finding that segregation psychologically harmed black children, cited a number of works, including Gunnar Myrdal's classic study of racism, **An American Dilemma** (1944) and Kenneth B. Clark's highly controversial studies of negative self-image among black children.[102] Warren himself later said, "It was only a note," but critics seized on it as proof that the Court had not interpreted law but had applied its own sociological views. Former Associate Justice and now governor of South Carolina, James F. Byrnes, derided footnote eleven as communist-inspired. The temerity of the bench in citing a foreigner, the Swede Gunnar Myrdal, raised southern hackles; the Georgia attorney general denounced Myrdal because one of his teachers had been the black radical W. E. B. DuBois, "who sent a message of condolence on the death of Stalin."[103]

Even conceding that at the time social science research in this area could best be described as limited and its methods primitive,[104] should the Court have even used this material? Edmund Cahn, who certainly supported equal rights for African Americans, declared that "I would not have the constitutional rights of Negroes—or of any other Americans—rest on such flimsy foundation as some of the scientific demonstrations in these [trial] records."[105] The respected columnist James Reston called *Brown* "A Sociological Decision," and said it "read more like an expert paper on sociology than a Supreme Court opinion."[106] Why Warren felt constrained to include the note is puzzling. NAACP lawyers themselves felt uneasy about the social science evidence, and did not play them up in oral argument. John W. Davis, counsel for South Carolina, tore the studies apart, and there were no questions from the bench, indicating that the Justices probably cared little about them. Ever since, footnote eleven has been a prime target of critics not only of *Brown,* but of what they consider the Warren Court's judicial activism. Footnote eleven was not only unnecessary, one liberal scholar has written, "it was stupid," and deprived the opinion of much of its force.[107]

Critics also accused the Court of excessive judicial activism. Whether one agreed with *Brown* or not, the Court had obviously departed dramatically from its previous rulings in this area. It had admittedly been chipping away at *Plessy* for some time, but its recent decisions had given little indication that it would abandon the fifty-year-old doctrine of separate but equal so precipitately. Unlike most Court opinions, the decision contained practically no citations to precedents, because so few existed. Critics charged the Court with engaging in the same type of policy-making activism as in *Lochner, Adair, Adkins,* and the anti-New Deal cases.[108] In *Brown,* however, the Court overturned its own prior ruling in *Plessy,* a decision that today nearly everyone agrees had been wrongly decided; in the reform cases, the Court interposed its own views over that of the legislature. Granted, the whole edifice of segregation statutes relied on that decision, but if *Plessy* was wrong, then so too were the laws that resulted from it.

Warren also presented two very different and contradictory ideas of constitutional interpretation in the opinion. When he announced that "separate educational facilities are inherently unequal," he seemed to be saying that racial segregation violated the constitutional mandate at all times and in all places. In essence, he intimated that constitutional meaning is unchanging, and that the Equal Protection Clause had always meant what the Court now said it meant, that racial discrimination had been unconstitutional since 1868, and that cases to the contrary, such as *Plessy*, had been wrongly decided.

But Warren also implied an opposing view of constitutional interpretation, that constitutional meaning changes with changing times and circumstances. Chief Justice John Marshall had lectured the American people to always remember that the Constitution is intended "to be adopted to the various crises of human affairs." This notion of a "living constitution" could be seen in Warren's dismissal of what the framers of the Fourteenth Amendment had intended regarding schooling, since public education had been practically non-existent in the South in 1868. By this view, although the Court overruled *Plessy*, one could argue that at the time it had been correctly decided.[109]

One of the most serious attacks came from a respected scholar who not only opposed segregation, but had advised the NAACP in several cases. Professor Herbert Wechsler of Columbia Law School did not object to the fact that the high court had departed from precedent nor to the fact that it insisted on viewing the Fourteenth Amendment in the light of current conditions rather than those that governed at the time of its adoption. Rather, the Justices had reached the conclusion that separate schools, because "inherently unequal," were unconstitutional. But how did they get there? What reasoning, what rules of constitutional interpretation, had the Court used to get from A (separate schools) to B (are inherently unequal) to C (and therefore unconstitutional)? Would all laws that segregated one group from another (such as men from women) be unconstitutional? Would all conditions that created inequality (such as poverty) be subject to constitutional remedy? The Court had failed, Wechsler claimed, to ground its conclusions in "neutral principles." Decisions must rest "on reasons with respect to all the issues in the case . . . that in their generality and their neutrality transcend any immediate result that is involved." Only if society could see that such far-reaching decisions such as *Brown* had, in fact, been reached through a rational and explainable method of legal reasoning would society be willing to accept the changes imposed by those decisions. The integrity of the judicial process outweighed any particular results.[110]

Defenders of the Court conceded most of these points, but insisted that the Justices had followed the right moral as well as legal course. One did not need fancy studies to see what must be plain to everyone, that "racial segregation under government auspices inevitably inflicts humiliation." In response to southern charges that the Court had promulgated a lawless decision, some scholars responded that massive racial discrimination constituted so great a violation of moral law as to make lawful a court ruling against it. Since neither Congress nor the states showed any inclination to promote civil rights, the Court's action may have been the only way to get the country moving on the road toward full racial equality. While that path has at times been painful and even violent, without *Brown* it is doubtful if legal segregation could have been ended except through massive protest and violence, such as afflicted South Africa in the 1980s.

As for the high-sounding idea of "neutral principles," one can surely ask if process is enough? Is Justice or society served if the courts only concern themselves with neutral principles? What about right results? For many, the "rightness" of *Brown* was sufficient. Professor Edward Beiser defended *Brown* as properly decided "because racial segregation was a grievous evil. Were this not so, the Supreme Court's decision would have been unjustified." Another legal scholar, Paul Bender, agreed that *Brown* had not been "tightly reasoned," but so what? The opinion had been "right," and if the Court had waited until it could write an "airtight opinion . . . it would have sadly failed the country and the Constitution."[111]

J. Harvie Wilkinson, now a federal judge on the Court of Appeals for the Fourth Circuit, dismisses much of this criticism when he reminds us that *Brown* "was humane, among the most humane moments in all our history. It was, with the pardonable exception of a footnote, a great political achievement, both in its uniting of the Court and in the steady way it addressed the nation." That it had flaws and might have been a more passionate document will continue to be debated, but this misses the point. Instead of grieving for what it might have been, "better we be thankful for what it was."[112] As Kenneth L. Karst noted: "If *Brown v. Board of Education* reflected a change in the American civic culture, it also generated further changes. *Brown* was the Supreme Court's most important decision of the twentieth century. Today it stands as much more than a decision about schools, or even a decision about segregation. *Brown* is our leading authoritative symbol for the principle that the Constitution forbids a system of caste."[113]

⌘

Warren's strategy assumed that the states would accept the inevitability of desegregation by the time the Court handed down the implementation decree, and initial signs seemed encouraging. Some southern communities did not wait for the Court to act, but began desegregating schools by the time the 1954 academic year began. Baltimore adopted a freedom of choice plan, which enabled 3,000 blacks to attend previously all-white schools that September. Louisville changed over its school system within a semester, while St. Louis initiated a two-year plan. Counties in West Virginia, junior colleges in Texas, and public schools in Washington, D.C., and Wilmington, Delaware, all enrolled blacks in previously segregated schools.

Ominous signs soon appeared, however. Governor Stanley abandoned his earlier moderation and announced in June that he would do everything he could to continue segregation in Virginia. In Mississippi, White Citizens Councils began to form in July, pledged to total war in defense of segregation. For the most part, though, a wait-and-see attitude in the South marked the twelve months following *Brown.* After all, no one knew exactly what the Court would order, and until then the schools would remain racially segregated.

The Court heard arguments on proposed remedies that winter and again in April. The subject was controversial enough on its own, but the Justices realized that they also had to decide whether to abandon, at least in this area, the Court's traditional policy of ruling only on the case before it. Normally, if someone raises a valid claim that his or her constitutional rights have been violated, the decree is directed only to that petitioner's case; other persons "similarly situated" do not immediately gain the benefit of the decision. Lower federal courts then take notice of the ruling and apply it prospectively to future petitioners raising the same issue. In the school cases, however, this would mean that every black child wishing to enroll in a previously all-white school would have to go to court in order to secure the same rights that Linda Brown now enjoyed in Topeka. Determined states and localities, armed with sufficient resources, could tie up the desegregation process for years by litigating every such claim.

Moreover, the Court usually takes little notice of practical matters of implementation. Once a right has been defined, it has to be available to all citizens, despite any institutional dislocations. But circumstances in public education varied enormously, and the Court understood that in some schools desegregation would mean a few blacks sitting in predominantly white classrooms and in other schools just the opposite—and it made a difference. Finally, how long could the Court give the South? Every day that black children continued to attend segregated schools they suffered a loss of their constitutional rights in violation of the Fourteenth Amendment's assurance of the equal protection of law. But too precipitate an order might lead to widespread obstruction, perhaps even violence.

The NAACP pushed for full integration in the shortest possible time; blacks had been waiting three and a half centuries to be treated as equals and should not have to wait any longer to claim their constitutional rights.

The South seemed equally intransigent. Virginia urged the Court to face the "reality" of major differences between the two races and offered statistics to prove the inferiority of blacks. Florida had commissioned a poll and ominously informed the Court that only one out of seven police officers would enforce attendance at racially mixed schools. The state also put forward such a complicated plan that, according to Richard Kluger, "the most ungainly camel in Islam would have had an easier time passing through the eye of a needle than a black child getting into a white school in Florida."[114]

The attorney for South Carolina said that whites in his district (which was overwhelmingly African American) would not abide by any decree sending their children to schools with Negroes. The Chief Justice asked "But you are not willing to say that there would be an honest attempt to conform?" To which the attorney replied, "Let us get the word 'honest' out of there." Warren acidly replied, "No, leave it in," and got a blunt answer: "No, because I have to tell you that right now we would not conform; we would not send our white children to the Negro schools." Warren did not like the answer, but as it turned out, it was one of the most prescient statements made at oral argument.[115]

The federal government, appearing as *amicus* at the request of the Court, urged a middle position between "integration now" and "segregation forever." The states should submit timetables within ninety days, and implementation should be supervised by the local district courts. The courts would have the discretion to make adjustments in the schedules depending on local conditions. Communities would thus have a chance to change their attitudes and accept desegregation as necessary in order for all Americans to enjoy their full constitutional rights. An immediate start would have to be made, however, and the decision would have to be enforced by federal, state, and local officials, all of whom had taken an oath to support the Constitution.

On May 31, 1955, Chief Justice Warren, again for a unanimous Court, handed down a seven-paragraph implementing decision, commonly known as *Brown II*. School segregation had to be ended everywhere, but the Court recognized that varying local conditions required different solutions. Local school districts must "make a prompt and reasonable start toward full compliance," and oversight would be lodged in the federal district courts. The local judges should exercise the "practical flexibility" traditionally associated with equity, but delay and noncompliance should not be contemplated. Desegregation of public schools should proceed "with all deliberate speed."[116]

The opinion, like that in *Brown I,* was short, less than four pages, and was designed to avoid provoking the South. Optimism by the Justices infused the opinion; if the Court showed appropriate sympathy, then perhaps the South would show appropriate restraint. Nonetheless the Court reminded the southern states that "it should go without saying that the vitality of these constitutional principles cannot be allowed to yield simply from disagreement with them."[117] Yet as many scholars have noted, the Court did in fact delay full implementation of *Brown I* because it feared the extent of southern disagreement with those principles, and may have created the worst of all worlds—promising hope to millions of African Americans still shackled by Jim Crow while reassuring the South that it understood the problem and was not pushing it.[118]

The Court did not fix a date for the end of segregation, nor even require that initial plans be filed within ninety days, as the federal government had suggested. In fact, it gave the South far more than the segregationists had expected, raising hopes that the actual implementation of the decree could be delayed indefinitely. Assignment of primary responsibility to the local district courts led some southerners to assume that the decree could be completely ignored. Lieutenant governor Ernest Vandiver of Georgia rejoiced when he heard the news. District judges, he declared, "are steeped in the same traditions that I am. . . . A 'reasonable time' can be construed as one year or two hundred. . . . Thank God we've got good Federal judges."[119]

Within a short time, however, many federal judges in the South made it quite clear that they took their oath to support the Constitution seriously. John Minor Wisdom, John R. Brown, Elbert Tuttle and Richard Rives of the United States Court of Appeals for the Fifth Circuit, as well as district court judges Frank Johnson of Alabama and J. Skelly Wright of Louisiana defied friends and associates to become forceful advocates of integration.[120] By January 1956, federal judges had rendered opinions in nineteen cases, and in every one, they reaffirmed the Supreme Court's ruling that segregation denied equal protection of the law. School segregation laws fell in Florida, Arkansas, Tennessee, and Texas. District Judge J. Skelly Wright, born and educated in New Orleans, struck down a Louisiana plan that would have retained completely segregated schools. He expressed his sympathy for all the problems white state officials faced and spoke of the need for "the utmost patience" on everyone's part. "But the magnitude of the problem may not nullify the principle. And that principle is that we are, all of us, freeborn Americans, with a right to make our way, unfettered by sanctions imposed by man because of the work of God."[121] Inspired by such victories, the NAACP filed additional petitions for desegregation of 170 school districts in seventeen states.

Some southern judges, however, found integration distasteful and believed the Supreme Court had decided *Brown* wrongly. With neither the Congress nor the president eager to push desegregation, they tended to emphasize the "deliberate" rather than the "speed," and perhaps little more could have been expected of them. For a few, their devotion to segregation proved stronger than their oath of office. In Dallas, Texas, for example, the NAACP started suit in September 1955, and Judge William Atwell, an outspoken defender of segregation, refused to act for two years. Time and again the NAACP had to appeal to the Fifth Circuit Court of Appeals, which consistently overruled Atwell and ordered him to move ahead with desegregating the city's school system. Atwell finally retired, but another segregationist took over the case. T. Whitfield Davidson admonished blacks to recognize "that the white man has a right to maintain his racial integrity and it can't be done so easily in integrated schools."[122] Again, the NAACP had to appeal over and over again to get around Davidson's obstructionary tactics.

A major problem facing the NAACP involved the local nature of public education. Local school boards, not the states, controlled the schools and determined policy, and this made it especially difficult and expensive to press for desegregation. Most small black communities could not afford to undertake a desegregation suit. Even when local attorneys volunteered their services or the NAACP Legal Defense Fund sent in one of its lawyers, it cost plaintiffs approximately $15,000 to take a desegregation suit through federal courts. As a result, as late as 1961 few southern school districts in the Deep South had faced a school desegregation suit.

Encouraged by all these obstacles to implementing desegregation, the South dug in its heels. Presses ground out articles and books purporting to demonstrate not only the error of footnote 11, but how "science" proved the basic inferiority of black people.[123] The Citizens Council movement spread and soon claimed 500,000 members in eleven states. Whites and blacks who signed desegregation petitions lost their jobs and found they could not get credit from stores or banks. In 1956, 101 members of Congress, including all but three of the Senators from the former Confederate states, signed a belligerent "Southern Manifesto" opposing the Court's decision, thus giving an imprimatur of respectability to segregationist resistance. The *Richmond News-Leader* defended Southern intransigence by charging that "the inept fraternity of politicians and professors known as the United States Supreme Court chose to throw away the established law. These nine men repudiated the Constitution, spit upon the Tenth Amendment, and rewrote the fundamental law of this land to suit their own gauzy concepts of sociology. If it be said now that the South is flouting the law, let it be said to the high court, *You taught us how.*"[124]

In Virginia, usually seen as moderate in its race relations, Senator Harry F. Byrd called for "massive resistance" to desegregation, and soon after, political leaders resurrected the long-discarded theories of John C.

Calhoun.[125] Alabama claimed that it had the right of interposition to protect its citizens from unconstitutional federal action, and the state legislature resolved *Brown* to be "null, void and of no effect." Georgia adopted a similar resolution, adding that it intended to ignore the Court. Mississippi condemned *Brown* as "unconstitutional and of no lawful effect," and set up a commission to prohibit compliance. Although avoiding the word "nullification," South Carolina protested against "the illegal encroachment of the central government." Both houses of the Louisiana legislature unanimously endorsed interposition, while North Carolina adopted a "resolution of protest."

Aside from the rhetoric, southern states enacted measures designed to thwart the courts and prevent compliance. Georgia, for example, made it a felony for any school official to use tax money for mixed-race schools, while Mississippi declared it unlawful for the races to attend school together at the high school level or below. Several states adopted plans to evade integration by substituting some form of private school system. Mississippi and South Carolina actually amended their constitutions to abolish public schools. Some states set up grant programs to support private schools, and nearly all of them amended their laws to shift full responsibility for pupil placement to local school boards, thus making it necessary to sue each district separately, rather than entering a single suit against the state. Because *Brown* proscribed only segregation based on race, states instituted all sorts of other health and welfare criteria, which could be manipulated to keep white and black children in separate classes. "There is no one way, but many," John Temple Graves of Alabama proclaimed. "The South proposes to use all of them that make for resistance. The decision tortured the Constitution—the South will torture the decision."[126]

When school opened in September 1956, 723 school districts in the seventeen border and southern states had accomplished some measure of desegregation, 186 more than the previous year. But 3,000 school districts remained totally segregated. About 300,000 Negroes went to school in so-called "integrated situations," which could mean many things; 2,400,000 remained entirely segregated. In Alabama, Florida, Georgia, Louisiana, Mississippi, North and South Carolina, and Virginia, total segregation remained the rule. In that fall's election, candidates who had urged moderation went down to defeat in one state after another. When the new state legislatures met in early 1957, they passed dozens of additional measures to cause delay. In the wake of the *Brown* decision, the Ku Klux Klan came alive again, and bombings, beatings, murders, and cross burnings spread across the southern states. In Mississippi three prominent civil rights activists were murdered during the summer and fall of 1955, and in 1957 a group of whites in Birmingham, Alabama savagely beat and castrated a black man and then told him, "This is what will happen if Negroes try to integrate the schools." All over the South, as the noted southern-born scholar C. Vann Woodward lamented, "the lights of reason and tolerance began to go out under the resistent demand for conformity [and] a malaise of fear spread over the region."[127]

~

It is now fifty years since the Supreme Court handed down what must surely rank as one of the most important decisions not only in the twentieth century, but in our nation's history as well. Implementation proved difficult, and the Warren Court has been roundly criticized for adopting the "all deliberate speed" standard in *Brown v. Board of Education II* (1955).[128] The South dug in its heels, and enforced racial segregation remained the rule well into the 1960s. The rule of law prevailed, however, and gradually the entire legal structure of Jim Crow gave way to the Equal Protection Clause's demand that all persons shall be treated equally before the law. There was resistance and some violence, but compared to the blood shed to bring down apartheid in South Africa, the elimination of state-sponsored racial discrimination in this country proved a relatively peaceful revolution.

The decision in *Brown* struck down legal segregation in the schools, and then the courts did away with laws separating blacks and whites in parks, on buses, in restaurants, and elsewhere. But what the Court could not do was eliminate racism, and fifty years after the decision the United States is still grappling with the lingering effects of more than three centuries of slavery and racial discrimination. For some people, as other essays in this book show,[129] the reality of life for people of color in the United States fifty years after *Brown* does not measure up to the dreams they had when Chief Justice Earl Warren announced that separate could never be equal. It is safe to say, however, that even those disappointed by the slow pace of progress in racial relations would not wish to return to the days of Jim Crow. The promise of equality may remain elusive, but it is a promise made by our Constitution, and eventually one that we all must keep.

Endnotes

1. *Brown v. Board of Education of Topeka,* 347 U.S. 483, 495 (1954).
2. C. Vann Woodward, **The Strange Career of Jim Crow** (3rd rev. ed., New York, 1974), 26.
3. 14 *Statutes at Large* 428 (1967).
4. 18 *Statutes at Large* 335 (1875).
5. Woodward, **Jim Crow,** 38.
6. *See* National Association for the Advancement of Colored People, **Thirty Years of Lynching in the United States, 1889–1918** (New York, 1919).
7. Howard N. Rabinowitz, **Race Relations in the Urban South, 1865–1890** (New York, 1978), *passim.*
8. One should not get the impression that blacks were treated that much better in the North. Prior to 1865, although not enslaved, free blacks in the northern states labored under a myriad of social, political and economic restrictions that in many ways anticipated the Jim Crow laws of the South. *See* Leon F. Litwack, **North of Slavery: The Negro in the Free States, 1790–1860** (Chicago, 1961).
9. William Gillette, **Retreat from Reconstruction, 1869–1879** (Baton Rouge, 1979), 191.
10. 109 U.S. 3 (1883).
11. 109 U.S. at 33 (Harlan, J., dissenting).
12. *Shelley v. Kraemer* 334 U.S. 1 (1948).
13. 94 U.S. 113 (1877).
14. 95 U.S. 485 (1878).
15. *Id.* at 489.
16. 133 U.S. 587 (1890).
17. 163 U.S. 537 (1896). The best analysis of the case is Charles A. Lofgren, **The *Plessy* Case: A Legal-Historical Interpretation** (New York, 1987).
18. 163 U.S. at 544.
19. *Id.* at 552, 555, 560, 563 (Harlan, J., dissenting)
20. Woodward, **Jim Crow,** 97–102.
21. *Berea College v. Kentucky,* 211 U.S. 45 (1908).
22. Alexander M. Bickel and Benno C. Schmidt, Jr., **The Judiciary and Responsible Government, 1910–21** (New York, 1984), 739.
23. John Milton Cooper, Jr., **Pivotal Decades: The United States, 1900–1920** (New York, 1990), 70 ff.

24. Mark V. Tushnet, **The NAACP's Legal Strategy against Segregated Education, 1925–1950** (Chapel Hill, 1987); *see also* Loren Miller, **The Petitioners: The Story of the Supreme Court of the United States and the Negro** (Cleveland, 1966), and above all, the magisterial study by Richard Kluger, **Simple Justice: The History of *Brown v. Board of Education* and Black America's Struggle for Equality** (New York, 1976, 2004).

25. *Missouri ex rel. Gaines v. Canada,* 305 U.S. 339 (1938).

26. *The New York Times,* 6 December 1946, p. 26.

27. **To Secure These Rights: The Report of the President's Committee on Civil Rights** (Washington: Government Printing Office, 1947).

28. William C. Berman, **The Politics of Civil Rights in the Truman Administration** (Columbus, 1970), *passim*.

29. Mary L. Dudziak, **Cold War Civil Rights: Race and the Image of American Democracy** (Princeton, 2000) 101; *see also* Dudziak, "Desegregation as a Cold War Imperative," 41 *Stanford Law Review* 61 (1988). For a broader evaluation of the impact of the Cold War on domestic liberal accomplishments, see H. W. Brands, **The Strange Death of American Liberalism** (New Haven, 2001)

30. 321 U.S. 649 (1944).

31. The strategy had first been outlined by Nathan Margold in the early 1930s; see Mark V. Tushnet, **Making Civil Rights Law: Thurgood Marshall and the Supreme Court, 1936–1961** (New York, 1994), ch. 8.

32. *Mitchell v. United States,* 313 U.S. 80 (1941).

33. For the road away from *Plessy, see* Catherine A. Barnes, **Journey from Jim Crow: The Desegregation of Southern Transit** (New York, 1983).

34. *Morgan v. Virginia,* 328 U.S. 373, 386 (1946).

35. Quoted in Kluger, **Simple Justice,** 238.

36. Burton apparently would have been happy if his colleagues had been willing to tackle separate but equal directly, and he stood ready to overturn *Plessy.* Frances Howell Rudko, **Truman's Court: A Study in Judicial Restraint** (Westport, 1988), 56.

37. 328 U.S. at 394.

38. 333 U.S. 28 (1948).

39. *Id.* at 30.

40. Felix Frankfurter to Wiley Rutledge, 2 January 1948 (2 letters), Wiley Rutledge Papers, Library of Congress.

41. *Id.* at 44; see also William O. Douglas, Conference notes, 20 December 1947, William O. Douglas Papers, Library of Congress.

42. C. Herman Pritchett, **Civil Liberties and the Vinson Court** (Chicago, 1954), 128.

43. 333 U.S. at 42. Justice Black joined in the concurrence.

44. *Buchanan v. Warley,* 245 U.S. 60 (1917).

45. D. O. McGovney, "Racial Residential Segregation by State Court Enforcement of Restrictive Agreements, Covenants or Conditions in Deeds is

Among the Most Humane Moments in All Our History 41

Unconstitutional," 33 *California Law Review* 5 (1945). McGovney sent a copy of this article to Justice Frankfurter.

46. Minutes of lawyers conference, 26 January 1947, Papers of the National Association for the Advancement of Colored People, Library of Congress.

47. 334 U.S. 1 (1948). Justices Reed, Jackson and Rutledge did not participate in this case, presumably because each owned property covered by a restrictive covenant. Jackson to Irving Brant, 9 February 1948, Robert H. Jackson Papers, Library of Congress.

48. *Hurd v. Hodge,* 334 U.S. 24 (1948). For a contemporary legal analysis of these cases, *see* Mark V. Tushnet, "*Shelley v. Kraemer* and Theories of Equality," 33 *New York Law School Law Review* 383 (1988); *see also* the older but still useful broader study, Clement E. Vose, **Caucasians Only: The Supreme Court, the NAACP, and the Restrictive Covenant Cases** (Berkeley, 1959).

49. Using the state action doctrine, the Warren Court voided the exclusion of blacks from a private theater located in a public park [*Muir v. Louisiana Park Theatrical Assn.,* 347 U.S. 971 (1955)], from a private restaurant in a court house [*Derrington v. Plummer,* 353 U.S. 924 (1957)], and from a private restaurant in a municipally-owned and operated parking garage [*Burton v. Wilmington Parking Authority,* 365 U.S. 715 (1961)].

50. *Barrows v. Jackson,* 346 U.S. 249 (1953).

51. *Brotherhood of Railway Trainmen v. Howard,* 343 U.S. 768 (1952).

52. For the full story of Ada Sipuel and her case, *see* the article below by David W. Levy, at p. 67.

53. *Sipuel v. Oklahoma State Board of Regents,* 332 U.S. 631 (1948).

54. Vinson, Memorandum to the Conference, 13 February 1948, Jackson MSS.

55. *Fisher v. Hurst,* 333 U.S. 147 (1948). Sipuel had recently married, and so the case came under her married name, Ada Fisher. She continued to fight for admission, and in the end was admitted to and graduated from the University of Oklahoma Law School.

56. Rutledge to Aubrey Williams, 26 February 1948, Rutledge MSS.

57. Kluger, **Simple Justice,** 258–59.

58. 339 U.S. 816 (1950).

59. *McLaurin v. Oklahoma State Regents for Higher Education,* 87 F. Supp. 528 (W.D. Ok. 1949).

60. Clark, Memorandum to the Conference, [7] April 1950, Douglas MSS.

61. Douglas, Conference notes of 8 April 1950, *id.*

62. Frankfurter to Vinson, 19 May 1950, Felix Frankfurter Papers, Harvard Law School.

63. *McLaurin v. Oklahoma State Regents,* 339 U.S. 637, 641 (1950).

64. *Id.*

65. *Sweatt v. Painter,* 339 U.S. 629, 634 (1950).

66. Tushnet, **NAACP's Strategy,** 135.

67. 321 U.S. 649 (1944).

68. 345 U.S. 461, 469 (1953). *See* Darlene Clark Hine, **Black Victory: The Rise and Fall of the White Primary in Texas** (Millwood, 1979).
69. 345 U.S. at 484, 485–86. Minton's dissent may well be ascribed to his long-time activism in the Democratic Party; Frankfurter once characterized him as "an almost pathological Democrat." Minton otherwise proved to be a staunch advocate of civil rights.
70. This account is also followed in the admirable and admiring study of the Warren Court, Bernard Schwartz, **Super Chief: Earl Warren and His Supreme Court—A Judicial Biography** (New York, 1983), and to a large extent in Howard Ball and Phillip J. Cooper, **Of Power and Right: Hugo Black, William O. Douglas, and America's Constitutional Revolution** (New York, 1992).
71. Schwartz, **Super Chief,** 72; Kluger, **Simple Justice,** 614, 581.
72. Douglas, Memorandum for the File, 17 May 1954, Douglas MSS.
73. *See*, for example, a similar memorandum to the file, 8 October 1958, detailing Frankfurter's obstructionism in the Little Rock case [*Cooper v. Aaron,* 358 U.S. 1 (1958)], *id.*
74. *See* in particular Philip Elman, "The Solicitor General's Office, Justice Frankfurter, and Civil Rights Litigation, 1946–1960: An Oral History," 100 *Harvard Law Review* 817 (1987). Elman, a former clerk to Frankfurter, was then in the solicitor general's office, spoke with Frankfurter on a regular basis, and has supported the notion that it was Frankfurter who masterminded the strategy that eventually led to a unanimous decision.
75. Mark Tushnet with Katya Lezin, "What Really Happened in *Brown v. Board of Education,*" 91 *Columbia Law Review* 1867 (1991); *see also* Dennis J. Hutchinson, "Unanimity and Desegregation: Decisionmaking in the Supreme Court, 1948–1958," 68 *Georgetown Law Journal* 1 (1979).
76. James F. Simon, **The Antagonists: Hugo Black, Felix Frankfurter and Civil Liberties in Modern America** (New York, 1989), 216–17.
77. Frankfurter to Paul Freund, 18 December 1947, Frankfurter MSS.
78. William T. Coleman, Jr., "Mr. Justice Frankfurter: Civil Libertarian as Lawyer and as Justice: Extent to which Judicial Responsibilities Affected His Pre-Court Convictions," in Ronald D. Rotunda, ed., **Six Justices on Civil Rights** (New York: Oceana, 1983), 85–105.
79. The piece was so good that Bickel, with Frankfurter's blessing and encouragement, published it in slightly modified form as "The Original Understanding and the Segregation Decision," 69 *Harvard Law Review* 1 (1955).
80. Quoted in Leonard Baker, **Brandeis and Frankfurter: A Dual Biography** (New York, 1984), 479.
81. Elman, "Oral History," 832.
82. Frankfurter, Memoranda to the Conference, 27 May and 4 June 1953, and Frankfurter to Vinson, 8 June 1953, Frankfurter MSS.
83. Hutchinson, "Unanimity and Desegregation," 87.

84. Tushnet and Lezin, "What Really Happened . . . ," 1902–04.
85. Philip B. Kurland, "Earl Warren, the 'Warren Court,' and the Warren Myth," 67 *Michigan Law Review* 353, 356 (1968).
86. Kluger, **Simple Justice,** 656.
87. *Id.* at 671.
88. *Id.* at 673.
89. *Id.* at 674.
90. The brief can be found in 49 **Landmark Briefs and Arguments of the Supreme Court of the United States** 23 (Philip B. Kurland and Gerhard Casper, eds., 1975).
91. *See* G. Edward White, **Earl Warren: A Public Life** (New York, 1982), 164–69.
92. The full text of the opinion can be found below at 171.
93. *Brown v. Board of Education of Topeka, Kansas,* 347 U.S. 483, 492–93 (1954).
94. *Id.* at 494.
95. *Id.* at 495.
96. In the companion case of *Bolling v. Sharpe,* 347 U.S. 497 (1954) the Court struck down segregation in the District of Columbia as well. Finding that segregation deprived the plaintiff of "liberty under law," the Court ruled that such discrimination violated the Fifth Amendment. The Constitution could not permit the federal government to operate segregated schools when it forbade the states to do so.
97. White, **Warren,** 167.
98. Kluger, **Simple Justice,** 708, 709–10.
99. *Id.,* 711.
100. Dewey W. Grantham, **The South in Modern America: A Region at Odds** (New York, 1994), 206.
101. *See* Alfred H. Kelley, "The Fourteenth Amendment Reconsidered: The Segregation Question," 54 *Michigan Law Review* 1049 (1956), and Bickel, "Original Understanding."
102. Footnote 11 reads in its entirety: "K. B. Clark, **Effect of Prejudice and Discrimination on Personality Development** (Midcentury White House Conference on Children and Youth, 1950); Witmer and Kotinsky, **Personality in the Making** (1952), c. VI; Deutscher and Chein, "The Psychological Effects of Enforced Segregation: A Survey of Social Science Opinion," 26 *J. Psychol.* 259 (1948); Chein, "What are the Psychological Effects of Segregation Under Conditions of Equal Facilities?," 3 *Int. J. Opinion and Attitude Res.* 229 (1949); Brameld, "Educational Costs, in Discrimination and National Welfare" (MacIver, ed., 1949), 44–48; Frazier, **The Negro in the United States** (1949), 674–681. And *see* generally Myrdal, **An American Dilemma** (1944)."

103. J. Harvie Wilkinson, III, **From *Brown* to *Bakke:* The Supreme Court and School Integration, 1954–1978** (New York, 1979), 33.

104. As social science studies have become more sophisticated, Clark's work has been increasingly dismissed as simplistic and methodologically flawed. *See,* however, Clark's defense of the use of this evidence in "The Desegregation Cases: Criticism of the Social Scientist's Role," 5 *Villanova Law Review* 224 (1959), as well as a response by Ernest Van den Haag, "Social Science Testimony in the Desegregation Cases," 6 *Id.* 69 (1960).

105. Edmund Cahn, "Jurisprudence," 30 *NYU Law Review* 150, 157 (1955).

106. James Reston, "A Sociological Decision," *The New York Times* (18 May 1954) 14.

107. Lucas A. Powe, Jr., **The Warren Court and American Politics** (Cambridge, 2000), 42.

108. *Lochner v. New York,* 198 U.S. 45 (1905); *Adair v. United States,* 208 U.S. 161 (1908); *Adkins v. Children's Hospital,* 261 U.S. 525 (1923); for the New Deal cases, *see Schechter v. United States,* 295 U.S. 495 (1935), and *United States v. Butler,* 297 U.S. 1 (1936).

109. *See* Morton J. Horwitz, **The Warren Court and the Pursuit of Justice** (New York, 1998), ch. 2.

110. Herbert Wechsler, "Toward Neutral Principles of Constitutional Law," 73 *Harvard Law Review* 1 (1959). The article generated an immediate controversy over its attitude toward *Brown. See* Louis H. Pollak, "Racial Discrimination and Judicial Integrity: A Reply to Professor Wechsler," 108 *University of Pennsylvania Law Review* 1 (1959), and Charles L. Black, Jr., "The Lawfulness of the Segregation Decisions," 69 *Yale Law Journal* 421 (1960). Although the notion of neutral principles enjoyed a vogue in the 1960s, it later came under attack for its supposed impracticability. *See* John Hart Ely, **Democracy and Distrust: A Theory of Judicial Review** (Cambridge, 1980).

111. Both quoted in Wilkinson, **From *Brown* to *Bakke,*** 35.

112. *Id.,* 39.

113. Kenneth L. Karst, **Belonging to America: Equal Citizenship and the Constitution** (New Haven, 1989), 73–74.

114. Kluger, **Simple Justice,** 725

115. 49A *Landmark Briefs* 1168.

116. *Brown v. Board of Education,* 349 U.S. 294, 301 (1955).

117. *Id.* at 300.

118. *See,* for example, Powe, **The Warren Court,** 56.

119. Woodward, **Jim Crow,** 153.

120. *See* Jack W. Peltason, **Fifty-Eight Lonely Men: Southern Federal Judges and School Desegregation** (New York, 1961), for a sympathetic account of the role of federal judges following *Brown II.*

121. *Bush v. Orleans Parish School Board,* 138 F. Supp. 337, 342 (E.D. La. 1956).

122. Melvin I. Urofsky and Paul Finkelman, 2 **A March of Liberty** 787–88 (New York, 2002).

123. *See*, for example, James J. Kilpatrick, **The Southern Case for School Seg-regation** (New York, 1962).

124. Cited in William E. Leuchtenburg, **A Troubled Feast: America Since 1945** (rev. ed., Boston, 1983), 83.

125. Benjamin Muse, **Virginia's Massive Resistance** (Bloomington, IN, 1961).

126. Woodward, **Jim Crow,** 159.

127. *Id.,* 165.

128. 349 U.S. 294 (1955).

129. *See* below Gerald N. Rosenberg, **African American-Rights after *Brown,*** 203.

✿ A N D R E W   K U L L [1]

Post-Plessy, Pre-Brown

"Logical Exactness" in Enforcing Equal Rights

In May 1896, the Supreme Court of the United States held in *Plessy v. Ferguson*[2] that a Louisiana statute requiring that black and white railroad passengers be transported in "equal" but separate cars was consistent with the Fourteenth Amendment's guarantee of the equal protection of the laws. Actually the majority opinion implied much more than this. The message of *Plessy*, if you read it carefully, was not just that a law requiring segregated transportation facilities was constitutional; nor did the Court remotely suggest that whatever was separate had to be precisely equal. What the Court said, and meant, was that a racial classification was like any other classification under the Fourteenth Amendment— it was constitutional if reasonable—and that a law separating the races was, in the nature of things, an appropriate exercise of the state's police power.[3]

Alone in dissent, the first Justice John Marshall Harlan protested that the Constitution prohibited any law drawing a racial distinction: "Our Constitution is color-blind, and neither knows nor tolerates classes among citizens." *Plessy* has been regarded ever since as the case confirming the legality of segregation, and Harlan's dissent as its quintessential refutation. This dual land-mark of constitutional law was reported by *The New York Times* as a brief item in its regular weekly column of railroad news—as Profes-sor Lofgren discovered—"sandwiched between reports of another Supreme Court railway decision, which overturned an Illinois law ordering minor rerouting of interstate passenger trains, and a request by the receivers of the Baltimore & Ohio for authority to issue new improvement bonds."[4]

In May 1954, the Court held in *Brown v. Board of Education* that racially segregated public schools violated the Equal Protection Clause.[5] The opinion by Chief Justice Earl Warren put the decision on the nar-rowest possible ground, short of naked fiat: it dealt with *Plessy* by saying that *Plessy* was a case about railroads, not schools. This time the country was intensely interested. Informed observers immediately inferred that the Court had reached conclusions about government-sponsored race classifications going much further than any it was prepared to announce. An editorial in the next Sunday's *New York Times* explained that the decision in *Brown* had made Justice Harlan's dissent in *Plessy* "in effect . . . a part of the law of the land." This was exactly what the Court had been careful not to say, but it was true, and it would remain true for more than a decade thereafter.[6]

Juxtaposing these two cases in a constitutional law casebook or a lecture series carries several perfectly natural implications. The dis-tance between them seems to define a period, post-*Plessy* and pre-*Brown,* that can conveniently be called "the 'separate-but-equal' era."[7] One of the Court's most reviled decisions (*Plessy* ranks with *Dred Scott* in this regard) is implicitly answered by the decision that is the most revered in the history of the Court. If we assume that this transforma-tion in doctrine is like the other long-running stories in constitutional history—the expansion of the Commerce Clause, or the incorporation of the Bill of Rights—we might expect to find a course of decisions by which the old view of equal protection is criticized, reworked, and reformed to yield, eventually, the new understanding. Actually we find no such thing.

I have three ideas to propose about this post-*Plessy,* pre-*Brown* interval, and the first is in some sense to quarrel with the topic. *Plessy* does not begin a period, and *Brown* does not end one. Rather, these

famous decisions are emblematic of two adjacent periods in the constitutional history of race: 1937, the year of the Court-packing crisis, marks
a symbolic dividing line. The first of the two periods begins not in 1896
but in 1883, with *The Civil Rights Cases*[8]—when the Court held that the
Civil Rights Act of 1875 (prohibiting segregation in transportation and
public accommodations) was unconstitutional because it was beyond the
power of Congress to enact. The Fourteenth Amendment restricts states,
not individuals ("No state shall make or enforce any law . . ."). The Court
held in 1883 that the congressional power to enforce this prohibition
on the states did not carry with it the power to legislate directly concerning the rights and duties of individuals. This, of course, was the
formal announcement of the "state action doctrine—a problem to
which we shall return shortly." But for our purposes just now, defining
periods, the 1883 decision was an announcement that the Court would
not thereafter go out of its way to interpret the Fourteenth Amendment
in a manner that was helpful to the cause of racial equality. The former
slave, wrote Justice Joseph P. Bradley, must finally "[take] the rank of a
mere citizen, and [cease] to be the special favorite of the laws."[9] This
meant, so far as his constitutional protection was concerned, that he
must henceforth be content with what the text of the amendment necessarily required. Congress in 1866 had been careful to draft the Fourteenth Amendment in such a way that what it necessarily required was
relatively little.[10]

By contrast, the period that followed—starting around 1937—
was one in which the civil rights plaintiff did for a time become, as
Justice Bradley would certainly have complained, "the special favorite of
the laws." It was a "civil-rights era" of approximately thirty-five years,
lasting into the mid-1970s, during which the Court was visibly unwilling that the cause of civil rights for racial minorities should be seen to
be defeated in any significant case that came before it.[11] To this end
the Court was fully prepared to set aside history and precedent,[12] to
overturn or manipulate settled doctrine,[13] to decide cases without giving reasons,[14] to create new constitutional rights,[15] or—*in extremis*—to
refuse to decide cases that it found no means to decide as it wished.[16]
Plessy was a routine case and a foregone conclusion under the first of
these constitutional regimes. *Brown* was anything but a routine case,
but its outcome was equally a foregone conclusion, under the second.

The dramatic advance of civil rights on the agenda of the Supreme Court coincides with a revolution in constitutional law that we already know about: the Court-packing crisis, the abandonment of federalism, the (temporary) surrender of substantive due process. My idea about what happened is very simple. For the remade Supreme Court that emerged from the constitutional crisis of 1937, putting the Court and the Constitution on the side of racial equality was a matter of first priority. The political convictions of the new majority coincided, as it happened, with the need to identify and assert a new institutional role. The Supreme Court had just been forced to surrender what had been, for 150 years, its central constitutional responsibility—the role of "umpire to the federal system," or guardian of state prerogatives against expansive national power—and it was publicly mulling over the question of what to take up next. The self-conscious choice of a new role for the Court appears in the famous *Carolene Products* footnote in 1938, where Justice Harlan Fiske Stone suggested that the Court might properly devote special attention to the rights of "discrete and insular minorities"—particularly where those rights were unlikely to be vindicated by ordinary political processes.[17]

A post-1937 majority that had decided to make constitutional adjudication into an instrument of racial equality faced obstacles of two kinds. There were problems of constitutional doctrine, and problems of political means—meaning simply, the problem faced by any court of enforcing compliance with its mandate. Under the heading of doctrine, the two biggest roadblocks were "separate but equal" and "state action." The obstacle on the political side was the obvious difficulty of calculating how far and how fast the Court might go in ordering a change in the country's racial arrangements without provoking successful resistance. The evidence suggests that it was primarily this practical question of judicial power, rather than the doctrinal difficulties, that gave the Court reason to hesitate.

The very first segregation case of this new era, *Missouri v. ex rel Gaines v. Canada,*[18] in 1938, about a whites-only law school at the University of Missouri—shows that *Plessy v. Ferguson* was no longer persuasive to a majority of the Court as a reading of the Fourteenth Amendment. Hindsight makes it easier to come to this conclusion, but we can see it even if we limit our view to 1938.

The University of Missouri had never admitted a black student. Lloyd Gaines applied for admission to the law school and was rejected because of his race. Missouri had an all-black university—Lincoln University—that had no law school. The State of Missouri claimed that it was ready to start a law school at Lincoln as soon as there was a demand for one, but no one had ever applied to study law at Lincoln. In the meantime, a Missouri statute provided that if a black student wanted to study a subject not offered at Lincoln, the state would pay his tuition at the university of any adjoining state to which he might be admitted. The Supreme Court held that this was not good enough: white students were able to study law without going out of state, and black students were entitled to the same treatment.

The result in *Gaines* seems so obvious today that we will miss the real implications of the decision unless we can see it from the defendant's point of view—the way a segregationist would have seen it. The implication of *Plessy* was that there was nothing intrinsically wrong with a racial classification; more specifically, that racial segregation was a legitimate legislative purpose, a reasonable exercise of the police power. If those propositions were still valid in 1938, it was hard to see why Missouri was not making a reasonable accommodation for Lloyd Gaines by offering to pay his tuition out of state. Of course he was not given the same treatment as a white law student. But that is not a sufficient objection, because our constitutional entitlement to the equal protection of the laws does not mean that we are entitled to the same treatment our neighbor receives. It turns out that "equal protection" is not really about treating people the same, but about the reasonableness of the lines that the government inevitably draws in treating people differently. A racially segregated state university system is unacceptable and unconstitutional today because we have rejected the idea that a racial classification, drawn for the purpose of segregation, is a permissible exercise of legislative power. That means rejecting *Plessy*, at least in its broader implications. And that means that the Court rejected *Plessy* in 1938, though of course it did not say so at the time.

With the second of the two doctrinal roadblocks, the problem of "state action," the post-1937 shift was just as abrupt. Judged by both text and history, "state action" is a real and significant limitation on the reach of the Fourteenth Amendment. This is something the Court has never denied. One of the distinguishing features of the post-1937 civil rights era, however, is the Court never found that discriminatory conduct was not state action in any case it agreed to decide.

The first example of the new approach came in the "white primary" cases. Black registered voters in Texas were not allowed to vote in the Democratic primary. This was a blatant violation of the Fourteenth and Fifteenth Amendments, if the discrimination was the action of the state; but a series of well-known Supreme Court decisions had marked out what seemed to be a clear distinction. If the Texas Democrats themselves, without state intervention, decided that only white Democrats should choose the party's nominees, there could be—the Court had made clear—no constitutional objection. Liberals and conservatives on the Court split sharply at earlier stages of the white primary controversy, but the decision to draw the line here—putting the internal procedures of a political party in the private rather than the public sphere—won unanimous support in *Grovey v. Townsend* in 1935.[19] The line so carefully drawn was then unceremoniously erased in *Smith v. Allwright* only nine years later: this time the vote was nearly unanimous the other way.[20] Justice Owen J. Roberts, dissenting, protested that the decisions of the Court were being put in "the same class as a restricted railroad ticket, good for this day and train only."[21]

Justice Roberts was right when he complained that nothing in the constitutional analysis had changed in the intervening nine years. What was different was the relative weight of the competing political principles involved. We tend to think of "state action" as a purely negative concept, a reason for not doing something, but the idea has a positive side to it as well: it affirms the existence of a private sphere of activity in which the laws of the states, and not the federal judiciary, retained paramount authority. As late as 1935, the Court was unanimously agreed on the importance of maintaining this public/private distinction, with its implications for federalism, even at the cost of a political outcome—the exclusion of black voters from any real participation in Texas politics—that many members of the Court in *Grovey v. Townsend* undoubtedly found repugnant. Nine years later, the balance between these competing principles was altogether different. The values of federalism protected by "state action" had been in eclipse since 1937. And on the other side of the scale—given the overtones for domestic politics

of our wartime ideology—a political outcome that had been repugnant in 1935 had become literally intolerable.

Shelley v. Kraemer[22] offers an even better example, because the state
action issue here was not nearly as close as in the white primary cases.
The question was the status of a "restrictive covenant" on a piece of
real estate—in this case, a prohibition on occupancy "by people of
the Negro or Mongolian Race." This was a covenant "running with
the land" and validly attached, under Missouri law, to a piece of property in St. Louis. Neither the City of St. Louis nor the State of Missouri could have imposed racial zoning by statue or ordinance, but it
was settled law that there was no constitutional objection to a private
restriction. Conceding that the covenant itself might be valid, the
Court in *Shelley v. Kraemer* made restrictive covenants effectively illegal by holding that the judicial enforcement of such a covenant would
be unconstitutional state action.

The difficulty here is very substantial. If *judicial enforcement* of a real
property covenant is state action, it is hard to see why the enforcement
or protection of any other property right is not also state action. (A law
school hypothetical would ask what happens if as a private landowner I
choose to prosecute trespassers of one race and not another. That hypothetical became a real-life question, one that the Court was unable to
resolve, in the series of sit-in cases that arose in the early 1960s.)[23]

Because *Smith v. Allwright* and *Shelley v. Kraemer* are decisions that
stretched the settled conception of state action to meet a political
imperative, they bear a certain resemblance to the *Jones & Laughlin
Steel* case[24] of 1937—if we can take *Jones & Laughlin* to symbolize the
point at which the Court officially renounced its opposition to expanding federal regulation on Commerce-Clause grounds. The problem of
defining the internal limits to the commerce power resembles the problem of defining state action in a number of respects. Both issues turn on
a fundamental constitutional distinction that is clear at its core but is
difficult or impossible to enforce at the margin. Both issues relate
directly to the question of federalism, meaning the allocation of political authority between state and national governments. ("State action"
is essentially a federalism question, as I have suggested, because if the
Court imposes constitutional restraints on private conduct it is exercising the general legislative power that the Fourteenth Amendment

had left with the states.) Both issues turned on a question of abstract constitutional principle, and in both cases the central interest protected by the abstract principle was the political position of the states in the federal system. Yet in both settings, the practical controversy at hand—economic regulation in one case, racial equality in the other—was one in which dominant public opinion was looking to the federal government for a solution, and not to the states. The cases are not usually discussed in the same lecture, but I think it is not too fanciful to suggest that *Jones & Laughlin* made *Shelley v. Kraemer* substantially easier—not to mention *Brown* itself.

ᘑ

The most interesting academic debate currently being pursued on the topic of *Brown v. Board of Education* is not about the constitutional legitimacy of the decision, but about how much difference it actually made. Michael Klarman, of the University of Virginia Law School, reminds us of the significance of nonjudicial developments affecting the status of black Americans at midcentury:

> There exists a widespread tendency to treat *Brown* as the inaugural event of the modern civil rights movement. Nothing could be farther from the truth. The reason the Supreme Court could unanimously invalidate public school segregation in 1954 . . . was that deep-seated social, political and economic forces had already begun to undermine traditional American racial attitudes. . . . [T]he same underlying forces that made *Brown* a realistic judicial possibility in 1954 also rendered it unnecessary from the point of view of long-term racial change.

The factors that Klarman proceeds to identify include "World War II, the ideological revulsion against Nazi fascism, the Cold War imperative, the growing political empowerment of northern blacks, the increasing economic and social integration of the nation, and changing southern racial attitudes."[25]

The Court's decision in *Brown* and its presumed consequences stand today as the cornerstone of the Supreme Court's political influence, indeed of our whole conception of the function of American constitutional law; so Professor Klarman's suggestion that we reconsider the relations of cause and effect surrounding *Brown* has been received in

some quarters as a form of *lèse-majesté.* The debate over the practical significance of *Brown* and its measurable consequences lies outside my
assigned topic, and I will not pursue it here. But that debate is part of
a broader puzzle, about the workings of judicial power in our political
system, which forms one of the pervasive themes in the case law of our
post-*Plessy,* pre-*Brown* interval. The cases remind us of certain fundamental constraints on the Court's power to make things happen.

This theme is announced very early in the century in the context of
voting rights. The case is *Giles v. Harris* in 1903.[26] Black citizens of
Alabama alleged that they had been excluded from registering to vote,
solely because of race, pursuant to a scheme designed to eliminate black
voters. Of course the allegations were true (this was 1903); of course
there was state action; of course there was a violation of the express terms
of the Fifteenth and Fourteenth Amendments. But what exactly would
we have the Supreme Court do about it in 1903, even judged with the
benefit of hindsight? *Giles v. Harris* is an extraordinary case because Justice Holmes, with his characteristic impatience and lack of tact,
described candidly why the Court was refusing to issue an injunction:

> The bill imports that the great mass of the white population intends to
> keep the blacks from voting . . . If the conspiracy and the intent exist, a
> name on a piece of paper will not defeat them. Unless we are prepared
> to supervise the voting in that State by officers of the court, it seems to us
> that all the plaintiff could get from equity would be an empty form.
> Apart from damages to the individual, relief from a great political wrong,
> if done, as alleged, by the people of a State and the State itself, must
> be given by them or by the legislative and political department of the
> Government of the United States.[27]

Present-day biographers and commentators quote these words of
Holmes with reactions that range from dismay to outrage. I call them to
your attention, on the contrary, because from our privileged perspective
at the end of the twentieth century we can see that "Holmes" description of the judicial dilemma was extraordinarily prescient. Of course a
more liberal court in 1903 could have given the plaintiffs in *Giles v.
Harris* what Holmes contemptuously called "a name on a piece of
paper." The Court post-1937 did everything it could, ruling in *Smith v.
Allwright* that the Texas Democratic Party was an agency of the state,
even managing to find in *Terry v. Adams*[28] that a local political club

violated the Fifteenth Amendment when it excluded blacks from its slate of recommended candidates. Of course the white primary cases made a difference. But judicial decrees could not finally remedy what Holmes called the "great political wrong": massive disfranchisement, on the basis of race, in defiance of the Fifteenth Amendment. They could not do so, because the wrong was accomplished—as it had been accomplished in *Giles v. Harris*—by the discriminatory administration of voter registration. That wrong could be remedied, as Holmes predicted, only by supervising or replacing the administrators and by removing, so far as possible, the possible grounds of discrimination. This was exactly the relief that was finally given by the Voting Rights Act of 1965—in "Holmes" words, "by the legislative and political department of the Government of the United States."

Holmes' dark vision in *Giles v. Harris* should make us think about two constraints on constitutional adjudication that explain a great deal about the course of Supreme Court decisions post-*Plessy* and pre-*Brown*. The first of these constraints is the sheer political necessity of avoiding the issuance of a mandate that can be successfully disobeyed. The problem is epitomized by Andrew Jackson's remark—supposedly uttered during a fight with the Court over Georgia's treatment of the Cherokee Indians in 1832—"Well, John Marshall has made his decision, now let him enforce it."[29] The Court's ultimate authority as expositor of the Constitution depends entirely, in our system, on the loyalty and acquiescence of the political branches. A Supreme Court that finds itself too far out in front, or that lags too far behind, will see its constitutional mandate ignored, defied, or repudiated. This is what almost happened in 1937 on the great question of federalism, and the Court was determined not to run any such risk again—for desegregation or any other cause. This is why the constitutional history that forms the prologue to *Brown* is preoccupied, not with questions of constitutional principle, but with judicial strategy and tactics; why the Court refused to take up the question of school segregation until it was convinced, in Justice Frankfurter's words, that public opinion had finally "crystallized against it";[30] why even then the Court hesitated—until it realized that it could declare a new rule of equal protection without having to enforce it. The Court waited until May 1955 before it announced that the school segregation cases would be remanded to the district courts, with instructions that they find the means to enforce the plaintiffs' constitutional rights "with all deliberate speed."[31]

A second major constraint on constitutional adjudication brings us back to the problem of state action. Discrimination in voting rights and school segregation presented problems that were subject to constitutional law—if not always subject to judicial remedy—because they resulted from the action of the state. Beyond this legal discrimination, however, lay all the rest of social relations, where the fact of racial inequality was reflected and reinforced by private choice.

By an expansive reading of what constituted state action, the Court might prohibit the judicial enforcement of a restrictive covenant, as it did in *Shelley v. Kraemer;* but a private refusal to sell real property is wholly self-enforcing. The refusal to sell can only be made illegal by legislation that constrains the private actor's usual freedom of choice: in this case, the federal Civil Rights Act of 1968 or comparable state legislation. In the case of employment discrimination—an even greater barrier to social and economic equality than segregated housing—the inherent limits to the judicial mandate were just as plain. The constitutional guarantee of equal protection or privileges and immunities conveyed no protection against a private entity's racially motivated refusal to make a contract. Like the Civil Rights Act of 1866, the Fourteenth Amendment undoubtedly secured to all persons "the same right . . . to make and enforce contracts . . . as is enjoyed by white citizens"—but that is only the right to make an enforceable contract with someone who wants to make one with you.[32] With employment as with housing, it would take plenary legislative authority to constrain a self enforcing private choice: in this case, Title VII of the Civil Rights Act of 1964.

Now by 1964, when it finally decided to act in this area, Congress possessed plenary legislative authority over the employment relationship—because the constitutional revolution of 1937 had changed the old enumeration of powers, granting the federal government full legislative authority at least in matters of economic regulation. (If the Civil Rights Act of 1964 had been enacted in 1934, it would have been held unconstitutional.) A case could be made that the Supreme Court's most important contribution to this century's unfinished revolution in racial equality was not *Brown v. Board of Education* but *NLRB v. Jones & Laughlin Steel.*

Looking back on it now, a generation after the modern civil-rights statutes were put in place, we can see that the fight over the state-action doctrine was a struggle by the Court to escape certain inherent limitations that distinguish the judicial from the legislative function. The Court took up an argument that was logically and historically awkward—attempting to cast the discriminatory choices of private actors as discrimination by the state—because it was determined to advance the cause of racial equality before Congress was ready to do so. Yet where the Court moved too far ahead of Congress, it laid claim to ground that it lacked the forces to occupy; with the result that this territory was not really gained for the cause of civil rights until it was retaken, in the 1960s, by "the legislative and political department of the Government of the United States." As Justice Holmes had pointed out in 1903, there was really no other way to do it.

⁓

One of the characteristic features of the post-*Plessy,* pre-*Brown* interval is the Court's occasional willingness to declare constitutional law exceeding the reach of its mandate. This means, of course, that in evaluating the accomplishments of the Court in the area of race we must try to measure the influence of the Court's pronouncements as distinct from the immediate force of its decrees. The pros and cons of "all deliberate speed" make this a familiar controversy for the civil-rights era at mid-century, but we encounter the same problem, very unexpectedly, in our earlier period as well. The first two decades of the twentieth century saw cases in which the Court clearly went out of its way to suggest the existence of constitutional principles of equality and nondiscrimination that it was not yet prepared, perhaps not yet even inclined, to enforce. Let me describe the three instances that I find most intriguing.

The first episode is a dog that did not bark: This was the Court's treatment of the *Berea College* case in 1908.[33] *Berea College* was a small, private institution in rural Kentucky that taught black and white students together. The Kentucky legislature passed a statute outlawing the practice. The Supreme Court upheld this segregation law against a constitutional challenge, but on a narrow, almost painfully artificial ground. Berea College was a Kentucky corporation, and the Supreme

Court ruled that the state was merely exercising its power to limit the activities of corporations it had chartered. To judge by the majority opinion, in other words, this was not a segregation case at all.

Why did the Court in *Berea College* not even mention *Plessy v. Ferguson?* Narrowly construed, the decision twelve years earlier had been about segregated railroad cars, not segregated education. But nobody construed it that narrowly. As I suggested at the outset, *Plessy* taught that the Fourteenth Amendment imposed no special barrier to a legislative classification on racial lines; moreover, that a law separating the races might be a reasonable and valid exercise of the police power. In upholding the validity of the Berea College statute, the Supreme Court of Kentucky read and cited *Plessy* in exactly this way.[34] When the College appealed, the state pressed the same argument before the U.S. Supreme Court. Since the Court had decided to let the Kentucky result stand, why not adopt the Kentucky reasoning as well?

Berea College draws our attention to a curious and significant fact about *Plessy v. Ferguson*. On the narrow issue of segregating railroad passengers, and on this issue alone, *Plessy* was treated as authoritative.[35] But the avowed reasoning of the majority opinion—and, I would argue, the plain meaning of the decision to anyone who read it in May 1896— proved to have no vitality whatsoever in the Court that had issued it. Apart from two railroad cases, *no subsequent decision by the United States Supreme Court ever referred to* Plessy v. Ferguson *as a guide to the meaning of the Fourteenth Amendment.* It is true that the Court before 1937 showed no inclination to revisit the question of segregation in transportation and public education, the two areas where segregation had been the status quo well before *Plessy*.[36] But the Court never once referred to *Plessy* as authority to support either another form of segregation or any other type of racial discrimination. *Berea College* is interesting because the Court so noticeably kept its distance from the reasoning the Kentucky judges had enthusiastically embraced—going out of its way to avoid reaffirming what it had said only twelve years earlier.

My second example is *McCabe v. Atchison, Topeka & Santa Fe Railway*,[37] decided in 1914. Here the Court considered an Oklahoma statute of the *Plessy* kind, mandating separate but equal facilities for black and white railroad passengers. But the Oklahoma law had a peculiarity: it provided that first-class accommodations, in sleeping and parlor cars, might be provided exclusively for passengers of one race, with no equivalent provision for the other. By a vote of 5-4, in an opinion by Justice Charles Evans Hughes, the Court declared this law unconstitutional. The railroad tried to justify, the reasonableness of the statute by pointing to the relative lack of demand among black passengers for first-class accommodations: a separate black Pullman car would have run empty most of the time. Hughes declared such considerations irrelevant, on the ground that "it is the *individual* who is entitled to the equal protection of the laws."[38]

McCabe was not a ruling against segregation, in practical effect: Railroads could still create a "separate but equal" Pullman or dining car by installing a curtain or a removable partition at one end of the car. And yet the decision carried extraordinary implications. Part of what makes the case extraordinary is that Hughes' opinion, for a narrow majority of the Court, was transparently *obiter dictum*. After giving what was in effect an advisory opinion about the constitutionality of the Oklahoma statute, the Court announced that the case would be dismissed because the plaintiffs had no standing to sue. (They had not bought tickets since the effective date of the law.) Obviously, the Court's 5-4 majority was going far out of its way to make a point. What was the point? Hughes' opinion in *McCabe* meant more than it said, because what it said cannot be taken at face value. It is simply not true that "it is the individual that is entitled to the equal protection of the laws," if that means that each of us has a constitutional claim to whatever benefits the law may provide to others. *McCabe* makes sense only if we understand it to mean something quite different: that a law requiring racial segregation is constitutionally permissible only if the segregated facilities are kept rigorously equal. But that is a strained reading of *Plessy*, very different from the rule that was actually announced in 1896—which was that a segregation law would be constitutional so long as it was reasonable in the eyes of the Court.

I do not wish to overstate the point. The decision in *McCabe* does not begin to prove that five members of the Court, had they had the power to do so, would have outlawed all forms of segregation in 1914. And yet the decisions in *Berea College* and *McCabe* show us something extremely interesting. Not two decades after *Plessy*, more than half the members of the Supreme Court had shown themselves to be uncomfortable with the reasoning of the case that was the leading authority for the legality of segregation under the Fourteenth Amendment. At a bare minimum, I would argue, the Hughes opinion in *McCabe* is a statement that a racial classification is *not* like any other classification, constitutionally valid if reasonable. On the contrary, Hughes and his colleagues treat a racial classification as inherently suspect—though without acknowledging any such judgment.

Justice Holmes, who saw precisely what Hughes was up to, accused him in correspondence of insisting on "logical exactness" in enforcing equal rights.[39] This was not meant as a compliment. The usual test of equal rights incorporates what might be called a rule of reason: the standard guarantee of the Fourteenth Amendment is not that all persons be treated identically in all circumstances, but that legislative classifications resulting in different treatment be drawn on reasonable lines. *Plessy* applied this rule of reason to the question of racial segregation, treating it as self-evident that, for purposes of a statute regulating railroad passenger facilities, the race of the passenger was a meaningful distinction. Hughes reached his result in *McCabe* by tacitly rejecting this rule of reason where a racial classification was concerned.

Whether the Hughes approach is called "logical exactness" or "stricter scrutiny," the result is that a racial classification is, to some extent at least, disfavored. Because *Plessy* had implied just the opposite, *Plessy* was, to that extent, tacitly disapproved. To find these implications in a Supreme Court opinion written in 1914—an opinion that five members of the Court persisted in issuing, while admitting that they had no case or controversy to decide—has to make us rethink what we think we know about "the era of separate but equal."

The last of my three instances is the Court's unanimous opinion in *Buchanan v. Warley*[40] in 1917. The case arose from a growing movement in southern and border-state cities to reinforce racially segregated housing patterns by municipal ordinance. Louisville, Kentucky, had adopted an ordinance with typical provisions: a house on a city block predominantly occupied by white residents could not be sold to a black purchaser, and vice-versa. In a unanimous opinion by Justice William R. Day, the Court in *Buchanan v. Warley* held that this ordinance violated the Fourteenth Amendment.

Buchanan was (among other things) a case about the right of an owner to dispose of his property, and it is reasonable to surmise that the decision would not have been unanimous if the case had lacked this implicit appeal to substantive due process. The rights of the aggrieved property owner are mentioned in the opinion, but they are not the basis on which Justice Day placed the reasoning of the Court.

The Fourteenth Amendment, the Court declared in 1917, "ordains that no State shall deprive any person of life, liberty, or property, without due process of law, or deny to any person within its jurisdiction the equal protection of the laws. *What is this but declaring that the law in the States shall be the same for the black as for the white; that all persons, whether colored or white, shall stand equal before the laws of the States, and, in regard to the colored race, for whose protection the amendment was primarily designed, that no discrimination shall be made against them by law because of their color?*"[41]

Justice Day was reading from *Strauder v. Virginia,*[42] a case decided in 1880 about racial discrimination in selecting juries; but he spoke in the present tense, about the meaning of the Constitution in 1917. It was an extraordinary thing to say. *If the Fourteenth Amendment declares that the law in the States shall be the same for the black as for the white,* many people would conclude that it prohibits not only Louisville's housing ordinance but every other form of segregation as well. Even if we give the words the most modest interpretation they will bear, they still imply that constitutional law in 1917—meaning the practical reality of the Court's mandate at the time—fell somewhere short of the constitutional command.

The suggestion that the Constitution sometimes requires more than the Court can yet deliver is the same that we see in the words of Chief Justice Stone in 1943, when he declared—in the bitterly ironic context of the Japanese Relocation Cases—that "Distinctions between citizens solely because of their ancestry are by their very nature odious to a free people."[43] We see it again in 1955, when the Court conceded that the Fourteenth Amendment rights of black schoolchildren could only be enforced in an indefinite future, "with all deliberate speed."

An implicit if intermittent promise of future mandates forms one of the primary stories of the interval between *Plessy* and *Brown.* A later generation of civil-rights lawyers would find these implications in *McCabe's* unstated but unmistakable hostility to Jim Crow practices; in *Buchanan's* evocation of an older nondiscrimination principle as the basis for a decision against segregated housing; in the seemingly unequivocal denunciation of "Distinctions between citizens solely because of their ancestry," even as such distinctions were being reluctantly upheld. Given the helpful fact that the original, expansive reasoning of *Plessy* had never reappeared in any subsequent decision of the Court, these recurring intimations over the years were what permitted the civil-rights forces, in the years immediately preceding *Brown*, to argue that *Plessy* had long since been abandoned, and that not only segregation but any legally-imposed racial classification had become plainly unconstitutional. So in their final consolidated brief in the *School Segregation Cases*, filed on the eve of the *Brown* decision in late 1953, the lawyers for the NAACP Legal Defense Fund, led by Thurgood Marshall, summarized their principal argument by stating that "Distinctions drawn by state authorities on the basis of color or race violate the Fourteenth Amendment." They reiterated in closing: "[T]hat the constitution is colorblind is our dedicated belief."[44]

Throughout the interval between *Plessy* and *Brown* it was Justice Harlan's dissenting opinion, and not the reasoning of the *Plessy* majority, that represented the meaning of racial equality for anyone who cared about racial equality. The majority in 1896 had shown how easily the command of equal protection might be accommodated to the existing state of race relations in America; Harlan's dissent anticipated a time when the Court might seek to change them. The constitutional law of race between *Plessy* and *Brown* reminds us that the political significance of constitutional doctrine sometimes falls short of the Court's mandate, and sometimes outruns it. This makes the question of the Court's influence a more complex and a more interesting one than if the Justices could simply tell us what to do.

NOTE: *This article is reprinted from 1999* **Journal of Supreme Court History** *vol. 24 no. 2.*

Endnotes

1. Readers familiar with the literature will recognize in the present essay the influence of two historians in particular Benno C. Schmidt, Jr., and Michael J. Klarman. Professor Schmidt's studies of the Supreme Court's race-related cases in the Progressive Era are collected in Alexander M. Bickel & Benno C. Schmidt, Jr., **The Judiciary and Responsible Government 1910–21**

[vol. 9 of the Holmes Devise History of the Supreme Court of the United States] chs. viii–x (1984). Professor Klarman is currently at work on a comprehensive study of the period that is the subject of this essay, tentatively titled **From Jim Crow to Civil Rights: The Supreme Court and the Struggle for Racial Equality.** For some of his preliminary conclusions *see* Klarman, "An Interpretive History of Modern Equal Protection," 90 *Mich. L. Rev.* 213 (1991); "*Brown,* Racial Change, and the Civil Rights Movement," 80 *Va. L. Rev.* 7 (1994); "Civil Rights Law: Who Made It and How Much Did It Matter?," 83 *Geo. L.J.* 433 (1994); "Race and the Court in the Progressive Era," 51 *Vand. L. Rev.* 881 (1998); "The *Plessy* Era," 1998 *Sup. Ct. Rev.* 303.

2. 163 U.S. 537 (1896).

3. *See* Andrew Kull, **The Color-Blind Constitution,** ch. 7 (1992).

4. Charles A. Lofgren, **The *Plessy* Case: A Legal-Historical Interpretation** 197 (1987).

5. 347 U.S. 483 (1954).

6. *See* Andrew Kull, **The Color-Blind Constitution** ch. 7 (1992).

7. Gerald Gunther & Kathleen M. Sullivan, **Constitutional Law** 671 (13th ed., 1997).

8. 109 U.S. 3 (1883).

9. *Id.* at 25

10. *See* Kull, *supra* note 3, ch. 5.

11. The close of what is here called the "Court's civil-rights era" is marked by the decisions in *Milliken v. Bradley,* 418 U.S. 717 (1974) (declining to consolidate school districts as a remedy for racially identifiable school systems), and *Washington v. Davis,* 426 U.S. 229 (1976) (finding the "disparate impact" of government policy insufficient to establish a violation of equal protection).

12. *See, e.g., Brown v. Board of Educ.,* 347 U.S. 483 (1954).

13. *See, e.g., Shelley v. Kraemer,* 334 U.S. 1 (1948) (judicial enforcement of private restrictive covenant as prohibited state action).

14. *See, e.g., Mayor & City Council of Baltimore v. Dawson,* 350 U.S. 877 (mem.) (1955) (segregation of public beaches and bathhouses); *Holmes v. City of Atlanta,* 350 U.S. 879 (mem.) (1955) (municipal golf courses); *Gayle v. Browder,* 352 U.S. 903 (mem.) (1956) (city buses).

15. *See NAACP v. Alabama ex rel. Patterson,* 357 U.S. 449 (1958) (freedom of association protected by First and Fourteenth Amendments).

16. *See, e.g., Naim v. Naim,* 197 Va. 80, 87 S.E.2d 749, vacated and remanded, 250 U.S. 891 (1955), reinstated and aff'd, 197 Va. 734, 90 S.E.2d 849, app. dismissed, 350 U.S. 985 (1956) (declining to pass on constitutionality of a statute prohibiting interracial marriage).

17. *United States v. Carolene Products Co.,* 304 U.S. 144, 152–53 n. 4 (1939).

18. 305 U.S. 337 (1938).

19. The sequence of cases is *Nixon v. Herndon,* 273 U.S. 536 (1927); *Nixon v. Condon,* 286 U.S. 73 (1932); *Grovey v. Townsend,* 295 U.S. 45 (1935).

20. 321 U.S. 649 (1944).
21. *Id.* at 669.
22. 334 U.S. 1 (1948).
23. *See, e.g., Bell v. Maryland,* 378 U.S. 226 (1964); *Hamm v. City of Rock Hill,* 379 U.S. 306 (1964).
24. *NLRB v. Jones & Laughlin Steel Corp.,* 301 U.S. 1 (1937).
25. Klarman, *supra* note 1, 80 *Va. L. Rev.* at 13–14.
26. 189 U.S. 475 (1903).
27. *Id.* at 488.
28. 345 U.S. 461 (1953).
29. 1 Charles Warren, **The Supreme Court in United States History** 759 (rev. ed. 1926).
30. Frankfurter's remark, quoted in a memorandum by Justice Douglas, was made in a Supreme Court conference in 1960. *See* Klarman, *supra* note 1, 83 *Geo. L.J.* 433, 455 and n. 107.
31. *Brown v. Board of Edu., (Brown II),* 349 U.S. 294, 301 (1955).
32. The Court's holding to the contrary in a case involving housing discrimination, *Jones v. Alfred H. Mayer Co.,* 392 U.S. 409 (1968), is singularly unpersuasive. The Civil Rights Act of 1968, forbidding racial discrimination in housing, had been enacted shortly before the decision was announced, *Jones* reveals the determination of a majority of the Court, at the height of the Court's civil rights ear, not to relinquish its placer in the vanguard even to a coordinate branch of the federal government.
33. *Berea College v. Kentucky,* 211 U.S. 45 (1908).
34. *Berea College v. Commonwealth,* 123 Ky. 209, 94 S.W. 623 (1906).
35. *Chesapeake & O. Ry. v. Kentucky,* 179 U.S. 388 (1900); *Chiles v. Chesapeake & O. Ry.,* 218 U.S. 71 (1910).
36. *Gong Lum v. Rice,* 275 U.S. 78 (1927), which assumes (without directly addressing) the constitutionality of segregated schools, cites *Plessy* merely for its cross-reference to the earlier state cases on school segregation.
37. 235 U.S. 151 (1914).
38. *Id.* at 161–62.
39. Holmes' letter to Hughes has not survived, but its content may be inferred from Hughes' reply. This letter is reproduced among the illustrations to Bickel & Schmidt, *supra* note 1, following page 592.
40. 245 U.S. 60 (1917).
41. *Id.* at 77 (emphasis added).
42. 100 U.S. 303 (1880).
43. *Hirabayashi v. United States,* 320 U.S. 81, 100 (1943).
44. Brief for Appellants in Nos. 1, 2 and 4 and for Respondents in No. 10 on Reargument, *Brown v. Board of Educ.,* et al. (Oct. Term 1943), at 16, 65.

   D A V I D W. L E V Y

Before Brown: The Racial Integration of American Higher Education

The landmark case of *Brown v. Board of Education of Topeka*[1] is known, at least in its general outline and result, to millions of American citizens. It may, in fact, be the most universally recognized of all of the decisions ever handed down by the Supreme Court of the United States. No reputable high school or college textbook in American history fails to mention it as one of those monumental determinations of the High Court that changed forever the fabric of American life. And there can be no doubt that the *Brown* case—followed as it was by spirited debate, invigorated efforts on behalf of integration, and bitter resistance by many whites—fully deserves the notice it has received since 1954. How is it possible, after all, to *overestimate* the importance of the decision that declared unconstitutional the long-established practice of racial segregation in elementary and high school public education?[2]

  But while the *Brown* case resulted in a flood of commentary and debate and anger and violence, and while the *Brown* case has been retold many times and from numerous perspectives by historians, participants, textbook writers, and others, the prior episode, centering around the legal attack on racial segregation in higher education, has been relatively little studied. Perhaps because the demolition of segregation in the nation's colleges and universities was accepted rather more calmly by the general public, it has tended to be given much less attention. But that story too was an important one. It was a dramatic and profoundly significant episode in the history of race relations in our country. It too was characterized by enormous courage and heavily freighted with implications and lessons about the complicated connections between law and social change. In the battle to rid American colleges and universities of the injustices of segregation, moreover, the Supreme Court played a decisive role . . . and one which paved the way for the Justices' monumental opinion of 1954.

و

In the late 1930s, when for practical purposes the effective attack on segregated higher education began in earnest, the availability of post-secondary education for African Americans was largely a matter of region. In the North, no state university prohibited the entrance of black students. Once they were on campus, however, they were subjected to various sorts of discrimination, often connected with the university's social and extra-curricular life. Some of that discrimination was formal, but most of it was unwritten, quietly understood, and traditional. Northern private schools had varying policies, but Gunnar Myrdal, in his classic study of 1944, **An American Dilemma,** offered this generalization: "Private universities in the North restrict Negroes in rough inverse relation to their excellence: the great universities—Harvard, Chicago, Columbia, and so on, restrict Negroes to no significant extent if at all. . . . Most of the minor private universities and colleges prohibit or restrict Negroes. Some of these permit the entrance of a few token Negroes, probably to demonstrate a racial liberalism they do not feel." Probably there were fewer than a dozen or so African-American faculty members in all northern colleges and universities.[3]

In the South, of course, things were very different. At the outbreak of World War II, seventeen states and the District of Columbia maintained, by law, separate school systems at all levels. The post-secondary education of African Americans in southern states was carried out in

117 all-black colleges. Thirty-six of these were public schools; of the private ones, only seven were not church-related.[4] Attendance in these black southern colleges had been growing steadily: they had 2,600 students in 1916, 7,600 in 1924, 34,000 in 1938, and 44,000 in the 1945–46 academic year. Although this was an impressive rate of growth, it must be remembered that by 1940, one out of every twelve southern white youths received some college education, while only one out of a hundred southern black youths did. Just as important, moreover, is that despite their healthy rate of growth, and despite the myth that black public schools were required by constitutional law to be "equal" if they were going to be "separate," these all-black colleges were, by most standards, inferior operations—starved for funds, poor in staff, buildings, and equipment. In 1943, the **National Survey of Higher Education of Negroes** studied twenty-five representative black colleges, applying the criteria of the North Central Association, and concluded that "colleges for Negroes in general are below par in practically every area of educational service."[5] Two years later, Charles Thompson, the crusading black editor of *The Journal of Negro Education,* wrote that not a single black college "offers work that is even substantially equal to that offered in the corresponding state institutions for whites."[6]

And if the conditions under which most southern African-American *undergraduates* tried to get an education were inferior and deplorable, the situation in graduate and professional education was a major scandal. The graduate and professional educational opportunities offered to African Americans were so few and so bad, in fact, that it was precisely there that the legal attack on segregation was about to unfold.

Up until 1936, only 139 African Americans had earned the PhD degree in the United States. In 1939, when Fred McCuistion undertook a thoroughgoing study entitled **Graduate Instruction for Negroes in the United States,** only seven black colleges in America offered any graduate work whatsoever; nine southern states had no provision whatsoever for black graduate education. No all black college in the South offered work beyond the M.A. degree until the 1950s. As far as professional education was concerned, in 1945 the South had fifteen medical schools for whites and none for blacks; four dental colleges for whites and none for blacks; sixteen law schools for whites and one for blacks; seventeen engineering schools for whites and none for blacks;

fourteen pharmacy schools for whites and none for blacks.[7] This deficiency, of course, made itself felt deeply in the professional assistance
available to American blacks. By 1945 each African-American doctor,
dentist, or lawyer had to provide services for a vastly greater number of
patients or clients than white practitioners of the same profession.[8]

These statistics clearly indicate the enormous disadvantages under
which African Americans, particularly in the South, were suffering
when it came to gaining higher education, and especially when it came
to getting graduate or professional training. It goes without saying that
this system of segregated southern education reflected the racial attitudes of most white southerners. In many southern states, therefore, the
system of separated higher and professional education (like the separation of public education at the elementary and high school levels) was
embedded not only in tradition and in persistent popular attitudes,
but heavily fortified in state law, in state constitutions, and in the rules
and regulations laid down by the governing bodies of southern colleges and universities as well.

In view of all of the formidable obstacles raised against quality, integrated higher education, those who undertook to challenge and reform
his system had a very serious task awaiting them. In a report done a
decade before the end of World War II, *The Journal of Negro Education* asserted that in the seventy years since the end of the Civil War,
forty-four lawsuits had challenged segregated education (at all levels)
and that all forty-four had been lost in the nation's courts.[9]

၁

Even before the outbreak of World War II, some attempts at breaking
down segregated higher education in the South had begun. Not counting a disastrous failure to force the integration of the pharmacy school
at the University of North Carolina in 1933,[10] two of these early comes
deserve some notice. The first occurred in Maryland in 1935, and was
aimed at the University of Maryland Law School, which was located in
Baltimore. A young African American named Donald Murray had
graduated from Amherst College in Massachusetts and hoped to practice law in Baltimore, his hometown. He applied to the Maryland
Law School and was turned down by the president of the University on

the grounds of race and race alone—and this despite the fact that Maryland had no law requiring segregation at the University. The state had no law school for African Americans. The National Association for the Advancement of Colored People took an interest in this case, and Murray was represented by two of the NAACP's ablest lawyers, Charles H. Houston and young Thurgood Marshall. The latter had a special interest in the case: Marshall was also from Baltimore, and he too had been denied the opportunity to study at the University of Maryland law school.[11]

Murray's attorneys did not attack segregation as such. Instead, on the basis of shrewd calculation, they rested their argument on a much less radical ground. They simply argued that if Maryland was going to provide legal education for its white citizens, it was obligated under the separate-but-equal formula of *Plessy v. Ferguson*[12] to provide it for black citizens too. The case was heard before the Baltimore City Court, which ordered that Murray be admitted to law school. The state promptly appealed to the Maryland Court of Appeals where the original decision was upheld.[13] At that point Maryland gave up and admitted Murray to its law school. Thus this case, for all of its pioneering importance, never reached the federal court system, much less the Supreme Court of the United States.

One more thing should be noted in connection with the Murray case. The Maryland legislature established out-of-state scholarships to pay the tuition expenses of black Maryland students who wanted to pursue graduate programs that they could not pursue in their own state, but that were available at home to white students. The legislature hoped by this means to satisfy the separate-but-equal formula, by being able to argue that no black student was being deprived of graduate or professional education simply because he or she could not get it in Maryland. These scholarships were not actually funded by the legislature, however, until Murray was rejected; and the court ruled, in addition, that tuition expenses alone were inadequate for students who had to bear the costs of travel and of living away from home. Nevertheless, several other southern states seized upon this device of out-of-state scholarships for African Americans as a way of forestalling integration. One state that tried it was Missouri, and it was in Missouri that a second significant pre-World War II case occurred.

In June 1935, Lloyd Gaines had graduated from Lincoln University, the all-black state school in Missouri. Like Donald Murray in Maryland, Gaines also wanted to go to law school in his home state and he too was denied admission because of his race alone. The Maryland precedent, of course, was not binding in another state and Missouri argued that there were some real differences anyway. In the first place, in Missouri, the out-of-state scholarships were real and adequate and several black students were already studying with these scholarships in other states. And second, Missouri was so anxious to maintain its segregated law school that it was willing to build a black law school at Lincoln—therefore, if Gaines was suffering a disability, it was merely a temporary one, until the Lincoln law school could get up and functioning.

Both the trial court and the appeals court in Missouri ruled in favor of the state's segregated system and to deny Gaines' request for admission.[14] The NAACP attorney—once again the intrepid Charles Houston—expected this outcome in the state courts and, perhaps, even hoped for it. Gaines went straight to the Supreme Court.[15] In 1938, by a vote of 6-2, the Missouri courts were reversed and the state was directed to admit Gaines to the existing law school—only the High Court's most reactionary Justices, James C. McReynolds and Pierce Butler, dissented from Chief Justice Charles Evans Hughes's majority opinion. As far as the plan to someday build a law school for black Missourians was concerned, the Chief Justice wrote, "we cannot regard the discrimination as excused by what is called its temporary character."[16] Hughes also made short work of the out-of-state tuition option that Missouri offered to provide: "We think that these matters are beside the point. The basic consideration is not as to what sort of opportunities other States provide, or whether they are as good as those in Missouri, but as to what opportunities Missouri itself furnishes to white students and denies to negroes solely upon the ground of color."[17]

The decision in the *Gaines* case set a precedent of enormous importance in the growing effort to break down race separation in southern higher education. Henceforth *Gaines* would be cited as one of the central arguments in every subsequent suit brought by those attempting to destroy segregation. It is important to reiterate, however, that none of the early cases directly attacked segregation itself. They simply contended that facilities available to black citizens were not equal to those available to white ones and that this was inconsistent with both the Fourteenth Amendment and the doctrine of separate-but-equal set forth in the old *Plessy* case back in 1896.

World War II intervened in this process of battling segregated higher education, however, and no cases came to the Supreme Court between 1938 (the *Gaines* decision) and 1948. When the struggle resumed, it resumed in Oklahoma and at the state's leading institution, the University of Oklahoma.

ॐ

Oklahoma was not a state at the time of the Civil War, of course, but by the time statehood came in 1907, the racial mores and attitudes of the old Confederate states had insinuated themselves firmly into Oklahoma's social life. Fearing the rejection of their work by the Republicans in Washington, D.C., the authors of the constitution of 1907 contented themselves with merely mandating separation of the races at school, content to turn over the real work of legally segregating Oklahoma society, to the first legislatures, and the new lawmakers did not disappoint. Before they were finished, Oklahoma had race laws that emulated many of the harshest practices of the deep South. A law of 1915, to take just one example, mandated the Corporation Commission to require telephone companies to provide separate phone booths for white and black users![18]

As the constitutional provision indicated, there was a special desire to keep school children of the different races apart, and Oklahomans produced at every level a segregated school system that survived for nearly half a century. As far as higher education was concerned, the state relied on Langston University, established in 1897, one year after *Plessy* and ten full years before statehood, to accommodate black youth. But through the years the legislature so starved Langston for funds that it could scarcely be considered an institution of higher learning. It offered no professional or graduate education and was not accredited. In 1935, the legislature—with one eye on the trouble being caused in Maryland by Donald Murray—set aside $5,000 to pay out-of-state tuition for African-American students who wanted to pursue graduate work. By the late 1940s, the sum was $50,000 and nearly two thousand black

Oklahomans had studied in other states, in various fields that white students could learn at home.

The Oklahoma legislature passed statutes in 1941 designed to protect absolutely the tradition of racial segregation in state schools.[19] The law now made it a misdemeanor to admit blacks into white schools, a misdemeanor to teach in a classroom that contained both whites and blacks, and a misdemeanor to be a student in such a mixed-race classroom. Administrators, teachers, or students were liable for stiff fines if they violated these laws, and each fresh day that they violated them was to be considered a new crime. On November 7, 1945, the University of Oklahoma's Board of Regents directed President George Lynn Cross "to refuse to admit anyone of Negro blood as a student in the University."[20] If all of this were not sufficiently daunting to potential African-American students, they had to also bear in mind one other fact: the University was located in Norman, a town that had probably never had a single black resident and whose citizens boasted that right up until World War II, no black person had ever spent the night within the town's boundaries.[21]

The first sign of trouble ahead occurred in 1945, less than a month after the end of World War II. Thurgood Marshall arrived from New York to attend the state's NAACP meeting in McAlester, Oklahoma.[22] On September 3 he told reporters that the group had decided to mount a challenge to Oklahoma's segregation laws by attempting to enroll a black student in the state's higher education system. A careful search was begun for the right candidate. On January 14, 1946, just before the start of the second semester, three African Americans appeared in President Cross's office. Two of them were state NAACP officials; sitting between them, across the desk from Cross, was Ada Lois Sipuel Fisher, a twenty-two-year-old Langston University honors graduate from Chickashaw, Oklahoma. Years later, Cross recalled "The young woman was chic, charming, and well poised as she entered my office, and I remember thinking that the association had made an excellent choice of a student for the test case."[23] Fisher—like Murray and Gaines before her—wanted to go to law school.

Cross told his visitors that, whatever his own views about segregation (and there can be no doubt that he privately regarded the system as absurd and unjust), he was prohibited by state law and by the directive of the University's Regents from admitting any African American. They said that they understood this fully. All they wanted from him was a letter stating that it was race—and only race—that prevented Fisher's admission. Cross quickly reviewed her credentials and dictated the requested letter in their presence.[24] On the basis of this acknowledgment that the candidate was acceptable on all grounds but one, the legal assault began. An unsuccessful attempt to secure a writ of mandamus from the Cleveland County District Court consumed the spring and early summer of 1946. From there the case was appealed to the Oklahoma Supreme Court, which, on April 29, 1947, rejected Fisher's request. The court held that Fisher should not insist on entering the all-white school, in opposition to the constitution and the laws of Oklahoma, but should instead apply to the proper authorities (presumably the State Regents for Higher Education[25]) to provide her with a legal education substantially equal to that being given to whites. In short, the Oklahoma Supreme Court ruled that she had asked for the wrong remedy.[26] Marshall and the others went to the Supreme Court of the United States.

The nation's highest court disposed of the state's claims with stunning speed. The arguments were heard on January 7 and 8, 1948, and a scant four days later, on January 12, the Supreme Court ruled unanimously that the Equal Protection Clause of the Fourteenth Amendment required Oklahoma to give black students training in law or to stop immediately giving such training to white students.[27] Thus the Supreme Court was able once again to dodge the underlying question of whether segregation was, itself, unconstitutional. An editorial in *The New York Times* said of the *Sipuel* decision: "So far, so good. But not far enough. The Court again begged the issue as to whether states' segregation laws are constitutional. . . ."[28]

If the Justices in Washington, D.C., thought that this settled the matter and that Fisher would now be admitted to the University of Oklahoma Law School, they had not sufficiently calculated the stubborn determination of the Oklahoma authorities to maintain segregation. Within a week of the High Court's ruling, the state's attorney general asserted that the Supreme Court's ruling did not, in his opinion, invalidate Oklahoma's race laws; the state supreme court declared that the State Regents had to provide a legal education for Fisher while still preserving the separation required by Oklahoma's constitution; and the State

Regents proclaimed the establishment of the Langston University School of Law—a school for one student that would have to be made ready in a week in order to coincide with the beginning of the second semester at the law school for white students in Norman. The black "law school" was to occupy three rooms on the fourth floor of the State Capitol building, the student body (i.e., Fisher) was to have access to the State Library, and the Regents hired, in unseemly haste, a "faculty" consisting of two Oklahoma City lawyers and a former Oklahoma attorney general.[29] On January 24, the State Board of Regents for Higher Education announced—apparently with a straight face—that the Langston Law School was "substantially equal in every way" to the one in Norman![30] Fisher and her attorneys, of course, quickly made it clear that she would have nothing whatever to do with this patent fraud.

Instead she and her lawyers returned to the judicial system, arguing that the makeshift arrangement concocted by the State Regents did not, in fact, actually constitute substantially equal educational opportunity. Despite an impressive array of expert witnesses (including the law deans from Harvard and the University of Pennsylvania) testifying that it was impossible to regard the two schools as being even remotely equal, the Cleveland County District Court decided that they were, in fact, equal—a conclusion that President Cross would later call "incredible." Naturally, Fisher and her lawyers headed off again to the Supreme Court.

But before the Supreme Court could rule, the question was settled in Fisher's favor in another way, by two other closely linked cases. These two are particularly important because they indicate a critical transition in the argument of those seeking to end segregated higher education and, in the process of shifting the argument, these two point the way to the future.

ॐ

The first of the cases also arose in Oklahoma. Having been encouraged by the Supreme Court's ruling in *Sipuel,* in January 1948, six other African Americans appeared in Norman to apply for admission into various graduate and undergraduate programs that were not available at the black college at Langston. Among them was George W. McLaurin, himself a faculty member at Langston and mature in years.[31] He wanted to work toward a doctorate in education. In October 1948, the federal district court handed down another curious opinion in the McLaurin case: admittedly, Oklahoma must provide training leading toward the doctorate in education for McLaurin or else discontinue that program for white students—that much was clear from the *Sipuel* ruling back in January; *but* this did not necessarily mean that Oklahoma's segregation statutes could not be enforced.[32] This language (and the fact that the district court refused to grant the injunction for which McLaurin's attorneys had asked) opened the way for the state to continue its attempt to escape integration of the races.

The "solution" to the problem of granting admission while maintaining segregation was defined by the legislature (which amended the 1941 statute[33]) and was worked out by the University's Board of Regents and the University's administration. (The University's administrators had little or no sympathy with the absurdities they were about to enact, but felt that Oklahoma law, with its system of heavy fines, left them little choice.) All of McLaurin's classes were to be held in the same room—a medium sized lecture hall with an anteroom at its north corner. McLaurin would sit in the anteroom where he could see and hear the teacher and see the blackboard, but still be considered "separated" from the whites, i.e., receiving instruction, as the newly amended law required, in a "separate classroom." A table with McLaurin's name on it was set aside for study in the University library; he was to eat by himself in a specially designated area in the student union; he had his own toilet.[34] A week after these arrangements had been perfected, Thurgood Marshall returned to Oklahoma and was asked what he thought of the measures taken to segregate McLaurin. With typical directness he characterized them as being "stupid."[35] Nevertheless, two months later, when Marshall and McLaurin petitioned the court to end the segregation, the federal district court refused, stating that the bizarre arrangements did not violate the provisions of the Fourteenth Amendment.[36] That decision was promptly appealed to the Supreme Court.

Meanwhile, three things were occurring back in Oklahoma that influenced the outcome. First, after McLaurin was admitted, even under these grotesque conditions, African Americans kept coming. They applied for admission to the University of Oklahoma in a steady stream, so that by the summer session of 1949, there were eleven enrolled in graduate work and more indicating their intention to apply for the fall semester. Each time that such a student applied, the University directed the application to the state's attorney general for an opinion.[37]

Second, it was becoming clearer with each passing week that the presence of black students on the campus was not causing trouble. From the outset it was obvious that there was overwhelming support for integration among the University's faculty. The students were more divided, but substantial support for the admission of African Americans was also present in the student body. There were some opinion polls taken at the time, but they were of a rather unscientific nature. It appears that around half of the student body favored the admission of African Americans. The highest percentage of those consisted of returned World War II veterans, graduate students, seniors, and students in the College of Arts and Sciences; the lowest support for integration was to be found among freshmen and business and engineering majors.[38] Those students who favored integration, however, were much more active and vocal in expressing their views. They formed organizations and held large demonstrations. They carried off the ropes and barriers erected to separate the black students. They walked over to shake hands and to offer welcome when new African-American students arrived. They ate at their table with them and studied side-by-side in the library.

Finally, public opinion in Oklahoma was gradually coming around. In part this was due to the increasing evidence that integration did not lead automatically to catastrophic disorder. In part, everyday Oklahomans, even the most rabid racists among them, came to see both the absurdity of the present system and the terrible expense that would be involved in setting up alternative programs at Langston every time any black student in Oklahoma requested one. What if an African American wanted to be a doctor or an atomic physicist? Could the state afford a medical school or a cyclotron in those eventualities? In part, moreover, Oklahomans were stung by the national ridicule their measures were drawing. As pictures of the roped off George McLaurin—dignified and grandfatherly, clad always in coat and tie—were published in the national media, the rest of the country expressed their views forcefully.[39] Undoubtedly many Oklahomans remained unconvinced of either the justice or the expediency of integration, but more and more of the Regents, educational leaders, members of the legislature, and other officeholders called publicly for an end to the absurdity.

Nevertheless, for a full academic year the University had to endure this business of divided rooms, separate tables, set-aside toilets. It devised policies to cover bringing African American guests to the student Union for lunch, their attendance at football games, their right to University housing. By the time the Supreme Court spoke in *McLaurin v. Oklahoma State Regents,*[40] the Oklahoma system of higher education was desperate for an end to what Cross called "this ridiculous and extremely embarrassing situation."[41]

But *McLaurin v. Oklahoma State Regents* was only half of a pair of closely related cases. The second case emanated from Texas, but it seemed in many ways (although not in all) the same old story.[42] Heman Sweatt, a mailman, wanted to go to the University of Texas Law School, and he applied for admission in February 1946. The District Court ruled, of course, that to deny him legal education was unconstitutional, but it gave Texas six months to build a law school for African Americans. A dingy little place in Houston was chosen, near the offices of two black attorneys who were to constitute the faculty. When it was obvious that this makeshift arrangement could not possibly be construed as being "substantially equal" to the University of Texas Law School, which was probably the best in the entire region, the legislature appropriated enough money to move the Houston operation to Austin, near the University of Texas. So far, it was the old tale of the petitioner claiming that the "separate" facility was far from being "equal." Despite widespread support from white Texas students and the appearance of high-powered experts who testified that the new law school was not "substantially equivalent" to the white law school, the District Court ruled against Sweatt, and the Court of Civil Appeals agreed.[43] Naturally, Marshall and his client were off to the Supreme Court. The Court decided to hear arguments in both *McLaurin* and *Sweatt* on the same day—April 4, 1950.

ॐ

Richard Kluger writes that "Thurgood Marshall had been in the fight too long not to see that he could spend the rest of his life trying to prove that white school boards in a thousand counties were failing to provide an equal-but-separate education for their resident Negroes."[44] It would be an endless endeavor, arguing that such-and-such a separate arrangement was not "equal" enough to satisfy the *Plessy* formula—that such-and-such a building or library or faculty or length of school year or expenditures for students or salaries for teachers or amount of available scholarship money was less for blacks than for whites. Moreover, in the McLaurin suit, the case of the Oklahoman who sat in his roped-off classroom, the matter of "equality" was not as clear as in the other cases: McLaurin, after all, had access to the same library, the same classroom, the same faculty at the University of Oklahoma as any white student.

Therefore, the NAACP attorneys, after intense and thorough discussion, adopted a new strategy as they argued *McLaurin* and *Sweatt*.[45] They were careful, of course, to make the same, laboriously documented contention that McLaurin and, particularly, Sweatt were being treated unequally; but they also, this time, made an additional argument: that segregation, in and by itself, was inherently unconstitutional, that the old doctrine in *Plessy v. Ferguson,* permitting separation if the conditions were substantially equal, was wrong and had been perniciously and disastrously wrong for more than half a century. Thus the brief before the Supreme Court began with these words:

> This case is believed to present for the first time in this Court a record in which the issue of the validity of a state constitutional or statutory provision requiring the separation of the races in professional schools is clearly raised. It is the first record which contains expert testimony and other convincing evidence showing the lack of any reasonable basis for racial segregation. . . .[46]

To make this part of their case, the lawyers for McLaurin and Sweatt introduced large quantities of expert testimony from social scientists, sociologists, psychologists, educators—all confirming the harmful effects of a policy of segregated education upon the lives and minds and self-evaluations of those being segregated and excluded. The Supreme Court, in short, was being given the opportunity in 1950 to declare that segregation—even in those instances where the conditions were relatively equal had no place in education.

The twin decisions in *McLaurin* and *Sweatt* were announced on the same day, June 5, 1950. Both of the opinions were the product of a unanimous Court, and both were read by Chief Justice Fred Vinson. But although the High Court edged hesitantly toward the more radical position that Marshall and the NAACP were hoping for, the Justices were unwilling to go the whole way. They still insisted on settling the cases in terms of the inequalities in Texas and Oklahoma. At the start of his opinion in *Sweatt,* Vinson addressed the matter directly: "Broader issues have been urged for our consideration," he admitted, "but we adhere to the principle of deciding constitutional questions only in the context of the particular case before the Court. We have frequently reiterated that this Court will decide constitutional questions only when necessary to the disposition of the case at hand, and that such decisions will be drawn as narrowly as possible." As a result of this self-imposed limitation, Vinson decreed, "much of the excellent research and detailed argument presented in these cases is unnecessary to their disposition."[47]

In the Texas case of Heman Sweatt, the Supreme Court ruled that the Austin facility was obviously not equal to the magnificent one at the University of Texas. This was entirely obvious from the hard facts. The white law school at the University of Texas had sixteen full-time and three part-time professors, 850 students, and a library with 65,000 volumes in it. The white school also had a law review, moot court facilities, scholarship funds, opportunities to specialize, many distinguished alumni, and other important advantages. The black law school, by contrast, had five full-time professors, twenty-three students, and a library of 16,500 volumes; it boasted one alumnus in the Texas bar.[48] On the face of it, therefore, the inequalities were glaring and unconstitutional. But Vinson's opinion went on to add some significant words:

> What is more important, the University of Texas Law School possesses to a far greater degree those qualities which are incapable of objective measurement but which make for greatness in a law school. Such qualities to name but a few, include reputation of the faculty, experience of the administration, position and influence of the alumni, standing in the community, traditions and prestige. It is difficult to believe that one who had a free choice between these laws schools would consider the question close.[49]

Clearly, when one begins to consider matters such as "prestige," "tradition," and "influence of the alumni," it is hard to see how any makeshift segregated facility would be able to stand the equality test.

In the *McLaurin* case from Oklahoma, the Court's reasoning was even more strained. The Justices concluded that, despite McLaurin's access to the same facility, the same library, and the same faculty as the white students, at the University of Oklahoma, the segregated conditions under which he was forced to go to school rendered him less than equal to his fellow students. True, there was no physical inequality, Chief Justice Vinson said, but the restrictions imposed upon McLaurin "impair and inhibit his ability to study, to engage in discussions and exchange views with other students and, in general, to learn his profession. . . . Those who will come under his guidance and influence must be directly affected by the education he receives. Their own education and development will necessarily suffer to the extent that his training is unequal to that of his classmates."[50] Thus the decision in *McLaurin* was that, once a student was admitted into a university, he or she could not be treated differently than other students simply on account of race. But, in the end, the *McLaurin* decision was also framed in terms of inequalities, not in terms of the unconstitutionality of segregation itself.

The Supreme Court of the United States was not to rule against segregation itself, until the *Brown* case, four years later. Then, on May 17, 1954, the Court spoke decisively through Chief Justice Earl Warren:

> We come then to the question presented: Does segregation of children in public schools solely on the basis of race, even though the physical facilities and other "tangible" factors may be equal, deprive the children of the minority group of equal educational opportunities? We believe that it does. . . . We conclude that in the field of public education the doctrine of "separate but equal" has no place. Separate educational facilities are inherently unequal.[51]

Perhaps we may leave the story of the legal struggle against segregated higher education at this point. We must not minimize, of course, the legal battles that lay ahead—the cases of George McLaurin and Heman Sweatt may have destroyed segregated *graduate* education, but they said little about normal *undergraduate* work. Nor should we minimize the dramatic integration struggles that remained to be won on the actual battle ground of the deep South. After all, the confrontation between Alabama's governor George Wallace and prospective college student James Meredith on the doorstep of the University of Alabama occurred a full dozen years after the Court's rulings in *McLaurin* and *Sweatt*. Nevertheless, by the end of 1950, and certainly by the end of 1954 with *Brown,* the important principles had all been laid down and enunciated; what remained was a kind of mopping-up operation against very difficult and stubborn white resistance in many places, but that part of the war against segregation is another and a distinct matter.

ॐ

Like every other important transformation of the American legal environment, this one too illustrates the complex, double-sided relationship between social change and the law. The simple rule—so simple that one is almost embarrassed to express it—has two parts: the first is that changes in our law spring from change in American life. As Oliver Wendell Holmes, Jr., put it in that famous first paragraph of his 1881 book, **The Common Law,**

> . . . the life of the law has not been logic: it has been experience. The felt necessities of the time, the prevalent moral and political theories, intuitions of public policy, avowed or unconscious, even the prejudices which judges share with their fellow-men, have had a good deal more to do than the syllogism in determining the rules by which men should be governed. The law embodies the story of a nation's development through many centuries, and it cannot be dealt with as if it contained only the axioms and corollaries of a book of mathematics.[52]

In his case, vast social forces were afoot, tending in the direction of the general breakdown segregation. The massive migration of thousands of southern blacks to northern states permitted them to assemble enough political power to make judges and presidents and legislators listen to grievances that it had long been possible to ignore. The rise of a group of African-American personalities that captured national admiration and sympathy had the effect of helping to neutralize negative stereotypes, humanizing a race that had been practically invisible to most whites—one thinks of Jesse Owens, Marian Anderson, Joe Louis, Jackie Robinson, Paul Robeson, and others. The crucible of World War II made unmistakable the hypocrisy of fighting against the Nazi racists while at the same time brutally segregating an entire race of American citizens. The constant humiliation that American race policies brought upon the nation at the height of the Cold War, the disadvantage those policies brought in the competition for the political and military allegiance of the non-white peoples of the earth, caused many Americans, including those in high political and diplomatic positions, to wonder if there were not more admirable, less ridiculous ways to conduct a nation's race relations. Above all, perhaps, the rising militancy of the African-American community itself—the attacks all across the nation on everything from housing covenants to separate entrances to federal buildings, from unequal pay for white and black teachers to segregation in the armed forces, from the all-white Democratic primary to the all-white jury to the all white section of the bus. Everywhere in the late 1930s and through the 1940s and early 1950s, thousands of black men and women and their leaders were determined that enough was enough. The assault on segregated higher education can be seen as a part of this gigantic wave of social change.

But the second part of that embarrassingly simple rule about law and social change also is true and comes into play in this case too. Transformations in the law might indeed be brought about by vast social changes; but once in place, the new law often goes on to have quite spectacular social effects itself. In this case, they are obvious. The new armies of African Americans who graduated from first-class, accredited colleges fueled the civil rights movement of the 1960s at all levels, entered the professions and politics and business, and established a powerful African-American middle class. How this change in the law recast American colleges and universities—their curricula, their social and athletic life, their hiring and harassment policies, the attitudes and experiences of the white students—is a breathtaking story in itself. Law, in short, makes changes as well as being caused by changes and one would be hard-pressed to think of a clearer example than this one.

This story has some symbolically satisfying footnotes. The new and slick brochures for the law schools at the state universities of Maryland, Missouri, Texas, and Oklahoma now all boast of the schools' commitment to "diversity" and to increasing the representation of minorities in the legal profession. Their catalogues indicate required courses in "Race, Gender and the Law," and elective courses in "Employment Discrimination" or "Affirmative Action" or "Civil Rights Law." Full color photographs show black faculty members of both sexes teaching to relaxedly integrated classrooms.

Another poignant and symbolically satisfying footnote is from the University of Oklahoma. Ada Lois Sipuel Fisher graduated from the Law School in 1951. After a few years of practice she went to work for

Langston University. She earned a Master's degree in History from the University of Oklahoma in 1968 and taught at Langston and served as chair of her department there. On April 27, 1992, Governor David Walters named her to a vacancy on the University of Oklahoma's Board of Regents, the seven-member body that governs all aspects of University life. It was, of course, the very Board that worked so hard to exclude her from attending the University in 1948. The appointment won applause from every corner of the state. If there was any criticism whatever, it never reached the level of public expression.[53]

We must be careful not to minimize the distance that still separates blacks and whites in American society, and we are not yet at the position where we can pretend that the journey to full equality is completed. Indeed, there is a very long way to go in many areas of American life. That having been acknowledged, however, there is still some merit in looking back over the last half-century and, while always remembering how much is left to do, taking some satisfaction in what the partnership of law and social change has made better.

NOTE: *This article was originally published in 1999* **Journal of Supreme Court History** *vol. 24, no. 3.*

Endnotes

1. 347 U.S. 483 (1954).
2. For the story of the case, *see* Richard Kluger, **Simple Justice: The History of Brown v. Board of Education and Black America's Struggle for Equality** (New York: Alfred A. Knopf, 1976); for the aftermath, *see* Numan V. Bartley, **The Rise of Massive Resistance: Race and Politics in the South during the 1950s** (Baton Rouge: Louisiana State University Press, 1969), Jennifer L. Hochschild, **Thirty Years after *Brown*** (Washington, D.C.: Joint Center for Political Studies, 1985) or Raymond Wolters, **The Burden of *Brown:* Thirty Years of School Desegregation** (Knoxville: University of Tennessee Press, 1984).
3. Gunnar Myrdal, **An American Dilemma: The Negro Problem and Modern Democracy** (New York: Harper & Brothers, 1944), 633.
4. *Id.,* 632, 951. In the thirty non-southern states, there were only four all-black colleges, two of them founded before the Civil War.
5. Myrdal reports (951n) that in the eleven states under the southern Association of Colleges and Secondary Schools, 46 percent of the white colleges were accredited in 1939, but only 22 percent of the black colleges were.

6. The best source for these statistics, problems, and descriptions of higher education for African Americans in this period are the pages of *The Journal of Negro Education,* edited since 1932 by Charles H. Thompson. *See also,* Horace Mann Bond, **The Education of Negroes in the American Social Order** (New York: Prentice Hall, 1934) and "Enrollment in Negro Colleges and Universities," *School and Society,* 50 (July 29, 1939): 141.

7. Fred McCuistion, **Graduate Instruction for Negroes in the United States** (Nashville: George Peabody College, 1939). For the figures ten years later, in 1948, *see* Kluger, **Simple Justice,** 257.

8. For example, Myrdal reports (326) that in 1930 there were six black lawyers in Mississippi and four in Alabama, compared to more than 1,200 and 1,600 white lawyers in those states, and (172) in the South in 1937 about 35 percent of black babies were delivered by doctors, compared to 90 percent of white babies.

9. Kluger, **Simple Justice,** 169.

10. *Id.* at 155–58, 806n. *Hocutt v. Wilson,* North Carolina Superior Court (March 28, 1933).

11. Mark V. Tushnet, **Making Civil Rights Law: Thurgood Marshall and the Supreme Court, 1936–1961** (New York: Oxford University Press, 1994), 11.

12. 163 U.S. 537 (1896).

13. *Pearson v. Murray,* 169 Md. 478 (1936). *See also* Kluger, **Simple Justice,** 186–94, and Tushnet, **Making Civil Rights Law,** 11–15.

14. 342 Mo. 121 (1937).

15. *Missouri ex rel. Gaines v. Canada,* 305 U.S. 337 (1938). S.W. Canada was the registrar at the University of Missouri. *See also,* Kluger, **Simple Justice,** 202–204, 213.

16. *Id.* at 352.

17. *Id.* at 49. The *Gaines* case had a bizarre footnote: Lloyd Gaines never entered the University of Missouri Law School; he disappeared mysteriously and was never found, causing some to speculate that he had been murdered.

18. Law of Mar. 30, 1915, ch.262, 1915 Okla. Sess. Laws 513.

19. Okla. Stat. tit. 70, Sec. 452–64 (1941).

20. University of Oklahoma Board of Regents, "Minutes," November 7, 1945, 1932–33.

21. George Lynn Cross, **Blacks in White Colleges: Oklahoma's Landmark Cases** (Norman: University of Oklahoma Press, 1975). 5–10.

22. This account of the *Sipuel* case relies on Cross, **Blacks in White Colleges,** and Ada Lois Sipuel Fisher, **A Matter of Black and White: The Autobiography of Ada Lois Sipuel Fisher** (Norman: University of Oklahoma Press, 1996). *See also* Kluger, **Simple Justice,** 258–60, and Tushnet, **Making Civil Rights Law,** 12–30.

23. Cross, **Blacks in White Colleges,** 35.

24. "One of the NAACP officials quoted President Cross as saying that he would write whatever "you feel will get you into court" in the rejection letter (Tushnet, **Making of Civil Rights Law,** 129). Had Cross felt otherwise, he could simply have denied admission to Fisher on the grounds that she had graduated from Langston, which was not an accredited college.

25. A body different from the University of Oklahoma Board of Regents.

26. 199 Oklahoma 36, 1947.

27. *Sipuel. Board of Regents of the University of Oklahoma, et al.,* 332 U.S. 631 (1948). Miss Sipuel had married Warren Fisher in March 1944, but her transcripts bore her maiden name and the case proceeded forward as *Sipuel.*

28. *The New York Times,* January 15, 1948.

29. Fisher, **A Matter of Black and White,** 125–26.

30. Cross, **Blacks in White Colleges,** 54.

31. His age is variously reported; Cross (**Blacks in White Colleges,** 85) gives his age as fifty-four; Kluger (**Simple Justice,** 266), quoting Thurgood Marshall, puts him at sixty-eight. The NAACP chose McLaurin purposefully as their test case, hoping to neutralize the racist argument that black men were only applying to white colleges to hunt for white women they could date or marry!

32. *McLaurin v. Oklahoma State Regents for Higher Education 87 F.* Supp. 526 (1948).

33. 70 Okla. Stat. Ann. (1950) Nos. 455, 456, 457.

34. Cross, **Blacks in White Colleges,** 89–95.

35. *Id.,* 96; Tushnet, **Making of Civil Rights Law,** 130. By the time McLaurin's case came to the Supreme Court, there were some modifications in his situation. He was removed from the anteroom and allowed to sit in the regular classroom, but in a row specified for African Americans; his library table was removed from the Library's mezzanine to the main floor, where the other students studied; and he was allowed to eat in the cafeteria at the same time as the other students—but, of course, at a separate table.

36. *McLaurin v. Oklahoma State Regents for Higher Education 87 F.* Supp. 526 (1948).

37. Cross, **Blacks in White Colleges,** 107–110.

38. Earnestine Beatrice Spears, **Social Forces in the Admittance of Negroes to the University of Oklahoma** (University of Oklahoma, MA thesis, 1951), 34–36.

39. President Cross quotes some of the letters he received in his book, **Blacks in White Colleges,** 118ff.

40. 339 U.S. 637 (1950).

41. Cross, **Blacks in White Colleges,** 118–28, the quotation is at 126.

42. *Sweatt v. Painter et al.,* 339 U.S. 629 (1950). The case is discussed in Kluger, **Simple Justice,** 262–84, and in Tushnet, **Making of Civil Rights Law,** 128–38.

43. *Sweatt v. Painter et* al., 210 S.W. 2d 442 (1948).
44. Kluger, **Simple Justice,** 275.
45. In part, the new arguments were put forward by the numerous *amici* briefs that were filed in these two cases.
46. *Sweatt v. Painter et al.,* petition and Brief in Support of Petition for Writ of Certiorari, 2.
47. *Sweatt v. Painter et al.,* 339 U.S. 629, 631 (1950).
48. *Id.* at 632–33.
49. *Id.* at 634.
50. *McLaurin v. Oklahoma State Regents,* 339 U.S. 637,641 (1950).
51. *Brown v. Board of Education,* 347 U.S. at 493, 495.
52. Oliver Wendell Holmes, Jr., **The Common Law** (Boston: Little, Brown and Co., 1881).
53. *See* her autobiography, **A Matter of Black and White.**

    ❧ J E F F R E Y   D .   H O C K E T T

Justice Robert H. Jackson and Segregation

A Study of the Limitations and Proper Basis of Judicial Action

The ruling in *Brown v. Board of Education of Topeka*[1]—that racially segregated public schools violate the Equal Protection Clause of the Fourteenth Amendment—has rightfully come to be one of the most celebrated decisions ever rendered by the Supreme Court.[2] When announced, however, the form as well as the substance of Chief Justice Earl Warren's opinion drew bitter criticism.[3] Despite its moderate and non-accusatory tone, negative commentary was directed at the opinion even by those who strongly approved of its purpose.[4] The apparent lack of a legal basis for the ruling, and Warren's reference to sociological studies purporting to demonstrate the harmful effects of segregation on black children,[5] struck many as evidence of a policy-making Court or an instance of judicial usurpation of the legislative function.[6] While the form of Warren's opinion was not the primary reason for the protracted noncompliance that followed the ruling,[7] the misgivings engendered by the decision were undoubtedly exacerbated by the vulnerability of the Court's argument.

Many of the criticisms leveled at *Brown* could have been avoided or blunted had some of Justice Robert H. Jackson's ideas been incorporated into the Court's opinion. Jackson's working papers on the case reveal that he possessed a certain prescience concerning public reaction to judicial attempts to depart from long-standing constitutional doctrine and to reinterpret provisions in light of current presumptions and conditions. And he believed that this case, more than most cases, demanded consideration of the limitations of the judicial process in dealing with complex social issues.[8] Jackson's careful attention to the inherent limitations of judicial efforts to reform society and the informal restraints placed on these efforts by public opinion resulted, paradoxically, in a sounder approach to securing the rights of the plaintiffs in *Brown*. This is not to say that Jackson afforded an ideal means to effect the needed change in constitutional doctrine. Significant revisions of his argument would have been necessary, and Chief Justice Warren anticipated certain criticisms not accounted for by Jackson. Nevertheless, an examination of Jackson's writings provides valuable insights into the politics of constitutional revision by the judiciary— insights that would have facilitated the implementation of *Brown* and that are relevant to contemporary circumstances.

Justice Jackson, Segregation and the Fourteenth Amendment

Several scholars, in reconstructing the judicial deliberations in *Brown,* have noted Jackson's reservations and concerns which complicated the quest for Supreme Court unanimity.[9] However, there has been no thorough analysis of Jackson's views concerning the unconstitutionality of segregation which were formed after he resolved his doubts. Jackson's argument for ending segregation was set forth at length in an unpublished memorandum which he composed in 1954.[10] This opinion probably was suppressed in the interest of Court unanimity and because of Jackson's debilitated condition following his heart attack of the same year.[11]

The first section of Jackson's memorandum provides a brief discussion of the complexity of the situation before the Court. The eradication of segregation presents a formidable task, he believed, since it "involves nothing less than a substantial reconstruction of legal institution[s] and of society." Segregation is established not only in the laws of seventeen states and the nation's capital but also is embedded in the social customs of a large part of the country. Segregation persists, according to

Jackson, because of fears, prides and prejudices, "which even in the North are latent," and which the Court cannot efface. And however sympathetic the members of the judiciary may be "with the resentments of those who are coerced into segregation, we cannot, in considering a recasting of society by judicial fiat, ignore the claims of those who are to be coerced out of it." The tendency toward separation is fundamental in mankind and is not limited to this country or to racial considerations. "It has seemed almost instinctive with every race, faith, state or culture to resort to some isolating device to protect and perpetuate those qualities, real or fancied, which it especially values in itself." Separatism is sometimes desired even by minorities. It is currently practiced on a voluntary basis by certain religious groups that forbid intermarriage, establish separate denominational schools and "seek to prevent contacts which threaten dilution of blood or dissipation of faith." This "instinct for self-preservation," Jackson argued, accounts for the existence of segregation in several northern states as well as in the South.

The southern situation, in Jackson's view, is complicated by antagonisms toward blacks that do not exist in the North. The white South still deeply resents the program of reconstruction and the humiliation of carpetbag government. Whatever the necessity or merit of these reconstruction measures, "the North made the Negro their emotional symbol and professed beneficiary, with the material consequence of identifying him with all that was suffered from his northern champions." The race problem in the South thus involves more than mere racial prejudice; it is characterized by the enmity resulting from "a white war and white politics."

Consideration of the conditions which brought about and sustained segregation, Jackson believed, should deter the Court from adopting "a Pharisaic and self-righteous approach" to these cases and from promulgating a "needlessly ruthless decree."

After appraising the complexity of the controversy before the Court, Jackson turned in the second part of his memo to the question of whether existing law condemned segregation:

> Layman as well as lawyer must query how it is that the Constitution this morning forbids what for three-quarters of a century it has tolerated or approved. He must further speculate as to how this reversal of its meaning [could have been initiated] by the branch of the Government

supposed not to make new law but only to declare existing law and which has exactly the same constitutional materials that so far as the states are concerned have existed since 1868 and in the case of the District of Columbia since 1791.

Since segregation has existed in this country for so long, Jackson argued, it is difficult to believe "that the states which have maintained segregated schools have not, until today, been justified in understanding their practice to be constitutional."

Several considerations, according to Jackson, support the notion that segregated schools are constitutional. The language of the Fourteenth Amendment does not furnish a definitive basis for outlawing segregated schools, as ratification of the Fifteenth Amendment was required even to assure equal voting rights to blacks. With the deficiencies of the Equal Protection Clause obvious, the Fifteenth Amendment included no language referring to either segregation or education.

Historical analysis reinforces the view that the Fourteenth Amendment does not prohibit segregated schools. It is difficult to support the contention, Jackson argued, that any influential body of the movement behind the Fourteenth Amendment intended this provision to eradicate segregated schools or had even thought about either segregation or the education of blacks as a current problem. Although a few individuals involved in the framing and passage of that provision hoped it would establish complete social equality between the races and assimilation of liberated blacks into the American population, a majority of those who supported the Amendment were concerned merely with "ending all questions as to the constitutionality of the contemporaneous statutes conferring upon the freed men certain limited civil rights."[12]

If deeds are consulted as evidence of purpose, Jackson argued, the behavior of neither Congress nor the states indicates that the Fourteenth Amendment was aimed at prohibiting segregation in education. The very Congress that proposed the Amendment, and every subsequent Congress, maintained segregated schools in the District of Columbia. Furthermore, while Confederate states were readmitted to the Union only upon acceptance of the Fourteenth Amendment, Congress never indicated that segregated schools violated the conditions of reinstatement. It is true that five states abandoned segregated schools when the Amendment was submitted to them, and four states which had segregated schools refused to ratify the provision. But nine north-ern states and two border states continued or established segregated educational facilities after ratifying the Fourteenth Amendment, and the eight reconstructed states all instituted segregated schools. "Plainly," Jackson concluded, "there was no consensus among state legislators or educators ratifying the Amendment any more than in Congress that it was to end segregation."

Judicial precedent, in Jackson's view, also supports the view that seg-regation is constitutional. Indeed, almost a century of case law confirms this view. Even northern state judges and the northern members of the Supreme Court of the United States have held continuously that the Fourteenth Amendment does not of its own force prohibit the states from establishing separate educational facilities for the races.

An examination of the language, history and case law of the Fourteenth Amendment led Jackson to conclude:

> Convenient as it would be to reach an opposite conclusion, I simply can-not find in the conventional material of constitutional interpretation any justification for saying that in maintaining segregated schools any state or the District of Columbia can be judicially decreed, up to the date of this decision, to have violated the Fourteenth Amendment.

In the next section of this memorandum, Jackson focused on the dif-ficulties attending the enforcement of a judicial decision invalidating seg-regation. In view of the Court's inability to ensure the equality of separate facilities after *Plessy v. Ferguson*,[13] he argued, there is "no reason to expect a pronouncement that segregation is unconstitutional will be any more self-executing or any more efficiently executed." This pes-simistic prediction is warranted since the Court lacks the power to enforce general declarations of law by applying sanctions against persons not before it in a particular case. Furthermore, the school districts can be expected to continue segregation without the aid of legislation, since racial separation "exists independently of any statute or decision as a local usage and deep-seated custom." If the Court must rely entirely upon its own resources, a decision invalidating segregation is thus likely to "bring the court into contempt and the judicial process into discredit."

Any constructive policy for abolishing segregation, Jackson believed, must come from Congress. The power of this branch to imple-ment its decisions far exceeds that of the Court. Congress can enact laws binding all states and districts and can delegate supervision to administrative agencies that may apply sanctions against those who fail to comply with the law. Moreover, Congress can supply federal funds to facilitate changes that are beyond the means of particular communities. Finally, Congress can assume the burden of expensive litigation against recalcitrant states.

Jackson rejected the argument of the Eisenhower Administration that the federal District Courts must assume the burden of implementing a decision invalidating segregation since Congress may refuse to act.[14] In Jackson's view, the belief that the courts must act because the representative system has failed is an insufficient basis for judicial action. The judiciary must first be capable of supervising educational authorities on a continuing basis. This task, however, is "manifestly beyond judicial power or functions," as "[a] gigantic administrative job has to be undertaken." "Local or state or federal action will have to build the integrated school systems if they are to exist." Another reason the judiciary should not be asked to implement a ruling invalidating segregation is that the federal government offered no guidance to determine when and how school systems should be reconstructed. Jackson refused to

> be a party to thus casting upon the lower courts a burden of continued litigation under circumstances which subject district judges to local pressures and provide them with no standards to justify their decisions to their neighbors whose opinions they must resist.

While most of his opinion was devoted to an examination of the difficulties attending the execution and justification of a decision invalidating segregation, Jackson explained in the final section of this memorandum why the constitutionality of the practice could be maintained no longer. He began this section with the conciliatory statement that "[u]ntil today Congress has been justified in believing that segregation does not offend the Constitution." Congress and the states have relied on the Court's holdings that the requirement of equal protection does not prohibit reasonable classifications of citizens nor require government to accord identical treatment to all. In its holding in this case, Jackson argued, the Court does not invalidate the principle that equal protection allows classifications that "rest upon real not upon feigned distinctions" and that have a "rational relation to the subject matter for which the classification is adopted."

What the Court does invalidate, however, are classifications in education based upon race. It is now possible to see, according to Jackson, that the primary basis of these classifications—that there are "differences between the Negro and the white races, viewed as a whole, such as to warrant separate classification and discrimination" in educational facilities—is incorrect. Jackson conceded that he did not know whether this presumption was warranted in earlier times. When first liberated, blacks had little opportunity to demonstrate their capacity for education or even for self-support. Consequently, Jackson did not want

> to stigmatize as hateful or unintelligent the early assumption that Negro education presented problems that were elementary special and peculiar and that the mass teaching of Negroes was an experiment not easily tied in with the education of pupils of more favored background.

The spectacular progress made by blacks, however—"one of the swiftest and most dramatic advances in the annals of man"—has enabled them "to outgrow and to overcome the presumptions on which it [segregation] was based." In other words,

> [t]he handicap of inheritance and environment has been too widely overcome today to warrant these earlier presumptions based on race alone. I do not say that every Negro everywhere is so advanced, nor would I know whether the proportion who have shown educational capacity is or is not in all sections similar. But it seems sufficiently general to require one to say that mere possession of colored blood in whole or in part no longer affords a reasonable basis for a classification for educational purposes and that each individual must be rated on his own merit. Retarded or subnormal ones, like the same kind of whites, may be accorded separate educational treatment. All that is required is that they be classified as individuals and not as a race for their learning aptitude and discipline.

The necessity for judicial action on this subject thus "arises from the doctrine concerning it which is already on our books."

The breakdown of racial distinctions in American society also contributes to the unreasonableness of segregation. "Blush or shudder, as many will," Jackson noted, "mixture of blood has been making inroads on segregation faster than change in law." An increasing population with mixed blood baffles anyone attempting to classify the races.

The fact that segregation had been upheld for so many years is insufficient reason for the Court to continue to place its imprimatur upon the practice. "It is neither novel nor radical doctrine," Jackson argued, "that statutes once held constitutional may become invalid by reason of changing conditions, and those held to be good in one state of facts may be held to be bad in another."

Jackson ended his memorandum with the statement that he favored "going no farther than to enter a decree that the state constitutions and statutes, relied upon as requiring or authorizing segregation merely on account of race or color, are unconstitutional." He called for re-argument on the nature of the decree that would provide a remedy to the petitioners in this case. But Jackson anticipated that the Court would have to allow for varying periods of compliance. In view of the complex and diverse circumstances surrounding the issue, Jackson held that "only a reasonably considerate decree would be an expedient one for the persons it has sought to benefit hereby."

The Jackson Memorandum:

A Statement of the Limitations and Proper Basis of Judicial Action

The most fundamental difference between the opinions of Warren and Jackson was the challenge posed in the latter to the underlying premise of segregation. Jackson's opinion was predicated upon the accurate assumption that the primary justification for racial classifications was a belief in the inferiority of blacks. The notion of black intellectual and moral infirmity was widely accepted by individuals and groups (both northern and southern) whose views dominated public discourse during the latter part of the nineteenth century. These allegedly immutable racial distinctions were thought to necessitate and justify segregation in general (so as to avoid the debilitation of the white race through interbreeding) and separation of the races for purposes of education in particular (since blacks could not benefit from the education afforded to whites).[15] Jackson's bold decision to examine the sensitive issue of racial differences contrasted with Warren's strategy of focusing on the harms caused by segregation.[16]

Before examining the implications of these strategies, it must be noted that the boldness of the final section of Jackson's memorandum was offset by a marked concern evident throughout much of the opinion with the vexing difficulties of enforcement and justification. The cautious tone of Jackson's memorandum disturbed E. Barrett Prettyman, Jr., Jackson's law clerk during the 1953–54 Term and Justice Harlan's clerk during the 1955 Term. In a reply memo, Prettyman told Jackson that his argument was unlikely to generate public or political support because of its "negative attitude" and preoccupation with "doubts and fears." "If you are going to reach the decision you do," he wrote to Jackson, "you should not write as if you were ashamed to reach it."[17] Prettyman's criticisms of Jackson's memorandum are compelling. He was justified in pointing out to the Justice that it is one thing to express numerous concerns about a difficult decision, but "it is another thing to state them at such length and in such precedence over your affirmative views that the result you reach is swallowed up in them." Jackson would have been wise to heed Prettyman's suggestion that the memo begin with a clear, affirmative, and extended discussion of the legal position adopted in the final section of the opinion.[18] Without these revisions (and others to be discussed shortly), it is unlikely that Jackson's opinion would have generated public and political support.

Yet, an opinion which failed to take Jackson's concerns into account would not have generated much support, either. Jackson anticipated intense opposition to a decision invalidating segregation, and he wisely counseled his brethren to concern themselves with the limitations of the judicial process and the difficulties attending the execution of the Court's rulings. As Walter Murphy suggests, a Justice of the Supreme Court "is not often in a particularly favorable position to exert the dynamic sort of leadership which can mobilize effective reform or counterreform movements,"[19] since the Court has control of neither purse nor sword. For this reason, Jackson believed the considerable powers of Congress would have to be enlisted to aid in desegregation efforts. His discussion of congressional power, his confession of judicial incapacity to direct the implementation of *Brown,* and his statement that a solitary judicial effort to eradicate segregation would ultimately damage the institutional prestige of the courts were intended to solicit the aid and enlist the moral authority of Congress.[20]

Jackson's suggestion that *Brown* would remain an empty gesture without congressional involvement was borne out. In 1964, ten years after the decision, only slightly more than 1 percent of southern black children attended school with whites, and several states had no public school integration. Significant progress toward desegregated schools was made only in the late 1960s, after the fiscal power of Congress was brought to bear on recalcitrant states.[21] Of course, a judicial appeal for congressional assistance in desegregation efforts was unlikely to be successful in 1954, given that southern Congressmen held influential positions on important committees.[22] A slightly more promising strategy would have been to combine the appeal for congressional support with a plea for assistance from the Executive, as President Eisenhower oftentimes stated that he was obligated to enforce the law as interpreted by the Court regardless of his personal beliefs.[23] Such a request might have served as the catalyst needed to activate an administration that was, for the most part, apathetic toward civil rights issues.[24] Jackson was correct, however, in assuming that congressional involvement was essential to the success of *Brown* (i.e., a President can only propose necessary legislation), and his opinion, unlike Warren's, was crafted to induce a legislative response.

Jackson's appeal for positive congressional action would not have been heeded unless the form or rationale of his opinion was compelling. His attempt to persuade representatives and their constituents of the unconstitutionality of segregated public schools differed considerably from the logic of *Brown*. And it is likely that, overall, Jackson's approach would have been less vulnerable to the attacks of segregationists and more persuasive in the minds of those who had no interest in perpetuating the practice but would insist that an exercise of judicial power be "legitimate." Jackson realized that the Justices could not invoke the specific intent of the framers of the Fourteenth Amendment to justify the desired change in constitutional doctrine. Contrary to Warren's contention that the circumstances surrounding the adoption of the Amendment are "[a]t best . . . inconclusive,"[25] Alexander Bickel's historical investigation (published in the year following the Court's ruling) demonstrated that segregation in educational facilities was present to the minds of the framers, but they chose not to ban the practice. Warren's dismissal of the constitutional record thus left the Court open to the charge that the Justices had willfully ignored history.[26]

Yet, Jackson's frank and protracted historical discussion also would have made the ruling vulnerable. He emphasized the history behind the Amendment so as to avoid the impression that the Court was accusing the states of behaving unconstitutionally in the past.[27] But it is doubtful the South would have looked upon the decision more favorably had the opinion dwelt upon this information. Indeed, this probably would have incited resistance by fostering a feeling that an injustice had been inflicted upon the states. A more prudent strategy—and a strategy more well founded than Warren's—would have been to acknowledge briefly the circumstances surrounding the Amendment while emphasizing the reasons segregation should still be viewed as a violation of the Equal Protection Clause. This would have required that Jackson juxtapose the second and final sections of his opinion to make the point explicit that the notion of constitutional intent has never been restricted to the particular conceptions of the framers of a provision. Jackson needed to emphasize that the general proscription of unreasonable classifications is part of the meaning of the equal protection requirement.[28]

These problems of emphasis and organization aside, Jackson's justification for invalidating segregation in public schools was less susceptible to the charge of judicial legislation than was the rationale employed in the Court's opinion. Prior to *Brown,* the Justices never challenged the *Plessy* standard itself; at most, they insisted that separate educational facilities be equal.[29] By maintaining that separate schools could never be equal,[30] *Brown* departed significantly from previous decisions. Jackson realized that "the holy rite of judges consulting a higher law loses some of its mysterious power," to use Walter Murphy's words, "[w]hen the Court reverses itself or makes new law out of whole cloth [and] reveals its policy-making role for all to see."[31] And he believed the Court could act to preserve its institutional integrity or prestige by resting its decision upon a "legal" foundation.[32] That is, while the Justices would reverse constitutional doctrine—invalidate the notion of "separate but equal"—they would do so by employing the standard used in previous equal protection cases, namely, classifications between groups or individuals are allowable only if they reasonably relate to legislative purpose and are based upon real distinctions.[33]

Jackson's expectation that the Justices would receive harsh criticism for deviating from past rulings was well founded. A common charge directed at the Court was that it "blatantly ignored all law and precedent."[34] Some suggest the Court could have strengthened its argument by elaborating upon Warren's point that the notion of "separate but equal" was actually a departure from earlier rulings, which held that the Fourteenth Amendment proscribed all state-imposed discriminations against blacks.[35] Warren's failure to follow this tack, however, was fortunate, and perhaps purposeful. These earlier rulings would have been subjected to severe and compelling historical critiques had the Justices based the decision on the claim that they were merely returning to the original understanding of the Amendment as articulated by an earlier Court.[36] The historical accuracy of the basis of Jackson's argument (i.e., that constitutional provisions should be interpreted as general concepts not restricted to the particular conceptions of the framers) has been debated recently.[37] But the idea that the Equal Protection Clause prohibits unreasonable classifications generally was not controversial and was unlikely to be challenged seriously.[38] Certainly, Jackson would have been criticized for departing from the understanding that racial classifications in education are reasonable. His approach, however, enabled him to use language emphasizing continuity with previous rulings that Warren could not employ.[39]

Another sense in which Jackson's argument was less susceptible to the charge of judicial legislation was that it did not appear to rely upon "extralegal" materials.[40] Conspicuously absent from Jackson's opinion were references to the sociological data that had figured prominently in the petitioner's arguments and were mentioned in Warren's opinion.[41] In view of the fact that studies demonstrating the harmful effects of segregation were irrelevant to Jackson's holding (i.e., his contention that racial classifications in education are unreasonable did not depend upon whether segregation created a feeling of inferiority in black children), he had no reason to refer to the data. In an earlier draft of his memorandum, however, Jackson expressed extreme skepticism concerning the wisdom of incorporating social science evidence into Fourteenth Amendment jurisprudence. "I do not think," he argued, that "we should read into the concept of equal protection the shadowy and changing doctrines relating to mental and emotional reactions."[42]

Jackson's skepticism concerning the wisdom of incorporating such evidence into the Court's opinion was warranted. Warren's use of sociological studies was taken by many as proof that *Brown* was a political decision, one that merely implemented the personal value preferences of the Justices.[43] Warren's opinion, according to one commentator, "read more like an expert paper on sociology than a Supreme Court opinion."[44] Although legal controversies are oftentimes bound up with empirical questions, and such cases should be decided in the context of facts derived from the most reliable sources, the public generally views law and science as insular disciplines. Most believe the Court's only legitimate function is to interpret law (without reference to "non-legal" sources), and judicial use of sociological data is regarded as evidence of policy-making Justices.[45]

Some scholars suggest that the sociological evidence was incidental to Warren's opinion and could have been dropped without weakening the Court's argument. The cruelty of segregation, they believe, was obvious and required only a common-sense discussion to rebut the antiquated psychology underpinning *Plessy.*[46] Other scholars argue quite persuasively, however, that the Court was obligated to make reference to the studies.[47] The proximity and number of prior rulings accepting the possibility that separate facilities can be equal compelled the Justices to move beyond common-sense arguments in explaining the sudden departure from precedent.[48] Warren's approach, then, was vulnerable whether or not reference was made to the findings of social science. By contrast, though Jackson based his opinion upon an empirical proposition (i.e., that blacks are not inferior to whites), he was not obligated to employ extralegal materials, since there were no direct recent rulings examining the basis of racial classifications.[49] Unlike Warren, Jackson was able to resort to a common-sense discussion of changed presumptions and conditions which necessitated a modification in constitutional doctrine.[50]

The basis of Jackson's holding was useful not only for the purpose of preserving the Court's institutional integrity. Jackson's argument also placed the right of the petitioners to equal protection of the laws on a secure foundation—a foundation more secure than that provided by the claim that segregation creates a feeling of inferiority in black children.[51] The shortcomings of Warren's approach were demonstrated by the efforts of segregationists to have *Brown* reversed. Proponents of segregation initially sought to have the decision overturned by claiming science had shown blacks to be an inferior race—a race undeserving of the rights and privileges accorded to whites. This unfounded assertion and unsuccessful tactic was followed by the accumulation of evidence ostensibly demonstrating the preferability of segregated to integrated schools.[52] Segregationists referred to the works of scholars such as A. James Gregor, who argued that racial separation actually enhances the development of a healthy personality in the black child "by reducing the psychological pressure to which the child is subjected" through contact with whites. In an ironic paraphrase of Warren's language in *Brown,* Gregor concluded that integration "gives every evidence of creating insurmountable tensions for the individual Negro child and impairing his personality in a manner never likely to be undone."[53] Criticism of the Court's argument was found not only in the writings of segregationists. Several scholars sympathetic to *Brown* doubted that the empirical basis of the Court's holding had been demonstrated convincingly by the findings of social science.[54]

While the effect of segregation on the personalities of black children was a matter of some controversy, the overwhelming weight of scientific opinion supported the view that all significant disparities in achievement between blacks and whites were traceable to environmental rather than biological causes. When *Brown* was rendered (and since then), scientific racism attracted little attention and virtually no support from the social science community.[55] Considering the segregationists' failure to demonstrate the inferiority of blacks,[56] Jackson's assumption that his declaration concerning the irrationality of segregation would withstand criticism or challenge was well founded.[57]

While Jackson's position on segregation survives the challenges of racists, it remains open (as does the Court's implementation decision)[58] to the criticisms of proponents of desegregation. Although he died before the Court heard arguments on the form of its remedial decree,[59] Jackson accepted the strategy ultimately adopted by the Justices. He was willing to defer relief to the victims of segregation by allowing for varying periods of compliance with the ruling as to accommodate diverse local conditions.[60] By failing to require immediate compliance with a declaration of unconstitutionality, Jackson essentially tolerated a deprivation of constitutional guarantees. The apology for this position—that compliance is only deferred and not evaded—is little consolation to those individuals who must hope for good faith efforts by state officials toward compliance and who are deprived of a public benefit that is rightfully theirs. It is arguable that the Justices must ensure that no individuals are deprived of their constitutional rights for reasons of expediency if the Court is to act in a principled manner.[61]

As Alexander Bickel argued, however, a large and heterogeneous society like ours would disintegrate if it were deprived of the art of compromise or were "principle-ridden." Our society cannot be governed entirely by principle in some matters and exclusively by expediency in others. Often, guiding principle must co-exist with expedient compromise. Universal, immediate compliance with a declaration of unconstitutionality, while attractive, may be impossible to achieve in a particular situation, given the complexity of the task involved, the intransigence of public opinion, or the vulnerability of the Court's institutional prestige. Bickel maintained, however (and there is no reason to believe Jackson would have disagreed), that if a principle enunciated by the Court cannot be the "immutable governing rule," it must affect or guide the tendency of policies of expediency.[62]

The Limitations of the Jackson Memorandum

While the form of Jackson's memorandum would have stifled or blunted much of the criticism directed at the Court's decision, his argument for ending segregation was vulnerable in ways that Warren's opinion was not. Jackson was correct in claiming that the primary justification for racial classifications was a belief in the inferiority of blacks.[63] Segregationists, however, proffered other justifications for the practice. Some defended the dubious claim that racial separation was merely the form of social organization preferred by both races.[64] Human beings, it was argued, find their greatest happiness when among people of similar cultural, historical, and social background.[65] Jackson would thus have been subject to the charge that his analysis of segregation was simplistic. The Court was particularly susceptible to this sort of criticism since most of its members were northerners.[66]

Alternatively, Jackson would have been criticized for failing to acknowledge the implications of the first section of his opinion, where he discussed the "instinctive" drive for separation present in every race,

faith or state.[67] Jackson intended to convince the South forthwith that
the Court was aware of the complexities of desegregation and to assuage
fears that the Justices sought to engage the wholesale dismantling of
southern culture.[68] He failed to realize, however, that by entertaining
the disingenuous arguments of segregationists, he undercut his efforts
to demonstrate the unreasonableness of racial classifications.[69]

Warren's opinion did not elicit charges of oversimplification or inconsistency, since he made no observations about the underlying premises
of segregation. His argument was limited to an inquiry concerning the
effects of the practice. True, the Court was implored during the hearings
on the nature of its remedial decree to respect the complex structure of
customs and traditions that had grown up around segregation.[70] But,
in declaring the practice unconstitutional, Warren did not incite resistance by fostering the impression that the Court had misunderstood the
distinctive culture of a significant portion of the country.

It is arguable that Warren's avoidance of any discussion of the
rationale underpinning segregation precluded him from expressing
a sufficiently strong judicial commitment to a philosophy of racial
equality.[71] Jackson's opinion—with its profession of the fundamental
sameness of the races[72]—may have been more appropriate for a ruling
that marked a long overdue change in American race relations.[73] But
Brown was and is generally regarded as a momentous decision and the
product of an egalitarian political philosophy.[74] Moreover, Jackson's
opinion would have had the unfortunate effect of subjecting blacks
to the demeaning and superficial arguments of racists. The post-*Brown*
developments demonstrated that certain proponents of segregation
did not hesitate to defend the notion of immutable racial
distinctions.[75] These repulsive arguments would have persisted and
received wider exposure had the Court's opinion struck at the roots
of the practice.[76]

Jackson's explicit challenge of the primary justification for segregation also would have made the Court's opinion appear somewhat self-
righteous. Jackson held that the irrationality of segregation was apparent
to all reasonable minds, and the obverse of this is that only unreasonable (or morally deficient) people continue to see any justification
for racial classifications. Warren's opinion (although non-accusatory)

also drew attention to the moral deficiency of segregationists. He maintained that segregation caused permanent harm, and all America knew where culpability lay.[77] Nevertheless, the psychological damage caused by segregation was not presented as a self-evident truth; social science data was used to demonstrate the existence of the harm. The infliction of this injury was thus less blameworthy than a belief in racial inferiority.[78]

Another problem stemming from Jackson's decision to challenge the underlying premise of segregation is the breadth of his ruling. Jackson's argument was likely to alarm the South since it effectively undercut all forms of segregation (i.e., if blacks are not inferior, the legal separation of the races cannot be justified in any social setting). By contrast, Warren narrowed the scope of his ruling by stressing the peculiar importance of public education and hence the need for vigilance in detecting inequality in this area alone.[79] This argument was expected to minimize the misgivings of those affected by the ruling.[80] *Brown,* however, could scarcely have engendered more controversy, as education was the most sensitive area in which desegregation could occur. School integration was viewed widely as a harbinger of what segregationists regarded as an execrable development in race relations—miscegenation. The period of adolescence was thought to be critical for the formation of social barriers between the races.[81] That segregation fell relatively easily in most areas except education suggests that the breadth of Jackson's opinion would not have generated significantly more opposition than Warren's ruling.[82]

While the drawbacks associated exclusively with Jackson's memorandum would have warranted concern, these problems were surmountable or were not as significant as the problems presented by Warren's opinion. Jackson minimized the accusatory or self-righteous tone of his opinion by noting that racial separation was not restricted to the South and stating that those who accepted the notion of racial distinctions should not be stigmatized or censured.[83] Charges that Jackson oversimplified the premises underlying segregation would have subsided as it became clear that alternative justifications were insupportable.[84] That this was likely to occur is demonstrated by the fact that efforts to prove the biological inferiority of blacks waned in part because of evidence to the contrary.[85] Arguments defending immutable racial distinctions would have persisted longer had the Court employed Jackson's reasoning. But it may be that significant progress toward equality in American society required that racists be challenged to defend their baseless arguments.

Conclusion

Since the problems associated with Jackson's opinion were not overwhelming, adoption of his argument by the Court would have been wise. The post-*Brown* developments demonstrated that the Court is only as powerful as its opinions are persuasive, and Jackson's argument for ending segregation was less susceptible to criticism than Warren's. Jackson's opinion was more consonant with constitutional history and accorded more closely with the public's conception of a permissible exercise of judicial power. Neither opinion could be characterized as a paean to the triumph of racial equality, as both "refused to lift the nation to the magnificence of the principle [they] had that day redeemed."[86] Even Jackson's opinion, which afforded a grand opportunity for such a statement,[87] seemed uncharacteristically hesitant and subdued.[88] Both Justices realized, however, that eloquence and incandescence had to be sacrificed to avoid the appearance of a pharisaical decree.[89]

If Jackson's opinion afforded a more promising strategy for securing the rights of the plaintiffs in *Brown,* it is reasonable to ask why the Court failed to adopt his approach. One possibility is that the Justices were unaware of this strategy, since Jackson's debilitating heart attack prevented him from presenting his case to his brethren.[90] This does not seem compelling, however, when one considers that during the *Brown* deliberations Warren proposed an argument for ending segregation similar to Jackson's. S. Sidney Ulmer, drawing upon the conference notes of Justice Harold H. Burton, suggests that the Chief Justice initially thought the Court should attack the underlying premise of segregation.[91] Ulmer provides no reason for Warren's abandonment of this tack. A likely explanation, however, may have been the need for unanimity. With three Justices from the South, the drawbacks of Jackson's argument may have led to its rejection. So, while the form of Warren's opinion drew public criticism that Jackson's approach may have avoided, the Chief Justice delivered something essential for the eventual success of a controversial ruling that Jackson may have been unable to furnish the force of a Court speaking with one voice.[92]

NOTE: *This article was originally published in the 1989* **Journal of Supreme Court History.**

Endnotes

1. 347 U.S. 483 (1954).
2. For a listing of articles extolling *Brown, see* Michael J. Perry, **The Constitution, the Courts, and Human Rights: An Inquiry into the Legitimacy of Constitutional Policymaking by the Judiciary** (New Haven: Yale University Press, 1982), p. 167 n. 8.
3. *See The New York Times,* 18 May 1954. Opinions for the Supreme Court are, of course, institutional products or negotiated documents, and Warren's opinion in *Brown* is no exception (*see* David M. O'Brien, **Storm Center: The Supreme Court in American Politics** (New York: W. W. Norton and Company, 1986), pp. 233–34, 240–62). Throughout this essay, however, I refer to the *Brown* opinion as "Warren's opinion," since the Chief Justice was the primary author of the document. Warren said he wrote "every blessed word" (*see* J. Harvie Wilkinson, III, **From *Brown* to *Bakke:* The Supreme Court and School Integration, 1954–1978** (New York: Oxford University Press, 1979), p. 30.
4. *See, e.g.,* Herbert Wechsler, "Toward Neutral Principles of Constitutional Law," *Harvard Law Rev.* 73 (1959): 26–35. *See also* Wilkinson, ***Brown* to *Bakke,*** pp. 34–39; and Richard Kluger, **Simple Justice: The History of *Brown v. Board of Education* and Black America's Struggle for Equality,** 2 vols. (New York: Alfred A. Knopf, 1975), 2:898–900.
5. 347 U.S. at 494–95.
6. I. A. Newby, **Challenge to the Court: Social Scientists and the Defense of Segregation, 1954–1966** (Baton Rouge, Louisiana: Louisiana State University Press, 1967), p. 186.
7. Significant progress toward fulfilling the promise of *Brown* was not made for over a decade (Charles A. Johnson and Bradley C. Canon, **Judicial Policies: Implementation and Impact** (Washington, D.C.: CQ Press, 1984), p. 256. The primary reason for noncompliance was, of course, white discontent with the result reached by the Court.
8. "Memorandum by Mr. Justice Jackson," 15 March 1954, p. 4, *The Papers of Robert H. Jackson,* Box 184, Library of Congress, Manuscript Division, Washington, D.C. (hereinafter cited as *Jackson Papers*).

9. *See* Dennis J. Hutchinson, "Unanimity and Desegregation: Decisionmaking in the Supreme Court, 1948–1958" *Georgetown Law Journal* 68 (1979): 34–44; S. Sidney Ulmer, "Earl Warren and the *Brown* Decision," *The Journal of Politics* 33 (1971): 689–702; and Kluger, **Simple Justice,** 2: 764–72.

10. "Memorandum by Mr. Justice Jackson," 15 March 1954, *Jackson Papers,* Box 184. Work on the argument contained in this memorandum began early in the 1953 Term, as Jackson believed then, according to his law clerk, E. Barrett Prettyman, Jr., that "Most of the Justices would eventually have to write the case" ("Notes re Segregation Decision. December 15, 1954," The Papers of E. Barrett Prettyman, Jr., Box 1, University of Virginia Law School Library, Rare Books Room, Charlottesville, Virginia) (hereinafter cited as *Prettyman Papers*). I trace the argument of Jackson's final and most developed memorandum. Page references to this short document are omitted in this section for the reader's convenience.

    Richard Kluger devotes several (primarily descriptive) pages to Jackson's memorandum, but he concludes: "Whatever its virtues . . . the Jackson memo left a good deal to be desired as a state paper" (Kluger, **Simple Justice,** 2: 869–73). Kluger is critical of the cautious tone of Jackson's writing. I attempt to demonstrate that while the memo is flawed in several respects, Jackson's argument for ending segregation has the earmarks of a piece of judicial statesmanship. The concerns which led to the cautious tone of Jackson's opinion (i.e., the inherent limitations of judicial efforts to reform society and the restraints placed on these efforts by public opinion) gave him insight into securing the rights of the plaintiffs in *Brown*.

11. Prettyman contends Jackson "was about to start reworking [the draft] when he had a heart attack in March." While Jackson was in the hospital, Warren personally delivered his own segregation opinion to the Justice. Jackson suggested minor revisions but agreed to support the opinion) ("Notes re Segregation Decision. December 15, 1954," *Prettyman Papers,* Box 1). Given Jackson's physical condition, Richard Kluger's contention seems reasonable that the Justice "would have a been likely to activate his concurrence memorandum only if Warren's opinion seemed to him a piece of irresponsible butchery" (Kluger, **Simple Justice,** 2:880–81). Warren's desire for and efforts to achieve unanimity are discussed in *Ibid.,* pp. 880–83.

12. Jackson did say historical analysis "yields for me only one sure conclusion: it was a passionate, confused and deplorable era" ("Memorandum by Mr. Justice Jackson," 15 March 1954, p. 6, *Jackson Papers,* Box 184). And in an earlier version of his memorandum, he seemed even more inclined to accept the view that history was unhelpful (Memo dated 1/6/54, p. 6 *Jackson Papers,* Box 184). But the definite import of his final version is that history supports the views of segregationists.

13. 163 U.S. 537 (1896). *Plessy* held that separate facilities for the races were permissible under the Fourteenth Amendment so long as the facilities were equal.

14. The Department of Justice filed an *amicus* brief in favor of the plaintiffs in *Brown* (Kluger, **Simple Justice,** 2: 705–09).

15. Charles O. Lofgren, **The *Plessy* Case: A Legal-Historical Interpretation** (New York: Oxford, University Press, 1987), pp. 93–115; *see also* Wilkinson, **Brown to Bakke,** p. 36.

16. 347 U.S. at 493–95.

17. *Ibid.,* pp. 1–4.

18. *Id.*

19. Walter F. Murphy, **Elements of Judicial Strategy** (Chicago: University of Chicago Press, 1964), p. 208. *See also* Johnson and Canon, **Judicial Policies,** p. 259.

20. *See* Murphy, **Elements of Judicial Strategy,** pp. 123–29.

21. Johnson and Canon, **Judicial Policies,** pp. 256–61; Kluger, **Simple Justice,** 2: 948–82.

22. *See* Barbara Hinckley, **The Seniority System in Congress** (Bloomington, Indiana: Indiana University Press, 1971), pp. 35–52; Barbara Hinckley, **Stability and Change in Congress,** 4th ed. (New York: Harper & Row, 1988), pp. 105–70; and Kluger, **Simple Justice,** 2: 950.

23. Murphy, **Elements of Judicial Strategy,** pp. 146–47.

24. Kluger, **Simple Justice,** 2: 950–52; C. Vann Woodward, **The Strange Career of Jim Crow,** 3d. rev. ed. (New York: Oxford University Press, 1974), pp. 163–68.

25. 347 U.S. at 489.

26. Alexander M. Bickel, "The Original Understanding and the Segregation Decision," *Harvard Law Rev.* 69 (1955): 1–65 (For a Recent Study of Fourteenth Amendment history, *see* Raoul Berger, **Government by Judiciary: The Transformation of the Fourteenth Amendment** (Cambridge, Massachusetts: Harvard University Press, 1977). Berger contends that the framers did not intend to proscribe segregated schools (*Ibid.,* pp. 117–33, 243–45)). Bickel's essay was the product of research conducted in 1952 when he served as a law clerk for Justice Frankfurter. The Justice had copies of Bickel's memorandum distributed among his brethren, and it is likely that Bickel's work informed Jackson's discussion of Fourteenth Amendment history (Kluger, **Simple Justice,** 2: 825–28). In his law review article, Bickel did not reject *Brown* or brand it as entirely inconsistent with history. But he concluded, contrary to Warren, that history is "anything but inconclusive" on the issue of whether the framers thought segregated schools were constitutional. Bickel suggested Warren may have meant merely that history is inconclusive on whether the framers understood that the Court could, in light of future conditions, have power to abolish segregation (as this was how Bickel squared *Brown* with the historical record) Bickel, "The Original Understanding," pp. 56–65). This interpretation of Warren's meaning, however, is too kind. Warren's language certainly suggests that no firm conclusion can be reached

on what the framers thought about the constitutionality of segregated schools (*see* 347 U.S. at 489–90).

27. Kluger, **Simple Justice,** 2: 771.

28. *See above,* pp. 94–95.

29. *Missouri ex rel. Gaines v. Canada,* 305 U.S. 337 (1938); *Sipuel v. Oklahoma,* 332 U.S. 631 (1948); *Fisher v. Hurst,* 333 U.S. 147 (1948); *Sweatt v. Painter,* 339 U.S. 629 (1950); *McLaurin v. Oklahoma State Regents,* 339 U.S. 637 (1950).

30. 347 U.S. 495.

31. Murphy, **Elements of Judicial Strategy,** p. 204.

32. According to E. Barrett Prettyman, Jr., Jackson believed Warren's opinion was flawed since it did not appear to have a legal basis ("Notes re Segregation Decision. December 15, 1954," p. 1, *Prettyman Papers,* Box 1).

33. *See, e.g., Lindsley v. Natural Carbonid Gas Co.,* 220 U.S. 61 (1911); *F. S. Royster Guano Co. v. Virginia,* 253 U.S. 412, 415 (1920); *Railway Express Agency v. New York,* 336 U.S. 106 (1949); and *Walters v. City of St. Louis,* 347 U.S. 231 (1953). Richard Kluger and S. Sidney Ulmer contend that Jackson believed the Court should indicate that its ruling in *Brown* as a "political decision" (Kluger, **Simple Justice,** 2: 860–61; Ulmer, "Earl Warren and the *Brown* Decision," 2: 860–61; Ulmer, "Earl Warren and the *Brown* Decision," p. 695). In Kluger's words: "As a political decision, [Jackson said] he could go along with it, but he would insist that it be so defined or he would have to protest. Almost certainly, Jackson was telling the conference that he would file a separate concurring opinion if whoever wrote the opinion of the Court feigned that the Justices were doing anything other than declaring new law for a new day" (Kluger, **Simple Justice,** 2:861). This conclusion is drawn from Justice Burton's terse and sometimes cryptic conference notes. If Kluger means that Jackson wanted to announce that the Justices had decided to outlaw segregation without any justification other than their personal values, such an interpretation is difficult to accept. An examination of Jackson's memorandum indicates that a more reasonable interpretation of Jackson's position is that he believed the Court had to acknowledge that it was making new law (was departing from precedent) and that the states had been justified in believing their past actions were constitutional. The Justices, however, had to demonstrate that the Court's decision was justified in law and that the classifications made by the states in the past were no longer acceptable. Ulmer seems to suggest this interpretation, but he fails to elaborate upon it (*see* Ulmer, "Earl Warren and the *Brown* Decision," p. 695).

34. *See, e.g.,* "Ruling Tempers Reaction of South" *The New York Times,* 18 May 1954, p. 20. *See also* Kluger, **Simple Justice,** 2: 897–98, 947.

35. Kluger, **Simple Justice,** 2: 899. *See* 347 U.S. at 490–91. These earlier cases include *Strauder v. West Virginia,* 100 U.S. 303, 307–08 (1880), *Virginia v. Rives,* 100 U.S. 313, 318 (1880), and *Ex Parte Virginia,* 100 U.S. 339, 344–45 (1880).

36. While Warren's assertion that the history of the Fourteenth Amendment is not enlightening is misleading, the claim that the Amendment was intended to proscribe all forms of racial discrimination is patently false (*see above,* n. 26, and accompanying text). Had the Court based its decision upon this claim, there would have been no need to refer to controversial social science data (*see below,* pp. 100–101). Consequently, all attention would have focused on the historical accuracy of the earlier rulings.

37. *See* Ronald Dworkin, **Taking Rights Seriously** (Cambridge, Massachusetts: Harvard University Press, 1977), pp. 131–37; Perry, **Constitution, Courts, and Human Rights,** pp. 70–75; Berger, **Government by Judiciary,** pp. 363–72, 414–18; H. Jefferson Powell, "The Original Understanding of Original Intent," *Harvard Law Rev.* 98 (1985): 885–948; and Raoul Berger, " 'Original Intention' in Historical Perspective," *George Washington Law Review* 54 (1986): 296–337. A majority of the Court has never accepted the view that the only legitimate basis for constitutional decision-making is the specific intentions of the framers, and even those who purported to do so apparently thought it necessary at times to deviate from the original understanding. For example, Justice Hugo L. Black's book, **A Constitutional Faith** (New York: Alfred A. Knopf, 1968), is a testimony to the importance of judicial fidelity to the intent of the framers. But his position in *Reynolds v. Sims,* 377 U.S. 533 (1964) (among other decisions), can only be characterized as a departure from this interpretive model (*see* Berger, **Government by Judiciary,** pp. 69–98). A Court that is liberated from the specific intent of the framers can certainly abuse its power. On the other hand, judicial adherence to a rigid form of interpretivism or originalism prevents the Court from acting when changed presumptions and conditions reveal the injustice of a governmental practice, and resort to the political process offers no hope for reform. Raoul Berger believes the original intent must be followed whatever the consequences: "I cannot bring myself to believe that the Court may assume a power not granted in order to correct an evil that the people were, and remain, unready to cure." (**Government by Judiciary,** p. 409).

38. *See above,* n. 33, and John Nowak, Ronald D. Rotunda, and J. Nelson Young, **Constitutional Law,** 3d ed., Hornbook Series (St. Paul, Minnesota: West Publishing Co., 1986), pp. 523–26.

39. *See above,* pp. 92–93.

40. The term "extralegal" is, in a sense, a misnomer, as legal questions oftentimes cannot be separated from empirical questions (*see* below, n. 45, and accompanying text).

41. 347 U.S. at 494–95.

42. Memorandum dated 1/6/54, p. 11, *Jackson Papers,* Box 184.

43. Paul Rosen, **The Supreme Court and Social Science** (Chicago: University of Illinois Press, 1972), p. x; Newby, **Challenge to the Court,** p. 186; Kluger, **Simple Justice,** 2: 891–92; Wilkinson, ***Brown*** to ***Bakke,*** pp. 27, 31.

44. James Reston, "A Sociological Decision," *The New York Times,* 18 May 1954, p. 14.

45. Rosen, **Supreme Court and Social Science,** pp. 3–22.

46. Edmond Cahn, "Jurisprudence," *New York University Law Rev.* 30 (1955); 157–61; Monroe Berger, "Desegregation, Law, and Social Science," Commentary 23 (1957): 475–76; Charles L. Black, Jr., "The Lawfulness of the Segregation Decisions," *Yale Law Journal* 69 (1960): 421–30; Kluger, **Simple Justice,** 2: 892–93, 900. In his opinion for the Court in *Plessy,* Justice Brown said: "We consider the underlying fallacy of the plaintiff's argument to consist in the assumption that the enforced separation of the two races stamps the colored race with a badge of inferiority. If this be so, it is not by reason of anything found in the act, but solely because the colored race chooses to put that construction upon it" (163 U.S. 537, 55 (1896)). Brown was unaware that the second sentence in this passage conceded the possibility that segregation causes psychological harm.

47. William B. Ball, "Lawyers and Social Scientists–Guiding the Guides," *Villanova Law Rev.* 5 (1959); 221; Kenneth B. Clark, "The Desegregation Cases: Criticism of the Social Scientist's Role," *Villanova Law Rev.* 5 (1969): 234–35; Herbert Garfinkel, "Social Science Evidence and the School Segregation Cases," *The Journal of Politics* 21 (1959): 43.

48. *See above,* n. 29. The import, if not the holding, of *Sweatt v. Painter,* 339 U.S. 629 (1950), is that separate higher educational facilities for blacks cannot be equal, given the beneficial intangibles afforded exclusively by white schools. This decision, however, could not have served as the basis of a common sense argument that separate facilities at the elementary school level are inherently unequal, since *Sweatt* emphasized intangibles unique to a law school environment (*viz.,* reputation of the faculty, experience of the administration, position and influence of the alumni, standing in the community, and tradition and prestige) (*Ibid.* at 634).

49. Acceptance of the reasonableness of racial classifications was only implicit in the Court's rulings addressing the notion of "separate but equal."

50. *See above,* p. 96.

51. One might argue that Justice Jackson's approach involved improper judicial behavior—since his discussion of the underlying premise of segregation and events demonstrating the unreasonableness of racial classifications required him to go beyond the Court record (*see above,* pp. 95–96). The long-established doctrine of "judicial notice," however, allows judges to take broad societal conditions and events into account. The Model Code of Evidence of the American Law Institute holds that judges may on their own motion take notice of such things as "specific facts so notorious as not to be the subject of reasonable dispute, and . . . specific facts and propositions of generalized knowledge which are capable of immediate and accurate demonstration by resort to easily accessible sources of indisputable accuracy"

(as quoted in Walter F. Murphy and C. Herman Pritchett, Court, **Judges, and Politics: An Introduction to the Judicial Process,** 4th ed. (New York: Random House, 1986), pp. 360–61. The historical and contemporary information upon which Jackson drew could reasonably fall within these guidelines.

52. 347 U.S. at 493–95.

53. Newby, **Challenge to the Court,** pp. 185–204.

54. A. James Gregor, "The Law, Social Science, and School Segregation: An Assessment," *Western Reserve Law Rev.* 14 (1963): 626–29. Compare Warren's language in *Brown,* 347 U.S. at 494.

55. Cahn, "Jurisprudence," pp. 161–65 (Cahn's critique of the sociological studies employed by the Court was quoted frequently by segregationists; Newby, **Challenge to the Court,** pp. 188–89); M. Berger, "Desegregation, Law, and Social Science," pp. 475–76; Black, "The Lawfulness of the Segregation Decisions," pp. 421–30. (*See also* Rosen, **Supreme Court and Social Science,** pp. 182–96; and Wilkinson, *Brown to Bakke,* pp. 32–33.) These scholars maintained that the Court was not obligated to refer to social science evidence, since the cruelty of segregation was obvious and capable of judicial notice (*see above,* n. 46, and accompanying text). This claim, however, was weakened by sociological studies suggesting that integration causes psychological harm in black children.

56. Rosen, **Supreme Court and Social Science,** pp. 186–89; Newby, **Challenge to the Court,** pp. 192–93.

57. *See above,* p. 101.

58. Jackson might have been criticized for improperly applying the baseline equal protection requirement or "rational basis" test. That is, segregation must stand under this test if racial classification have "*some* reasonable basis in terms of *some* rational view of the public interest." Second, "[I]f a set of facts could conceivably exist that would render a [racial] classification reasonable, their existence must be assumed" Archibald Cox, **The Role of the Supreme Court in American Government** (New York: Oxford University Press, 1976), p. 59–60, emphasis in original; *see also* John Hart Ely, **Democracy and Distrust: A Theory of Judicial Review** (Cambridge, Massachusetts, Harvard University Press, 1980), p. 31. The Court could have envisioned and segregationists could have put forth several arguments to demonstrate the existence of some reasonable basis for racial classifications: (1) *some* studies suggest that there may be immutable racial distinctions (Newby, **Challenge to the Court,** pp. xi–xii); (2) even if there is no basis to scientific racism, the presence of disadvantaged blacks in white classrooms could hinder the educational development of white students (this was the argument put forth by the state of Virginia after *Brown;* Kluger, **Simple Justice,** 2: 913–14); (3) *some* evidence suggests that racially segregated schools promote healthy personalities in black children (*see above,* p. 102). Jackson, however, could (and should) have noted that the Court considered racial classifications "suspect" (ironically, this

principle was first articulated in the Japanese exclusion case, *Korematsu v. United States,* 323 U.S. 214, 216 (1944)). With suspect classifications, the traditional presumption of constitutionality is reversed. The state's goal must be "compelling," and the burden is on the state to demonstrate the validity of the arguments supporting the classification and to prove that alternative means are not available to accomplish the stated legislative goal (Novak, Rotunda, and Young. **Constitutional Law,** pp. 530–31). None of the above justifications for segregation would survive strict scrutiny.

59. *Brown v. Board of Education of Topeka,* 349 U.S. 294 (1955).

60. *Kluger,* **Simple Justice,** 2: 903.

61. *See above,* p. 96. In its implementation decision, the Court did not fix a date for the end of segregation, nor did it direct the courts below to require the defendant school boards to submit desegregation plans within a certain period of time. It merely ordered the lower courts to "require that the defendants make a prompt and reasonable start toward full compliance with our May 17, 1954, ruling" (349 U.S. at 300; *see also* Kluger, **Simple Justice,** 2: 939–41; and Woodward, **Strange Career of Jim Crow,** pp. 152–53).

62. This was the argument of the NAACP after *Brown* (Kluger, **Simple Justice,** 2: 926–28).

63. Alexander Bickel, **The Least Dangerous Branch: The Supreme Court at the Bar of Politics,** 2d ed. (New Haven: Yale University Press, 1986), pp. 64–72, 247–54.

64. According to C. Vann Woodward: "[W]hile they did comply, blacks were neither happy nor voluntary in their acquiescence [to racial restrictions] and . . . they resisted where it was possible" ("The Mississippi Horrors," *New York Review of Books,* 36 (June 29, 1989): 15).

65. Wilkinson, ***Brown to Bakke,*** p. 36; Woodward, **Strange Career of Jim Crow,** pp. 167–68. The Court appeared to accept this justification in *Plessy* (163 U.S. at 550–51).

66. Only Hugo L. Black (Alabama), Stanley F. Reed (Kentucky), and Tom Clark (Texas) were southerners.

67. *See above,* p. 91.

68. He also sought to avoid the appearance of self-righteousness (*see above,* p. 91).

69. These arguments were disingenuous and unsupportable since the justification which fit racial classifications most closely was the exclusion of a race because of the supposed inferiority of its members. In other words, a philosophy of racial inequality would surely produce this sort of legislation. Other reasons advanced to support segregation do not fit the classification as closely. Alternative means to accomplish these goals are apparent (*see* Ely, **Democracy and Distrust,** pp. 145–46. Under strict scrutiny, the alternative justifications would not support the classification. Jackson, of course, would have had to revise significantly the first section of his opinion.

70. Kluger, **Simple Justice,** 2: 913.

71. *Ibid.,* pp. 900–01; Johnson and Canon, **Judicial Policies,** p. 257; Wilkinson, ***Brown* to *Bakke,*** p. 39.

72. *See above,* p. 95.

73. Jackson's opinion, however, was not a particularly strong statement of racial equality either.

74. *See above,* n. 2; "Historians Laud Court's Decision," *The New York Times,* 18 May 1954, p. 17; and Kluger, **Simple Justice,** 2: 895–96.

75. *See above,* p. 102.

76. The segregationists relented in their attempts to defend the notion of immutable racial distinctions in part because Warren's opinion presented other targets (*see above,* pp. 101–102). These targets were not present in Jackson's memorandum.

77. Wilkinson, ***Brown* to *Bakke,*** p. 53.

78. Warren's controversial use of social science evidence, then, helped the Court avoid the appearance of self-righteousness. The common sense discussion of the harmful effects of segregation desired by some commentators (*see above,* pp. 100–101) would have had the opposite result.

79. 347 U.S. at 492–93.

80. Kluger, **Simple Justice,** 2: 948.

81. Rosen, **Supreme Court and Social Science,** pp. 173–74.

82. Kluger, **Simple Justice,** 2: 948.

83. *See above,* pp. 90–91.

84. *See above,* n. 69.

85. *But see above,* n. 76.

86. Although Wilkinson's language refers only to Warren, it applies as well to Jackson (Wilkinson, ***Brown* to *Bakke,*** p. 29).

87. Jackson's critical examination of racist tenets afforded an excellent occasion for a powerful statement on human equality.

88. *See* his beautiful language in *West Virginia State Bd. of Educ. v. Barnette,* 319 U.S. 624 (1943).

89. It is probably for this reason that neither Warren nor Jackson employed language from the ringing dissent of the first Justice Harlan in *Plessy* (*see* 163 U.S. 537 at 552–64). It has been suggested that the tone of *Brown* would have been elevated had the Court borrowed from this great opinion (*see* Wilkinson, ***Brown* to *Bakke,*** p. 29).

90. *See above,* p. 90.

91. Ulmer, "Earl Warren and the *Brown* Decision," pp. 692–94.

92. For sources examining Warren's efforts to achieve unanimity in *Brown, see above,* n. 9. For a discussion of unanimous Court opinions, *see* O'Brien, **Storm Center,** pp. 214–15, 273–74.

✖ J O H N D . F A S S E T T

A Plea for the Demise of a Stubborn Myth

Simple Justice,[1] Richard Kluger's comprehensive treatise regarding the *School Segregation Cases* which were decided by the Supreme Court on May 17, 1954, includes many details regarding the Court's deliberations leading to the opinions in *Brown v. Board of Education*[2] and *Bolling v. Sharp.*[3] Among such details is that the first formal vote during the 1953 Term by the Justices on the issues presented by the cases, a vote which Kluger surmised most likely occurred in late March, resulted in "eight to strike down segregation and one, Reed, to uphold it."[4] Accordinging to Kluger's reconstruction, Justice Stanley F. Reed continued in opposition until a date in early May when Chief Justice Earl Warren met with Reed and said, "Stan, you're all by yourself in this now. You've got to decide whether it's really the best thing for the country." Kluger added that the "only condition" Reed "extracted from Warren for going along . . . was a pledge that the Court implementation decree would allow segregation to be dismantled gradually instead of being wrenched apart."[5] These details were attributed to "Reed's clerk, George Mickum, who was 'on hand' " during the meeting. The treatise also reported that the same clerk "saw tears on his Justice's face as the last words of the two opinions were spoken."[6]

These details have formed the basis for a myth that has been repeated so often that it is now widely accepted as historical fact. There are four aspects to the myth. First, with respect to timing, the myth has Reed holding out and preventing unanimity until only a short period before May 17. Second, the myth has Reed capitulating only upon his confrontation by Warren. Third, the myth asserts that Reed obtained as consideration for his reluctant capitulation a concession regarding the dismantling of segregation. Fourth, the myth has Reed so distraught by the action of the Court that he cried during the reading of the opinions. One corollary of all four aspects of the myth is that, even though he joined the decision, Reed was an ardent supporter of the segregation of races.

All of these aspects of the myth are false. They represent fundamental distortions and misrepresentations of historical facts. Nevertheless, the myth continues to be propagated. The sole object of this essay is to describe the creation and proliferation of the myth and to establish that it does not have any reliable historical foundation. This essay will not join in the vigorous debate that has raged both before and since the publication of **Simple Justice** regarding the roles of Robert H. Jackson and Felix Frankfurter with respect to the segregation cases. That debate has involved scrutiny of the actions of the present Chief Justice while serving as Jackson's law clerk during the 1952 Term and much questioning of the amount of credit attributed by **Simple Justice** and other writings to Frankfurter for accomplishment of the unanimous decision.[7]

Origin of the Myth

I had the good fortune to be one of Reed's two law clerks for the 1953 Term. When I departed the Court in late July, 1954, upon completion of my appointment, I took with me a file of materials I had accumulated regarding my work for the Justice on the segregation cases. I first revealed publicly the contents of this file in a talk I delivered to a small group of judges, law professors, and lawyers in New Haven in 1966. In confidence, I told the group known as "the Benchers" that I had retained the materials because "I had the feeling that it might be desirable if such materials were preserved for history by a person outside the court,"[8] and I sought their advice regarding disposition of the materials and revelation of my knowledge regarding the development of the momentous decisions. My audience was unanimous in opining that I owed a responsibility to the demands of history to preserve the papers and, at an appropriate time, to reveal the facts as I knew them to historians.

My prime concern in 1966 was that the press and most of academia had accorded virtually undivided credit for the decisions and the Court's unanimity to the Chief Justice; that the Chief had "somehow coerced or persuaded Justice Reed and other potential dissenters into making the decisions unanimous."[9] I concluded my presentation by noting that a recently published exposé by Ted Sorensen regarding the Kennedy administration had been justified as appropriate "to dispel myths about the late President." I asked, "Is it really any more desirable that myths be dispelled about a president dead less than two years than about one of the most important judicial decisions in the history of man?"[10]

Despite my concern about the fairness of many of the published commentaries, I chose not to reveal further the facts known to me until almost twenty years after my clerkship. In June 1974, I received a letter from Kluger identifying himself as "a journalist, editor, and publisher" and stating that "For the past five years I have been researching what I hope will prove a major book on the origin, course, and consequence of the *School Segregation Cases.* . . ." He sought my help in his research—"with full awareness of the proprieties of a clerk's relationship to the Justice he serves"—in the "hopes that the interests of history and accuracy may be served by such an inquiry."

In my response, I acknowledged that "I was quite deeply involved in the *Brown* decision" and that, shortly after my clerkship, "I assembled my recollections and materials" regarding it. I added that to date I had "never felt the time was appropriate for their publication." I noted that, in 1957, based on a recommendation by Reed, I had reviewed, solely for the purpose of pointing out any inaccuracies for Rutgers University Press, the manuscript of **Desegregation and the Law,**[11] but added, "While Justice Reed lives, despite changes in attitudes toward disclosures of confidentialities since 1954, I would want his approval before I did anything on the subject beyond what he authorized on the prior occasion."

I did not advise Kluger that in 1958, the year following Reed's retirement from the Court, I had received a communication from the

Justice advising that he had agreed to be interviewed as part of an oral history project of Columbia University "about my experiences in life, particularly those relating to the Government and people whom I have known in Washington." He stated that his interviewer would also "like to have the comments of my law clerks" and concluded that "I commend his interest and ask that you give him such assistance as you think proper in his work." Since I was never contacted by the interviewer, I had no occasion to determine the intended scope of this authorization.

Residing in Connecticut, I met with the Justice and my former fellow clerk, who practiced in Washington, between 1958 and 1974 on only the few occasions when I was able to attend reunion dinners for the Justice and his law clerks. The last such occasion I attended was in 1970 during which, having been asked about his role in *Brown,* Reed merely responded, as he had on other occasions, that he considered the decisions "appropriate" and "inevitable." Prodded by the host of the occasion, Reed's first clerk Harold Leventhal, I related the incident early in my Term when the Justice sent me to his dictionary to learn the meaning of "krytocracy." The following week, I received a telephone call from Leventhal requesting that I refresh his memory as to the word involved since he wished to relate the incident to several judges with whom he was lunching.[12] The reunions ended after the Reeds moved in the mid-1970s from the apartment they had occupied in the Mayflower Hotel throughout his Washington career to a nursing home in New York.

In response to my proposal that he obtain approval from Reed, Kluger agreed to contact the Justice again. Kluger reported that Reed had previously denied an interview, as had William O. Douglas, whereas Warren and Tom Clark had granted interviews. He also reported that he had succeeded in interviewing a number of 1953 Term clerks, and he provided a number of references among my Yale Law School acquaintances. A subsequent letter detailed Kluger's lack of success in contacting Reed and, as an alternative to obtaining such authorization, offered to demonstrate the seriousness of his project by submitting a memorandum which "would summarize my understanding of the disposition of the Justice toward the desegregation question along with my sources for such assessment." The memorandum would be based in part on the conference notes of Frankfurter and Jackson. He concluded that he was "trying to avoid guesswork and flimsy surmise— without being pompous about it."

After receiving Kluger's materials and discussing them and his project at length with him, I provided him with a copy of the confidential memorandum I had written in 1956 which had been the source of my 1966 talk. My action was based on my conclusions that Kluger had done extensive research, that his book would be a scholarly work, and that omission of the facts regarding Reed's participation could result in further distortions of the historical record and misperceptions regarding Reed's role. When I advised Mickum of my action, he responded:

> I have your letter of September 24th in which you indicated that you had reversed yourself and had spoken to Mr. Kluger. While I doubt that I could add very much to what you have already told him, I, too, would be willing to speak with him inasmuch as you have done so. . . .

I never had an opportunity for a discussion with either Kluger or Mickum regarding the interview that apparently ensued.

In December 1975, I received from Kluger an inscribed copy of **Simple Justice** which shows its publication date of 1976. The book was well received by reviewers, and it was widely accepted as the most authoritative treatise regarding the *School Segregation Cases*. It is an impressive and careful work and the author accurately quoted and, except as to one detail hereinafter discussed, incorporated the information he obtained from me.

Rather than contributing to a dispelling of misperceptions about the roles of the Chief Justice and Reed in the accomplishment of unanimity, **Simple Justice** unfortunately accorded even greater credence to the misperceptions by relating the two purported incidents that were attributed to Mickum. In support of the contention that Reed did not agree to join the decisions until just prior to May 17, Kluger wrote that in "the middle of May" the following occurred:

> At the end, Warren put it to him directly, according to Reed's clerk, George Mickum, who was on hand at one of the Chief Justice's final interviews with the Kentuckian. He said, "Stan, you're all by yourself in this now," Mickum recalls. "You've got to decide whether it's really the best thing for the country." . . .
> After the Chief had left, Reed asked Mickum, who had been raised in a community with segregated schools, how he felt about the Justice's

going along with the rest of the Court. Mickum, a man not notably more convinced of the natural equality of the Negro than Reed himself was, suggested that the demands of conscience seemed to require his going beyond the knowable facts in the case and asking himself, as Warren had, what was best for America. . . . The only condition he extracted from Warren for going along, Mickum believes, was a pledge that the Court implementation decree would allow segregation to be dismantled gradually instead of being wrenched apart.[13]

In recounting the reading of the opinions by Warren, Kluger reported, "Stanley Reed's clerk George Mickum saw tears on his Justice's face as the last words of the two opinions were spoken."[14] These two incidents have been more frequently cited and quoted in subsequent writing regarding *Brown* than virtually any other aspect of the development of those decisions.

Regrettably, Reed never chose personally to refute the developing myth. In November 1975, he was interviewed in his chambers at the Court for the Fred Vinson oral history collection being assembled by the University of Kentucky. During the interview, Reed, who was then ninety years old, was asked for his impression of the fact that "Many historians of the Vinson Court question whether or not the *Brown* decision would have been reached if Vinson would have lived." The following ensued:[15]

> Reed: Wasn't the *Brown* case a unanimous case?
> Birdwhistell: Yes, sir.
> Reed: I don't think there was an opposition in the *Brown* case.
> Birdwhistell: If Vinson had lived and had still been Chief Justice, do you think the *Brown* case would have still been handed down at the same time?
> Reed: I don't see how you could have an idea about that. I should say offhand that yes, it would have been handed down. There were several Justices on here who were not people who were supporters of the equality of the blacks. Yes, I think that was on its way, that there were too many black people to think of classifying them as a lower order of beings.
> Birdwhistell: Did you ever discuss the Civil Rights issue with Chief Justice Vinson at any time, in terms of particular cases, or just in general?
> Reed: Civil Rights? What do you mean by that?
> Birdwhistell: In terms of school integration . . .
> Reed: Black and white?

Birdwhistell: Black and white, yes, sir.

Reed: No, I don't remember ever having any discussion of that. That was a unanimous case, wasn't it?

Birdwhistell: Yes, sir.

Reed: That doesn't mean that the decision that was made there, that color could make no difference . . . It seems so obvious and so much a part now. Well, there's still a good deal of opposition. But there it is. I don't think his being here or not being here would have had anything to do with it. They don't have any blacks up in his country.

Birdwhistell: Right. I think what it is that so many historians of the Supreme Court have raised this issue, just in speculation. It's one that I don't think has ever been answered yet. And it's the kind of question that, possibly, can't be answered specifically. But they have raised the question as to whether or not a Vinson Court would have gone ahead with the *Brown* decision considering all the circumstances involved and the politics involved.

Reed: I guess that we have so completely accepted it that now it only seems to be very natural that everybody in the country should have the same rights and the same privileges and the same punishments, and so forth. Don't you think that we have accepted the equality of the peoples?

Birdwhistell: OK, yes, sir, I believe so.

That conversation constitutes, I believe, Reed's last public commentary relating to *Brown*. Obviously, it provides no support for the myth. Reed's earlier interview by a Columbia University professor,[16] as to which he had communicated with me, covered much of his government career but nothing with respect to *Brown*.

My initial concern that a serious misperception of Reed's course of participating in *Brown* would result from the **Simple Justice** version was ameliorated considerably when more accurate accounts appeared during the final few years of Reed's life in the writings of two of the other participants, Warren and Douglas. In addition, biographies of Warren, Hugo L. Black, and Harold H. Burton, based on interviews as well as authoritative documents, also were published and did not adopt or confirm the myth.

Warren's **Memoirs,**[17] published in 1977, included his detailed recollection regarding development of the *Brown* decisions. He recounted that actual voting on the decision was deferred after the reargument in December until February, when "on the first vote, we unanimously agreed that the 'separate but equal' doctrine had no place in public education."[18] As in his interview with Liva Baker during her research for her biography of Frankfurter published in 1969,[19] he mentioned no ultimatum to or coercion of Reed and no last-minute concession with respect to enforcement decrees. Consistent with his Baker interview, he again opined:

> The real credit for achieving unanimity, in my opinion, should go to the three Justices who were born and reared in the part of the nation where segregation was a way of life and where everyone knew the greatest emotional opposition to the decision would be forthcoming. They were Justices Hugo L. Black of Alabama, Stanley F. Reed of Kentucky, and Tom C. Clark of Texas. . . .[20]

Warren emphasized the many steps taken during the 1953 Term to assure secrecy of the Court's actions including confining any communications among the Justices "to the fewest possible people as a matter of security."[21]

The first full biography to undertake a detailed analysis of the development of *Brown* subsequent to **Simple Justice,** while citing that source in its bibliography, did not adopt its version of events. The analysis in Professor Gerald Dunne's biography of Hugo L. Black,[22] also published in 1977, repeated that, at the Justices' conference on December 12:

> Only two of the Justices present seemed disposed to dispute their new Chief. Stanley Reed, conceding that the Constitution of *Plessy* and 1896 might not be the Constitution of today, denied Warren's assumption that segregation necessarily rested on an assumption of racial inferiority and suggested the arrangement might be justified as an application of the police power of the state. A far harder opposition seemed to lie with Robert Jackson. . . .[23]

Discussing the accomplishment of unanimity, Dunne concluded:

> . . . a unanimous opinion is the product of all participants, and the role of the Chief Justice was essentially that of orchestral intermediary. Perhaps some members of the Court were more open to his advocacy than others, as for example, Justice Reed, whose concession on a changing Constitution had stipulated away half the intellectual opposition and whose heart had already demonstrated it was in the right place. Notwithstanding a rural Kentucky background, Reed was the one who wrote the landmark opinions ending the color ban in party primaries and integrating common passenger carriers in interstate commerce.[24]

Following Warren, Dunne reported no coercion or intimidation nor a last-minute capitulation.

As had Dunne, Professor Berry in writing her biography of Burton,[25] published in 1978, briefly acknowledged **Simple Justice** in an endnote but did not adopt the myth. Based on documents from the files of Burton and Frankfurter and information from Burton's law clerk, Berry recounted Reed's role during the discussion at the December 12 conference as follows:

> Reed understood Warren's position that equal protection had not been satisfactory; but he believed that the issue was not whether blacks were inferior, because "there is no inferior race." To Reed, the issue was a matter of long-exercised state police power, and he would leave the "entrenched aspects and wait to see what the rest of the court does." . . . There was a clear majority for Warren's position in the conference. However, at this point, Reed was reluctant; he did not want to announce his decision until the remainder of the justices had indicated firm positions. Frankfurter was tentatively with the majority, and Jackson would go along with the majority if a rational legal opinion could be worked out. . . .[26]

According to Berry's reconstruction, "By January 15, 1954, the issues were resolved; and the justices were concerned mainly with the decree." With respect to the Justices' deliberations, Berry reported:

> The clerks were told very little about the discussions in order to minimize the danger of the information leaking to the public. When Warren circulated his draft in May, Burton thought it was a "magnificent job that may win a unanimous court," a result which would have been impossible the year before with Vinson, Jackson, and Reed in opposition and with Frankfurter wavering. After Warren's opinion was accepted in final form by the conference, the justices personally handed back the circulated drafts, again to avoid possible leaks.[27]

Berry made no attempt to reconcile her reconstruction with the myth.

Whereas Dunne and Berry relied on a variety of research sources, in writing his biography of Warren,[28] published in 1979, journalist Jack Pollack actually had the benefit of extensive personal interviews with the former Chief Justice. He quoted Warren as having again verified that the initial conference vote "was unanimous," although Pollack placed the timing as "early in March."[29] As in his memoirs, Warren did not suggest the occurrence of any last-minute ultimatum or conference with Reed.

The second volume of Douglas's autobiography,[30] published in 1980, while confirming that Reed initially challenged the overruling of *Plessy v. Ferguson,* states that Jackson was the last holdout against unanimity.[31] It also confirmed the stringent efforts of the Justices to maintain tight security with respect to their actions on the cases. Unlike Douglas's own account, which ignored **Simple Justice,** Professor James Simon's biography of the Justice,[32] also published in 1980, relied upon that source for those aspects of the *Brown* process involving the relationship between Douglas and Frankfurter. Noting that, during the 1952 Term, Vinson and Reed were prepared to uphold *Plessy,* Simon reported that "Frankfurter was unabashedly playing for time, attempting to coax a unanimous opinion out of his colleagues."[33] He did not adopt nor mention the **Simple Justice** version of the accomplishment of unanimity.

While the Warren, Douglas, Dunne, Berry, Pollack, and Simon accounts ameliorated my concern regarding the details presented in **Simple Justice,** the fact that its version had not been dispelled was apparent with the publication contemporaneously in the *Georgetown Law Journal* of a book-length article[34] discussing the unanimity issue. While Professor Dennis Hutchinson repeated none of the details attributed to Mickum (a Georgetown graduate), the professor did conclude that "Kluger has demonstrated convincingly that Stanley Reed was the last holdout to Warren's opinions."[35] This conclusion, which must have been based on acceptance of the occurrence of the supposedly overheard ultimatum, was reached despite these other conclusions:

> There is almost no hard evidence of the Court's deliberations between the December conference and early May. Secrecy and fear of early leaks became obsessions.[36] . . . Even for its wealth of illuminating detail, **Simple Justice** cannot be denominated the definitive account of the decision making process in the *Brown* cases. . . .[37]

Despite these admonitions by Hutchinson and the other publications following the release of **Simple Justice,** the happenings attributed to Mickum commenced a process of unchallenged acceptance by academics during the 1980s. First, in 1982, Professor G. Edward White published his Warren biography.[38] It stated that the "conversation" between Warren and Reed occurred "between the seventh and the twelfth of May."[39] However, a detailed endnote refers to conflicting sources with respect to the date and concludes, "[N]o sources are authoritative on this point."[40]

White's book was followed by the first of five pertinent volumes written by Professor Bernard Schwartz. The first publication,[41] released in 1983, adopted the details of the accomplishment of unanimity as related by Kluger. However, it added drama to the scene as follows:

> After Warren had gently soaped up Reed, he rinsed him abruptly under a cold shower. "Stan, you're all by yourself in this now," he said bluntly . . .[42]

Schwartz identified the event as occurring at "the end of April" when "Reed's law clerk was at a meeting."[43]

Also in 1983, Schwartz published **Super Chief**,[44] his acclaimed biography of Warren, in which he related that "there are indications that Reed persisted in standing alone until the end of April," when the same admonition by Warren to Reed occurred. Again, the detail is attributed to "Reed's law clerk, who was present at the meeting" and the sole source cited is **Simple Justice.** While accepting this version regarding unanimity, Schwartz rejected a plethora of evidence "about Frankfurter's being ready to file a separate concurrence or dissent."[45] He also concluded that Jackson's work on a separate opinion had been interrupted by that Justice's heart attack on March 30 and then abandoned during hospitalization. In **The Unpublished Opinions of the Warren Court,** published in 1985, Schwartz parroted his adopted version of the events.[46]

Initial Refutation Effort

Concerned that the repetition of details from **Simple Justice** by Professors Hutchinson, White, and Schwartz had given credence to an inaccurate historical record, I concluded in 1985 that it was then appropriate that I publish my account of Reed's role in the event and make the supporting documents public. Accordingly, I submitted to the Supreme Court Historical Society the text of the talk I had delivered in 1966. Without modification, it was published as an article entitled "Mr. Justice Reed and *Brown v. Board of Education*" in the 1986 *Yearbook* of the Society. Of course, having been written a decade prior to the publication of **Simple Justice,** the article merely stated the facts as then known to me;

no answer to the Mickum details was added. At the same time, I donated to the Society for its archives all of the documentation I had retained from the 1953 Term relating to Reed's work on a possible dissent.

To my disappointment, the *Yearbook* article did not deter the continued repetition of the myth in further publications. As noted at the outset, even prior to publication of **Simple Justice,** a controversy had existed regarding Frankfurter's role with respect to the *Brown* decisions. His law clerk from the 1952 Term, Professor Bickel, fanned the flame when he wrote in 1970 that "when the inner history of that case [*Brown*] is known, we may find he [Frankfurter] was a moving force in its decision."[47] And the publication five months prior to **Simple Justice** of excerpts from Frankfurter's diaries included an essay which credited Frankfurter with taking Warren "to school on the issues in the *Brown* case in lengthy talks. . . ."[48] Neither that essay nor a biography of Frankfurter published in 1981[49] repeated or directly endorsed the myth. However, Professor Hirsch's tome constituted an indirect endorsement since it included an endnote reading, "For a thorough description of the decision-making process in *Brown,* and Frankfurter's crucial role in that process, see" **Simple Justice.**[50]

Whereas Hirsch had been indirect, when Professor Melvin I. Urofsky published his Frankfurter biography[51] in 1991, he led a series of explicit repetitions of the myth. Citing Kluger's "magisterial history of the *Brown* case," Urofsky reported:

> By early May only Stanley Reed still supported *Plessy.* Warren, with eight votes, confronted Reed directly and told him that he now had to decide whether to stand alone in defense of racial segregation or join the others. Reed capitulated. . . .

Interestingly, while adopting that aspect of the **Simple Justice** version, Urofsky challenged that book's failure to give proper recognition to Frankfurter's role. With respect to *Brown,* Urofsky suggested:

> Frankfurter may have suggested the strategy and then relied on Warren's political skills to pull it off. Essentially, the chief justice would avoid having the Court decide any of the issues in the cases until he could be sure of unanimity. Between December and the following May, Warren, with behind-the-scenes help from Frankfurter, gradually forged a consensus among the justices. . . . [note omitted][52]

Urofsky's description of the strategy employed accorded with Warren's authoritative version. The fact of unanimity when the vote was ultimately taken in March, as Warren affirmed, is fully consistent with that strategy. The confrontation in May introduced by the myth directly conflicts with the decision to assure unanimity before voting. Since Urofsky's focus during his analysis was on the role of Frankfurter, he did not discuss the inconsistencies between his analysis and the myth.

In disputing Kluger's interpretation of the Frankfurter role in *Brown,* Urofsky squarely relied on the extensive research and analysis by Professor Mark Tushnet revealed in an article entitled "What Really Happened in *Brown v. Board of Education,*" published in the 1991 *Columbia Law Review.*[53] While Kluger, Hutchinson, and Schwartz in their analyses had relied primarily on existing papers of Black, Burton, Clark, and Frankfurter, Tushnet also considered "new information available in the papers of" Warren, Douglas, and Jackson. While Tushnet's key conclusion was that "The standard interpretation of Frankfurter's role . . . overstates his contribution to the deliberation process, at least to the extent that it attributes to him substantial influence over his colleagues' positions,"[54] and he undertook no analysis of the veracity of the myth, a number of his conclusions were in conflict with aspects of the myth. He interpreted Reed's comments during the December 12 conference as not being "a commitment to fight their decision vigorously" and, while concluding that "Warren made his most important contribution to the unanimity of the decision . . . in persuading Reed not to dissent," he implied that such had been accomplished well before the formal conference vote. He revealed:

> The Court began to focus on the definition of the remedy in a conference held on January 16, 1954. In some ways the most notable thing about the conference discussion was that it occurred at all. The Court had not yet taken a formal vote on the merits in *Brown,* but Warren seems to have been confident enough of the ultimate outcome to direct discussion to the question of remedy, apparently believing that it was possible for the Court to dispose of the cases completely during the 1953 term. He was mistaken, because agreement on the terms of a gradualist remedy could not be reached. . . .[55]

Contrary to the myth, Tushnet's article did not assign any significant role to Reed in the discussions of the proposed decrees.

Like my *Yearbook* article, Tushnet's scholarship had no apparent effect on the spreading of the myth. Professor Schwartz's attempt at a "good one-volume history" of the Supreme Court,[56] published in 1993, not surprisingly repeated the version of *Brown* he had adopted in his three prior books. While citing Tushnet's study in one endnote, Schwartz wrote:

> In his posthumously published memoirs, the Chief Justice stated that the Court voted in February and that the vote was unanimous against the separate-but-equal doctrine. In later interviews Warren indicated that the vote came in March. The question of the exact date is less important than that of how the vote went. Despite Warren's statement in his memoirs, it is probable that the vote was eight to one, with Justice Reed voting to follow the *Plessy* case.
>
> That Reed did vote to uphold segregation is indicated by his working on the draft of a dissent during February, asserting that segregation by itself did not violate equal protection. In addition, there are indications that the Justice persisted in standing alone until the end of April. Warren continued to work on him to change his vote, both at luncheon meetings and in private sessions. Then, toward the end, the Chief Justice put it to Justice Reed directly; "Stan, you're all by yourself on this now. You've got to decide whether it's really the best thing for the country." As described by Reed's law clerk, who was present at the meeting, Warren was typically restrained in his approach . . . [note omitted].[57]

As do all other commentators, Schwartz emphasized the strong security adopted by the Justices with respect to the *Brown* deliberations:

> The Justices also took steps to ensure that the way they voted would not leak out. No record of action taken in *Brown* was written in the docket book that was kept by each Justice and was available to his clerks. Warren tells us that, at the conference at which the opinion was assigned, "the importance of secrecy was discussed. We agreed that only my law clerks should be involved, and that any writing between my office and those of the other Justices would be delivered to the Justices personally. This practice was followed throughout." . . .
>
> Toward the end of April, after he had secured Justice Reed's vote, the Chief Justice was ready to begin the drafting process. . . . As soon as Warren had finished his *Brown* draft and had it typed, he called in his three law clerks and told them that the decision of the Court was to overturn *Plessy,* and that the decision was unanimous. He enjoined them to the strictest secrecy, saying that he had not told anyone outside the Justices what the decision was—not even his wife. . . . It was now the end of April . . . [note omitted].[58]

With respect to decision day, Schwartz reported:

> Warren had advised his law clerks to be in the courtroom that morning. . . . Justice Frankfurter had also told his clerks that *Brown* was coming down. The other Justices' clerks had not been informed in advance, but they all sensed that this was to be more than the usual decision day. On his way to the robing room, Justice Clark had stopped to say to the clerks, "I think you boys ought to be in the courtroom today" [note omitted].[59]

By 1993, not only had the **Simple Justice** version found acceptance in legal literature, but its veracity had been accepted and repeated in more popular literature. Thus David Halberstam's **The Fifties,**[60] a volume heavily marketed that year, describing the *Brown* decisions, stated that "As late as April, Reed was still holding out. . . ." It added:

> Finally, the Chief Justice made his move: "Stan, you're all by yourself in this now," he said. "You've got to decide whether it's really the best thing for the country." In the end he caved in; all he asked was for a decision that made the dismantling gradual rather than violent and quick.[61]

The only Reed clerk Halberstam identified was myself, described as, like Reed, "also from the South,"[62] an obvious error since I was born and raised in New York State.

Second Refutation Effort

Subsequent to my retirement, I received a request from Clare Cushman to prepare, for a volume to be published under the sponsorship of the Supreme Court Historical Society, a brief biographical sketch of Reed. With respect to *Brown,* the five-page summary included in the volume of illustrated biographies[63] published in 1993 reported only that "His greatest impact came in the watershed case of *Brown* . . . , when, despite misgivings about the Court's role in desegregating public schools, he ultimately abandoned a dissent so the Court could issue its groundbreaking decision unanimously."[64] Not surprisingly, editor Cushman chose Bernard Schwartz to write the Warren chapter, which included three paragraphs regarding *Brown,* described as "the watershed case of the century." It concluded that "The unanimous decision was a direct result of Warren's considerable efforts."[65]

My cursory research for my chapter confirmed for me not only that, despite Reed's interesting career, no one had undertaken to publish a comprehensive biography, but that many references to his actions in other books, as with his role in *Brown,* were inaccurate or distorted. Encouraged by the staff at the Society, I decided to undertake the research required to produce an accurate biography. My assumption that such a volume would not be lengthy was exploded when I found that 379 boxes containing Reed's files and other materials had been deposited by Reed's sons in the archives at the library of the University of Kentucky.

The boxes contained no materials pertinent to Reed's participation in *Brown* for the 1953 Term.[66] The omission did not surprise me since Helen Gaylord, the Justice's secretary during his entire tenure on the Court, had advised me that he proposed to destroy his files regarding those decisions.

The prevalence of the myth posed a difficult dilemma for me when I commenced writing the chapter of my biography of Reed[67] that covered the development of the school segregation decisions. I entitled that chapter "The Evolution of a Reluctant Krytocrat" and in it primarily summarized the material included in my 1966 talk. However, I was perplexed as to an appropriate handling of details attributed to my fellow clerk in **Simple Justice,** one of which I knew to be untrue and the other I felt virtually to a certainty was either a grave misunderstanding or a fabrication. Regrettably, Mickum had suffered an untimely demise in 1985, many years prior to my undertaking the research for the biography, which was published in 1994, and I had never had an opportunity to discuss the matter with him.

With respect to the date when unanimity was achieved, I wrote:

> While Chief Justice Warren's recollection in his **Memoirs** that the formal votes on the school cases occurred in February was almost certainly mistaken, [51] the votes probably not having occurred until the following month, his recollection that "on the first vote, we unanimously agreed that the 'separate but equal' doctrine had no place in public education," and that he thereupon undertook to draft opinions for the Court appears to be accurate.[68]

Endnote 51 cited Kluger's comment that "Warren himself gave conflicting information on the date of the vote," that both Kluger and

Hutchinson placed the vote in either February or March, and that Warren was not confirmed until March 1. Kluger had, correctly I believed, noted the unlikelihood that Warren would schedule such a vote until he had been "fully and properly invested with the authority of his high office."[69]

Convinced both by the record and by my personal involvement of the veracity of my conclusion, I was faced squarely by the oft-quoted alleged overheard conversation between Reed and Warren. In view of his demonstrated careful scholarship, I felt certain that Kluger was reporting accurately what had been related to him by some source. On the other hand, I was unwilling to conclude that Mickum invented or hypothesized the incident to impress someone. During our term together, as well as on the few occasions when Reed's clerks met with him and questions were posed regarding *Brown,* Mickum appeared somewhat to resent the fact that he had been excluded by Reed from matters relating to the cases. While Kluger asserted that "from December to February" Reed put both myself and Mickum "to work researching for the dissent he intended to write,"[70] as related in my 1966 talk, the only assignment Mickum performed relating to the matter was delegated by me and not by Reed.[71] I alluded to that situation in my talk as follows:

> An interesting aspect to me of developments was the fact that George was not assigned any jobs related to the decision nor invited to join in the discussions the Justice and I had regarding the cases. Since he was more sympathetic with reaffirmation of *Plessy v. Ferguson,* while the Justice never so stated, this arrangement convinced me that Justice Reed was not looking for support but analysis and he welcomed the challenge of answering my arguments.[72]

I resolved my dilemma by writing:

> Based on a conversation that Reed's other law clerk reported to author Kluger that he overheard between Reed and Warren in May, that author and many subsequent writers have concluded that Reed did not join the majority until just prior to the release of the unanimous opinions in *Brown v. Board of Education* and *Bolling v. Sharp* on May 17th. However, it appears that the chief justice's recollection on this point was accurate and that the conversation apparently overheard must have related solely to the form of the Court's decree, the only aspect of the decisions still being seriously debated by early May other than by Justice Jackson, who

had been confined to a hospital since suffering a heart attack on March 30th and had not yet agreed not to file a concurring opinion [notes omitted].[73]

Referring to the period prior to the unanimous vote, the chapter reported that Warren:

> . . . did engage in a number of low key but effective conversations regarding the cases with Reed. Most of these conversations occurred in the justices' dining room, but on the few occasions when the chief justice strode down the hallway to the Reed chambers for a discussion during the period, the door between the offices of the justice and his clerks was closed and neither clerk was invited to participate. . . . The exclusion even of the law clerk deeply involved with Reed with respect to the cases from the discussions with the chief justice was consistent with the strict rules regarding extra secrecy the conference had adopted with respect to the cases [notes omitted].[74]

With respect to the not quite as frequently reported tale that Reed's clerk "saw tears in his Justice's face as the last words of the two opinions were spoken," which I knew to be untrue, I chose not to dignify it in the text, but to answer it in an endnote. I was present in the courtroom on the occasion and saw no tears, only a very serious mien. No other observer of the event, including those other law clerks and secretaries who were present, reported any unusual deportment by Reed. There were many journalists present with opportunities to observe the Justices and none of them wrote of any such occurrence.

In the text, as had most other commentators, I emphasized the stringent efforts devoted by the Court to the prevention of any leak of news regarding either the substance or the timing of the *Brown* decisions:

> . . . in keeping with their pledge to secrecy, most of the justices did not even advise their secretaries and law clerks that a historic event was about to occur. Justice Reed, like Justice Clark, was an exception in that, as he departed for the session just prior to noon, he suggested to Fassett that it would be a good day to attend an opinion session [60].[75]

Endnote 60 added:

> Reed also obviously alerted Helen Gaylord because she also observed the opinion session on May 17. Mr. Mickum had departed for a luncheon date at the Court of Appeals prior to Reed's cryptic comment so he missed the opening of the opinion session. Mrs. Warren, a daughter, and a

nephew also were in attendance at the opinion session on May 17, but she has said that the chief justice did not even tell her of the Court's plan. She came because Douglas was giving a luncheon for the Belgian ambassador following the Court session. . . .[76]

Had I been aware at the time I was writing the book of the observation of one other person beside myself who was focusing specifically on Reed, I certainly also would have incorporated that information. Thurgood Marshall's direct observation was related to journalist Juan Williams for a *Washington Post Magazine* article. Thereafter, it became part of a volume of tributes to that Justice collected by Roger Goldman and David Gallen[77] as follows:

> As the decision came down, Marshall was watching Reed's eyes. "When Warren read the opinion," he says, Reed "looked me right straight in the face the whole time because he wanted to see what happened when I realized that he didn't write that dissent. I was looking right straight at him, and I did like that [a nod of the head], and he did like that [a nod in response]."[78]

When Williams's own biography of Marshall was published in 1998,[79] he added some details regarding the incident based on his extensive interviews with the Justice. He reported that, at the outset of the opinion session, "Marshall, seated in the lawyers' section, focused a glare at Justice Stanley Reed" and explained:

> Marshall heard that Reed had prepared a dissent, with the help of a privately hired law clerk. He wanted to watch Reed's face as a clue to what was going to happen. Reed only stared back at him, wide-eyed. . . . "When Warren read the opinion," Marshall recalled, "Reed looked me right straight in the face the whole time because he wanted to see what happened when I realized that he didn't write that dissent and I was looking right straight at him. I'm sure Reed laughed at that."[80]

Marshall's erroneous belief[81] that Reed had "hired a separate law clerk to write his dissent" was also reported in the Marshall biographies of Carl Rowan (1993)[82] and Professor Howard Ball (1998).[83] The latter volume quoted Mickum's tale of Reed crying during the reading of the opinions and added:

> And the rumor Marshall heard about Reed bringing on an extra law clerk was correct. Jack Fassett, according to Mickum, helped Reed prepare

"lots of drafts of dissents" that Reed was considering using in the *Brown* case. "It was the Earl Warren influence that brought him around. . . . It was a sense on Reed's part that it was in the best interests of the country that the opinion be unanimous [46]."[84]

I was intrigued by the fact that, rather than citing **Simple Justice,** Ball's endnote 46 cited only a Reed oral history project at the University of Kentucky.

I was not aware of the Reed oral history project when I was doing research at the University of Kentucky for **New Deal Justice.** The "oral history interviews file" (box 282) included among the materials made available to me at the Kentucky archives contained only transcripts of the Reed interview for the Vinson project, of his extensive interview for the Columbia University project, and of an interview for a Herbert Hoover project. The detailed index to the Reed collection prepared by the library staff made no reference to a Reed project. Alerted by Ball's reference, I learned that in 1981, following Reed's death, the Modern Political Archives Division of Special Collections at the university undertook a project of collecting oral histories regarding Reed's career. During the ensuing four years twenty-one interviews were conducted, including one of Mickum. The interviews are now available on the Internet.[85]

Had I been aware that Mickum had been interviewed prior to his death, I certainly would have referred to its contents in discussing the allegedly overheard conversation which is fundamental to the myth. Speaking with Mickum in March, 1981, in Washington, the interviewer first confirmed that Mickum had clerked during the Term of the *Brown* decisions and continued:

> Gilson: Tell me a little about that if you . . . if you can. Was it agonizing for Reed? Did he have a hard time with it?
> Mickum: Let me say this. I . . . I've always followed a principle that I just would prefer not to talk about, you know, a case.
> Gilson: Okay.
> Mickum: I know that I have been quoted in a book that was written and I refused to take the call of the man who wrote the book at least seven times, and I don't know where he got those quotes.
> Gilson: Seriously?
> Mickum: Deadly serious.
> Gilson: Oh, I'm . . . I'm sure you're serious. I'm just . . .

Mickum: But I . . . you know, I can tell you that it was not an easy case for Reed. I think I . . . I think it's public knowledge that one . . . at the commencement of the term he was really in dissent in that case. So, I think I can answer the question I think you asked—no, it was not . . .

Gilson: Okay.

Mickum: . . . an easy decision for him.

Gilson: Okay.

Mickum: The fact is, I . . . I could tell you that when that opinion was read from the bench, he cried.

Gilson: He cried?

Mickum: Yes, sir.

Gilson: Whew!

Mickum: He was really very troubled by it. But I don't think I want to go into the ins and outs of . . .

Gilson: Okay.

Mickum: . . . what he . . . my God, you know, I think I told you he was in dissent and there were lots of drafts of dissents and I believe Jack Fassett still has copies of most. Indeed, one draft was published in the book I averted to in Reed's own handwriting. But that's not a game I'm going to play.

Gilson: Okay. Well, I was working on two angles there. Another angle is, it was originally argued in the '52 term with [Frederick] Vinson as chief justice. Then it came back in the '53 term for re-argument. Was it really . . . I was just . . . well, I was wondering, was it . . . was it a different forms of arguments each time or was it more the Earl Warren influence that brought him around?

Mickum: Oh, I think it was the Earl Warren influence. In fact, I don't think it, I know it.

Gilson: You know it?

Mickum: Yes, sir.

Gilson: Is there any reason for that other than, perhaps, Warren was able to write a . . .

Mickum: Well, . . .

Gilson: . . . an opinion that he liked?

Mickum: . . . no. If you're asking me if Earl Warren overwhelmed Reed . . .

Gilson: No, I'm not.

Mickum: . . . either by the power of his personal or written eloquence, the answer is no.

Gilson: Umhmm.

Mickum: It was a sense on Reed's part that it was in the best interests of the company . . . country that the opinion be unanimous.

Gilson: And since . . . well, not that . . .
Mickum: And he was alone. He was . . .
Gilson: Yeah.
Mickum: . . . he was a lone dissenter at that point in the game.[86]

While this confusing interview primarily muddies the water, it also clearly contradicts the contention that Mickum overheard the claimed Warren admonition as well as that Mickum was present at the meeting in question. I would undoubtedly have been less reticent about refuting the myth in **New Deal Justice** had I been aware of the interview. However, it appears unlikely that any evidence I might have added to the discussion in my tome, no matter how definitive, would have deterred the continued propagation of the myth. My belief that the publication would stem the tide of acceptance of the myth proved to be naïve. I should have known that history is made by what historians report and not necessarily by what occurred. An intriguing myth sometimes will fit more snugly into a historian's concept of an event than the less interesting reality.

Continued Proliferation of the Myth

In 1996, Bernard Schwartz again included an account of the *Brown* decision in one of his books:[87] he reported the details of the supposed meeting between Reed and Warren "As described by Reed's law clerk, who was present at the meeting."[88]

The following year, the Indiana Historical Society published a biography by Professors Gugin and St. Clair of Sherman Minton.[89] While it referred to **Simple Justice** as an "epochal study" and endorsed Kluger's description of Minton's role in *Brown,* it did not adopt the details of the myth. To the contrary, it concluded that "Sometime in March or April, the exact date is not known, the Justices met to take their final vote on the case, reaching a compromise that resulted in a unanimous decision."[90] The authors emphasized Minton's role in accomplishment of the unanimity as follows:

> . . . Warren was convinced that the decision to overturn segregated schools had to have the moral force of a unanimous decision. For the next few months Warren worked on two levels—the personal and the conference—to get that unanimity. Minton, of course, was a good candidate for helping with the personal strategy. The luncheon grouping,

fostered by Minton when Vinson was chief justice, proved a valuable tool since Reed, the most reticent justice, was one of the regular participants. At these gatherings, Warren, Minton and Burton worked on Reed to join with the majority. Minton, along with Burton, was the most congenial with Reed and the most likely to influence Reed's vote. As the Court's strongest team player, Minton no doubt stressed to his colleague the unfortunate effects of a split decision.

These authors also stressed the exceptional secrecy involved:

> Court proceedings leading up to *Brown* were shrouded in secrecy. Regarding all the Court's business, but especially pertaining to *Brown,* Minton was adamant that neither he nor his law clerks would discuss the deliberations of the Court with outsiders, either then or in the future. One clerk, recalling the drama surrounding *Brown,* acknowledged that "the Court generally maintained much stricter confidentiality even with respect to law clerks in regard to *Brown* than in regard to the general run of cases. . . ."[91]

The Minton biography, like my Reed biography, did not noticeably impede the proliferation of the myth. Thus, when Professor Ed Cray's biography of Warren[92] appeared during the same year, it followed Schwartz's lead. Citing **Simple Justice,** it repeated the tale of the incident with the introduction that "Near the end of April, Warren walked down the hall to confront the Kentuckian one last time."[93]

Professor Lucas Powe's treatise on the Warren Court,[94] published in 2000, also relied on Kluger in relating its version:

> As April was nearing its end, Reed remained the lone holdout. At a meeting with Reed, Warren went for the clinching argument.[95]

It then repeated verbatim the allegedly witnessed conversation.

In 2001, Oxford University Press published a massive compilation of selected Supreme Court conference notes,[96] edited by Professor Del Dickson, covering the period 1940 to 1985. While the volume constitutes neither a commentary on *Brown* nor a biography of a participant, it does contain annotations by the editor to a reconstruction of the conference of December 12, 1953. The reconstruction was based on the private papers of Douglas and Burton. The lead annotation reads:

> Result: Led by Earl Warren, the Justices continued to discuss the case informally among themselves, without voting. They talked about the case together in chambers, at meals, and during conferences on other

cases [72]. A formal vote was finally taken in February or March, with all the Justices agreeing that the doctrine of separate by equal had no place in public schools [73].[97]

Footnote 72 cited **Simple Justice** and stated, "One of Stanley Reed's clerks, George Mickum, claimed to have witnessed Earl Warren pressuring Reed to secure a unanimous vote. According to Mickum, Warren cornered Reed and told him, 'Stan, you're all by yourself in this now.'" Footnote 73 cited Warren's **Memoirs.** It seems clear that Dickson was not only skeptical about the Mickum tale but rejected the key elements of the myth.[98]

Regrettably, the most recently published pertinent commentary[99] was not similarly skeptical of the myth. Titled *Brown v. Board of Education* and also published in 2001, it was written by Professor James Patterson. He cited both **Super Chief** and **Chief Justice** for the following version of the accomplishment of unanimity:

> . . . In the end the still-torn justices took no action on December 12. They agreed to keep talking about the issues among themselves.
>
> That they did over the next three months, with Warren working hard to bring his colleagues together. Like Frankfurter, he much wanted the Court to reach a unanimous opinion or, if Reed held out, to announce a decision with only one dissent. He labored especially assiduously to woo the argumentative Frankfurter and he regularly sought out Reed for lunch. He assured Reed that he [Reed] would in the end "really do the best thing for the country."
>
> By late March, Warren was sure that he would have his way—all but Reed seemed prepared to support a decision against segregation. . . .
>
> Warren then set to work drafting opinions . . . he hand-delivered drafts to his colleagues early in May. . . . At some point the Chief even won over Reed, reminding him that he stood alone and that a dissent would encourage resistance in the South. Did Reed really wish to do that? Reed, assured that Warren's opinion would give the South time to dismantle segregation, gave in. . . .[100]

While Patterson did not quote the Mickum version nor identify him as his source, Mickum's tale was the basis for the accounts in the two cited sources and the summary of events Patterson adopted followed the **Simple Justice** model. It is apparent that Patterson, unlike Ball, but like all of the other authors including myself, was either not aware of or chose to disregard Mickum's oral history interview.

Summing Up and Final Plea

Myths have lives of their own! The myth regarding Reed's performance in the *School Segregation Cases* has so often been repeated at this point that it may be impossible to dispel. When I gave my 1966 talk, which was published in the 1986 *Yearbook,* I stated that I had "little doubt that eventually the true facts should be available to historians." At that time, I was concerned merely with some exaggeration of Warren's role; I certainly did not anticipate a distortion such as has been perpetrated by the proliferation of the myth. I also mentioned during the talk that a number of actions by Reed, such as his recommendation of me in 1957 to the director of a university press to review a manuscript dealing with desegregation, indicated that he "counted on me eventually putting the record straight."[101] While Reed never chose to describe publicly his role in *Brown,* even when directly questioned as during the Vinson project interview, he did not intrude or object when I gave my response, including my reference to krytocracy, to an inquiry during the 1970 gathering of his law clerks.

In any event, both because of my respect for Reed and in fairness to his memory, as well as because I wish to do what I can to correct the historical record of an event in which I participated, I am making this final effort to destroy the myth.

The issue is not whether Reed initially planned, or, more accurately, seriously considered writing a dissent to a decision overruling *Plessy.* There is no doubt that, during the 1952 Term while Fred Vinson was still Chief, the Court was sharply divided. Three days after the *Brown* decision, Frankfurter wrote Reed that "I have no doubt that if the *Segregation Cases* had reached decision last term there would have been four dissenters—Vinson, Reed, Jackson and Clark—and certainly several opinions for the majority view."[102] That analysis conflicts with the perceptions of several of the other participants[103] and may well have been an early step in the campaign to enhance Frankfurter's role in *Brown.* Nevertheless, it probably was accurate with respect to Reed.

In their biography of Vinson published in 2002,[104] Professors St. Clair and Gugin summarized the situation during the 1952 Term as follows:

> The conference on the school desegregation cases was held on December 13, 1952. Various efforts to document what transpired in the conference

have produced some conflicting stories, but some aspects of the conference deliberations seem clear. The first attempt to document the conference debate was Kluger's extensive work on the *Brown* case, but since publication of that work, more data have become available and subsequent investigations have provided different interpretations. . . . One thing that is certain about the December 13 conference is that there was no clear consensus among the justices about the issues raised in the desegregation cases; had the justices been asked to decide that day, odds are good that there would not have been a unanimous decision. However, the extent of disagreement among the justices is in dispute. . . .[105]

Relying heavily on Tushnet's analysis, the authors concluded that "What stood in the way of unanimity was not differences over merits, 'but division over how to justify the results.' "[106]

In any event, my personal experience working for Reed during the summer and fall of 1953, which was detailed in the 1986 *Yearbook* and **New Deal Justice,** confirms that Reed was still considering a possible dissent up to the time of the reargument during the week of December 7, 1953. Those writings also show that Reed's concerns, like Jackson's and apparently those of Frankfurter, were with the fundamental issue of the power of the Court in view of the teachings of history to outlaw segregation and, additionally, with reliance on the Equal Protection Clause to accomplish that result. He was indeed concerned that his Court, like the Court before which he had argued the early New Deal cases,[107] would be guilty of assuming the role of krytocrats. Apropos of his concerns, during the reargument Reed suggested to counsel that the failure of Congress to act over the years with respect to the matter indicated an intention to leave the matter to the states. He also pointed out that the Court that decided *Plessy* was composed of Justices who "were thoroughly familiar with all the history" underlying the Fourteenth Amendment.[108]

Based on all published accounts, including Tushnet's detailed analysis and Dickson's reconstructed conference notes[109] as well as **Simple Justice,**[110] Reed's role at the December 12 conference, during which the cases were first discussed with Warren, was neither adversarial nor adamant. Tushnet's summary in his article, which drew on the widest range of sources, was repeated in his subsequent biography of Thurgood Marshall[111] as follows:

By the discussion's end, and probably before it began, it was clear that a majority was prepared to hold segregation unconstitutional, and that the justices would be interested in developing a remedy allowing some delay in implementation. Justice Reed reiterated his view that segregation was constitutional because it was "not done on inferiority but on racial differences," for "of course there is no inferior race," although, [Reed] said, African-Americans "may be handicapped by lack of opportunity." Rather, segregation "protects people against [the] mixing of races." History and the contemporaneous understanding of the Fourteenth Amendment meant that segregation was constitutionally permissible. Still, even Reed said that the Constitution was "dynamic," and *Plessy* "might not be correct now" because the states had not provided equal facilities to African-Americans. The tone of Reed's comments is not easy to capture, but he seems not to have committed himself to a vigorous fight.[112]

No new projects with respect to *Brown* were undertaken between December 12 and the vote taken during the Court's recess, which went from February 9 to March 9. Reed attended, but apparently was not a major advocate at, the conference on January 16 when the manner of achieving a gradualist remedy was discussed. If a dissent had still been seriously considered during this period, much work would have been required to organize and polish the materials assembled prior to December 12. The handwritten paper as to which Reed solicited my comments at the outset of the recess clearly had not been written recently. I believe it was the product of his cogitations the previous summer. In any event, prior to my analysis, it had not even been reduced to typewritten form, and Reed thereafter did not seek to reclaim it from me. As related in the *Yearbook* article, following the discussion of my analysis, Reed and I had no further discussions of any aspect of *Brown* prior to May 17, and Helen Gaylord confirmed to me that he made no further independent effort to prepare any opinion.

The obvious conclusion is that, as reported by Warren, Reed had, after thorough consideration, agreed during the initial vote to support decisions overruling *Plessy.* No special concession was made to him at that time with respect to the decrees since there had for some time been general agreement that the matter of appropriate remedies should receive additional consideration. Only the precise wording of the proposed orders was still unsettled.

The absence of any factual basis for the crying aspect of the myth is too clear to warrant reiteration. However, the implication that the decisions were deemed either a public or a personal disaster by Reed is equally ludicrous. From his first Term on the Court, when he joined Chief Justice Hughes's opinion in *Missouri ex rel. Raines v. Canada,*[113] the first case in which the Court actually faced the issue of racial segregation in education, Reed had supported decisions requiring fair treatment for Negroes. He was the author of the landmark decision in *Smith v. Allwright,*[114] which overruled a contrary holding by the Court and upheld the right of Negroes to participate in previously exclusively white primary elections. He also authored less well-known decisions prohibiting racial discrimination by motor carriers[115] and by labor organizations.[116] He often expressed the view, as he had at the December 12 conference, that an end to segregation was "an inevitability."[117]

In response to Frankfurter's post-decision letter expressing "deep gratitude for your share in what I believe to be a great good for our nation," Reed promptly replied:

> While there were many considerations that pointed to a dissent, they did not add up to a balance against the Court's opinion. From Canada through Smith and Allwright, Sweatt, Morgan, Steel to Jay Bird, the factors looking toward a fair treatment for Negroes are more important than the weight of history. While "due process" seemed a better ground to me, there really isn't much difference. Equal protection comes close to this situation.[118]

That is not the writing of a gravely disappointed or disheartened Justice. To the contrary, it accurately reflects precisely what occurred: Reed presented his concerns about the Court's power and the rationale for the decision, but, in the final analysis, when the vote was finally taken in early March, he joined the unanimous result and did so willingly and without coercion. It constitutes no derogation of the leadership afforded by Warren to acknowledge that the myth and all of its implications have no factual basis and it should not continue to be repeated.

During my 1966 talk, I expressed the view that Reed's action with respect to *Brown* "was an act of judicial statesmanship." I adhere to that view and have been troubled that both his and the historic record have been tarnished and distorted by the proliferation of the myth. As we approach the fiftieth anniversary of the *Brown* decisions, it is particularly appropriate that the myth be refuted.

Endnotes

1. Richard Kluger, **Simple Justice: The History of *Brown v. Board of Education* and Black America's Struggle for Equality** (Alfred A. Knopf 1976, c 1975), hereinafter "**SJ.**"
2. 347 U.S. 483 (1954).
3. 347 U.S. 497 (1954).
4. **SJ** 694.
5. **SJ** 698.
6. **SJ** 708.
7. *See* Mark Tushnet, with Katya Lezin, "What Really Happened in *Brown v. Board of Education*," 91 *Columbia Law Review* 1867 (1991), for the most detailed analysis of the roles of Jackson and Frankfurter based on the most extensive use of source materials.
8. John D. Fassett, "Mr. Justice Reed and *Brown v. Board of Education*," 1986 *Yearbook,* Supreme Court Historical Society 48, 62, hereinafter "*Yearbook.*"
9. *Yearbook* 61.
10. *Yearbook* 63.
11. Albert P. Blaustein and Clarence Clyde Ferguson, Jr., **Desegregation and the Law; The Meaning and Effect of the School Segregation Cases** (Rutgers University Press 1957). *See Yearbook* 62.
12. Query whether it was from Leventhal that Warren Burger heard of this incident. As Chief Justice he related the story in a memorial tribute to Reed. Warren E. Burger, "Stanley F. Reed," 1981 *Yearbook* 11.
13. **SJ** 698.
14. **SJ** 708.
15. Stanley F. Reed Collection, University of Kentucky Library, box 282.
16. *Ibid.*
17. Earl Warren, **The Memoirs of Earl Warren** (Doubleday & Company 1977), hereinafter "**Memoirs.**"
18. **Memoirs** 285.
19. Liva Baker, **Felix Frankfurter** (Coward-McCann 1969) 317.
20. **Memoirs** 4.
21. **Memoirs** 286.
22. Gerald T. Dunne, **Hugo Black and the Judicial Revolution** (Simon and Schuster 1977).
23. *Id.* 318–319.
24. *Id.* 321.

25. Mary Frances Berry, **Stability, Security and Continuity: Mr. Justice Burton and Decision-Making in the Supreme Court 1945–1958** (Greenwood 1978).
26. *Id.* 155–156.
27. *Id.* 157–158.
28. Jack Harrison Pollack, **Earl Warren: The Judge Who Changed America** (Prentice-Hall 1979).
29. *Id.* 174.
30. William O. Douglas, **The Court Years 1939–1975: The Autobiography of William O. Douglas** (Random House 1980).
31. *Id.* 115. Cf. the "Memorandum to the File" dated May 17, 1954, by Douglas, reproduced in Del Dickson, editor, **The Supreme Court in Conference (1940–1985): The Private Discussions Behind Nearly 300 Supreme Court Decisions** (Oxford University Press 2001) 660–661, wherein Douglas wrote that "Everyone thought that at least Justice Reed was going to write a dissent but he finally agreed to leave his doubts unsaid and to go along."
32. James F. Simon, **Independent Journey: The Life of William O. Douglas** (Harper & Row 1980).
33. *Id.* 357, 480.
34. Dennis J. Hutchinson, "Unanimity and Desegregation: Decisionmaking in the Supreme Court, 1948–1958," 68 *Georgetown Law Journal* 1–96 (1979).
35. *Id.* 43.
36. *Id.* 41.
37. *Id.* 33.
38. G. Edward White, **Earl Warren: A Public Life** (Oxford University Press 1982).
39. *Id.* 167.
40. *Id.* 400.
41. Bernard Schwartz with Stephan Lesher, **Inside the Warren Court** (Doubleday & Company 1983).
42. *Id.* 87.
43. *Id.* 86.
44. Bernard Schwartz, **Super Chief: Earl Warren and His Supreme Court— A Judicial Biography** (New York University Press 1983).
45. *Id.,* at 94, 95.
46. Bernard Schwartz, **The Unpublished Opinions of the Warren Court** (Oxford University Press 1985) 447.
47. Alexander M. Bickel, **The Supreme Court and the Idea of Progress** (Harper & Row 1970) 33.
48. Joseph P. Lash, **From the Diaries of Felix Frankfurter with a Biographical Essay and Notes** (W. W. Norton 1975) 84.

49. H. N. Hirsch, **The Enigma of Felix Frankfurter** (Basic Books 1981).
50. *Id.* 246.
51. Melvin I. Urofsky, **Felix Frankfurter: Judicial Restraint and Individual Liberties** (Twayne Publishers 1991).
52. *Id.* 134, 136, 137, 139.
53. Tushnet, *supra* n.7.
54. *Id.* 1868, 1875.
55. *Id.* 1914, 1922, 1924.
56. Bernard Schwartz, **A History of the Supreme Court** (Oxford University Press 1993), preface.
57. *Id.* 298.
58. *Id.* 298–300.
59. *Id.* 304–305.
60. David Halberstam, **The Fifties** (Villard Books 1993).
61. *Id.* 423.
62. *Id.* 422.
63. Clare Cushman, editor, **The Supreme Court Justices: Illustrated Biographies, 1789–1993** (Congressional Quarterly, 1993).
64. *Id.* 385.
65. *Id.* 438–439.
66. Tushnet, *supra* n.7 at 1868, studied Reed's papers for his article. He noted only one item pertinent to the 1954 Term.
67. John D. Fassett, **New Deal Justice: The Life of Stanley Reed of Kentucky** (Vantage 1994), hereinafter "**NDJ.**"
68. **NDJ** 572.
69. **SJ** 694.
70. **SJ** 691.
71. *Yearbook* 57.
72. *Yearbook* 55–56.
73. **NDJ** 572.
74. **NDJ** 571–572.
75. **NDJ** 573.
76. **NDJ** 745.
77. Roger Goldman with David Gallen, **Thurgood Marshall: Justice for All** (Carroll & Graf 1992).
78. *Id.* 151.
79. Juan Williams, **Thurgood Marshall: American Revolutionary** (Random House 1998).
80. *Id.* 226.
81. Reed selected me to be his law clerk based on the recommendation of the Dean of Yale Law School, exactly as he had selected clerks for preceding Terms. As noted in my 1966 talk, my first conversation with Reed about

Brown occurred after I reported for work. During the 1953 Term, each Associate Justice was authorized two law clerks.

82. Carl T. Rowan, **Dream Makers, Dream Breakers: The World of Justice Thurgood Marshall** (Little, Brown and Company 1993) 218.

83. Howard Ball, **A Defiant Life: Thurgood Marshall and the Persistence of Racism in America** (Crown 1998).

84. *Id.* 133.

85. The Stanley Forman Reed Oral History Project, Division of Special Collections and Archives of the University of Kentucky Libraries, http://kdl.kyvl.org/cgi/t/text/text-idx?tpl=kukohsfr.tpl.

86. http://kd.kyvl.org/cgi/t/text/text-idx?c=oralhist;xc=1&idno=81oh40&view=toc.

87. Bernard Schwartz, **Decision: How the Supreme Court Decides Cases** (Oxford University Press 1996).

88. *Id.* 98.

89. Linda C. Gugin and James E. St. Clair, **Sherman Minton: New Deal Senator, Cold War Justice** (Indiana Historical Society 1997).

90. *Id.* 264.

91. *Id.* 263–264.

92. Ed Cray, **Chief Justice: A Biography of Earl Warren** (Simon & Schuster 1997).

93. *Id.* 284.

94. Lucas A. Powe, Jr., **The Warren Court and American Politics** (Harvard University Press 2000).

95. *Id.* 28.

96. Dickson *supra* n. 31, hereinafter "Dickson."

97. *Id.* 661–662.

98. Another Dickson footnote commented that "the heroic representation of Frankfurter" in many writings about *Brown* "is at best exaggerated." He noted that "After *Brown* was decided, Frankfurter had a personal army of ex-clerks and academic protégés to rebuild his reputation as the intellectual leader of the Court and the strategic mastermind behind the segregation cases." Dickson 651–652.

99. James T. Patterson, ***Brown v. Board of Education*: A Civil Rights Milestone and Its Troubled Legacy** (Oxford University Press 2001).

100. *Id.* 64–65.

101. *Yearbook* 62.

102. **NDJ** 575.

103. Berry *supra* n. 25 at 125 concluded that "If the votes had been counted, Burton, Minton, Clark, Douglas and Black would have been in favor of the black petitioners; and Reed, Frankfurter, Vinson and Jackson would have been opposed." *See also* Dickson, *supra* n. 31 at 646–653; Tushnet, *supra* n. 7 at 1902.

104. James E. St. Clair and Linda C. Gugin, **Chief Justice Fred M. Vinson of Kentucky** (University Press of Kentucky 2002)
105. *Id.* 319.
106. *Id.* 321.
107. **NDJ** chapters 7–12.
108. Mark V. Tushnet, **Making Civil Rights Law: Thurgood Marshall and the Supreme Court, 1936–1961** (Oxford University Press 1994) 207, 208.
109. Dickson, *supra* n. 31 at 654–660.
110. **SJ** 680.
111. Tushnet, *supra* n. 108 at 210–211.
112. *Id.* 210–211.
113. 305 U.S. 337 (1938).
114. 321 U.S. 649 (1944).
115. *Morgan v. Virginia,* 328 U.S. 373 (1946).
116. *Railway Mail Association v. Corsi,* 326 U.S. 88 (1945).
117. **NDJ** 580. *See also* Roger K. Newman, **Hugo Black: A Biography** (Pantheon 1994) 438.
118. **NDJ** 575. *See also* Fassett, "The Buddha and the Bumblebee: The Saga of Stanley Reed and Felix Frankfurter," 28 *Journal of Supreme Court History* 165 (2003).

❧ B R A D L E Y D . H A Y E S

Linda Brown and the Fight for Educational Equality

Linda Brown's name heads one of the most famous and, arguably, important cases in Supreme Court history. *Brown v. Board of Education of Topeka*[1] laid the foundation for later efforts to dismantle racially segregated society in southern America and that served as a catalyst for the civil rights movement. Moreover, *Brown* marked the start of a new role for the federal judiciary as the institution most engaged in the protection of minority rights. Yet, behind all the grandeur of *Brown,* stood an eight-year-old-girl who had little understanding of her case when it was initiated. That girl would grow up to become a citizen activist who would keep pushing for equality in education.

By all accounts, Linda Brown (1943-) was a happy and beloved child growing up in Topeka, Kansas. The Brown family was headed by Oliver and Leola Brown who also had two younger daughters: Terry, and Cheryl. Oliver worked as a boxcar welder at the Santa Fe Railroad. In 1951, he was ordained as an African Methodist Episcopal minister and served as an assistant pastor at their local church.

The Browns lived in a modest, multiracial neighborhood. While the neighborhood itself was not highly segregated, the schools which the neighborhood children attended were. Linda recalled,

> I lived in a neighborhood that was integrated and I had playmates of all nationalities . . . that I played with . . . and then when school started we would go these opposite directions and, of course, your playmates who you played with everyday wanted to know "Well, why don't you go to school with us?"[2]

Seven block from the Brown's house was the Sumner Elementary School—an all-white public elementary school. Instead of being allowed to enroll in Sumner, Linda was forced to attend Monroe Elementary School. In order to get to Monroe, Linda had to walk through an active railway switching yard for about five blocks to get to her bus station. The bus then took a circuitous route to the school and would occasionally arrive before the school was open, leaving the children outside to battle whatever weather the season brought. According to Oliver Brown, Linda departed an hour and twenty minutes before school started in order to get there on time.

In 1950, Oliver Brown attempted to enroll Linda at the Sumner Elementary School so that she would no longer have to make the precarious and lengthy trip to Monroe. The Browns were quickly turned away by school administrators. The stress of the event was not lost on young Linda:

> I remember walking up the steps and how big the building seemed to me . . . but [also] this excitement inside of me. And I remember [my father] going inside with the principle and talking to him. Being young . . . I really didn't know what was going on but I knew something was wrong because walking home I could feel the tension . . . when he took me by the hand that something was going on.[3]

Angered and frustrated, Oliver Brown, who idolized heavyweight boxing champion Joe Lewis, agreed to join a fight of a different kind. Oliver and Linda Brown became one of thirteen families the National Association for the Advancement of Colored People (NAACP) enlisted to challenge the constitutionality of the segregated schooling system in Topeka. The NAACP took the lead in pursuing the case and Linda had very little involvement with the case at trial or on appeal.

Linda Brown's first foray into constitutional litigation resulted in defeat but not a wholesale loss. The three-judge federal district court held that conditions among black and white schools in Topeka were similar and, therefore, there was no unconstitutional discrimination in the segregated system. However, the court wrote that it believed the segregation of white and black children adversely affected black children. It seems quite clear from the district court's opinion that had *Plessy v. Ferguson*[4] (1896) and its doctrine of "separate but equal" not been the governing precedent, the court would have ruled in favor of Linda Brown.

The NAACP lawyers leading the Brown case appealed the district court's decision, in coordination with four other cases, directly to the Supreme Court of the United States. The Court heard oral arguments twice before rendering its decision on May 17, 1954. Chief Justice Earl Warren read the opinion for a unanimous Court. Warren posed the question before the Court and gave its answer in the following, now famous, passage:

> Does segregation of children in public schools solely on the basis of race, even though the physical facilities and other 'tangible' factors may be equal, deprive the children of the minority group of equal educational opportunities? We believe that it does . . . We conclude that in the field of public education the doctrine of 'separate but equal' has no place. Separate educational facilities are inherently unequal.[5]

The Court's decision made the lead headline in every major newspaper in the country. There was high praise by African-American leaders, progressive politicians, and world leaders. There was harsh criticism from white segregationists and southern politicians, who mocked the Court's use of sociological data. Similar, if more tempered, praise and criticism followed the Court's issuance of a legal remedy in *Brown II*.[6] The same newspapers that covered *Brown* so extensively largely ignored the named petitioners such as Linda Brown and their reaction to judicial victory.

Yet, Linda recalled the jubilation she and her family felt the day the decision was issued:

> I was at school the day the decision was handed down. Mother was home. I remember her talking about [the *Brown* decision] and being so excited. Then when my father came in, he was overjoyed. My mother said that she remembers him embracing us and saying "Thanks be to God for this" and just being overwhelmed.[7]

African-American families across the South (and beyond) shared the Brown family's joy while realizing that *Brown* marked the start of significant social change.

In the fall of 1954 Linda began 7th grade at a junior high school that was already integrated. Although she was too old to attend Sumner Elementary School, her younger sister Cheryl enrolled there in 1961. At the time, Linda did not give the case much thought. At age eleven, she did not fully understand what the case had accomplished: her parents worked to keep the milestone low key.

Yet Linda came to recognize the responsibility attached to the legacy of *Brown.* Consequently, the Supreme Court's decisions in 1954 and 1955 were not the last judicial decrees under the case entitled *Brown v. Board of Education.* In 1979, at the urging of attorney Richard Jones and financial backing from the American Civil Liberties Union, Linda, now age 36, agreed to re-open the case on behalf of her own children. Linda claimed that the Topeka school district had not completed desegregation in the system as mandated by the Supreme Court. At times it appeared as if Linda's legacy would be pushing for change that would not come. "It's disheartening that we are still fighting," she reasoned, "But we are dealing with human beings. As long as we are, there will always be those who feel the races should separate."[8] Linda's oldest son, Charles Smith, was quoted as saying, "I had a funny feeling when I heard the judge agreed to reopen the case. I began to wonder whether my kids will be in this lawsuit too someday."[9]

Linda's son may have been closer to the mark than many would have liked. The case languished in the courts for eight years before federal District Court Judge Richard Rogers ruled that the school district could not control where people lived and found that there was no "illegal, intentional, systematic or residual separation of races"[10] within the Topeka school district. Brown and her co-plaintiffs, determined to realize the aspirations announced in *Brown,* appealed the decision. Two years later, they won in a 2-1 decision handed down by the Tenth Circuit Court of Appeals.[11] However, following an appeal by the Topeka school board, the U.S. Supreme Court ordered the Tenth Circuit to reconsider its decision.[12] In 1992, the circuit court upheld its decision; the next year, the Supreme Court refused to review the case.[13]

Finally, in 1994, Judge Rogers approved a new desegregation plan: Topeka Unified School District 501.[14] The plan included a transfer program designed to level the racial balance throughout the school district, shifting some of the past boundaries, moving students who received English as a second language classes into schools with higher white student percentages, and proposed construction of three new schools within the district. On July 29, 1999, Judge Rogers closed the case twenty years after Linda Brown had re-opened *Brown* and nearly fifty years after the *Brown v. Board of Education* case was first filed.

It would be incomplete to describe Brown's legacy as defined exclusively by her role as litigant. In 1988 Linda Brown, now Linda Brown Thompson, and her sister, Cheryl Brown Henderson, founded the Brown Foundation for Educational Equity, Excellence and Research. Cheryl serves as executive director and Linda as a program associate. The mission of the Brown Foundation is to provide educational resources regarding the significance of *Brown v. Board of Education* and to record the experiences of the attorneys and plaintiffs involved in the five lawsuits that were combined under the heading of *Brown.* The Foundation's accomplishments include passage of the *Brown v. Board of Education* National Historic Site Act of 1992, which turned the Monroe School into a historic landmark, and the creation of the *Brown v. Board of Education* 50th Anniversary Presidential Commission.

Linda Brown went from a child who had little understanding of a case that bore her last name to an activist for educational opportunity and the preservation of *Brown*'s legacy. As Linda's sister, Cheryl Brown Henderson, observed, "Being the family of the namesake of this judicial turning point comes with a responsibility to teach and never let the country forget what it took for some of its citizens to be afforded their constitutional rights."[15] It is clear that Linda, and the Brown family, have fought so that Americans will never forget the aspirations embedded in *Brown v. Board of Education* or the people who sought to realize those aspirations. Linda's deeds match her call to arms: "The struggle has to continue."[16]

NOTE: *This essay is adapted from* **One Hundred Americans Making Constitutional History: A Biographical History** *(CQ Press, 2004). It is reprinted with permission.*

Endnotes

1. 347 U.S. 483 (1954).

2. Linda Brown, "School, The Story of American Public Education: Episode 3—A Struggle for Educational Equality"; Sarah Mondale (Director), 5:45.
3. *Id.* at 10:31.
4. 163 U.S. 537 (1896).
5. 347 U.S. 483, 493–495 (1954).
6. 349 U.S. 294 (1955).
7. *Supra* note 2 at 12:32.
8. Sudo, Phil. 1994 "Forty Years and Counting," *Scholastic Update* 157:2–3.
9. *Washington Post,* November 30, 1975, A17 (Bill Richards).
10. *Oliver Brown et al. v. Board of Education of Topeka,* Shawnee County, et al., 671 F. Supp. 1290, 1309 (1987).
11. 892 F.2d 851 (1989).
12. 503 U.S. 978 (1992).
13. 978 F.2d. 585 (1992).
14. *Brown et al. v. Board of Education of Topeka, Shawnee County, Kansas et al.,* 1994 U.S. Dist. LEXIS 4206 (1994).
15. Brown Henderson, Cheryl, 2003 "Personal Perspective," *The Brown Quarterly* 5:3.
16. Sudo, Phil, 1994 "Forty Years and Counting" *Scholastic Update* 127:2–3.

∞ PAUL E. WILSON

A Time to Lose

It has been a long time since I first came to this chamber to speak about *Brown v. Board of Education of Topeka.*[1] In 1952, I stood facing this bench and urged that a Kansas statute that permitted racial segregation in some of the state's public schools was not unconstitutional. I lost. This evening I have a different purpose. I have no case to argue, no ax to grind. I shall not talk about constitutional law. My remarks will be personal and anecdotal—some even trivial. They will concern matters not written about by scholars, but they will reflect some of my recollections about *Brown.*

In Richard Kluger's book, **Simple Justice,** the author introduces me by writing, "By Eastern standards, Paul Wilson was a hayseed. His background and practice did not seem to qualify him very well . . . as a reluctant dragon [in] defending his state's Jim Crow public schools."[2] I do not take exception to Mr. Kluger's assessment. I was a country lawyer. I had practiced in the county seat of the rural Kansas county where I was born. My clients there were farmers and tradespeople and the proprietors of small businesses, most of whom found litigation distasteful. I served as prosecuting attorney but my constituents were law abiding people and serious crime was minimal. Felony prosecutions were rare. Racial discrimination cases were unknown because there was no one to discriminate against. We were all white. My courtroom experience was largely limited to the local county and district courts. I had never argued an appeal, either on the federal or state level. After four years, I had left this prairie nirvana to become an assistant state attorney general. My objective was twofold. I had an interest in state politics and wanted to extend my statewide acquaintance. Also, I wanted to broaden my professional experience. Particularly, I wanted to get some experience as an appellate lawyer. A year later I made my first argument before an appellate court. The court was the Supreme Court of the United States. My case was *Brown v. Board of Education of Topeka.*

In the language of civil rights, *Brown v. Board of Education of Topeka* means not a single case, but the rule drawn from the consolidation of four, or perhaps five, cases. During the second week in December 1952, the Supreme Court heard appeals from the states of Kansas,[3] South Carolina,[4] Virginia,[5] Delaware,[6] and from the District of Columbia.[7] Although each was a separate case and was appealed on its own discrete record, all raised the issue of the constitutionality of laws requiring or permitting racial segregation in the public schools. The four state cases were decided in a single opinion bearing the caption *Brown v. Board of Education of Topeka.* Kansans are often embarrassed that their state is so conspicuously known as a place where racial discrimination was sanctioned by law. They ask why couldn't it have been South Carolina or Virginia where the issue was more critical and the impact of the decision was greater. The answer is that the Kansas case was the first docketed for argument in the Supreme Court. It was not the first to be appealed. The South Carolina case was appealed earlier but was returned to the trial court for further proceedings. Meanwhile, the *Brown* appeal reached the Supreme Court and was assigned a place in the docket. Thus the free state of Kansas and not Clarendon County, South Carolina, became identified as the place where public school segregation made its last stand. My remarks here will be limited to the Kansas case.

In 1951, the laws of Kansas prohibited racial discrimination in the public schools, except in cities of the first class where boards of education were empowered, not required, to segregate in the elementary grades only.[8] Cities of the first class are those with 15,000 or more inhabitants. In 1951 there were twelve such cities. The elementary grades were grades one through six. Of the twelve cities affected by the statute, one had never segregated its schools, two had abandoned their earlier policies of segregation, and three others were in the process of desegregating. Thus, in only six districts of the state were there established policies of segregation with no plan for abandonment. Topeka was one of those cities. Its schools were governed by a board of education of six elected members.

In 1951, there were twenty-two elementary schools in Topeka— four were for African-American students only and the rest were almost, but not quite, lily white. Hispanics, Native Americans and other non-African children attended the white schools. The external facilities of all schools were substantially equal, the only difference being that transportation was provided for students attending the black schools and was not provided for the whites.

In the fall of 1950, Oliver Brown, who lived in a racially mixed neighborhood, attempted to enroll his eight-year-old daughter, Linda, in their neighborhood elementary school. The child was denied admission solely because of her color. Instead, she was assigned to attend an all-black school twenty-two blocks away. Other families were experiencing similar rejections as part of a coordinated effort. With the support and assistance of the NAACP the aggrieved families prepared and filed a lawsuit claiming that the segregation policy of the board of education and the state statute permitting it, violated the Equal Protection Clause of the Fourteenth Amendment. Thirteen parents representing twenty children joined as plaintiffs. The names of Oliver and Linda Brown appeared first on the caption of the complaint. Because of this fortuitous circumstance, Linda Brown has become an icon of the civil rights movement while the names of the other plaintiffs are seldom remembered.

The defendants named in the complaint were the Board of Education, the Superintendent of Schools, and the principal of the school that rejected Linda Brown's application. The state of Kansas was not sued. Still, the heart of the plaintiffs claim was the unconstitutionality of a state statute. At the urging of the Board of Education, the governor and other state and local officials, the attorney general, whose personal sympathies were with the plaintiffs, reluctantly intervened on the state's behalf less than two weeks before the date set for trial. The state's answer denied that the state statute was unconstitutional. It neither admitted nor denied the plaintiffs' claims concerning the Topeka school system. The case was tried in Topeka before a three-judge federal court in mid-summer 1951. An assistant attorney general was present at the trial but his role was passive. He produced no evidence, examined no witnesses nor made any argument. Judgment was for the defendants. The court found that the facilities for the education of black and white children were substantially equal and that under the rule in *Plessy v. Ferguson*[9] there was no denial of equal protection. But the court added as its Finding of Fact no. 8:

> Segregation of white and colored children in public schools has a detrimental effect upon the colored children. The impact is greater when it has the sanction of the law; for the policy of separating the races is usually interpreted as denoting the inferiority of the negro group. A sense of inferiority affects the motivation of a child to learn. Segregation with the sanction of law, therefore, has a tendency to retard the educational and mental development of negro children and to deprive them of some of the benefits they would receive in a racial[ly] integrated school system.[10]

This finding was a gratuitous one, irrelevant in view of the court's narrow interpretation of *Plessy*. But as I have later realized, the judges, who had no sympathy for separate but equal, were deliberately laying the foundation for reversal on appeal. In due time, the decision was appealed to the Supreme Court and assigned a place on the October 1952 docket.

I became an assistant attorney general in December 1951. The *Brown* case was among my early assignments. As the attorney general discussed the case with me, he explained that he wanted me to become familiar with the case and prepare a suggested draft of the state's brief. He stated that he expected to make the oral argument to the Court but that I should accompany him to Washington, sit at the counsel table, and be admitted to the Supreme Court Bar. The suggestions pleased me and I set about my task.

When I was satisfied that I understood the case and the issues it raised, I began to prepare for briefing. As I came to understand the law, it supported our position. The precedents were abundant. History, the traditions and attitudes of our culture, were on our side. The law, I felt could not permit us to lose but as I reflected on the problem

I also thought we probably would not win. Whether precedent and tradition of the law would prevail over the twentieth-century conscience was the question the Court would decide. It might find that the separate-but-equal concept had outlived its usefulness.

Along with my substantive preparation, I undertook to learn something of Supreme Court procedure and protocol. I read Stern and Gressman on **Supreme Court Practice,** then a single, not-very-thick, volume. I read about Courtroom decorum—where I should sit, when I should stand, how I should address the court, what I should wear. It was the matter of proper garb that gave me pause. I was pleased to learn that the traditional formal dress was no longer required but a little disturbed to read that the acceptable alternative was a conservative business suit "in a dark color in keeping with the dignity of the court." My dark suit had been purchased several years before and no longer fit. My more recent purchases had been a tan gabardine, a pepper and salt tweed, and miscellaneous sport jackets and trousers. These served well in Kansas, but I had a date in the Supreme Court and nothing to wear. Seeking assistance, I went to the Palace Clothing Store, then the Topeka counterpart of Brooks Brothers, where I found a midnight-blue suit of worsted wool; a perfect fit. I was assured by the salesman that a garment of that quality was a bargain at forty-five dollars. But this only partially solved the problem. In 1951 the state of Kansas was not a lavish paymaster. With house payments, a car payment, a wife, three children, and a household, I could ill-afford an unplanned-for expenditure of forty-five dollars. The era of the credit card had not yet arrived. Hence, this solution. With a five dollar deposit, the suit was removed from the display rack and laid away to be picked up and paid for when I needed it. Eventually I wore the suit during the argument. Forty-six years later, my blue suit, in good condition and an approximate fit, reposes in the Kansas Museum of History to remind posterity of the time, place, and by whom it was worn. This is hardly the kind of immortality to which I aspired, but, I suppose, it beats oblivion.

When I advised the attorney general that I was ready to commence composing the brief, he told me to wait. It was his thought that as the Board of Education was the principal defendant and we were in the case for a limited purpose, our effort should be coordinated with the board's and we should not proceed until its position was known. But the board had not determined its position. As public school segregation began to attract national interest and publicity, Kansans who had been largely indifferent began to inquire why the free state of Kansas would stand before the Supreme Court to defend a scheme based on an assumption of racial inequality. Some, I think, were merely embarrassed. Others, on reflection, could find no justification for the Topeka board's policy. The position of the state and the policy of the board were becoming politically unpopular and both the board and the attorney general were politically sensitive. To an observer it was clear that their enthusiasm for their lawsuit was waning. But neither seemed to know what to do. In consequence, neither did anything.

In April 1952, three incumbents stood for reelection. All were defeated. While segregation had not been an overt issue in the campaign, the vote was a clear repudiation of the status quo. And the result of the election was that a majority of the board's members did not favor the position it was defending in the appeal.

For me, the summer was a season of uncertainty. We received and studied the briefs and other documents filed by the appellants as well as the responses of South Carolina and Virginia. A dozen organizations, with our consent, filed briefs as friends of the Court. None of them were our friends. The most unkind cut of all came when the Attorney General of the United States appeared with a brief suggesting that the separate-but-equal doctrine be reexamined and overruled.

Toward the end of summer, the new board members took office. The superintendent of schools resigned and the board fired the law firm that had successfully represented it in the trial. A new attorney was employed and there were rumors that the board would not resist the appeal. Although I had begun to be concerned about our position, the attorney general continued to say that in due time we would move. As late as September 10, he wrote to Governor Byrnes of South Carolina that "we shall defend in every way the validity of our state statute."[11] Still I knew he was struggling to reconcile his sense of official duty and his understanding of the law with his personal lack of sympathy for the traditional Topeka policy and his political aspirations. Meanwhile, I waited and wondered. Arguments in the Kansas, South Carolina, and Virginia appeals were originally scheduled to commence on October 14. Early that month the date was continued to December 8.

On October 6, the board of education announced that it would make no defense in the Supreme Court. It instructed its attorney to advise the Court that Topeka would not appear. Upon learning of the board's decision, the attorney general announced that he had changed his mind and that the state would make no appearance. He reasoned that the board was the principal defendant, that the policy under attack had been established and enforced by the board, that the board had power to discontinue its segregated schools, and that if the board was unwilling to defend the policy that it and its predecessors had enforced for nearly a century, the state ought not to assume that burden. Moreover, election day was only a month away and the attorney general was running for re-election.

My views were somewhat different. I felt that as members of the bar representing a party before the Supreme Court of the United States, we had a duty to make some response—either to defend the trial court's decision or admit that it was wrong. I found it hard to reconcile our inaction with my notions of professional responsibility. Besides, I had a new blue suit on layaway at the Palace with apparently no place to wear it. The attorney general was adamant. He listened to me patiently and said we would not appear.

As we procrastinated, our eastern counterparts, particularly those in South Carolina and Virginia, became restive. Their frequent letters and phone calls were referred to me, and I didn't know what to say. *Brown* would be the first of the cases called for argument. They were concerned with the impact that a default by Kansas might have on their cases. When they learned of the decision not to appear, their concern deepened. The pressure became more intense. Virginia offered to send lawyers to Topeka to assist in preparing a brief but the attorney general said no. Kansas would not appear. Then, on November 24, the Supreme Court on its own motion entered an order that required that we evaluate our position. The Court's order took notice of the pendency of the case, the decision of the board not to appear, and the failure of the state to respond. The order continued, "Because of the national importance of the issue presented and because of its importance to the state of Kansas, we request that the state present its views at oral argument."[12]

The attorney general was out of the office when we learned of the Court's order. I spoke with him by telephone but because of the intervening Thanksgiving holiday we were not able to discuss the matter until the 28th. By that time he had decided that we were obliged to defend the constitutionality of the statute. After reviewing the file he returned it to me with the admonition "Do what you can with the damn thing." I had already begun to assemble the material for a brief and, with his approval, I started writing. I had ten days to write the brief, have it printed, filed and served on opposing counsel. This was in the pre-computer era when procedures were less streamlined than now, and I, a somewhat bewildered country lawyer, was in charge. Four days later, the board relented a bit and allowed its attorney to collaborate with me and to join in submitting the brief.

On the afternoon of December 4, the brief was ready and I took it to the attorney general for his approval. He thought it adequate and wanted to discuss our further action. While writing the brief I had assumed that in spite of his personal views, the attorney general would appear for the state or, perhaps, waive oral argument. But on that Thursday afternoon, I learned that his thoughts were different. He told me that he felt the state ought to be present for argument, that his schedule would not permit him to be in Washington at that time, and that I was familiar with the case so he wanted me to make the state's argument. It was then Thursday afternoon. I would have a weekend to prepare. As I think about the events of that Thursday afternoon, I sometimes recall something that I first read in my college Shakespeare course sixty-five years ago: "Some [men] are born great; some achieve greatness; and some have greatness thrust upon them."

My first act was to visit the Palace and pick up my blue suit. Then I called the Clerk of the Supreme Court to report that I would be present at the docket call. After that were the logistical arrangements. In Washington, I would stay at the Carlton, now the Sheraton-Carlton. I would travel to Washington by train. The twenty-six hour train ride alone would give me the opportunity to think and to plan an argument. Saturday at noon, I boarded the east bound Santa Fe Chief.

My argument, as I thought it through, would not be very imaginative. We would not urge or approve segregation as a matter of policy. We would only assert that the statute permitting it was not unconstitutional. I would argue precedent, of which there was an abundance on our side. I would argue history and tradition and the need for stability in the law. I would point out that implicit in the laws passed by more than a score of legislatures including the Congress of the United States was reliance on the Court's prior interpretation of the Equal Protection Clause. I would argue for the right of the sovereign state of Kansas and its local governments to fix policies for the management of their local schools. Then I would say that if the state's public schools were to be within the purview of the Fourteenth Amendment, under Section 2 it would be for Congress, not the judiciary, to prescribe standards. To rebut Finding no. 8 that segregation was harmful to black children, I would argue that the evidence did not support the finding and that, in any case, there was no evidence to show that any of the plaintiffs had suffered or was in jeopardy of irreparable injury; that mere membership in a class does not entitle one to injunctive relief.

By the time the train reached Harper's Ferry, I knew what I wanted to say to the Court. As we headed toward Washington, I relaxed, subconsciously wishing that the train ride would go on forever. It didn't. I left the train at Washington's Union Station and as I waited to retrieve my luggage, I bought a newspaper. The banner headline read "Legal Giants to Vie in Segregation Case." That, I thought, is my case, and I was a little surprised to be so described. As I read the story, I found that the writer had in mind John W. Davis and Thurgood Marshall, who would argue the South Carolina case. Kansas and its counsel were barely mentioned. Another story, which identified me by name, suggested that the Kansas case might be the most difficult to decide since in Kansas the physical facilities had been found equal, but the court had made the further finding that segregation was detrimental. Only the Kansas case presented the issue of constitutionality of segregation per se.

After checking into my hotel, I delivered copies of my brief and met Mr. Robert Carter who would be my adversary in the Supreme Court. There I also met Thurgood Marshall and a dozen other lawyers whose names have been prominent in civil rights history. These were gracious and agreeable men. They were confident they would win. Later that evening, I met the lawyers who would sit on my side of the table. They too were gracious and agreeable men who expected to win. I learned from them that the arguments had been postponed until Tuesday. This would give me an extra day for preparation.

Monday, I found the courthouse, filed my brief, and met Mr. Willey, the Clerk, who showed me the courtroom. In the evening, I met in a strategy session with the other attorneys who would sit on my side of the table. This was a high point in the experience. Then I met and talked with John W. Davis who would argue for South Carolina. Mr. Davis, sometimes said to have been the greatest appellate advocate of this century, was a friend of South Carolina's governor and was representing the state without retainer or fee. For several minutes, perhaps half an hour, he talked with me about the case, discussing my oral presentation, anticipating questions, and suggesting answers that might please the court. He spoke with no impatience or condescension. He made me feel important. Near the end of our conversation he offered to act as my sponsor and move for my admission to the Supreme Court Bar. I gratefully accepted his offer.

On the next day, as the time for argument approached, the attorneys moved to their positions. I sat immediately left of the podium, where I waited to make my first appellate argument. To my immediate left sat Mr. Davis, who would make his 140th Supreme Court argument. To his left were the other distinguished lawyers who would argue for their states. Robert Carter, my adversary, sat next to the podium on the right. Next to him was Thurgood Marshall and beyond him were other lawyers who have made history. When the arguments began, Mr. Carter spoke first. When he had finished, the Chief Justice, with a disarming smile, addressed me as General Wilson. I stood and spoke and I think I was generally coherent.

I was able to present the argument that I had planned en route. Five Justices interrogated me. None seemed hostile; indeed, most were helpful in developing my argument. In response to a question by Justice Felix Frankfurter, candor required me to say there would be no serious consequences in Kansas if the segregation law were struck down. When I had spoken for a little more than half an hour, the Justices stopped asking questions, which I took as a signal that they had heard enough. So I sat down feeling that I had said all that could be said for Kansas and that I had said it as well as I could.

Richard Kluger, who read the transcript twenty years later, described my argument as perfectly able but somewhat simplistic.[13] I suspect I agree with Mr. Kluger. To me, *Brown* was a fairly simple case.

Notwithstanding my personal misgivings about segregated schools in mid-twentieth century Kansas, to me it was clear that it was permitted by law. As I saw it, my oath and my duty was to uphold the law. Moral and social issues were to be decided by others. I don't know how I would stand today. I hope that age has not diminished my commitment to duty. But time and reflection may have mellowed my perception.

The Kansas case was only a preliminary. The South Carolina case featuring Thurgood Marshall and John W. Davis was the main attraction. I sat through those arguments, which must be ranked as one of the great debates in Supreme Court history. When the argument ended, I took the train home to wait. When the word came, it was different from what I had expected. The cases would be restored to the docket for re-argument. Counsel would give special attention to the Fourteenth Amendment's impact on segregated schools intended by the Congress that proposed and the legislatures that ratified it.[14]

This time there was no procrastination or equivocation. Kansas would respond. The Board of Education would proceed independently and would not defend against the claims of unconstitutionality. With plenty of time and the help of a law professor from Washburn, we prepared what I thought to be a good brief and filed it on time. We found no evidence that either Congress or the ratifying legislatures intended that the Fourteenth Amendment would preclude segregated schools. We found some evidence that it did not. We also pointed out the desegregation occurring in Kansas communities. Kansas, we argued, could take care of its own problems if permitted.

With the brief completed, I turned my attention to the oral argument. I did not often write speeches, but this time was special. I carefully wrote my tentative argument and placed the manuscript in a loose leaf binder carefully indexed and tabbed. Then I was ready.

During the late summer, other events occurred that were to have impact on the case. The first was the death of Chief Justice Fred Vinson and the appointment of Governor Earl Warren of California as his successor. My southern associates were disturbed. They had regarded the deceased Chief Justice, a Kentuckian, as their friend. They were dubious about the new appointee. Then, in Topeka, the board of education announced that it would terminate segregation "as rapidly as practicable."[15] This raised a question of mootness. I thought the case was not moot. Topeka had not conceded that the plaintiffs' claims were valid. Its elementary schools were still segregated. The board's resolution was only a promise to end segregation at some indefinite time in the future. Mr. Carter agreed with me. So our preparation had continued with scant attention to mootness.

I again traveled to Washington by train. This time I was accompanied by my wife and our six-month-old son. We again stayed at the Carlton. Upon arriving, we found that the order of argument had been rearranged. The South Carolina and Virginia cases had been consolidated and would be argued first, followed by a statement by the Attorney General of the United States, then Kansas, Washington, D.C., and Delaware.

When the Court assembled with the new Chief Justice presiding. I sat spellbound while the consolidated South Carolina–Virginia arguments were heard. I then heard Mr. Rankin, who appeared for the Department of Justice, argue that public school segregation was unconstitutional. Then it was Kansas' turn. Mr. Carter had spoken only a few words when Justice Frankfurter asked, "Isn't this case moot?" With Mr. Carter, the Justices pursued the mootness issue for several minutes. Finally, Mr. Carter asked leave to yield to the state (me) to hear what I had to say. I was embarrassed. There was nothing in my prepared argument about mootness. There was no one to whom I could yield. Thus, instead of going for the jugular vein, I began my argument with an extemporaneous effort to stay in Court. My reasoning did not satisfy Justice Frankfurter. He continued to pursue the matter. After several minutes and growing despair, the Chief Justice came to my rescue. He thought the case was not moot and directed me to proceed. I did proceed, but not with the speech I had prepared. I had begun to sense that the Court saw my argument as a mere rehash of arguments they had already heard, so I abbreviated, summarized and passed over points that were relevant but not critical, and as the Justices began to yawn, I picked up my carefully prepared speech and withdrew. Forty years later, I deposited my *Brown* papers in the library at my university. Among these contributions to future generations of scholars is the transcript of my speech that was never spoken.

When the arguments ended I again returned to Topeka and waited. The answer came on May 17, 1954. The world knows what it was. Kansas along with its sister states lost. Most interested Kansans were pleased. The plaintiffs were jubilant. Members of the Board of Education praised the opinion. The governor expressed satisfaction. The attorney general, whose name appeared above mine on the Kansas brief, wrote to the Chief Justice congratulating him on the Court's wise and courageous opinion. My own feelings were mixed. I could not disapprove the result. Early in *Brown* I concluded that there was no moral, social, or economic justification for segregated schools in Kansas in 1951. I agreed that the law should reflect the common idea of justice. I also thought it was the responsibility of the state legislature and the Board of Education to put their houses in order. It was a little saddening that they did so only when ordered by the Supreme Court. Such lethargy diminishes the stature of state and local government. Also, I had been a loser in an adversarial proceeding, and fifty-nine years as a lawyer have taught me that losing is less fun than winning.

There was a third argument in the spring of 1955. Often called *Brown II,* the concern was how and when the decision of 1954 would be implemented. In Kansas, there was no longer a controversy. The main issue was settled and Topeka and other Kansas cities were moving forward with desegregation plans. This time I went to Washington with the attorney general, he to make the oral argument and I to carry his papers. From this round of arguments came the order to desegregate "with all deliberate speed."[16]

Although Topeka readily accepted the *Brown* decision in principle, problems arose with its implementation. There was protracted litigation and the district court still retains jurisdiction. However, after nearly forty-eight years and twenty million dollars, Topekans are in agreement that the mandate of *Brown* has been fully complied with and the court's supervision is about to end. The motto of our state is *ad astra per Aspera*—"to the stars through difficulties." Stated differently, we often do things the hard way but we eventually succeed.

I did not participate in the case after *Brown II* so my story should end here. But before I stop, I ask license to make one further statement. I have been often asked whether I regret my role in *Brown*. The answer is, "I do not." *Brown* gave me the opportunity to represent my state before the Supreme Court of the United States, an honor that does not often come to a country lawyer. Here the Court was being asked to decide one of the most important issues of the century—to reverse a trend that was supported by precedent, by history, and by the traditional attitudes of our society. To decide the issue correctly, the Court had to be fully informed. Kansas had an important contribution to make to the case. Located in the heart of America, Kansas was different. Its history, traditions, and culture were different from those of the other states. Its laws were different and had been enacted in a different environment. These were considerations that the Court needed to complete its record, and had specifically requested. I said all that could be said for Kansas, and I said it as well as I could. So I have no regrets. Besides, had it not been for *Brown,* I would not have been invited to speak to you on this very pleasant occasion.

NOTE: *This article is reprinted from 1999 **Journal of Supreme Court History** vol. 24, no. 2. It was originally delivered in 1998 as a lecture at the Supreme Court sponsored by The Supreme Court Historical Society.*

Endnotes

1. 347 U.S. 483 (1954).
2. Richard Kluger, **Simple Justice** (New York, Alfred A. Knopf, 1976) 548.
3. *Brown v. Board of Educ.,* 98 F. Supp. 797 (Kan. 1951).
4. *Briggs v. Elliott,* 98 F. Supp. 529 (E.D.S.C. 1951); 103 F. Supp. 920 (E.D.S.C. 1952).
5. *Davis v. County School Bd. Of Price Edward County, Virginia,* 103 F. Supp. 337 (E.D. Va. 1951).
6. *Gebhart v. Belton* (S.C. Del), 91 A. 2d 137 (1952).
7. *Bolling v. Sharpe* (Cert. To U.S.C.A., D.C. Cir) 347 U.S. 497 (1954).
8. General Statutes of Kansas, 1949, 72–1724.
9. 163 U.S. 537 (1896).
10. Transcript of Record, Brown of. Board of Educ. of Topeka, Shawnee County, Kansas, Case No. T-316 Civil, United States District Court, District of Kansas, 245–246 (print ed.).
11. Letter, Fatzer to Byrnes, Sept. 10, 1952.
12. 344 U.S. 141 (1952).
13. *See* Kluger, *supra,* 565–71.
14. 345 U.S. 972 (1953).
15. *Topeka Daily Capital,* Sept. 6, 1953, 1.
16. 349 U.S. 294, 301 (1955).

Brown v. Board of Education of Topeka
347 U.S. 483 (1954)

JUDGES: Warren, Black, Reed, Frankfurter, Douglas, Burton, Clark, Minton, Harlan

MR. CHIEF JUSTICE WARREN delivered the opinion of the Court.

These cases come to us from the States of Kansas, South Carolina, Virginia, and Delaware. They are premised on different facts and different local conditions, but a common legal question justifies their consideration together in this consolidated opinion.[1]

In each of the cases, minors of the Negro race, through their legal representatives, seek the aid of the courts in obtaining admission to the public schools of their community on a nonsegregated basis. In each instance, they had been denied admission to schools attended by white children under laws requiring or permitting segregation according to race. This segregation was alleged to deprive the plaintiffs of the equal protection of the laws under the Fourteenth Amendment. In each of the cases other than the Delaware case, a three-judge federal district court denied relief to the plaintiffs on the so-called "separate but equal" doctrine announced by this Court in *Plessy v. Ferguson*, 163 U.S. 537. Under that doctrine, equality of treatment is accorded when the races are provided substantially equal facilities, even though these facilities be separate. In the Delaware case, the Supreme Court of Delaware adhered to that doctrine, but ordered that the plaintiffs be admitted to the white schools because of their superiority to the Negro schools.

The plaintiffs contend that segregated public schools are not "equal" and cannot be made "equal," and that hence they are deprived of the equal protection of the laws. Because of the obvious importance of the question presented, the Court took jurisdiction.[2] Argument was heard in the 1952 Term, and reargument was heard this Term on certain questions propounded by the Court.[3]

Reargument was largely devoted to the circumstances surrounding the adoption of the Fourteenth Amendment in 1868. It covered exhaustively consideration of the Amendment in Congress, ratification by the states, then existing practices in racial segregation, and the views of proponents and opponents of the Amendment. This discussion and our own investigation convince us that, although these sources cast some light, it is not enough to resolve the problem with which we are faced. At best, they are inconclusive. The most avid proponents of the post-War Amendments undoubtedly intended them to remove all legal distinctions among "all persons born or naturalized in the United States." Their opponents, just as certainly, were antagonistic to both the letter and the spirit of the Amendments and wished them to have the most limited effect. What others in Congress and the state legislatures had in mind cannot be determined with any degree of certainty.

An additional reason for the inconclusive nature of the Amendment's history, with respect to segregated schools, is the status of public education at that time.[4] In the South, the movement toward free common schools, supported [*490] by general taxation, had not yet taken hold. Education of white children was largely in the hands of private groups. Education of Negroes was almost nonexistent, and practically all of the race were illiterate. In fact, any education of Negroes was forbidden by law in some states. Today, in contrast, many Negroes have achieved outstanding success in the arts and sciences as well as in the business and professional world. It is true that public school education at the time of the Amendment had advanced further in the North, but the effect of the Amendment on Northern States was generally ignored in the congressional debates. Even in the North, the conditions of public education did not approximate those existing today. The curriculum was usually rudimentary; ungraded schools were common in rural areas; the school term was but three months a year in many states; and compulsory school attendance was virtually unknown. As a consequence, it is not surprising that there should be so little in the history of the Fourteenth Amendment relating to its intended effect on public education.

In the first cases in this Court construing the Fourteenth Amendment, decided shortly after its adoption, the Court interpreted it as proscribing all state-imposed discriminations against the Negro race.[5] The doctrine of "separate but equal" did not make its appearance in this Court until 1896 in the case of *Plessy v. Ferguson, supra*, involving not education but transportation.[6] American courts have since labored with the doctrine for over half a century. In this Court, there have been six cases involving the "separate but equal" doctrine in the field of public education.[7] In *Cumming v. County Board of Education*, 175 U.S. 528, and *Gong Lum v. Rice*, 275 U.S. 78, the validity of the doctrine itself was not challenged.[8] In more recent cases, all on the graduate school level, inequality was found in that specific benefits enjoyed by white students were denied to Negro students of the same educational qualifications. *Missouri ex rel. Gaines v. Canada*, 305 U.S. 337; *Sipuel v. Oklahoma*, 332 U.S. 631; *Sweatt v. Painter*, 339 U.S. 629; *McLaurin v. Oklahoma State Regents*, 339 U.S. 637. In none of these cases was it necessary to re-examine the doctrine to grant relief to the Negro plaintiff. And in *Sweatt v. Painter, supra*, the Court expressly reserved decision on the question whether *Plessy v. Ferguson* should be held inapplicable to public education.

In the instant cases, that question is directly presented. Here, unlike *Sweatt v. Painter*, there are findings below that the Negro and white schools involved have been equalized, or are being equalized, with respect to buildings, curricula, qualifications and salaries of teachers, and other "tangible" factors.[9] Our decision, therefore, cannot turn on merely a comparison of these tangible factors in the Negro and white schools involved in each of the cases. We must look instead to the effect of segregation itself on public education.

In approaching this problem, we cannot turn the clock back to 1868 when the Amendment was adopted, or even to 1896 when *Plessy v. Ferguson* was written. We must consider public education in the light of its full development and its present place in American life throughout the Nation. Only in this way can it be determined if segregation in public schools deprives these plaintiffs of the equal protection of the laws.

Today, education is perhaps the most important function of state and local governments. Compulsory school attendance laws and the great expenditures for education both demonstrate our recognition of the importance of education to our democratic society. It is required in the performance of our most basic public responsibilities, even service in the armed forces. It is the very foundation of good citizenship. Today it is a principal instrument in awakening the child to cultural values, in preparing him for later professional training, and in helping him to adjust normally to his environment. In these days, it is doubtful that any child may reasonably be expected to succeed in life if he is denied the opportunity of an education. Such an opportunity, where the state has undertaken to provide it, is a right which must be made available to all on equal terms.

We come then to the question presented: Does segregation of children in public schools solely on the basis of race, even though the physical facilities and other "tangible" factors may be equal, deprive the children of the minority group of equal educational opportunities? We believe that it does.

In *Sweatt v. Painter, supra*, in finding that a segregated law school for Negroes could not provide them equal educational opportunities, this Court relied in large part on "those qualities which are incapable of objective measurement but which make for greatness in a law school." In *McLaurin v. Oklahoma State Regents, supra*, the Court, in requiring that a Negro admitted to a white graduate school be treated like all other students, again resorted to intangible considerations: ". . . his ability to study, to engage in discussions and exchange views with other students, and, in general, to learn his profession." Such considerations apply with added force to children in grade and high schools. To separate them from others of similar age and qualifications solely because of their race generates a feeling of inferiority as to their status in the community that may affect their hearts and minds in a way unlikely ever to be undone. The effect of this separation on their educational opportunities was well stated by a finding in the Kansas case by a court which nevertheless felt compelled to rule against the Negro plaintiffs:

"Segregation of white and colored children in public schools has a detrimental effect upon the colored children. The impact is greater when it has the sanction of the law; for the policy of separating the races is usually interpreted as denoting the inferiority of the negro group. A sense of inferiority affects the motivation of a child to learn. Segregation with the sanction of law, therefore, has a tendency to [retard] the educational and mental development of negro children and to deprive them of some of the benefits they would receive in a racial[ly] integrated school system."[10]

Whatever may have been the extent of psychological knowledge at the time of *Plessy v. Ferguson*, this finding is amply supported by modern authority.[11] Any language in *Plessy v. Ferguson* contrary to this finding is rejected.

We conclude that in the field of public education the doctrine of "separate but equal" has no place. Separate educational facilities are inherently unequal. Therefore, we hold that the plaintiffs and others similarly situated for whom the actions have been brought are, by reason of the segregation complained of, deprived of the equal protection of the laws guaranteed by the Fourteenth Amendment. This disposition makes unnecessary any discussion whether such segregation also violates the Due Process Clause of the Fourteenth Amendment.[12]

Because these are class actions, because of the wide applicability of this decision, and because of the great variety of local conditions, the formulation of decrees in these cases presents problems of considerable complexity. On reargument, the consideration of appropriate relief was necessarily subordinated to the primary question the constitutionality of segregation in public education. We have now announced that such segregation is a denial of the equal protection of the laws. In order that we may have the full assistance of the parties in formulating decrees, the cases will be restored to the docket, and the parties are requested to present further argument on Questions 4 and 5 previously propounded by the Court for the reargument this Term.[13] The Attorney General of the United States is again invited to participate. The Attorneys General of the states requiring or permitting segregation in public education will also be permitted to appear as *amici curiae* upon request to do so by September 15, 1954, and submission of briefs by October 1, 1954.[14]

It is so ordered.

Endnotes

1. In the Kansas case, *Brown v. Board of Education*, the plaintiffs are Negro children of elementary school age residing in Topeka. They brought this action in the United States District Court for the District of Kansas to enjoin enforcement of a Kansas statute which permits, but does not require, cities of more than 15,000 population to maintain separate school facilities for Negro and white students. Kan. Gen. Stat. § 72-1724 (1949). Pursuant to that authority, the Topeka Board of Education elected to establish segregated elementary schools. Other public schools in the community, however, are operated on a nonsegregated basis. The three-judge District Court, convened under 28 U. S. C. §§ 2281 and 2284, found that segregation in public education has a detrimental effect upon Negro children, but denied relief on the ground that the Negro and white schools were substantially equal with respect to buildings, transportation, curricula, and educational qualifications of teachers. 98 F.Supp. 797. The case is here on direct appeal under 28 U. S. C. § 1253.

In the South Carolina case, *Briggs v. Elliott*, the plaintiffs are Negro children of both elementary and high school age residing in Clarendon County. They brought this action in the United States District Court for the Eastern District of South Carolina to enjoin enforcement of provisions in the state constitution and statutory code which require the segregation of Negroes and whites in public schools. S. C. Const., Art. XI, § 7; S. C. Code § 5377 (1942). The three-judge District Court, convened under 28 U. S. C. §§ 2281 and 2284, denied the requested relief. The court found that the Negro schools were inferior to the white schools and ordered the defendants to begin immediately to equalize the facilities. But the court sustained the validity of the contested provisions and denied the plaintiffs admission to the white schools during the equalization program. 98 F.Supp. 529. This Court vacated the District Court's judgment and remanded the case for the purpose of obtaining the court's views on a report filed by the defendants concerning the progress made in the equalization program. 342 U.S. 350. On remand, the District Court found that substantial equality had been achieved except for buildings and that the defendants were proceeding to rectify this inequality as well. 103 F.Supp. 920. The case is again here on direct appeal under 28 U. S. C. § 1253.

In the Virginia case, *Davis v. County School Board*, the plaintiffs are Negro children of high school age residing in Prince Edward County. They brought this action in the United States District Court for the Eastern District of Virginia to enjoin enforcement of provisions in the state constitution and statutory code which require the segregation of Negroes and whites in public schools. Va. Const., § 140; Va. Code § 22-221 (1950). The three-judge District Court, convened under 28 U. S. C. §§ 2281 and 2284, denied the requested relief. The court found the Negro school inferior in physical plant, curricula, and transportation, and ordered the defendants forthwith to provide substantially equal curricula and transportation and to "proceed with all reasonable diligence and dispatch to remove" the inequality in physical plant. But, as in the South Carolina case, the court sustained the validity of the contested provisions and denied the plaintiffs admission to the white schools during the equalization program. 103 F. Supp. 337. The case is here on direct appeal under 28 U. S. C. § 1253.

In the Delaware case, *Gebhart v. Belton*, the plaintiffs are Negro children of both elementary and high school age residing in New Castle County. They brought this action in the Delaware Court of Chancery to enjoin enforcement of provisions in the state constitution and statutory code which require the segregation of Negroes and whites in public schools. Del. Const., Art. X, § 2; Del. Rev. Code § 2631 (1935). The Chancellor gave judgment for the plaintiffs and ordered their immediate admission to schools previously attended only by white children, on the ground that the Negro schools were inferior with respect to teacher training, pupil-teacher ratio, extracurricular activities, physical plant, and time and distance involved in travel. 87 A. 2d 862. The Chancellor also found that segregation itself results in an inferior education for Negro children (*see* note 10, *infra*), but did not rest his decision on that ground. *Id.*, at 865. The Chancellor's decree was affirmed by the Supreme Court of Delaware, which intimated, however, that the defendants might be able to obtain a modification of the decree after equalization of the Negro and white schools had been accomplished. 91 A. 2d 137, 152. The defendants, contending only that the Delaware courts had erred in ordering the immediate admission of the Negro plaintiffs to the white schools, applied to this Court for certiorari. The writ was granted, 344 U.S. 891. The plaintiffs, who were successful below, did not submit a cross-petition.

2. 344 U.S. 1, 141, 891.

3. 345 U.S. 972. The Attorney General of the United States participated both Terms as *amicus curiae*.

4. For a general study of the development of public education prior to the Amendment, *see* Butts and Cremin, **A History of Education in American Culture** (1953), Pts. I, II; Cubberley, **Public Education in the United States** (1934 ed.), cc. II-XII. School practices current at the time of the adoption of the Fourteenth Amendment are described in Butts and Cremin, *supra*, at 269-275; Cubberley, *supra*, at 288-339, 408-431; Knight, **Public Education in the South** (1922), cc. VIII, IX. *See also* H. Ex. Doc. No. 315, 41st Cong., 2d Sess. (1871). Although the demand for free public schools followed substantially the same pattern in both the North and the South, the development in the South did not begin to gain momentum until about 1850, some twenty years after that in the North. The reasons for the somewhat slower development in the South (*e. g.*, the rural character of the South and the different regional attitudes toward state assistance) are well explained in Cubberley,

supra, at 408-423. In the country as a whole, but particularly in the South, the War virtually stopped all progress in public education. *Id.*, at 427-428. The low status of Negro education in all sections of the country, both before and immediately after the War, is described in Beale, **A History of Freedom of Teaching in American Schools** (1941), 112-132, 175-195. Compulsory school attendance laws were not generally adopted until after the ratification of the Fourteenth Amendment, and it was not until 1918 that such laws were in force in all the states. Cubberley, *supra*, at 563-565.

5. *Slaughter-House Cases*, 16 Wall. 36, 67-72 (1873); *Strauder v. West Virginia*, 100 U.S. 303, 307-308 (1880):

"It ordains that no State shall deprive any person of life, liberty, or property, without due process of law, or deny to any person within its jurisdiction the equal protection of the laws. What is this but declaring that the law in the States shall be the same for the black as for the white; that all persons, whether colored or white, shall stand equal before the laws of the States, and, in regard to the colored race, for whose protection the amendment was primarily designed, that no discrimination shall be made against them by law because of their color? The words of the amendment, it is true, are prohibitory, but they contain a necessary implication of a positive immunity, or right, most valuable to the colored race, the right to exemption from unfriendly legislation against them distinctively as colored, exemption from legal discriminations, implying inferiority in civil society, lessening the security of their enjoyment of the rights which others enjoy, and discriminations which are steps towards reducing them to the condition of a subject race."

See also *Virginia v. Rives*, 100 U.S. 313, 318 (1880); *Ex parte Virginia*, 100 U.S. 339, 344-345 (1880).

6. The doctrine apparently originated in *Roberts v. City of Boston*, 59 Mass. 198, 206 (1850), upholding school segregation against attack as being violative of a state constitutional guarantee of equality. Segregation in Boston public schools was eliminated in 1855. Mass. Acts 1855, c. 256. But elsewhere in the North segregation in public education has persisted in some communities until recent years. It is apparent that such segregation has long been a nationwide problem, not merely one of sectional concern.

7. See also *Berea College v. Kentucky*, 211 U.S. 45 (1908).

8. In the *Cumming* case, Negro taxpayers sought an injunction requiring the defendant school board to discontinue the operation of a high school for white children until the board resumed operation of a high school for Negro children. Similarly, in the *Gong Lum* case, the plaintiff, a child of Chinese descent, contended only that state authorities had misapplied the doctrine by classifying him with Negro children and requiring him to attend a Negro school.

9. In the Kansas case, the court below found substantial equality as to all such factors. 98 F.Supp. 797, 798. In the South Carolina case, the court below found that the defendants were proceeding "promptly and in good faith to

comply with the court's decree." 103 F.Supp. 920, 921. In the Virginia case, the court below noted that the equalization program was already "afoot and progressing" (103 F.Supp. 337, 341); since then, we have been advised, in the Virginia Attorney General's brief on reargument, that the program has now been completed. In the Delaware case, the court below similarly noted that the state's equalization program was well under way. 91 A. 2d 137, 149.

10. A similar finding was made in the Delaware case: "I conclude from the testimony that in our Delaware society, State-imposed segregation in education itself results in the Negro children, as a class, receiving educational opportunities which are substantially inferior to those available to white children otherwise similarly situated." 87 A. 2d 862, 865.

11. K. B. Clark, **Effect of Prejudice and Discrimination on Personality Development** (Midcentury White House Conference on Children and Youth, 1950); Witmer and Kotinsky, **Personality in the Making** (1952), c. VI; Deutscher and Chein, "The Psychological Effects of Enforced Segregation: A Survey of Social Science Opinion," 26 *J. Psychol.* 259 (1948); Chein, "What are the Psychological Effects of Segregation Under Conditions of Equal Facilities?," 3 *Int. J. Opinion and Attitude Res.* 229 (1949); Brameld, **Educational Costs, in Discrimination and National Welfare** (MacIver, ed., 1949), 44-48; Frazier, **The Negro in the United States** (1949), 674-681. And *see generally* Myrdal, **An American Dilemma** (1944).

12. *See Bolling v. Sharpe, post*, p. 497, concerning the Due Process Clause of the Fifth Amendment.

13. 4. Assuming it is decided that segregation in public schools violates the Fourteenth Amendment

(*a*) would a decree necessarily follow providing that, within the limits set by normal geographic school districting, Negro children should forthwith be admitted to schools of their choice, or

(*b*) may this Court, in the exercise of its equity powers, permit an effective gradual adjustment to be brought about from existing segregated systems to a system not based on color distinctions?

5. On the assumption on which questions 4 (*a*) and (*b*) are based, and assuming further that this Court will exercise its equity powers to the end described in question 4 (*b*),

(*a*) should this Court formulate detailed decrees in these cases;

(*b*) if so, what specific issues should the decrees reach;

(*c*) should this Court appoint a special master to hear evidence with a view to recommending specific terms for such decrees;

(*d*) should this Court remand to the courts of first instance with directions to frame decrees in these cases, and if so what general directions should the decrees of this Court include and what procedures should the courts of first instance follow in arriving at the specific terms of more detailed decrees?"

14. *See* Rule 42, Revised Rules of this Court (effective July 1, 1954).

Brown v. Board of Education of Topeka
349 U.S. 294 (1955)

JUDGES: Warren, Black, Reed, Frankfurter, Douglas, Burton, Clark, Minton, Harlan

MR. CHIEF JUSTICE WARREN delivered the opinion of the Court.

These cases were decided on May 17, 1954. The opinions of that date, declaring the fundamental principle that racial discrimination in public education is unconstitutional, are incorporated herein by reference. All provisions of federal, state, or local law requiring or permitting such discrimination must yield to this principle. There remains for consideration the manner in which relief is to be accorded.

Because these cases arose under different local conditions and their disposition will involve a variety of local problems, we requested further argument on the question of relief. In view of the nationwide importance of the decision, we invited the Attorney General of the United States and the Attorneys General of all states requiring or permitting racial discrimination in public education to present their views on that question. The parties, the United States, and the States of Florida, North Carolina, Arkansas, Oklahoma, Maryland, and Texas filed briefs and participated in the oral argument.

These presentations were informative and helpful to the Court in its consideration of the complexities arising from the transition to a system of public education freed of racial discrimination. The presentations also demonstrated that substantial steps to eliminate racial discrimination in public schools have already been taken, not only in some of the communities in which these cases arose, but in some of the states appearing as *amici curiae*, and in other states as well. Substantial progress has been made in the District of Columbia and in the communities in Kansas and Delaware involved in this litigation. The defendants in the cases coming to us from South Carolina and Virginia are awaiting the decision of this Court concerning relief.

Full implementation of these constitutional principles may require solution of varied local school problems. School authorities have the primary responsibility for elucidating, assessing, and solving these problems; courts will have to consider whether the action of school authorities constitutes good faith implementation of the governing constitutional principles. Because of their proximity to local conditions and the possible need for further hearings, the courts which originally heard these cases can best perform this judicial appraisal. Accordingly, we believe it appropriate to remand the cases to those courts.

In fashioning and effectuating the decrees, the courts will be guided by equitable principles. Traditionally, equity has been characterized by a practical flexibility in shaping its remedies and by a facility for adjusting and reconciling public and private needs. These cases call for the exercise of these traditional attributes of equity power. At stake is the personal interest of the plaintiffs in admission to public schools as soon as practicable on a nondiscriminatory basis. To effectuate this interest may call for elimination of a variety of obstacles in making the transition to school systems operated in accordance with the constitutional principles set forth in our May 17, 1954, decision. Courts of equity may properly take into account the public interest in the elimination of such obstacles in a systematic and effective manner. But it should go without saying that the vitality of these constitutional principles cannot be allowed to yield simply because of disagreement with them.

While giving weight to these public and private considerations, the courts will require that the defendants make a prompt and reasonable start toward full compliance with our May 17, 1954, ruling. Once such a start has been made, the courts may find that additional time is necessary to carry out the ruling in an effective manner. The burden rests upon the defendants to establish that such time is necessary in the public interest and is consistent with good faith compliance at the earliest practicable date. To that end, the courts may consider problems related to administration, arising from the physical condition of the school plant, the school transportation system, personnel, revision of school districts and attendance areas into compact units to achieve a system of determining admission to the public schools on a nonracial basis, and revision of local laws and regulations which may be necessary in solving the foregoing problems. They will also consider the adequacy of any plans the defendants may propose to meet these problems and to effectuate a transition to a racially nondiscriminatory school system. During this period of transition, the courts will retain jurisdiction of these cases.

The judgments below, except that in the Delaware case, are accordingly reversed and the cases are remanded to the District Courts to take such proceedings and enter such orders and decrees consistent with this opinion as are necessary and proper to admit to public schools on a racially nondiscriminatory basis with all deliberate speed the parties to these cases. The judgment in the Delaware case—ordering the immediate admission of the plaintiffs to schools previously attended only by white children—is affirmed on the basis of the principles stated in our May 17, 1954, opinion, but the case is remanded to the Supreme Court of Delaware for such further proceedings as that Court may deem necessary in light of this opinion.

It is so ordered.

Plessy v. Ferguson (1896) got more play in the local Louisiana newspaper *The Daily States* (right) than in *The New York Times*, which treated it in its regular column of railroad news. The lone dissent of Justice John Marshall Harlan (inset) would not become the law of the land for a half-century. Louisiana State Museum/ Library of Congress

The NAACP chose Ada Lois Sipuel Fisher, a twenty-two-year-old Langston University honors graduate, to mount a challenge to Oklahoma's segregation laws by applying to the University of Oklahoma's law school. She posed for the cameras with admissions director J.E. Fellows and NAACP lawyers Amos T. Hall (right) and Thurgood Marshall (middle) in 1946. Library of Congress

In the 1880s and 1890s one southern state after another adopted Jim Crow regulations that eventually reached into all aspects of life. Library of Congress

When George W. McLaurin applied to the University of Oklahoma for a doctorate in education, he was admitted on the condition that he be physically separated from white students in the classroom, the library and the cafeteria. His equal protection case, *McLaurin v. Oklahoma*, was reviewed by the Supreme Court in 1950 and generated one of two decisions that year holding that the psychological effects of schooling in a segregated setting amounted to inequality per se. Library of Congress

Paul E. Wilson was a country lawyer from rural Kansas who became an assistant attorney general in 1952 because of his interest in state politics and his desire to gain experience as an appellate lawyer. A year later he made his first argument before an appellate court. The case was *Brown v. Board of Education* and the court was the Supreme Court of the United States. Courtesy Paul E. Wilson

Seasoned advocate John W. Davis made his 140th—and last—Supreme Court argument in *Briggs v. Elliot* (representing South Carolina in one of the companion cases to *Brown*) for which he received neither a retainer nor a fee. Library of Congress

Louis L. Redding (left) and Thurgood Marshall (right) conferred during a recess in the school segregation arguments at the Supreme Court. Redding represented black schoolchildren in Delaware; Marshall was general counsel of the NAACP and argued the case against South Carolina. Library of Congress

The NAACP Legal Defense Fund team that prepared the plaintiffs' cases (left to right): John Scott, James M. Nabrit, Jr., Spottswood W. Robinson III, Frank D. Reeves, Jack Greenberg, Thurgood Marshall, Louis L. Redding, U. Simpson Tate, and George E.C. Hayes. Courtesy of the Legal Defense Fund

Oliver Brown attempted to enroll his daughter, Linda (pictured) in the neighborhood school, but she was denied admission because of her race. Instead, Linda was assigned an all-black school twenty-two blocks away. Oliver Brown and twelve other parents, representing twenty children as plaintiffs, filed a lawsuit claiming that the segregation policy violated the Equal Protection Clause. The Brown family's name appeared first on the caption of the complaint. AP Wide World

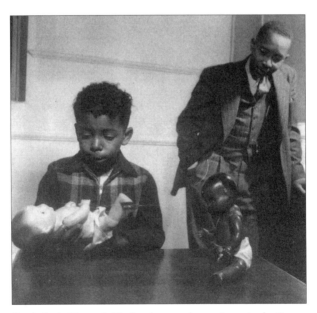

Psychologist Kenneth Clark, who served as a witness in the *Brown* case, conducted projective tests with schoolchildren. He concluded that segregation either made them pathologically conscious of race or forced them to evade reality. Library of Congress

Spottswood W. Robinson III and Thurgood Marshall prepared arguments for *Brown II* in 1955. Library of Congress

Some of the plaintiffs in the *School Segregation Cases* were photographed in 1964 at a press conference. From left to right are Harry Briggs, Jr., Linda Brown Smith, Spottswood Bolling, and Ethel Louis Belton Brown. Library of Congress

These black students were escorted to Central High School in Little Rock under protection from the U.S. Army in 1958. Library of Congress

Herbert Brownell (left) was sworn in as Attorney General by Chief Justice Fred Vinson (right) in 1953 as President Eisenhower looked on. As the head of the Justice Department, Brownell oversaw litigation stemming from the *School Segregation Cases*. Library of Congress

Instead of integrating its public schools in 1961, officials in Prince Edward County, Virginia chose to close them. White students (above) were sent to private schools financed by the state, county, and private donations made in lieu of tax payments, while black students (below) continued to attend school in a one-room shack. Library of Congress

cϐ HERBERT BROWNELL

Brown v. Board of Education Revisited

Today[1] I would like to fill in some missing pages (or at least some unrecorded pages) of history from the early days of the enforcement of *Brown v. Board of Education of Topeka*,[2] which surely was one of the most important constitutional decisions ever handed down by the Court. It posed an immense problem of law enforcement for the executive branch and that included us at the Justice Department.

The case—really five cases consolidated—was originally argued before the Court in the waning days of the Truman administration—in the period between Dwight D. Eisenhower's election and his inauguration. On Inauguration Day, the case had not been decided. The first intimation that the new administration was to have a significant role before the Supreme Court in the pending *Brown* case came just a few days after Eisenhower was sworn in as the new president.

A ceremony was being held at the Justice Department for the swearing in, by Chief Justice Fred Vinson, of the new deputy attorney general and two new assistant attorneys general. After the ceremony, the Chief Justice remained to visit with us informally about a number of matters affecting the judiciary as to which the previous Attorney General had been asked to take action. I was called out of the room at one point by a telephone call. The Chief Justice continued in my absence to speak to the new assistant attorney general for the Civil Division, Warren E. Burger, one of those who had just been sworn into office. As reported to me later by Burger, Chief Justice Vinson said that the Supreme Court would be interested in the views of the Eisenhower administration in the pending case of *Brown v. Board of Education.* I doubt if Chief Justice Vinson surmised that he was delivering this message to a future Chief Justice of the United States.

The significance of Vinson's seemingly offhand remark did not sink in at the moment. In retrospect, it appears that the Court was not at that point unanimous in favor of school desegregation as it would later be. Later history appears to bear that out. It strikes me as plausible that Vinson was soliciting the new administration's legal views to tip the balance, either by encouraging waiverers on the Court to overturn *Plessy v. Ferguson*[3] if the Eisenhower administration was on that side of the school desegregation issue, or to dodge the question until public and political support were more evident and the Court would not have to risk its prestige in such a controversial constitutional area. Furthermore, it can be reasoned that if a stronger majority or even unanimity among all the nine Justices could be attained, the country might be more willing to accept such a drastic change in its mores. This, of course, is speculation on my part. It is entirely within the realm of reason—although I think less plausible—that Vinson may have anticipated a negative response on the administration's part, which might have turned some Justices the other way.

Several months later, near the end of the Supreme Court Term in June 1953, instead of handing down a decision, the Court issued an order setting the *Brown* case for reargument in October of that year. It requested the Attorney General to appear for oral argument, as *amicus curiae,* and to respond to five specific questions listed by the Court.

The questions to the Attorney General were searching ones. Included among them were some dealing with methods of enforcement of any decree to be issued by the Court. The Court order read:

> In their briefs and on oral argument [on reargument] counsel are requested to discuss particularly the following questions insofar as they are relevant to the respective cases:

What evidence is there that the Congress which submitted and the State legislatures and conventions which ratified the Fourteenth Amendment contemplated or did not contemplate, understood or did not understand, that it would abolish segregation in public schools? . . .

Assuming it is decided that segregation in public schools violates the Fourteenth Amendment (a) would a decree necessarily follow providing that, within the limits set by normal geographic school districting, Negro children should forthwith be admitted to schools of their choice, or

(b) may this Court, in the exercise of its equity powers, permit an effective gradual adjustment to be brought about from existing segregated systems to a system not based on color distinctions?

[W]hat specific issues should the decrees reach[?]

[S]hould this Court appoint a special master to hear evidence with a view to recommending specific terms for such decrees[?]

[S]hould this Court remand to the courts of first instance with directions to frame decrees in these cases, and if so what general directions should the decrees of this Court include and what procedures should the courts of first instance follow in arriving at the specific terms of more detailed decrees?

The Attorney General of the United States is invited to take part in the oral argument and to file an additional brief if he so desires.[4]

I immediately notified the president of the Court's request. The Court's forthcoming answers to its own questions obviously would be of vital interest to the whole executive branch. President Eisenhower had already, as one of his first presidential acts, commenced, and was nearing completion of, desegregation of restaurants, hotels, theaters and other places of public accommodation in the District of Columbia to carry out a campaign pledge. But I think he was surprised at the Court's order in *Brown*.

His first reaction was that, since the federal government had not been, and was not, a party, to any of the five *Brown* cases, the Court's invitation should be declined under the doctrine of separation of powers. I argued otherwise and he accepted this advice.

The Department of Justice then formally appeared in the case. By that time, Chief Justice Earl Warren was presiding. We argued orally and in our *amicus* brief in favor of desegregation of the public schools and also submitted a detailed historical examination of the Fourteenth Amendment insofar as it might bear on school desegregation.

So much for the background of our subject today.

The Court handed down its unanimous and historic decision on May 17, 1954, but specifically left open the all-important decision of *how* the decision should be enforced—the enforcement problem was left in limbo for a year until the Court's decision in the second *Brown* case, *Brown II,* in 1955.[5]

In our brief and oral argument in *Brown II,* the Justice Department favored a plan to have each school district where a dispute arose—either from the school board or parents of school children—submit a desegregation plan to the local federal district court for approval. The plans might differ from school district to school district to meet local needs. The Supreme Court adopted this procedure. The alternative proposal before the Court, developed by the NAACP lawyers, was to require immediate desegregation of all school districts. The members of the Court, I believe, evidently believed, as did President Eisenhower, that this second proposal would meet with the massive resistance envisioned in the Southern Manifesto and would lead to having the federal government counter by sending in federal officials to supersede local officials. Our plan, on the other hand, had the definite advantage of decentralizing the resistance forces, and treating each district separately.

We also argued a second point in our brief—that all affected school districts should be required to submit a plan within a period of ninety days after the Court's decree. The executive branch would be empowered to step in as soon as the lower court approved the plan to enforce desegregation.

The Supreme Court adopted our first recommendation, as I said, but rejected our second when it handed down its decision, again unanimous, in *Brown II* in 1955. Power of enforcement was given to the federal district courts but with no timetable for presentation of plans or for their completion. Desegregation was to take place "with all deliberate speed." Although the intent of this phrase was surely otherwise for members of the Court, it was interpreted by political leaders in the South as being so ambiguous as to mean mañana at some indefinite date in the future. No statute existed for executive branch action independent of the Court's decree and in any event Congress had not appropriated any funds for enforcement. President Eisenhower immediately exercised his direct authority over the government of the District of Columbia and called for and obtained desegregation of the public schools in the nation's capital. But no such authority existed for the president to act with respect to the states of the Union.

In this connection, let me say the doctrine of separation of powers between the branches of the federal government is important. But the primary purpose of the doctrine should also be remembered—to check unbridled power by any individual or branch of government. Its aim is not to stymie or stall orderly government as Mr. Justice Jackson noted in the *Youngstown*[6] case:

> While the constitution diffuses power the better to secure liberty, it also contemplates that practice will integrate the dispersed powers into a workable government. It enjoins upon its branches separateness but interdependence, autonomy but reciprocity.[7]

Applied to the *Brown II* case, I believe the Court could well have set a timetable for enforcement, once it decided the constitutional issue. It does sometimes, in effect, by pronouncing whether a decision is to be applied retroactively or only prospectively and, for further example, in some antitrust cases it sets an enforcement timetable. Violation of a timetable would have enabled enforcement officials to act much earlier. As it was, *Brown II* created uncertainty among local education and political officials. It unwittingly sowed the seeds for the violence that ensued at Little Rock and during the administrations of Presidents Kennedy and Johnson. Many years had passed, when in 1969 Justice Hugo L. Black stated for the Court in *Alexander v. Holmes*[8] that " '[a]ll deliberate speed' has turned out to be only a soft euphemism for delay."[9]

After a brief period of calm, the strategy of the segregationist forces became clear. One hundred ten members of Congress issued the Southern Manifesto encouraging massive resistance to *Brown*. The Manifesto stated "we pledge ourselves to use all lawful means to bring about a reversal of this decision which is contrary to the Constitution and to prevent the use of force in its implementation." The Southern Manifesto spawned the formation throughout the South of White Citizens Councils seeking to nullify the *Brown* decision by delay—a strategy that had worked during Reconstruction after the Civil War. These so-called "Citizens Councils" in many cases condoned and even encouraged rioting to resist desegregation in the public schools.

I attempted to counteract the Manifesto by appealing to the attorneys general of the southern states as fellow law enforcement officers, at their convention held in Phoenix, Arizona. After my speech I asked the attorneys general from the states in the Deep South to meet with me at an off-the-record session at midnight. I asked their professional help in eliminating segregation in the schools and in interstate bus and railroad transportation now that the *Brown* case had been decided. Some expressed sympathy with my enforcement problem but told me every state attorney general was a potential candidate for governor and that it would be political suicide to make any move favoring integration. Without rancor they said the federal government should not expect any help from them.

It was clear at this point that the enforcement of *Brown* depended primarily on the actions of federal judges, especially in the southern states where resistance to any enforcement was concentrated, and where plans for desegregating the schools in a hotly contested atmosphere would be considered first.

Ordinarily the recommendation of a senator from the federal district involved was an important factor in selecting federal judges. But candidates recommended by southern senators during this period almost always had a public record of having been opposed to desegregation. As a result, we often made recommendations to the president for judicial positions in the southern states without senatorial confirmation were obvious if we didn't select persons were known to me personally so I could vouch for them. They had no record of opposing desegregation and would approach this problem with an open mind.

One was Frank Johnson of Alabama. President Eisenhower had appointed him United States Attorney shortly after his first inauguration. I knew Johnson and his father earlier in Republican circles. Another was Albert Tuttle of Georgia, also a friend from my political days and at the time Assistant Secretary of the Treasury. The third was John Minor Wisdom of Louisiana, a distinguished New Orleans attorney. The Wisdom appointment was especially significant in signaling the administration's commitment to enforcing desegregation because we selected Wisdom over Governor Kennon of Louisiana, a Democrat who had backed Eisenhower but remained a staunch segregationist. The fourth notable appointment was that of John Brown, a native of my own state of Nebraska, who practiced in Texas. All four were confirmed and bore the brunt of judicial enforcement of the *Brown* decision in the southern states, suffering social snubs and bitter attacks in the local media as a result. Belatedly, I was delighted to see them honored by the bench and bar at the Joint Conference in New Orleans in 1989 of the Fifth and Eleventh (southern) circuits.

Eisenhower realized the importance of appointing federal judges who would uphold the Constitution and who had not publicly opposed the desegregation decision. This is most clearly shown in the case of his nomination of Solicitor General Simon Sobeloff (who had argued for desegregation in the *Brown II* case) to be a judge of the Circuit Court of Appeals for the Fourth Circuit. The Sobeloff nomination was vigorously opposed by southern senators but insisted upon by the president. Eisenhower also strongly backed our other choices—Judge Harlen H. Grooms of Alabama was one of these—despite the strong lobbying of southern senators. I was usually the go-between in dealing with members of Congress dissatisfied with the president's judicial nominees. On occasion, they appealed directly to Eisenhower and were willing to trade legislative support for altering our suggested choices in favor of candidates who were unsupportive of civil rights. Eisenhower, however, resisted political temptation and supported our recommendations one hundred percent.

Sporadically, cases of rioting began to occur when local school board officials attempted to comply with the *Brown* decision. In one case, in Clinton, Tennessee, a man named John Kasper led a tumultuous mob that blocked the entry of black students into the local high school; the governor was forced to send the National Guard to restore order. The federal district court ordered Kasper to desist from obstructing the integration, but Kasper persisted in his actions and the court began contempt proceedings against him. The Justice Department then stepped in and assisted the federal district judge, at his request, in obtaining a contempt of court conviction against Kasper who was sent to jail.

Violence also came close to home. Shortly after the Kasper affair, unknown persons burned fiery crosses in the front of the Washington residences of a number of Supreme Court Justices. The following Sunday, early in the morning, I heard a commotion outside my own home and turned on a master light switch. I found that kerosene had been dumped on the ground under the bedrooms where my children slept, but the intruders were nowhere to be seen. Thereafter the FBI provided protection for a time for my residence and accompanied the children to school and to their social engagements. I might say my daughters did not like the idea of having an FBI agent in the front seat of the car when they went out on their dates.

During this period two legal theories for enforcing *Brown II* were being formulated and debated. One was pressed by the NAACP. It argued that *Brown I,* declaring public school segregation to be unconstitutional, was a sufficient basis for enforcement, without waiting for the District Court approval of a plan. It developed a test case based on its theory in a private action at Mansfield, Texas in October 1955. It sought to have the local school board, without seeking to have a prior approval of a federal court plan for desegregation, be required to desegregate. The local district court refused to order immediate desegregation. The circuit court on June 28, 1956 likewise refused to order immediate desegregation. It merely restated that *Brown I* had declared segregated schools to be unconstitutional and that the lower court should have so declared. It sent the case back to the district court saying that the school board should act with all deliberate speed. It also stated that the district judge "if he had deferred to a later date" the question of injunctive relief, "he might well have been within the bounds of his discretion." In other words, a broad hint that further delay was legally within bounds. That was the end of the Mansfield litigation. Later Governor Shivers, at the opening of the next school term, sent in the National Guard to support the local authorities who wanted to continue segregated schools. But no plan for desegregation was passed upon by the local district court.

The second legal theory for enforcement of *Brown II* (in the absence of voluntary compliance) was the one adopted by the Department of Justice. We were well aware that if we brought a case or intervened and were rebuffed, we could have played into the hands of the White Citizens Councils and set back the cause of desegregation. Our interpretation of *Brown II* concluded that the decision could not be enforced by the executive branch of the federal government until a plan of desegregation had been submitted to a federal district court, by a school board or by school parents, followed by court approval of the plan, followed by defiance of the court order, and a request from the court to the Department of Justice to intervene.

However that may be, Little Rock furnished the test. The Supreme Court later unanimously upheld President Eisenhower's action of sending in the federal troops to enforce the district court order in Little Rock, upholding the school board's plan to allow black children into high school classes. The Little Rock story has been told many times and need not be repeated here.

Suffice it to say, in that case, after the school board presented its plan for gradual desegregation to the local district court and the plan was approved by the Court, Governor Faubus of Arkansas defied the president's request and the local court's ruling. The Court ordered the governor to comply and called on the Department of Justice to enter the case as *amicus curiae*. We did so. When all else failed, President Eisenhower, as we all know, sent in the 101st Airborne Division.

There never was a doubt after Little Rock that the Constitution, as defined by the Supreme Court in *Brown I,* would be upheld by the full powers of the federal government. The old *Plessy v. Ferguson* decision was dead. Of course, it took more time, more Supreme Court decisions, more strong presidential actions and many heroic acts by individuals and lower court federal judges, to obtain general acceptance of *Brown.* But the story of the early exciting and controversial days of enforcement of *Brown,* I believe, is worth revisiting today.

NOTE: *This article is reprinted from the 1993 **Journal of Supreme Court History.***

Endnotes

1. This lecture was delivered on June 7, 1993, in the Supreme Court Chamber at the Annual Meeting of the Supreme Court Historical Society.
2. 347 U.S. 483 (1954).
3. 163 U.S. 537 (1896).
4. 345 U.S. 972–973 (1953).
5. 349 U.S. 294 (1955).
6. 343 U.S. 579 (1952).
7. *Id.* at 579, 635.
8. 396 U.S. 1219 (1969).
9. 396 U.S. 1218, 1219 (1969).

GERALD N. ROSENBERG

African-American Rights After Brown

Other chapters in this volume have focused on the U.S. Supreme Court and African-American rights in the years prior to the mid-twentieth century. That history shows the Court at its worst and at its best—as perpetuating racism and striving to overcome it. In this chapter, I will step back and ask if the Court's attempts to overcome racism made much difference to the lives of African Americans. In particular, I will focus on the Court's 1954 decision, *Brown v. Board of Education,*[1] which unanimously struck down race-based segregation in elementary and secondary schools as violating the Equal Protection Clause of the Fourteenth Amendment of the U.S. Constitution. *Brown* is an apt case for focus on the Court's contribution to change because it has received praise across the legal spectrum and is celebrated by scholars and social critics as a landmark. As the legal historian Michael Klarman puts it, "constitutional lawyers and historians generally deem *Brown v. Board of Education* to be the most important U.S. Supreme Court decision of the twentieth century, and possibly of all time."[2]

The question I address in this article is whether the decision in *Brown* made the contribution to American society that this comment suggests. In asking this question, I mean to disparage no one. Civil rights lawyers like Thurgood Marshall, Jack Greenberg and countless others dedicated their careers, and sometimes their lives, to a principled belief in justice for all. My question does not challenge their commitment nor their principles. It does ask whether litigation was the right strategic choice to further their goals, whether their understanding of the strengths and weaknesses of courts as agents of social change was subtle enough to guide them to the best strategy for change.

Underlying this question about *Brown* is a broader question about the role of the Supreme Court in the larger society. Since the mid-twentieth century, there has been a belief that courts can act to further the interests of the relatively disadvantaged. Starting with civil rights and spreading to issues raised by women's groups, environmental groups, political reformers, and others, American courts seemingly have become important producers of political and social change. Cases such as *Brown* and *Roe v. Wade*[3] are heralded as having produced major change. Further, such litigation has often occurred, and appears to have been most successful, when the other branches of government have failed to act. Indeed, for many, part of what makes American democracy exceptional is that it includes the world's most powerful court system, protecting minorities and defending liberty in the face of opposition from the democratically elected branches. Americans look to activist courts, then, as fulfilling an important role in the American scheme.

Courts, many also believe, can bring heightened legitimacy to an issue. Courts deal with rights. Judges, at their best, are not politically beholden nor partisan. Rather, they are independent and principled, deciding not what policy they want but rather what the Constitution requires. This gives judicial decisions a moral legitimacy that is missing from the actions of the other branches. Court decisions can remind Americans of our highest aspirations and chide us for our failings. Courts, Bickel suggests, have the "capacity to appeal to men's better natures, to call forth their aspirations, which may have been forgotten in the moment's hue and cry."[4] For Rostow, the "Supreme Court is, among other things, an educational body, and the Justices are inevitably teachers in a vital national seminar."[5] Bickel agrees, viewing courts as "a great and highly effective educational institution."[6] Courts, one commentator put it, can provide "a cheap method of pricking powerful consciences."[7]

In the confines of a single chapter, I can do little more than sketch out an answer to the question of whether *Brown* made a major contribution to civil rights. Readers who wish to see a more fully developed argument might consult **The Hollow Hope** and other work of mine.[8]

Reasons for Caution

Before uncritically accepting this view of the Court as correct, there are at least three reasons to be skeptical. First, it is almost entirely lawyers who make this argument. Although lawyers may be no less self-critical than other professionals, they may be no more self-critical either. That is, they may have deep-seated psychological reasons for believing in the importance of the institutions in which they work. This may lead to overvaluing the contribution of the courts to furthering the interests of the relatively disadvantaged.

Second, there is an older view of the role of courts which sees them as much more constrained. Under this view, courts are the least able of any of the branches of government to produce change because they lack all of the necessary tools to do so. They are the "least dangerous branch" because they lack budgetary or coercive power. That courts are uniquely dependent on the executive branch is a view that was most forcefully argued over two hundred years ago by Alexander Hamilton in *Federalist* 78. Hamilton wrote: the judiciary "has no influence over either the sword or the purse; no direction either of the strength or of the wealth of the society, and can take no active resolution whatever. It may truly be said to have neither FORCE nor WILL but merely judgment of and must ultimately depend upon the aid of the executive arm even for the efficacy of its judgments."[9] As President Jackson reportedly commented in response to *Worcester v. Georgia*,[10] in a decision with which he disagreed, "[Chief Justice] John Marshall has made his decision, now let him enforce it." This view suggests that Court decisions furthering the interests of the relatively disadvantaged will only be implemented when the other branches are willing to do so.

The third reason for skepticism about the role of courts as producers of progressive change comes from several decades of public opinion research. If courts are dependent on public and elite support for their decisions to be implemented, as Hamilton suggests, this requires both public knowledge of Court decisions and a public willingness to act based on them. Proponents of an activist, progressive Court assume this. According to one defender of the claim, "without the dramatic intervention of so dignified an institution as a court, which puts its own prestige and authority on the line, most middle-class Americans would not be informed about such grievances."[11] However, decades of public opinion research paint a mixed picture, at best. In general, only about 40 percent of the American public report having read or heard something contemporary about the Court.[12] As an example, in 1966, despite important Supreme Court decisions on race, religion, criminal justice, and voting rights, nearly half of respondents could not recall anything at all that the Court had done recently.[13] And when prompted with a list of eight "decisions," four of which the Court had recently made and four of which it had never made, and asked to identify which, if any, the Court had made, only 19 percent of a 1966 sample made five or more correct choices.[14] In 1973, 20 percent of respondents to a Harris poll, identified the Court as a branch of Congress, as did 12 percent of respondents with college degrees. In a culture in which personality is important, the public, too, is quite ignorant of the Justices' identity. In a 1989 *Washington Post* poll, for example, 71 percent of 1,005 respondents could not name any Justice while only 2 percent could correctly name all nine. Somewhat humorously, while 9 percent named the Chief Justice of the United States (Rehnquist), a whopping 54 percent, six times as many respondents, correctly identified the "judge of the television show 'The People's Court' " (Judge Wapner).[15] The Supreme Court is not in the forefront of the consciousness of most Americans.

This lack of knowledge is not limited to Americans in general, as was illustrated by a fascinating 1990 study reported in that great "scholarly" journal, *Spy Magazine.* In a cleverly designed study, the magazine called six Washington heavyweights claiming to be assistants to five other famous Washingtonians and one Hollywood power broker. The magazine then timed how long it took for the phone calls to be returned. Those called included U.S. Secretary of Defense Dick Cheney; Ben Bradlee, editor of the *Washington Post;* Jack Kent Cooke, owner of the football team the Washington Redskins; and Marlin Fitzwater, Press Secretary to President Bush. The caller claimed to be either the individual or an aid to, among others, Georgette Mosbacher (wife of Cabinet Secretary Robert Mosbacher and renowned for throwing the best parties in Washington); Ben Bradlee, the *Washington Post* editor; Oliver North, William H. Rehnquist, and Senator Moynihan. The results were stunning. The caller claiming to be an aid to Georgette Mosbacher was put immediately through to the Secretary of Defense whose secretary "suggested interrupting a meeting" to reach him. President Bush's press secretary, Marlin Fitzwater, returned the call an hour later. Chief Justice Rehnquist, alas, fared much less well. His calls were returned, on average, two days later than Mosbacher's. Jack Kent Cooke's secretary asked what company "Mr. Lindquist" was with. Fitzwater's secretary apologetically asked "Who is he?" Upon being told that he was the Chief Justice of the United States, it still took Fitzwater four days to return the call.[16]

The point of this discussion is that there are good reasons to be wary of claims that the Court can further the interests of the relatively disadvantaged. Lacking the power to implement their decisions, courts are dependent on other elite institutions and the public at large. And given the findings of the survey literature, this is not a comforting thought for those who believe in the efficacy of the courts to further the interests of the relatively disadvantaged. With this background in mind, I return to *Brown.*

Examining the effects of *Brown* raises questions of how to deal with complicated issues of causation. Because it is difficult to isolate the effects of court decisions from other events in furthering the interests of the relatively disadvantaged, special care is needed in specifying how courts can be effective. On a general level, one can distinguish two types of influence courts can exercise. Court decisions may produce significant social reform through a *judicial* path that relies on the authority of the court. Alternatively, court influence can follow an *extra-judicial* path that invokes court powers of persuasion, legitimacy, and the ability to give salience to issues. Each of these possible paths of influence is different and requires separate analysis.

The *judicial* path of causal influence is straightforward. It focuses on the direct outcome of judicial decisions and examines whether the change required by the courts was made. In civil rights, for example, if a Supreme Court decision ordering an end to public segregation was the cause of segregation ending, then one would see lower courts ordering local officials to end segregation, those officials acting to end it, the community at large supporting it, and, most important, segregation actually ending.

Separate and distinct from judicial effects is the more subtle and complex causal claim of *extra-judicial* effects. Under this conception of causation, courts do more than simply change behavior in the short run. Court decisions may produce significant social reform by inspiring individuals to act or persuading them to examine and change their opinions. Court decisions, particularly Supreme Court decisions, may be powerful symbols, resources for change. They may affect the intellectual climate, the kinds of ideas that are discussed. The mere bringing of legal claims and the hearing of cases may influence ideas. Courts may produce significant social reform by giving salience to issues, in effect placing them on the political agenda. Courts may bring issues to light and keep them in the public eye when other political institutions wish to bury them. Thus, courts may make it difficult for legislators to avoid deciding controversial issues.

In 1954, in *Brown v. Board of Education*,[17] the U.S. Supreme Court found that state laws requiring race-based segregation in public elementary and secondary schools violated the Equal Protection Clause of the Fourteenth Amendment. Overturning nearly sixty years of Court-sanctioned racial segregation, *Brown* is heralded as one of the Supreme Court's greatest decisions. In particular, *Brown* is the paradigm of the Court's ability to protect rights and bring justice to minorities. To the human rights activist Aryeh Neier, *Brown* is the great "symbol" of courts' ability to protect rights and produce significant social reform.[18] For Jack Greenberg, long-time civil rights litigator, *Brown* is the "principal inspiration to others" who seek change and the protection of rights through litigation.[19]

Given the praise accorded to the *Brown* decision, examining its actual effects produces quite a surprise. The surprise is that a decade after *Brown* virtually nothing had changed for African-American students living in the eleven states of the former Confederacy that required race-based school segregation by law. For example, in the 1963–1964 school year, barely one in one hundred (1.2%) of these African-American children was in a nonsegregated school. That means that for nearly ninety-nine of every 100 African-American children in the South a decade after *Brown*, the finding of a constitutional right changed nothing. A unanimous landmark Supreme Court decision had no effect on their lives. This raises the question of why there was no change.

The answer, in a nutshell, is that there was no political pressure to implement the decision and a great deal of pressure to resist it. On the executive level, there was little support for desegregation until the Johnson presidency. President Eisenhower steadfastly refused to commit his immense popularity or prestige in support of desegregation in general or *Brown* in particular. As Roy Wilkins, executive secretary of the National Association for the Advancement of Colored People (NAACP), put it, "if he had fought World War II the way he fought for civil rights, we would all be speaking German today."[20] And Jack Peltason summed up Eisenhower's position this way: "Thurgood Marshall got his decision, now let him enforce it."[21] Although President Kennedy was openly and generally supportive of civil rights, he took little concrete initiative in school desegregation and other civil rights matters until pressured by events to do so. He did not rank civil rights as a top priority and, like Eisenhower before him, was "unwilling to draw on the moral credit of his office to advance civil rights."[22]

Civil rights were not supported by other national leaders until late in the Kennedy administration. In March 1956, southern members of Congress, virtually without exception,[23] signed a document entitled a "Declaration of Constitutional Principles," also known as the Southern Manifesto. Its 101 signers attacked the *Brown* decision as an exercise of "naked power" with "no legal basis." They pledged themselves to "use all lawful means to bring about a reversal of this decision which is contrary to the Constitution and to prevent the use of force in its implementation."[24] This unprecedented attack on the Court demonstrated to all that pressure from Washington to implement the Court's decisions in civil rights would not be forthcoming.

If national political leaders set the stage for ignoring the courts, local politicians acted their part perfectly. A study of the 250 gubernatorial candidates in the southern states from 1950 to 1973 revealed that after *Brown* "ambitious politicians, to put it mildly, perceived few incentives to advocate compliance."[25] This perception was reinforced by Arkansas Governor Orval Faubus's landslide reelection in 1958, after he repeatedly defied court orders to prevent the desegregation of Central High School in Little Rock, demonstrating the "political rewards of conspicuously defying national authority."[26] Throughout the South, governors and gubernatorial candidates called for defiance of court orders. Any individual or institution wishing to end segregation pursuant to court order, that is, to obey the law as mandated by the Supreme Court, would incur the wrath of state political leaders and quite possibly national ones. The best they could hope for was a lack of outright condemnation. Political support for desegregation was virtually nonexistent.

At the prodding of state leaders, state legislatures throughout the South passed a variety of pro-segregation laws. By 1957, only three years after *Brown,* at least 136 new laws and state constitutional amendments designed to preserve segregation had been enacted.[27] These ranged from depriving policemen of their retirement and disability if they failed to enforce the state's segregation laws (Georgia), to denying promotion or graduation to any student of a desegregated school (Louisiana), to simply making it illegal to attend a desegregated school (Mississippi) to Virginia's massive resistance including closing public schools, operating a tuition grant scheme, suspending compulsory attendance laws, and building private segregated schools. In 1960–1961 alone, the Louisiana legislature met in one regular and five extraordinary sessions to pass ninety-two laws and resolutions to maintain segregated public schools. As the southern saying went, "as long as we can legislate, we can segregate."[28]

Along with opposition to desegregation from political leaders at all levels of government, there was hostility from many white Americans. Law and legal decisions operate in a given cultural environment, and the norms of that environment influence the decisions that are made and the impact they have. In the case of civil rights, decisions were announced in a culture in which slavery had existed and apartheid did exist. Institutions and social structures throughout America reflected a history of, if not a present commitment to, racial discrimination. Cultural barriers to civil rights had to be overcome before change could occur. And courts do not have the tools to do so. This is well illustrated in the decade after *Brown.*

One of the important cultural barriers to civil rights was the existence of private groups supportive of segregation. One type, represented by the Ku Klux Klan, White Citizens' Councils, and the like, existed principally to fight civil rights. Either through their own acts, or the atmosphere these groups helped create, violence against blacks and civil rights workers was commonplace throughout the South. Spectacular cases such as the murder of Medgar Evers, the attacks on the freedom riders, the Birmingham Church bombing that killed four black girls, and the murder of three civil rights workers near Philadelphia, Mississippi, are well known. But countless bombings and numerous murders occurred throughout the South.[29] During the summer of 1964 in Mississippi alone there were thirty-five shootings, sixty-five bombings (including thirty-five churches), eighty beatings, and six murders.[30] It was a brave soul indeed who worked to end segregation or implement court decisions.

Another tactic used by white groups to fight civil rights was economic coercion. Since whites controlled the economy throughout the South, this was extraordinarily effective.[31] In fact, so effective was this sort of intimidation that as late as 1961 *not a single* desegregation suit in education had been filed in Mississippi.[32]

A totally different kind of private group resisted civil rights by simply ignoring court decisions and going about their business as if nothing had changed. Public carriers, for example, even when owned by non-southerners, looked to the "segregationist milieu" in which they operated and thus took a "narrow view of desegregation decrees, implementing them minimally, if at all."[33]

The cultural biases against civil rights that pervaded private groups also pervaded local governments. Court-ordered action may be fought or ignored on a local level, especially if there is no pressure from higher political leadership to follow the law and pressure from private groups not to. It was common to find, for example, that where bus companies followed the law and removed segregation signs in terminals, state and local officials put them back up.[34] In the five Deep South states, as a matter of principle no school-board member or superintendent openly advocated compliance with the Supreme Court decision.[35] And despite *Cooper v. Aaron*,[36] and the sending of troops to Little Rock in 1957, as of June 1963, only sixty-nine out of 7,700 students at the supposedly desegregated, "formerly" white, junior and senior high schools of Little Rock were black.[37] Public resistance, supported by local political action, can almost always effectively defeat court-ordered civil rights.

In sum, in civil rights, court-ordered change confronted a culture opposed to that change. That being the case, the American judicial system, constrained by the need for both elite and popular support, constrained change.

The analysis above, however, omits one key institution and one key group: the judiciary, lawyers and their academic counterparts. The South, like the rest of the country, has both state and federal courts as well as lawyers. And the courts have a natural constituency in the American legal profession. Indeed, Justice Frankfurter believed that lawyers' support of the Court's decision in *Brown* would be decisive. As he put it in a letter to a friend, "it is the legal profession of the South on which our greatest reliance must be placed . . . because the lawyers of the South will gradually realize that there is a transcending issue, namely respect for law as determined so impressively by a unanimous court [in *Brown*]."[38] But Justice Frankfurter was to be doubly disappointed; both southern lawyers and elite lawyers and legal academics throughout the country condemned the case or offered only the most tepid support.

Lawyers and the Legal Profession

While there were undoubtedly some white southern lawyers who supported the Court, they were few and far between. Opponents, in contrast, were everywhere. And surprisingly, opposition was voiced not merely by white southerners but also by elite, northern lawyers as well. A notable example was the American Bar Association (ABA), which is the nation's major professional legal organization. Politically neutral, it claims the legitimacy of professional expertise. However, in the wake of *Brown,* it lent the pages of its journal, the *ABA Journal,* to condemnation of *Brown,* from the vicious to the technical. It published only the most tepid, rule-of-law, defenses of the decision. Not once, in either editorials or articles, was there an argument that *Brown* was morally, constitutionally, or substantively correct.

The ABA was not alone. In 1958, the Conference of Chief Justices of State Courts issued a report on the Court. While the body of the report was careful, the report finished with polemical conclusions that criticized the Supreme Court for legislating. "In the fields with which we are concerned [the report concluded] . . . the Supreme Court too often has tended to adopt the role of policy-maker without proper judicial restraint."[39] The report continued, "it has long been an American boast that we have a government of laws and not men. We believe that any study of recent decisions of the Supreme Court will raise at least considerable doubt as to the validity of that boast."[40] The report was adopted by a vote of 36-8 and won praise in an *ABA Journal* editorial for its "attitude of careful study, calm deliberation and temperate statement."

Elite legal academics also joined the fray "[S]peaking the rhetoric of institutional legitimacy, a significant number of northeastern, white, liberal lawyers joined with white, southern, never-say-die segregationists in questioning the Court's authority and legitimacy in *Brown*."[41] Although there was some support for the decision in law reviews immediately following *Brown,* it was found mostly in short pieces. In contrast, elite law reviews repeatedly blasted the Court. For example, the *Harvard Law Review* poured out a torrent of criticism, especially in its annual Forewords. *Brown* was criticized as poorly thought out, insufficient to support other cases, and unprincipled. The most important article was undoubtedly written by Herbert Wechsler, a law professor at Columbia University in New York City. Giving the Holmes Lecture at Harvard, and appearing as the Foreword to the 1959 *Harvard Law Review,*[42] *Brown* was criticized as unprincipled. *Brown* lacked a neutral principle, Wechsler argued, because separate but equal, if truly equal, was itself a neutral principle and there was no neutral way of deciding between it and equality. Wechsler's piece is the second most cited law review article in the period 1957 through March 1985! The popularity of his critique of *Brown* as unprincipled is a powerful indicator of the lack of support elite academic lawyers gave to *Brown*.

Local Courts

Judges seldom stepped in where politicians, lawyers, and the public at large were unwilling to go. The "fifty-eight lonely men" who served the federal judiciary in the South were being asked to dismantle a social system they had grown up with and of which they were a part. Even a judge as pro-civil-rights as John Minor Wisdom was sympathetic, finding it "not surprising that in a conservative community a federal judge may feel that he cannot jeopardize the respect due the court in all of his cases" by vigorously supporting civil rights.[43] Although there were some outstanding southern federal judges such as J. Skelly Wright, John

Minor Wisdom, Bryan Simpson, and Frank Johnson, there were also some who were not. For example, Judge Elliott (M. Dist. GA) stated that he did not want "pinks, radicals and black voters to outvote those who are trying to preserve our segregation laws."[44] Judge Cox (S. Dist. Miss.), speaking from the bench in March 1964, referred repeatedly to black voter-registration applicants in derogatory language (as "a bunch of niggers") who were "acting like a bunch of chimpanzees."[45] It is important to note that both judges Elliott and Cox were Kennedy appointees. In the Dallas school desegregation case, started in 1955 and still pending in 1960, in which the federal district court was reversed six times, Judge Davidson complained that the "white man has a right to maintain his racial integrity, and it can't be done so easily in integrated schools."[46]

On the state levels judges were even more biased. Chief Justice J. Edwin Livingston of the Alabama Supreme Court, speaking in 1959 to several hundred students and business leaders, announced: "I'm for segregation in every phase of life and I don't care who knows it. . . . I would close every school from the highest to the lowest before I would go to school with colored people."[47] Alabama circuit judge Walter B. Jones wrote a column in the *Montgomery Advertiser* that he devoted to the "defense of white supremacy." In June 1958 he told readers that in the case against the NAACP, over which he was presiding, he intended to deal the NAACP a "mortal blow" from which it "shall never recover."[48] It is no wonder, then, that despite clear Supreme Court rulings, Alabama was able to keep the NAACP in litigation for eight years and effectively incapacitated in the state. As Leon Friedman, who talked with scores of civil rights lawyers in the South concluded, "the states' legal institutions were and are the principal enemy."[49]

The use of the courts in the civil rights movement is considered the paradigm of a successful strategy for social change. Yet, a closer examination reveals that courts had virtually *no direct effect* on ending discrimination in education. Courageous and praiseworthy decisions were rendered, and nothing changed. *Brown* and its progeny stand for the proposition that courts are impotent to further the interests of the relatively disadvantaged. *Brown* is a paradigm, but for precisely the opposite view.

This, however, is not the end of the story. By the 1972–1973 school year, more than 91 percent of African-American children in the eleven states of the former Confederacy were in a nonsegregated school. Eighteen years after *Brown*, southern school systems were desegregated. How did this occur?

Change came to southern school systems in the wake of congressional and executive branch action. Title VI of the 1964 Civil Rights Act permitted the cut-off of federal funds to programs receiving federal monies where racial discrimination was practiced, and the 1965 Elementary & Secondary Education Act provided a great deal of federal money to generally poor southern school districts. By the 1971–1972 school year, for example, federal funds comprised from between 12 percent and 27.8 percent of southern state school budgets, up from between 4.6 percent and 11.1 percent in the 1963–1964 school year. This combination of federal funding and Title VI gave the executive branch a tool to induce desegregation when it chose to do so. When the U.S. Department of Health, Education, and Welfare began to threaten fund cut-offs to school districts that refused to desegregate, dramatic change occurred. By the 1972–1973 school year, more than 91 percent of African-American school children in the eleven southern states were in integrated schools, up from 1.2 percent in the 1963–1964 school year. With only the constitutional right in force in the 1963–1964 school year, no more that 5.5 percent of African-American children in any southern state were in school with whites. By the 1972–1973 school year, when economic incentives were offered for desegregation, and costs imposed for failure to desegregate, in no southern state were fewer than 80 percent of African-American children in integrated schools. School desegregation occurred in the years 1968–72, then, because a set of conditions provided incentives for it and imposed costs for failing to desegregate. When those conditions were lacking, as in the first decade after *Brown*, constitutional rights were flouted. What a Court decision was unable to accomplish, federal dollars were able to achieve. The Supreme Court, acting alone, lacked the power to produce change.

Indirect Effects

The judicial path of influence is not the only way an institution can contribute to civil rights. By bringing an issue to light courts may put pressure on others to act, sparking change. Thus *Brown* and its progeny may have been the inspiration that eventually led to congressional and executive branch action and some success in civil rights. According to one commentator, "*Brown* set the stage for the ensuing rise in black political activism, for legal challenges to racial discrimination in voting, employment, and education, as well as for the creation of a favorable climate for the passage of the subsequent civil rights legislation and the initiation of the War on Poverty."[50] Indeed, most commentators (and I assume most readers) believe this is the case and hold their belief with little doubt. As C. Herman Pritchert put it, "if the Court had not taken that first giant step in 1954, does anyone think there would now be a Civil Rights Act of 1964?"[51]

In the next few pages I examine these claims. What evidence exists to substantiate them? How important was *Brown* to the civil rights struggle? In examining these questions, it must be noted that social scientists do not understand well enough the dynamics of influence and causation to state with certainty that the claims of Court influence (or any other causal claims) are right or wrong. Similarly, social scientists do not understand fully the myriad of factors that are involved in an individual's reaching a political decision. Ideas seem to have feet of their own, and tracking their footsteps is an imperfect science. Thus, even if I find little or no evidence of extra-judicial influence, it is simply impossible to state with certainty that the Court did not contribute in a significant way to civil rights. On the other hand, claims about the real world require evidence. Otherwise, they are merely statements of faith.

Turning to the specifics, I have tried to delineate the links that are necessary for the Court to have influenced civil rights by the extra-judicial path. The bottom line, the last link, is that the action of the President and Congress resulted in change. That is, the passage of the 1964 Civil Rights Act brought about change. I have demonstrated this elsewhere[52] and it is assumed to be true throughout this chapter. The key question, then, is the extent to which congressional and presidential action was a product of Court action.

One hypothesized link postulates that Court action gave civil rights prominence, putting it on the political agenda. Media coverage of civil rights over time could provide good evidence to assess this link. A second link, put quite simply, is that Court action influenced both the President and Congress to act. The Court, in other words, was able to pressure the other branches into dealing with civil rights. A third hypothesized link proposes that the Court favorably influenced white Americans in general about civil rights and they in turn pressured politicians. By bringing the treatment of black Americans to nationwide attention, the Court may have fomented change. A final hypothesized link suggests that the Court influenced black Americans to act in favor of civil rights and that this in turn influenced white political elites either directly or indirectly through influencing whites in general.

Salience

When the Supreme Court unanimously condemned segregation in 1954, it marked the first time since 1875 that one of the three branches of the federal government spoke strongly in favor of civil rights on a fundamental issue. The Court, it is claimed, put civil rights on the political agenda. "*Brown,*" Neier writes, "launched the public debate over racial equality."[53] One important way in which the political agenda is created is through the press. Thus, one way in which the Court may have given salience to civil rights is through inducing increased press coverage of it and balanced treatment of blacks.

Press Coverage

Overall, there is no evidence of such an increase or major change in reporting in the years immediately following *Brown.* In general, newspaper coverage of civil rights was poor until the massive demonstrations of the 1960s. Numerous studies support this conclusion. C. A. McKnight, executive director of the Southern Education Reporting Service, found that in the years following *Brown* Supreme Court treatment of segregation received "minimum coverage."[54] In 1956, Ralph McGill, editor of the *Atlanta Constitution,* chided newspapers for failing to do "a good job of presenting and interpreting the segregation controversy."[55] This was particularly true in the South, where there was a "paucity" of coverage and where the wire services "seldom reported the story in its full dimensions and meaning."[56] And *Time* magazine criticized southern newspapers for doing a "patchy, pussyfooting job of covering the region's biggest running story since the end of slavery."[57] In general, the southern press did not greatly increase or balance its civil rights coverage in response to the Court.

The most powerful way to determine if there was a sustained increase in press coverage of civil rights in response to *Brown* is to actually count press stories over time. The evidence shows that while press coverage of civil rights, as measured by the number of stories dealing with the issue in the *Reader's Guide To Periodical Literature,* increased moderately in 1954 over the previous year's total, by 1958 and 1959 coverage actually dropped below the level found in several of the years of the late 1940s and early 1950s! In addition, if one examines the magazines in America in the 1950s and early 1960s with the largest circulations, *Reader's Digest, Ladies Home Journal, Life,* and the *Saturday Evening Post,* the same general pattern again repeats. And it was not until 1962 that *TV Guide* ran a story having to do with civil rights. Thus, press coverage provides no evidence that the Court's decision gave civil rights salience for most Americans.

It is possible, of course, that the political agenda is formed more by elites than by ordinary citizens. Thus, it may be that the magazines most likely read by elites would provide increased coverage of civil rights in the wake of the Court's decision. But this is not the case. The magazines most likely to be read by political elites, *The New York Times Magazine, Newsweek, Time,* and the *New Republic,* show the same pattern. In fact, for each of these magazines there was as much, if not more, coverage of civil rights in several of the years of the 1940s as in 1958 or 1959. The same general pattern holds for civil rights coverage in *The New York Times* as measured by the proportion of pages in the *Times Index* devoted to discrimination. In 1952, there was actually more coverage than in 1954 or 1955. Further, coverage in the years 1954, 1955, 1958, and 1959 was barely equal to or actually less than the coverage allotted to civil rights in four of the years of the 1940s! Here again, there is no evidence that the Court's action indirectly affected elites by putting civil rights on the political agenda through the press.

There was one media outlet that gave enormous coverage to *Brown;* Voice of America! The decision was immediately translated into thirty-four languages and broadcast around the world. In poignant contrast, Universal News-reels, the company that made news reports for movie theaters in the United States, never mentioned *Brown.*[58]

In sum, press coverage of civil rights provides no evidence for the claim that the Court has important extra-judicial-effects claim. This finding is striking since *Brown* is virtually universally credited with having brought civil rights to national attention.

Elites

The extra-judicial-effects argument claims that the actions of the Supreme Court influenced members of Congress, the President, and the executive branch. The argument might be that because of the "deference paid by the other branches of government and by the American public"[59] to the Supreme Court, its decisions prodded the other branches of the federal government into action. Further, the argument might run that the Court's actions sensitized elites to the legitimate claims of blacks. As Wilkinson puts it, "*Brown* was the catalyst that shook up."[60]

Legislation

A sensible place to look for evidence of indirect effects is in the legislative history and debates over the 1957, 1960, and 1964 civil rights acts, and in presidential pronouncements on civil rights legislation. If Court action was crucial to congressional and presidential action, one might reasonably expect to find members of Congress and the President mentioning it as a reason for introducing and supporting civil rights legislation. While it is true that lack of attribution may only mean that the Court's influence was subtle, it would cast doubt on the force, if not the existence, of this extra-judicial effect.

At the outset, the case for influence is supported by the fact that civil rights bills were introduced and, for the first time since 1875, enacted in the years following *Brown*. While this makes it seem likely that *Brown* played an important role, closer examination of the impetus behind the civil rights acts of 1957, 1960, and 1964, does not support this seemingly reasonable inference. The 1957 and 1960 bills were almost entirely driven by electoral concerns. Republicans attempted to court northern urban black voters and, at the same time, embarrass the Democrats by exposing the major rift between that party's northern and southern wings.[61] The press and political opponents understood the bills as a response to electoral pressures, not to constitutional mandates.

The story of the 1964 act is similar in that there is no evidence of Court influence and a great deal of evidence for other factors, in this case the activities of the civil rights movement. The Kennedy administration offered no civil rights bill until February 1963 and the bill it offered then was "a collection of minor changes far more modest than the 1956 Eisenhower program."[62] When a House subcommittee modified and strengthened the bill, Attorney General Robert Kennedy met with the members of the full Judiciary Committee in executive session and "criticized the subcommittee draft in almost every detail."[63] The President specifically objected to the prohibition of job discrimination that became Title VII, the provision making the Civil Rights Commission a permanent agency, the provision empowering the attorney general to sue on behalf of individuals alleging racial discrimination, and the provisions mandating no discrimination in federally funded programs and allowing fund cut-offs.[64] It was not until the events of the spring of 1963 that the administration changed its thinking.

In Congress, there is little evidence that *Brown* played any appreciable role. The seemingly endless congressional debates, with some four million words uttered in the Senate alone,[65] hardly touched on the case. References to *Brown* can be found on only a few dozen out of many thousands of pages of Senate debate.[66] While much of the focus of the debate was on the constitutionality of the proposed legislation, and on the Fourteenth Amendment, the concern was not with how *Brown* mandated legislative action, or even how *Brown* made such a bill possible. Even in the debates over the fund cut-off provisions, *Brown* was seldom mentioned.[67] This is particularly surprising since it would have been very easy for pressured and uncertain members of Congress to shield their actions behind the constitutional mandate announced by the Court. That they did not credit the Court with affecting their decisions prevents the debates from providing evidence for the indirect-effects thesis. Thus, there does not appear to be evidence for the influence of *Brown* on legislative action.

Reviewing the public pronouncements of Presidents Eisenhower, Kennedy, and Johnson on civil rights legislation, I do not find the Court mentioned as a reason to act. Neither Eisenhower nor Kennedy committed the moral weight of their office to civil rights. When they did act, it was in response to violence or upcoming elections, not in response to Court decisions. While President Johnson spoke movingly and eloquently about civil rights, he did not mention Court decisions as an important reason for civil rights action. In his moving speeches to Congress and the nation in support of the 1964 Civil Rights Act and the 1965 Voting Rights Act he dwelt on the violence that peaceful black protesters were subjected to, the unfairness of racial discrimination, and the desire to honor the memory of President Kennedy. It was these factors that Johnson highlighted as reasons for supporting civil rights, not Court decisions.

In sum, I have not found the evidence necessary to make a case of clear attribution for the Court's effects on Congress or the President. Students of the Civil Rights Acts of 1957, 1960, and 1964 credit their introduction and passage to electoral concerns, or impending violence, not Court decisions. The extra-judicial-effects claim is not supported with Congress or the President.

Whites

The extra-judicial-effects thesis views courts as playing an important role in alerting Americans to social and political grievances. The view here is that the Supreme Court "pricked the conscience"[68] of white America by pointing out both its constitutional duty and its short-comings. "Except for *Brown*," Aryeh Neier contends, white Americans "would not have known about the plight of blacks under segregation."[69] For this claim to hold, in order for courts to affect behavior, directly or indirectly, people must be aware of what the courts do. While this does not seem an onerous responsibility, I have shown earlier in this chapter that most Americans have little knowledge about U.S. courts and pay little attention to them. The specific question this leaves unanswered is whether this holds true for a case such as *Brown*.

Public Opinion—*Brown* and Civil Rights

Surprisingly, and unfortunately, there appear to be no polls addressing awareness of *Brown*. There are, however, polls charting the reaction to *Brown* by southerners over time. They show both very little support for desegregation and lessening support throughout the 1950s. By 1959, for example, support for desegregation actually dropped, with only 8 percent of white southerners responding that they would not object, down from 15 percent in 1954.[70]

If there is little evidence that *Brown* changed opinions about school desegregation in the South, perhaps it helped change white opinions more generally. It is clear that throughout the period from the beginning of the Second World War to the passage of the 1964 Act, whites became increasingly supportive of civil rights. Is there evidence that this change was the effect of Court action? The answer appears to be no. Writing in 1956, Hyman and Sheatsley found that the changes in attitude were "solidly based" and "not easily accelerated nor easily reversed."[71] Further, they found that the changes were not due to any specific event, such as Kennedy's assassination, or a Supreme Court decision. They found that changes in national opinion "represent long-term trends that are not easily modified by specific—even by highly dramatic—events."[72]

Another way of examining the indirect-effects claim on white Americans is to look at how the sensitivity of Americans to civil rights changed generally. According to one proponent of judicial influence, the "*Brown* decision was central to eliciting the moral outrage that both blacks and whites were to feel and express about segregation."[73] If the Court served this role, it would necessarily have increased awareness of the plight of blacks. The evidence, however, shows no sign of such an increase. Survey questions as to whether most blacks were being treated fairly resulted in affirmative responses of 66 percent in 1944, 66 percent in 1946, and 69 percent in 1956.[74] The variation of 3 percent is virtually meaningless. By 1963, when Gallup asked if any group in America was being treated unfairly, 80 percent said no. Only 5 percent of the sample named "the Negroes" as being unfairly treated while 4 percent named "the whites."[75] Most poignantly, in December 1958, when Gallup asked its usual question about the most admired men in the world, Governor Orval Faubus of Arkansas, who had repeatedly defied court orders a year earlier to prevent the desegregation of Central High School in Little Rock, was among the ten most frequently mentioned.[76] As Burke Marshall, head of the Justice Department's Civil Rights Division put it, "the Negro and his problems were still pretty much invisible to the country . . . until mass demonstrations of the Birmingham type."[77] These results, and the change over time, hardly show an America whose conscience is aroused. If the Court pricked the conscience of white Americans, the sensitivity disappeared quickly.

In sum, in several areas where the Supreme Court would be expected to influence white Americans, evidence of the effect has not been found. Most Americans neither follow Supreme Court decisions nor understand the Court's constitutional role. It is not surprising, then, that change in public opinion appears to be oblivious to the Court. Again, the extra-judicial-effects thesis lacks evidence.

Blacks

The indirect-effects thesis makes claims about the effect of the Supreme Court on black Americans. Here, a plausible claim is that *Brown* was the spark that ignited the black revolution. By recognizing and legitimizing black grievances, the public pronouncement by the Court provided blacks with a new image and encouraged them to act. This assumption is virtually universal among lawyers and legal scholars, and representative quotations can be found throughout this chapter *Brown* "begot," one legal scholar tells us, "a union of the mightiest and lowliest in America, a mystical, passionate union bound by the pained depths of the black man's cry for justice and the moral authority, unique to the Court, to see that justice realized."[78] Thus, *Brown* may have fundamentally re-oriented the views of black Americans by providing hope that the federal government, if made aware of their plight, would help. Black action, in turn, could have changed white opinions and led to elite action and civil rights. If this is the case, then there are a number of places where evidence should be found.

One area where this effect should be seen is in civil rights demonstrations. The evidence plainly indicates that civil rights marches and demonstrations affected both white Americans and elites and provided a major impetus for civil rights legislation. As Wilkinson puts it, "the Court sired the movement, succored it through the early years, [and] encouraged its first taking wing."[79] If this were the case, if, in the words of civil rights litigator Jack Greenberg, the direct-action campaign would not have developed "without the legal victories that we'd won earlier,"[80] then one would expect to see an increase in the number of demonstrations shortly after the decision. However, there is almost no difference in the number of civil rights demonstrations in the years 1953, 1954, and 1955. There was a large jump in 1956, due to the Montgomery bus boycott. But then the numbers drop. For example, 1959 saw fewer civil rights demonstrations than in four of the years of the 1940s! And the number of demonstrations skyrocketed in the 1960s, six or more years after *Brown*. This pattern does not suggest that the Court played a major role. The time period is too long and the 1960s increases too startling to credit the Court with a meaningful effect.

The Montgomery Bus Boycott

The 1956 Montgomery bus boycott created worldwide attention. Coming just a few years after *Brown,* it is quite plausible that it was sparked by the Court. If this were the case, one might trace the indirect effect of *Brown* to Montgomery to the demonstrations of the 1960s to white opinion to elite action in 1964 and 1965 to desegregation of public schools in the early 1970s. The problem is that there does not appear to be evidence even for this tortuous causal chain. The immediate crisis in Montgomery was brought about by the arrest, in December 1955, of Mrs. Rosa Parks, a black woman, for refusing to give up her seat to a white person and move to the back of a segregated city bus. Parks was the fourth black woman arrested in 1956 for such a refusal.[81] It is unclear why this particular incident sparked the boycott, although Parks was fairly well-known and commanded respect in the black community. Because the Montgomery bus boycott is mentioned by so many civil rights activists, and because it launched both Dr. King's and Reverend Abernathy's civil rights careers, it is worth examining briefly.

In the 1940s and early 1950s there were a number of black civil rights organizations in Montgomery. One of them, the Women's Political Council (WPC), began to focus on bus segregation and lodged complaints with the city at the end of 1953 and again in the spring of 1954, before *Brown*. Before *Brown* the WPC had prepared for a bus boycott by preparing a notice calling on the black community to act and by planning the distribution routes. "On paper, the WPC had already planned for fifty thousand notices calling people to boycott the buses; only the specifics of time and place had to be added."[82] The arrest of Rosa Parks provided the opportunity the WPC was waiting for.

There is another piece of evidence, as well, that suggests that *Brown* was not influential; the nature of the boycotters' initial demands. Despite the efforts of the WPC, and the evident anger of the black community, initially the boycotters did *not* demand an end to bus segregation. Rather, the principal demand called for modified seating by race, with blacks starting at the back and whites at the front. As late as April 1956 Dr. King was still willing to settle on these terms.[83] This led the NAACP to withhold support on the grounds that the demands were too "mild."[84] As Abernathy puts it, "at first we regarded the Montgomery bus boycott as an interruption of our plans rather than as the beginning of their fulfillment."[85] Again, this suggests that a host of local factors provided the inspiration for the boycott.

Finally, four additional parts of the historical context suggest that *Brown* had little influence. First, the idea of a bus boycott was not new, having been used successfully by blacks in Baton Rouge, Louisiana, during the summer of 1953. Dr. Martin Luther King, Jr., the leader of the Montgomery bus boycott, knew the leader of that boycott, T. J. Jemison, from college days, and spoke with him early in the boycott.[86] From the Baton Rouge boycott, Abernathy notes, Montgomery's blacks took "considerable inspiration."[87] Second, Montgomery's blacks "did know that other cities in the Deep South, notably Mobile and Atlanta, had already conceded the 'first come, first served' principle."[88] Third, in November 1955, Representative Adam Clayton Powell visited Montgomery and suggested that blacks use their economic power to force change. Characteristically, the flamboyant Powell took credit for instigating the bus boycott.[89] Finally, King specifically addressed the influence of *Brown* on the boycott. It was clear, he said, that *Brown* "cannot explain why it happened in Montgomery" and that the "crisis was not produced by . . . even the Supreme Court."[90] Although Montgomery may have inspired blacks, there does not appear to be much evidence that the Court inspired Montgomery.[91]

Sit-Ins

Another possible way in which *Brown* may have sparked change is through providing the inspiration for the sit-in movement and the demonstrations of the 1960s. The decision might have given blacks new hope that the federal government would work to end discrimination. It might have confirmed their own belief in the unfairness of segregation. If this were the case, one might plausibly expect to find participants in, and students of, the demonstrations talking and writing about the Court's decision as one reason for their actions. A review of biographies, autobiographies, and scholarly studies of the civil rights movement provides the evidence for assessing the claim.

The sit-in in Greensboro, North Carolina, in February 1960 started the sit-in movement of the 1960s. Organized by four black college students, it does not appear to have been Court-inspired. After Greensboro, the sit-ins spread quickly throughout the South. Within sixty days of Greensboro, sit-ins had spread to at least sixty-five southern cities."[92] For black students throughout the South, the inspiration was the action of other students, as well as Montgomery and King. Instead of looking to courts for inspiration and support, the demonstrators "appealed to a higher law" because they "weren't sure about the legality" of their actions.[93] When black students from Atlanta joined the sit-ins, they took out a full-page advertisement in Atlanta's newspapers listing their demands and defending their actions. Entitled "An Appeal For Human Rights," the detailed and lengthy list of grievances was supported by six separate justifications of the sit-ins. No mention of the Court, the Constitution, or *Brown* is found anywhere in the text.[94] The six-year time interval between *Brown* and the sit-ins, the lack of attribution to the Court, the crediting of several non-Court factors, and the rapidity with which the movement spread, all suggest it was unlikely that *Brown* played much of a role.

Why did the sit-ins work? Was it because white business owners, in the wake of *Brown,* saw the constitutional legitimacy of the protesters' claims? The evidence does not support this conclusion. In most places businesses rejected the demands and refused to alter their practices. Constitutional principle did not appear to motivate them. Rather, they tried to outlast the demonstrators. However, sit-ins and ensuing black boycotts took their toll. In Greensboro, for example, Wolff writes of the "tremendous economic pressure put on the stores by the Negroes' boycott, along with the reticence of whites to trade there because of fear of trouble." The Woolworth's store where the sit-ins started registered a $200,000 drop in sales in 1960.[95] Economic pressure, not constitutional mandate, appears the best explanation for the success of the sit-ins.

Dr. Martin Luther King, Jr.

One possible way in which *Brown* might have ignited the civil rights movement is by inspiring Dr. King. His ringing denouncements of segregation, his towering oratory, and his ability to inspire and move both blacks and whites appear to have played an indispensable role in creating pressure for government action. Was King motivated to act by the Court? From an examination of King's thinking, the answer appears to be no. King rooted his beliefs in Christian theology and Gandhian nonviolence, not constitutional doctrine. His attitude to the Court, far from a source of inspiration, was one of strategic disfavor. "Whenever it is possible," he told reporters in early 1957, "we want to avoid court cases in this integration struggle."[96] He rejected litigation as a major tool of struggle for a number of reasons. He wrote of blacks' lack of faith in it, of its "unsuitability" to the civil rights struggle, and of its "hampering progress to this day."[97] Further, he complained that to "accumulate resources for legal actions imposes intolerable hardships on the already overburdened."[98] In addition to its expense, King saw the legal process as slow. Blacks, he warned, "must not get involved in legalism [and] needless fights in lower courts because that is "exactly what the white man wants the Negro to do. Then he can draw out the fight."[99] Perhaps most important, King believed that litigation was an elite strategy for change that did not involve ordinary people. He believed that when the NAACP was the principal civil rights organization, and court cases were relied on, "the ordinary Negro was involved [only] as a passive spectator" and "his energies were unemployed."[100] Montgomery was particularly poignant, he told the 1957 NAACP annual convention, because, in Garrow's paraphrase, it demonstrated that "rank-and-file blacks themselves could act to advance the race's goals, rather than relying exclusively on lawyers and litigation to win incremental legal gains."[101] And, as he told the NAACP Convention on July 5, 1962, "only when the people themselves begin to act are rights on paper given life blood."[102] King's writings and actions do not provide evidence for the Dynamic Court view that he was inspired by the Court.

Black Groups

The founding of the Student Non-Violent Coordinating Committee (SNCC), the Congress of Racial Equality (CORE), and the Southern Christian Leadership Conference (SCLC), the organizations that provided the leadership and the shock troops of the movement, could quite plausibly have been inspired by the Court. Although SNCC was not founded until six years after *Brown,* and CORE was not revitalized until 1961, it may have taken that long for the effect to be felt.

However, it is quite clear that the Court played no role in inspiring these key groups of the civil rights movement to form. To the contrary, they were formed as an explicit rejection of litigation as a method of social change. The SCLC, for example, was founded in the winter of 1957. The moving force behind it was not the inspiration of *Brown* but an attempt to capitalize on the success of the Montgomery bus boycott.[103] The founding of SNCC in 1960 is similar and was aimed at helping students engaged in sit-ins to create at least some communication and organization network.[104] And CORE was founded in 1942 as a Gandhian-type movement of mass non-violent direct action.[105] As its Executive Director James Farmer told Roy Wilkins of the NAACP in response to Wilkins's opposition to the Freedom Ride, and preference for litigation, "we've had test cases and we've won them all and the status remains quo."[106] The point is that *Brown* is simply not mentioned as a source of inspiration.

If *Brown* is not mentioned by those who sat in, demonstrated, and marched, was anything? The answer is a clear yes. The participants pointed to a number of sources of inspiration for their actions. For some, the emergence of black African nations and the movements that accompanied their liberation had a "profound effect."[107] Over the twelve months from June 1960 to June 1961, eleven African countries gained independence. "We identified with the blacks in Africa," John Lewis of SNCC said, "and we were thrilled by what was going on."[108] Third-world liberation movements were also prominently mentioned by King in his classic *Letter From Birmingham Jail.*[109] For others, the Montgomery bus boycott was an "inspiration."[110] James Forman, a powerful force in SNCC, credits the bus boycott with having a "very significant effect on the consciousness of black people" and a "particularly important effect on young blacks." Montgomery, Forman believed, "helped to generate the student movement of 1960."[111] Participants in sit-ins also pointed to other sit-ins as inspiration, and to Dr. King, either by his actions or his writings.[112] *Brown* and the Supreme Court may have played a role in inspiring the activists of the early 1960s but they did not mention it in describing their inspiration for acting. And given the fact that they did point to other factors as inspiring them, the lack of attribution of *Brown* is all the more telling.[113]

In exploring the case for extra judicial effects with blacks, I looked for evidence in a variety of places, including the Court's ability to inspire black activists, black protest activity, and black leaders. In none of these places was evidence found for the claim and in a number of places the evidence seems to contradict it. Again, the extra-judicial-effects thesis lacks support.

Before I sum up these findings, it is important to note that while there is little evidence that *Brown* helped produce positive change, there is some evidence that it hardened resistance to civil rights among both elites and the white public. I have documented how, throughout the South, white groups intent on using coercion and violence to prevent change grew. Resistance to change increased in all areas, not merely in education but also in voting, transportation, public places, and so on. *Brown* "unleashed a wave of racism that reached hysterical proportions."[114] On the elite level, *Brown* was used as a club by southerners to fight any civil rights legislation as a ploy to force school desegregation on the South. In hearings and floor debates on the 1957 Civil Rights Act, southerners repeatedly charged that the bill, aimed at voting rights, was a subterfuge to force school desegregation on the South.[115] When Attorney General Brownell testified before a Senate committee on the 1957 bill, he was queried repeatedly and to his astonishment on whether the bill gave the President the power to use the armed forces to enforce desegregation.[116] By stiffening resistance and raising fears before the activist phase of the civil rights movement was in place, *Brown* may actually have delayed the achievement of civil rights.

In sum, the claim that a major contribution of the courts in civil rights was to give the issue salience, press political elites to act, prick the consciences of whites, legitimate the grievances of blacks, and fire blacks up to act is not substantiated. In all the places examined, where evidence supportive of the claim should exist, it does not. The concerns of clear attribution, time, and increased press coverage all cut against the thesis. Public-opinion evidence does not support it and, at times, clearly contradicts it. The emergence of the sit-ins, demonstrations, and marches, does not support it. While it must be the case that Court action influenced some people, I have found no evidence that this influence was widespread or of much importance to the battle for civil rights. The evidence suggests that *Brown*'s major positive impact was limited to re-inforcing the belief in a legal strategy for change of those already com-mitted to it. The burden of showing that *Brown* accomplished more now rests squarely on those who for years have written and spoken of its immeasurable importance.

Conclusion: The Fly-Paper Court

This chapter has examined whether the Supreme Court's decision in *Brown v. Board of Education* was able to desegregate schools. Surprisingly, the analysis showed the Court's decision, praiseworthy as it was, did not make much of a contribution. This is the case because, on the most fundamental level, courts depend on political support to produce such reform. Thus, political hostility doomed the Court's contributions.

Courts will also be ineffective in producing change, given any seri-ous resistance because of their lack of implementation powers. The structural constraints built into the American judicial system, make courts virtually powerless to produce change. They must depend on the actions of others for their decisions to be implemented. With civil rights, little changed until the federal government became involved. Where there is local hostility to change, court orders will be ignored. Community pressure, violence or threats of violence, and lack of mar-ket response all serve to curtail actions to implement court decisions. When Justice Jackson commented during oral argument in *Brown,* "I suppose that realistically this case is here for the reason that action couldn't be obtained from Congress,"[117] he identified a fundamental reason why the Court's action in the case would have little effect.

In general, then, not only does litigation steer activists to an insti-tution that is constrained from helping them, but also it siphons off crucial resources and talent, and runs the risk of weakening political efforts. In terms of financial resources, social reform groups do not have a lot of money. Funding a litigation campaign means that other strategic options are starved of funds. In civil rights, while *Brown* was pending in June 1953, Thurgood Marshall and Walter White sent out a telegram to supporters of the NAACP asking for money, stating "funds entirely spent."[118] Compare this to the half-million-dollar estimates of the cost of the freedom rides, largely due to fines and bail.[119] Further, the legal strategy drained off the talents of people such as Thurgood Marshall and Jack Greenberg. As Martin Luther King, Jr., complained: "to accumulate resources for legal actions imposes intolerable hardships on the already overburdened."[120]

It is important to note here that there were options other than litigation. Massive voter-registration drives could have been started in the urban North and in some major southern cities. Marches, demonstrations, and sit-ins could have been organized and funded years before they broke out, based on the example of labor unions and the readiness of groups like the CORE. Money could have been invested in public relations. Amazingly, in 1957 the NAACP spent just $7,814 for its Washington Bureau operations. Its entire "public relations and informational activities" spending for 1957 was $17,216. NAACP lobbyists did not even try to cultivate the black press or the black church, let alone their white counterparts. And even in 1959 the public relations budget was only $10,135.[121] When activists succumbed to the "lawyers' vision of change without pain,"[122] a "massive social revolution" was sidetracked into "legal channels."[123] Because the NAACP failed to understand the limits on U.S. courts, its strategy was bound to fail.

If this is the case, then there is another important way in which courts effect social change. It is, to put it simply, that courts act as "flypaper" for social reformers who succumb to the "lure of litigation." Courts, I have argued, can seldom produce significant social reform. Yet if groups advocating such reform continue to look to the courts for aid, and spend precious resources in litigation, then the courts also limit change by deflecting claims from substantive political battles, where success is possible, to harmless legal ones where it is not. Even when major cases are won, the achievement is often more symbolic that real. Thus, courts may serve an ideological function of luring movements for social reform to an institution that is structurally constrained from serving their needs, providing only an illusion of change.

This conclusion does not deny that courts can occasionally, though rarely, help social reform movements. Sometimes, too, litigation can remove minor but lingering obstacles to change. But here litigation is often a mopping-up operation, and it is often defensive. In civil rights, for example, when opponents of the 1964 and 1965 acts went to court to invalidate them, the courts' refusal to do so allowed change to proceed. Similarly, if there had never been a *Brown* decision, a southern school board or state wanting to avoid a federal fund cut-off in the late 1960s might have challenged its state law requiring segregation. An obliging court decision would have removed the obstacle without causing much of a stir, or wasting the scarce resources of civil rights groups. This is a very different approach to the courts than one based on using them to produce significant social reform.

Litigation can also help reform movements by providing defense services to keep the movement afloat. In civil rights, the NAACP Legal Defense and Educational Fund, Inc. (Inc. Fund) provided crucial legal service that prevented the repressive legal structures of the southern states from totally incapacitating the movement. In springing demonstrators from jail, providing bail money, and forcing at least a semblance of due process, Inc. Fund lawyers performed crucial tasks. But again, this is a far cry from a litigation strategy for significant social reform.

These findings also suggest that a great deal of writing about courts is fundamentally flawed. Treating courts and judges as either philosophers on high or as existing solely within a self-contained legal community ignores what they actually do. This does not mean that philosophical thinking and legal analysis should be abandoned. It emphatically does mean that the broad and untested generalizations offered by constitutional scholars about the role, impact, importance, and legitimacy of courts and court opinions that pepper this chapter must be rejected. When asking those sorts of questions about courts, they must be treated as political institutions and studied as such. To ignore social science literature and eschew empirical evidence, as much court writing does, makes it impossible to understand courts as they are.

American courts are not all-powerful institutions. They were designed with severe limitations and placed in a political system of divided powers. To ask them to produce significant social reform is to forget their history and ignore their constraints. It is to cloud our vision with a naïve and romantic belief in the triumph of rights over politics. And while romance and even naïveté have their charms, they are not best exhibited in courtrooms.

NOTE: *This article is reprinted from 1999* **Journal of Supreme Court History,** *vol. 24, no. 2.*

Endnotes

1. 347 U.S. 483 (1954).
2. Michael J. Klarman, "How Brown Changed Race Relations: The Backlash Thesis," *Journal of American History* 81 (1994): 81.
3. 410 U.S. 113 (1973).
4. Alexander M. Bickel, **The Least Dangerous Branch: The Supreme Court at the Bar of Politics.** 2nd ed. (New Haven: Yale University press, 1962) p. 26.
5. Eugene V. Rostow, "The Democratic Character of Judicial Review," 66 *Harv. L. Rev.* 193, 208 (1952).
6. Bickel, **Least Dangerous Branch,** p. 26.
7. Note. "Implementation Problems in Institutional Reform Litigation," 91 *Harv. L. Rev.* 428, 463 (1977).
8. **The Hollow Hope: Can Courts Bring About Social Change?** (Chicago: University of Chicago Press, 1991, 1993); "The Irrelevant Court: The Supreme Court's Inability to Influence Popular Beliefs about Equality (or Anything Else)," In **Redefining Equality,** eds. Neal Devins and Dave Douglas (New York: Oxford University Press, 1998): 172–190: "The Implementation of Constitutional Rights: Insights from Law and Economics," 64 *University of Chicago Law Review* 1215 (1997); "The Real World of Constitutional Rights: The Supreme Court and the Implementation of the Abortion Decisions," in **Contemplating Courts,** ed. Lee Epstein (Washington, D.C. Congressional Quarterly Press, 1995): 390–419; "*Brown* is Dead! Long Live *Brown!*: The Endless Attempt to Canonize a Case," 80 *Virginia L. Rev.* 161 (1994).
9. *The Federalist Papers.* Ed. Clinton Rossiter (New York: Mentor, 1961), p. 465.
10. 31 U.S. (6 Pet.) 515 (1832).
11. Ariah Never, **Only Judgment: The Limits of Litigation in Social Change** (Middletown: Wesleyan University Press, 1982) p. 23.
12. Sheldon Goldman and Thomas P. Jahnige, **The Federal Courts as a Political System,** 2nd ed. (New York: Harper & Row, 1976) p. 145; William J. Daniels, "The Supreme Court and Its Publics," 37 *Alb. L. Rev.*
13. Walter F. Murphy, Joseph Tanenhaus, and Daniel L. Kastner, **Public Evaluations of Constitutional Courts: Alternative Explanations** (Beverly Hills: Sage, 1973) p. 53.

14. Survey cited in Kenneth M. Dolbeare, "The Public Views the Supreme Court," in **Law, Politics, and the Federal Courts,** ed., Herbert Jacob (Boston: Little, Brown, 1967) pp. 199–201.

15. Lee Epstein, Jeffrey A. Segal, Harold J. Spaeth, Thomas G. Walker, **The Supreme Court Compendium** (Washington, D.C.: Congressional Quarterly Press, 1994) p. 609.

16. Findings reported in James Warren, "Hold for Mr. Bigwig," *Chicago Tribune* 12 Ap. 1990, sec. 5, p. 2.

17. 347 U.S. 483 (1954).

18. Neier, **Only Judgment,** p. 57.

19. Jack Greenberg, "Litigation for Social Change: Methods, Limits and Role In Democracy," 29 *Record of the Association of the Bar of the City of New York* 32, 331 (1974).

20. Roy Wilkins with Tom Mathews, **Standing Fast: The Autobiography of Roy Wilkins** (New York: Penguin, 1984) p. 222.

21. Jack W. Peltason, **Fifty-Eight Lonely Men** (Urbana: University of Illinois Press, 1971) p. 54.

22. Victor S. Navasky, **Kennedy Justice** (New York: Atheneum, 1977) p. 161.

23. The only southern senators not to sign the Manifesto were Johnson of Texas and Kefauver and Gore of Tennessee. And two North Carolina congressman who refused to sign, Charles B. Deane and Thurmond Chatman, lost their seats.

24. *Cong. Rec.* 12 March 1956; 4460 (Senate), 4515–16 (House).

25. Earl Black, **Southern Governors and Civil Rights; Racial Segregation as a Campaign Issue in the Second Reconstruction** (Cambridge: Harvard University Press, 1976) p. 299.

26. Black, **Southern Governors,** p. 299.

27. Gary Orfield, **The Reconstruction of Southern Education** (New York: Wiley, 1969) pp. 17–18.

28. Harrell R. Rodgers, Jr. and Charles S. Bullock III, **Law and Social Change: Civil Rights Laws and Their Consequences** (New York: McGraw-Hill, 1972) p. 72.

39. Peltason, **Fifty-Eight Lonely Men,** p. 5; Southern Regional Council, Law Enforcement in Mississippi (Atlanta: Southern Regional Council, 1964) pp. 7–17.

30. David J. Garrow, **Protest at Selma** (New Haven: Yale University Press, 1978) p. 21; Doug McAdam, **Freedom Summer** (New York: Oxford University Press, 1988) pp. 257–82.

31. Reed Sarratt, **The Ordeal of Desegregation** (New York: Harper, 1966) pp. 301–02; Peltason, **Fifty-Eight Lonely Men,** pp. 58, 60.

32. Sarratt, **Ordeal,** pp. 99–100.

33. Catherine A. Barnes, **Journey from Jim Crow: The Desegregation of Southern Transit** (New York: Columbia University Press, 1983) pp. 196, 195.

34. William Brink and Louis Harris, **The Negro Revolution in America** (New York: Simon, 1963) p. 41.
35. Robert G. Dixon, Jr., "Civil Rights in Transportation and the I.C.C.," 31 *Geo. Wash. L. Rev.* 198, 213–14 (1962).
36. 358 U.S. 1 (1958).
37. William Brink and Louis Harris, **The Negro Revolution in American** (New York: Simon, 1963) p. 41.
38. J. Frankfurter, letter to C. C. Burlingham, quoted in Mark G. Yudof, "Implementation Theories & Desegregation," in "Symposium, Judicially Managed Institutional Reform," 32 *Ala. L. Rev.* 441, 450 (1981).
39. "Report of the Committee on Federal-State Relationships as Affected by Judicial Decisions," *Congressional Record* 25 August 1958: A7782, at p. A7787.
40. *Id.,* p. A7788.
41. Gary Peller, "Neutral Principles in the 1950's," 21 *U. Mich. J.L.* Ref. 561, 563 (1988).
42. Herbert Wechsler, "Toward Neutral Principles of Constitutional Law," 73 *Harv. L. Rev.* 1 (1959).
43. John Minor Wisdom, "The Frictionmaking, Exacerbating Political Role of Federal Courts," 21 *Sw. L. Rev.* 411, 419 (1967).
44. Quoted in Note, "Judicial Performance in the Fifth Circuit," 73 *Yale L.J.* 90, 101 n. 71 (1963).
45. Southern Regional Council, **Law Enforcement** (Atlanta: The Council, 1964) pp. 19–20.
46. Quoted in Sarratt, **Ordeal,** p. 201.
47. Quoted in Peltason, **Fifty-Eight Lonely Men,** p. 66.
48. Quoted in Peltason, **Fifty-Eight Lonely Men,** p. 65, 67.
49. Leon Friedman, ed., **Southern Justice** (New York: Pantheon, 1965) p. 7.
50. Henry M. Levin, "Education and Earnings of Blacks and the *Brown* Decision," in **Have We Overcome? Race Relations Since *Brown*,** ed., Michael V. Namorato (Jackson: University of Mississippi Press, 1979) p. 80.
51. C. Herman Pritchett, "Equal Protection and the Urban Majority," *American Political Science Review* 58 (1964): 869.
52. *See* Rosenberg, **Hollow Hope,** chapter 2.
53. Neier, **Only Judgment,** pp. 241–42.
54. Quoted in Sarratt, **Ordeal,** p. 263.
55. Quoted in Roy E. Carter, Jr., "Segregation and the News: A Regional Content Study," *Journalism Quarterly* 34 (1957): 4, n. 4.
56. Pat Watters and Reese Cleghorn, **Climbing Jacob's Ladder** (New York: Harcourt, 1967) p. 73 n. 10.
57. "The Press—Dilemma in Dixie," *Time* 20 February 1956: 76.
58. Taylor Branch, **Parting the Waters: America in the King Years 1954–1963** (New York: Simon & Schuster, 1988) p. 113.
59. Neier, **Only Judgment,** p. 9.

60. J. Harvie Wilkinson, III, **From *Brown* to *Bakke:* The Supreme Court and School Integration, 1954–1978** (New York: Oxford University Press, 1979) p. 49.

61. *See* J. W. Anderson, **Eisenhower, Brownell, and the Congress: The Tangled Origins of the Civil Rights Bill of 1956–1957** (University, Ala: University of Alabama Press, 1964) pp. 3, 47, 133–35; Robert Fredrick Burk, **The Eisenhower Administration and Black Civil Rights** (Knoxville: University of Tennessee Press, 1984) pp. 6, 145, 165, 218; Richard Kluger, **Simple Justice** (New York: Knopf, 1976) p. 754; Steven F. Lawson, **Black Ballots: Voting Rights in the South, 1944–1969** (New York: Columbia University Press, 1976) chap. 6; Roy Wilkins, **Standing Fast,** p. 234.

62. Orfield, **Reconstruction,** p. 24.

63. Daniel M. Berman, **A Bill Becomes a Law: Congress Enacts Civil Rights Legislation** 2nd ed. (New York: Macmillan, 1966) pp. 21–22; Charles and Barbara Whalen, **The Longest Debate: A Legislative History of the 1964 Civil Rights Act** (Cabin John, Md: Seven Locks, 1985) pp. 44–45.

64. Berman, **A Bill Becomes a Law,** pp. 22–23; Jack Greenberg, "Preface, Blacks and the Law," *Annals of the American Academy of Political and Social Science* vol. 407 (1973): ix.

65. Whalen, **The Longest Debate,** p. 193.

66. References can be found in the following parts and on the following pages of volume 110 of the *Congressional Record,* 88th Congress, 2nd sess., 1964: Part 4: 4996, 5017, 5087, 5247, 5267, 5342; Part 5: 5695, 5703, 5705, 5935, 6540, 6813, 6814, 6821, 6837, 6838; Part 6: 8052, 8054; Part 7: 8620, 8621; Part 8: 10919, 10921, 10925, 10926, 11194, 11195, 11198; Part 9: 11597, 11875, 12339, 12579, 12580; Part 10: 12683, 13922; Part 11: 14294, 14296, 14447, 14457. Over 40% of these references are by Senators opposing the Bill.

67. Berman, **A Bill Becomes a Law;** Orfield, **Reconstruction,** pp. 33–45; Whalen, **The Longest Debate.**

68. Loren Miller, "Very Deliberate Speed," in **The Segregation Era 1863–1954,** ed., Allen Weinstein and Frank Otto Gatell (New York: Oxford University Press, 1970) p. 281.

69. Neier, **Only Judgment,** p. 23.

70. AIPO Poll in Hazel Gaudet Erskine, "The Polls: Race Relations," *Public Opinion Quarterly* 26 (1962): 140, 141.

71. Herbert H. Hyman and Paul B. Sheatsley, "Attitudes Toward Desegregation," *Scientific American* (July 1964): 38.

72. Herbert H. Hyman and Paul B. Sheatsley, "Attitudes Toward Desegregation," *Scientific American* (July 1964): 17.

73. Henry M. Levin, "Education and Earnings of Blacks and the *Brown* Decision," in **Have We Overcome? Race Relations Since *Brown*,** ed., Michael V. Namorato (Jackson: University of Mississippi Press, 1979) p. 110–11.

74. Hyman and Sheatsley, 1956, p. 39.

75. George H. Gallup, **The Gallup Poll: Public Opinion 1935–1971,** 3 vols. (New York: Random House, 1972) vol. 3: 1825.

76. Gallup, **The Gallup Poll,** vol. 2: 1584.

77. Quoted in Adam Fairclough, **To Redeem the Soul of America: The Southern Christian Leadership Conference and Martin Luther King, Jr.** (Athens, Ga.: University of Georgia Press, 1987) p. 135.

78. Wilkinson, **From *Brown* to *Bakke*,** p. 5.

79. Wilkinson, **From *Brown* to *Bakke*,** p. 3.

80. " 'Someone Has to Translate Rights into Realities': Conversation with Civil Rights Lawyer Jack Greenberg," 2 *Civil Liberties Rev.* (Fall, 1975): 111.

81. David Levering Lewis, **King: A Biography** (New York: Praeger Publishers, 1970) p. 48.

82. Jo Ann Gibson Robinson, **The Montgomery Bus Boycott and the WOMEN Who Started It: The Memoir of Jo Ann Gibson Robinson,** ed., David J. Garrow (Knoxville: University of Tennessee Press, 1987) p. 39.

83. Fairclough, **To Redeem the Soul of America,** p. 20.

84. Wilkins, **Standing Fast,** p. 228.

85. Ralph David Abernathy, **And the Walls Came Tumbling Down** (New York: Harper & Row, 1989) p. 169.

86. Branch, **Parting the Waters,** p. 145.

87. Abernathy, **And the Walls Came Tumbling Down,** p. 178; David J. Garrow, **Bearing the Cross: Martin Luther King, Jr., and the Southern Christian Leadership Conference** (New York: Morrow, 1986) pp. 26–27; Aldon D. Morris, **The Origins of the Civil Rights Movement: Black Communities Organizing for Change** (New York: The Free Press, 1984) p. x. Morris argues that the Montgomery bus boycott was "partly inspired by the Baton Rouge effort and to some extent modeled after it."

88. Fairclough, **To Redeem the Soul of America,** p. 12.

89. J. Mills Thornton III, "Challenging and Response in the Montgomery Bus Boycott of 1955–1956," *Alabama Review* 33 (July 1980): 194.

90. Martin Luther King, Jr., **Stride Toward Freedom: The Montgomery Story** (New York: Harper, 1958) pp. 64, 191–92. At a news conference in January 1956, King explained the boycott as "part of a world-wide movement. Look at just about any place in the world and the exploited people are rising against their exploiters. This seems to be the outstanding characteristic of our generation" (quoted in Garrow, **Bearing the Cross,** p. 54).

91. Morris, **Origins,** p. 25 credits the Baton Rouge boycott with more importance than the Court. However, the Supreme Court may have played a vital role in the final victory by allowing the city a way out of a boycott that was costly and damaging. In *Gayle v. Browder,* 352 U.S. 903, (1956), the Supreme Court upheld a lower-court decision prohibiting enforcement of Montgomery's bus segregation law. The Court's decision may have allowed the city to end segregation without "giving in" to the boycotters' demands.

On the other hand, without the strength of the boycott, there would have been little pressure on Montgomery to comply.

92. Southern Regional Council, **The Student Protest Movement** Winter 1960. Revised. (Atlanta: The Southern Regional Council, April 1, 1960) p. 1.

93. Remarks of Julian Bond, University of Chicago, 10 January 1990. In 1960 Bond was a student leader of the Atlanta sit-ins.

94. "An Appeal for Human Rights," *Atlanta Constitution* 9 March 1960: 13.

95. Miles Wolff, **Lunch at the Five and Ten** (New York: Stein and Day, 1970) pp. 173, 174.

96. Quoted in Garrow, **Bearing the Cross,** p. 87.

97. Martin Luther King, Jr. **Why We Can't Wait** (New York: Harper, 1963) pp. 23, 157.

98. King, **Why We Can't Wait,** p. 157.

99. Quoted in Garrow, **Bearing the Cross,** p. 78.

100. Quoted in Morris, **Origins,** p. 123.

101. Garrow, **Bearing the Cross,** p. 78.

102. Quoted in Branch, **Parting the Waters,** p. 598.

103. Garrow, **Bearing the Cross,** p. 85; Fairclough, **To Redeem the Soul,** pp. 30, 31.

104. Clayborne Carson, **In Struggle** (Cambridge: Harvard University Press, 1981) pp. 19, 20; Garrow, **Bearing the Cross,** pp. 131 ff; Mary King, **Freedom Song: A Personal Story of the 1960s Civil Rights Movement** (New York: Morrow, 1987) pp. 42–46; Juan Williams, **Eyes on the Prize: America's Civil Rights Years, 1954–1965** (New York: Penguin, 1988) p. 137; Paul Good, **"Odyssey of a Man—And a Movement,"** *The New York Times Magazine* 25 June 1967: 44; Cleveland Sellers, **The River of No Return** (New York: Morrow, 1973) p. 16.

105. James Farmer, **Lay Bare the Heart: An Autobiography of the Civil Rights Movement** (New York: Plume, 1985) Appendix A.

106. Quoted in Farmer, **Lay Bear the Heart,** p. 13.

107. Carson, **In Struggle,** p. 16; William, **Eyes on the Prize,** p. 11; James W. Vander Zanden, **"The Non-Violent Resistance Movement Against Segregation,"** *American Journal of Sociology* 68 (1963): 545; Howard Zinn, **Albany: A Study in National Responsibility** (Atlanta: Southern Regional Council, 1962).

108. Quoted in Williams, **Eyes on the Prize,** p. 139.

109. Martin Luther King, Jr., "The Negro is Your Brother" [Letter from Birmingham Jail] as published in 212 *Atlantic Monthly* (August, 1963) pp. 5, 11.

110. Howard Zinn, **SNCC: The New Abolitionists** (Boston: Beacon, 1964) p. 18.

111. Thomas Forman, **The Making of Black Revolutionaries** (New York: Macmillan, 1972) pp. 84, 85.

112. Thomas Gaither, "Orangeburg: Behind the Carolina Stockade," in **Sit-Ins: The Student Report,** ed., Jim Peck (New York: Congress of Racial

equality, 1960); Minnie Finch, **The NAACP: Its Fight for Justice** (Metuchen, N.J.: Scarecrow, 1981) p. 205; Martin Oppenheimer, "The Genesis of the Southern Negro Student Movement (Sit-In Movement): A Study in Contemporary Negro Protest." Ph.D. Diss. University of Pennsylvania, 1963 p. 103; C. Vann Woodward, **The Strange Career of Jim Crow.** Rev. ed. (New York: Oxford University Press, 1974) p. 197.

113. For confirmation of this analysis, *see,* for example, the following works by participants: Abernathy, **And the Walls Came Tumbling Down;** Farmer, **Lay Bare the Heart;** Foreman, **The Making of Black Revolutionaries;** King, **Stride Toward Freedom;** King, **Why We Can't Wait;** King, "The Negro is Your Brother" [Letter from Birmingham Jail]; King, **Freedom Song;** various participants in Peck, **Sit-Ins;** various participants in Howell Raines, **My Soul Is Rested: Movement Days in the Deep South Remembered** (New York: Putnam, 1977); Sellers, **The River of No Return;** Elizabeth Sutherland, ed. **Letters from Mississippi** (New York: McGraw-Hill, 1965). Studies of the movement that confirm this analysis include Branch, **Parting the Waters;** Carson, **In Struggle;** William H. Chafe, **Civilities and Civil Rights: Greensboro, North Carolina, and the Black Struggle for Freedom** (New York: Oxford University Press, 1980); Fairclough, **To Redeem the Soul;** Garrow, **Protest at Selma;** Garrow, **Bearing the Cross;** Henry Hampton and Steve Fayer, **Voices of Freedom: An Oral History of the Civil Rights Movement from the 1950s through the 1980s** (New York: Bantam, 1990); McAdam, **Freedom Summer;** August Meier and Elliott Rudwick, eds. **Black Protest in the Sixties** (Chicago: Quadrangle, 1970); Oppenheimer, "Genesis": Southern Regional Council, **The Student Protest Movement: A Recapitulation** (N.p.: Southern Regional Council, 1960); Pete Seeger and Bob Reiser, **Everybody Says Freedom: A History of the Civil Rights Movement in Songs and Pictures** (New York: W. W. Norton, 1989); Nancy J. Weiss, **Whitney M. Young Jr., and the Struggle for Civil Rights** (Princeton: Princeton University Press, 1989); Robin M. Williams, Jr., "Social Change and Social Conflict: Race Relations in the United States, 1944–1964," *Sociological Inquiry* 35 (1965): 8–25; Williams, **Eyes on the Prize;** Wolff, **Lunch at the Five and Ten;** Zanden, "Non-Violent Resistance"; Zinn, **SNCC.**

114. Fairclough, **To Redeem the Soul,** p. 21.

115. Civil Rights: Hearings Before the Subcomm. No. 5 of the House Comm. On the Judiciary, 85th Cong. 806, 1187 (1957).

117. Civil Rights—1957: Hearings Before the Subcomm. On Constitutional Rights of the Senate Comm. On the Judiciary, 85th Congress 214–16 (1957).

117. Quoted in Leon Friedman, ed., **Argument: The Oral Argument Before the Supreme Court in** *Brown v. Board of Education of* Topeka, **1952–1955** (New York: Chelsea House, 1969) p. 244.

118. Quoted in Kluger, **Simple Justice,** p. 617.

119. Sarratt, **Ordeal,** p. 333.

120. King, **Why We Can't Wait,** p. 157.
121. Gilbert Ware, "The National Association for the Advancement of Colored People and the Civil Rights Act of 1957," Ph.D. Diss. Princeton University, 1962, pp. 188–89, 189, 190, 13.
122. Stuart A. Scheingold, **The Politics of Rights: Lawyers, Public Policy, and Political Change** (New Haven: Yale University Press, 1974) p. 145.
124. Morton J. Horwitz, "The Jurisprudence of *Brown* and the Dilemmas of Liberalism," in **Have We Overcome? Race Relations Since *Brown,*** ed., Michael V. Namorato (Jackson: University of Mississippi Press, 1979) p. 184.

⚞ J E F F R E Y D . H O C K E T T

The Battle Over Brown's Legitimacy

Constitutional scholars have given few Supreme Court rulings the attention that they have lavished upon the celebrated decision in *Brown v. Board of Education.*[1] Yet the literature of public law is surprisingly unedifying with regard to the process by which the desegregation decision achieved iconic status in American legal culture. Scholarly inattentiveness to the history of *Brown's* reputation is startling, given that southern politicians were not the only persons in 1954 to characterize the decision as a manifest instance of judicial legislation. Even persons sympathetic to desegregation conceded that the Justices had circumvented traditional legal constraints in rendering *Brown.*[2] In the years immediately following the ruling, some scholars appealed to the notion of a "living Constitution" to defend *Brown* against charges that it conflicted with the original understanding of the Fourteenth Amendment and with the "separate but equal" doctrine that the Court had established in *Plessy v. Ferguson.*[3] But critics, some of whom even accepted the concept of the "living Constitution," also challenged the Court's reading of social fact—that is, its claims regarding the inherent inequality of segregated schools—which supposedly justified judicial recognition of a right that conflicted with precedent and with the intentions of the framers of the Equal Protection Clause.

If *Brown* reveals the role that discretion can play in the process of constitutional decision-making, however, the decision also demonstrates that the Court is limited in its ability to control the meaning of its rulings. Ironically, this limitation on the Court's power worked to the Justices' advantage in *Brown*. For the exalted status that the decision eventually achieved was, in part, a function of scholarly revisions of the basis of the ruling. More specifically, the fortunes of the *Brown* decision improved considerably when certain scholars recast the ruling as an attack upon an institution that, they argued, could only be characterized as a manifestation of white supremacy. The violence that greeted desegregation efforts in the South made benign characterizations of apartheid seem disingenuous and thus solidified the ethical appeal of *Brown*. The completeness of *Brown's* triumph as a political icon is reflected not only in a corresponding decline in the status of the *Plessy* decision, but also in the damage done to the reputations of those scholars who accepted the morality of *Brown* but continued to question the legality of the decision.

Scholarly Criticism of *Brown*

The Historical Critique

To place the debate over *Brown's* legitimacy in proper historical perspective, one should note that flexible interpretations of constitutional provisions were anything but novel in 1954. Indeed, the concept of the "living Constitution" had been an accepted part of American legal thought and Supreme Court doctrine at least since the end of the New Deal.[4] However, the criticism that some politicians, journalists, and scholars directed at Chief Justice Earl Warren's opinion for a unanimous Court in *Brown* revealed that the jurisprudential consensus regarding the idea that constitutional provisions are relative to time and circumstance applied only to the powers of government and did not extend to the realm of individual rights. Warren made no pretense in his opinion that the Court's ruling rested upon the intentions of the framers and ratifiers of the Fourteenth Amendment. His treatment of the historical sources that were the focus of reargument in 1953[5]—a statement that these sources were, "[a]t best, . . . inconclusive"[6]—prompted southern congressmen to emphasize what the Chief Justice merely implied: that constitutional history undermined the Court's holding that racial segregation in public schools violates the concept of equal protection of the laws. Indeed, the inconsistency between the Court's ruling and the history of the Fourteenth Amendment was the focus of the "Southern Manifesto" of March 1956. That statement of protest against the Court's ruling, which more than ninety southern congressmen signed, recalled the arguments of the lawyers for the defendant school boards and emphasized that "[t]he debates preceding the submission of the 14th amendment clearly show that there was no intent that it should affect the systems of education maintained by the States." The manifesto also noted, among other things, that "[t]he very Congress which proposed the amendment subsequently provided for segregated schools in the District of Columbia."[7]

Besides noting the Court's failure to respect the traditional sources of constitutional interpretation, certain commentators pointed up the novelty of the apparent basis of the holding in *Brown*. Of special concern to these individuals was Warren's reference in his eleventh footnote to the social-science evidence of the petitioners in the case as support for the conclusion that racially segregated public schools are inherently unequal and, thus, unconstitutional. Echoing the arguments of the NAACP's lawyers, who represented the petitioners, Warren maintained that segregation "generates a feeling of inferiority [in black children] as to their status in the community that may affect their hearts and minds in a way unlikely ever to be undone." In the sentence to which he attached the controversial footnote, Warren said: "Whatever may have been the extent of psychological knowledge at the time of *Plessy v. Ferguson,* this finding is amply supported by modern authority."[8] James Reston of *The New York Times* responded to the opinion with the observation that, in "ruling out racial segregation in the nation's public schools, [the Court] rejected history, philosophy and custom as the major basis for its decision and accepted instead Justice Benjamin N. Cardozo's test of contemporary social justice." Reston declared that "[t]he Court's opinion read more like an expert paper on sociology than a Supreme Court opinion."[9] In the same issue of the *Times,* the august constitutional scholar, Alpheus T. Mason, lamented: "Rather than rely

244 BLACK, WHITE, AND *BROWN*

on available judicial precedents, the Court invoked two of the flimsiest of all our disciplines—sociology and psychology—as the basis of its decision." Another venerable scholar, Carl Brent Swisher, observed that the "decision was based neither on the history of the amendment nor on precise textual analysis but on psychological knowledge."[10]

In an effort to defend the *Brown* decision against historical criticism, Alexander Bickel championed a broader, more flexible understanding of abstract constitutional rights although he did not use the term "living Constitution." Echoing the arguments that the NAACP's attorneys had used before the Court,[11] and drawing upon the research that he had conducted for Felix Frankfurter while serving as the Justice's law clerk in 1953,[12] Bickel drew a distinction between "the congressional understanding of the immediate effect of the [Fourteenth Amendment] on conditions then present" and "the long-range effect, under future circumstances, of provisions necessarily intended for permanence." With regard to the former notion, he conceded that "[t]he obvious conclusion to which the evidence . . . easily leads is that section I of the fourteenth amendment . . . was meant to apply neither to jury service, nor suffrage, nor antimiscegenation statutes, nor segregation." But, he insisted, "the fact that the proposed constitutional amendment was couched in more general terms could not have escaped those who voted for it." In other words, such language implied "a rejection presumably— as inappropriate in a constitutional provision—of such a specific and exclusive enumeration of rights as appeared in section I of the Civil Rights Act [of 1866]." Bickel hypothesized that the amendment's language may have been the result of a compromise between moderate and radical Republicans in the 39th Congress. The former individuals—in order to "defend themselves against charges that on the day after ratification Negroes were going to become white men's 'social equals,' marry their daughters, vote in their elections, sit on their juries, and attend schools with their children"—sought to avoid terms that explicitly endorsed radical changes in race relations. The radical elements in the party, however, would agree to nothing less than language that was "sufficiently elastic to permit reasonable future advances."[13]

Given the weightiness of the evidence against the view that the framers and ratifiers of the Fourteenth Amendment specifically intended to do away with segregation, Bickel suggested that Chief Justice Warren "must" have been considering the broader notion of the original under-standing "when he termed the [historical] materials 'inconclusive.' "[14] Warren, however, clearly directed his statement regarding the indetermi-nacy of historical investigation to the specific intentions informing the Fourteenth Amendment. For the Chief Justice followed this comment with the observation that "[t]he most avid proponents of the post-War Amendments undoubtedly intended them to remove all legal distinctions among 'all persons born or naturalized in the United States,' " while "[t]heir opponents, just as certainly, were antagonistic to both the letter and the spirit of the Amendments and wished them to have the most lim-ited effect." "What others in Congress and the state legislatures had in mind," he said, "cannot be determined with any degree of certainty."[15] That Warren would risk appearing disingenuous by declaring the spe-cific intentions of the framers and ratifiers of the Fourteenth Amendment inscrutable seems less impolitic when one considers that Bickel's argu-ment regarding the meaning of that amendment was entirely lacking in evidentiary support and was thus just as vulnerable to criticism.[16]

Four years after *Brown*, Judge Learned Hand challenged the view that the "living Constitution" concept should extend to the rights con-tained in the Fourteenth Amendment (although he did not focus upon the matter of the historical legitimacy of this model of constitutional interpretation). The former federal appeals court judge insisted that, in a democracy committed to the rule of law, it is "absolutely essential to confine the power [of judicial review] to the need that evoked it: that is, it was and always has been necessary to distinguish between the fron-tiers of another 'Department's' authority and the propriety of its choices within those frontiers." Hand, however, was at a loss to articulate a stan-dard that would limit the power of review when judges did not link the meaning of the Constitution's provisions to the original intentions of the framers of that document. Immediately after referring to the *Brown* decision, he confessed that he could not "frame any definition that will explain when the Court will assume the role of a third legisla-tive chamber and when it will limit its authority to keeping Congress and the states within their accredited authority." Stating that it was "quite clear that it has not abdicated its former function," he said he had "never been able to understand on what basis it does or can rest except as a *coup de main*."[17]

The Empirical Critique

In a famous response to Judge Hand, Herbert Wechsler suggested that the Supreme Court does not necessarily "function as a naked power organ" when exercises of judicial review are not grounded in the intentions of the framers. Echoing Hand's commitment to the rule of law, he said he did not "depreciate the duty of fidelity to the text of the Constitution, when its words may be decisive," or "deny that history has weight in the elucidation of the text," or "deem precedent without importance." Nevertheless, he did not "regret that interpretation [of the Due Process and Equal Protection Clauses] did not ground itself in ancient history but rather has perceived in these provisions a compendious affirmation of the basic values of a free society. . . ." In defense of the notion of a "living Constitution," he said that he preferred to see these and "the other clauses of the Bill of Rights read as an affirmation of the special values they embody rather than as statements of a finite rule of law, its limits fixed by the consensus of a century long past, with problems very different from our own." To identify "a middle ground between a judicial House of Lords" (which Hand feared would result when the Court left "room for adaptation and adjustment" in constitutional interpretation) "and the abandonment of any limitation on the other branches" (which Hand counseled when the traditional materials of interpretation do not afford adequate guidance to judges) Wechsler offered the following:

> I put to you that the main constituent of the judicial process is precisely that it must be genuinely principled, resting with respect to every step that is involved in reaching judgment on analysis and reasons quite transcending the immediate result that is achieved. To be sure, the courts decide, or should decide, only the case they have before them. But must they not decide on grounds of adequate neutrality and generality, tested not only by the instant application but by others that the principles imply?[18]

Wechsler did not deny the realist insight that judicial decisionmaking—even that rooted in neutral principles of adjudication—involves value choices or discretion. Indeed, he conceded "that courts in constitutional determinations face issues that are inescapably 'political' . . . in that they involve a choice among competing values or desires, a choice reflected in the legislative or executive action in question, which the court must either condemn or condone." But he rejected the conclusion that evidence of value choices on the part of judges necessarily renders courts and legislatures equivalent institutions. "No legislature or executive," he observed, "is obligated by the nature of its function to support its choice of values by the type of reasoned explanation that I have suggested is intrinsic to judicial action. . . ." While a decision that "rests on reasons with respect to all the issues in the case—reasons that in their generality and their neutrality transcend any immediate result that is involved," is not devoid of discretion, it is nevertheless distinguishable from "an act of willfulness or will." One would be mistaken to conclude that this contrast between methods of decision-making amounts to a distinction without a difference, Weschler believed. For the restraints that the requirement of principled decision-making places upon judges are substantive, not merely stylistic. "When no sufficient reasons of this kind can be assigned for overturning value choices of the other branches of the Government or of a state," Weschler explained, "those choices must . . . survive."[19]

Weschler was not so naïve as to believe that, invariably, judges remain passive in the absence of principled arguments for their rulings, strong though the social expectations for normatively appropriate judicial behavior may be. Indeed, he concluded that the *Brown* decision, with which he was careful to express his sympathy, represented just such an instance of result-oriented decision-making on the part of the Court. "[F]or one of my persuasion . . . ," he confessed, "the school decision . . . stirs the deepest conflict I experience in testing the thesis I propose." Besides agreeing with the result in the case, he emphasized (consistent with his defense of the "living Constitution") that he did not find troubling the Court's refusal to abide by the traditional materials of constitutional interpretation: "[T]he words [of the Fourteenth Amendment] are general and leave room for expanding content as time passes and conditions change." His "problem [with the decision] inhere[d] strictly in the reasoning of the opinion"—the fact that "the separate-but-equal formula . . . was held to have 'no place' in public education on the ground that segregated schools are 'inherently unequal,' with deleterious effects upon the colored children in implying their inferiority, effects which retard their educational and mental development." The Court's treatment of social fact, or the supposed harms of segregation, he believed, hardly seemed sufficient to justify the result in the present case, let alone to provide adequate guidance in cases that might follow. The social scientists and expert witnesses in the lower courts were not of one mind that segregation has the negative effects that the Court mentioned. And it was not clear whether the witnesses who acknowledged such harm compared the "position [of the black child] under separation with that under integration where the whites were hostile to his presence and found ways to make their feelings known," or whether the point of comparison was simply "an integrated school where he was happily accepted and regarded by the whites." Similarly, Wechsler wondered whether the Court denied the existence and relevance of "the benefits that [segregation] entailed," such as a "sense of security" for black children or "the absence of hostility," and whether the Justices thought that the perception in certain black communities that such benefits existed was insufficient to sustain segregation.[20]

In view of these obvious problems, Wechsler found "it hard to think the judgment [in *Brown*] really turned upon the facts." He also recognized the significance of subsequent per curiam decisions, in which the Court—citing *Brown* as precedent, but without explanation—invalidated state-maintained segregated parks, beaches and bath houses, golf courses, and public transportation. These later decisions, he thought, indicated that the Justices regarded *Brown* as based upon more than the negative effects of segregation upon black schoolchildren.[21] Anticipating the arguments of future defenders of *Brown*,[22] he hypothesized that the decision "rested [instead] on the view that racial segregation is, in principle, a denial of equality to the minority against whom it is directed; that is, the group that is not dominant politically and, therefore, does not make the choice involved." Yet he did not find this alternative assessment of social fact any less problematic. Such a position, he believed, "involve[s] an inquiry into the motive of the legislature, which is generally foreclosed to the courts" because of the vagaries of the enterprise. Moving from the motives of the alleged oppressors to the perceptions of the oppressed, he wondered whether it is "defensible to make the measure of validity of legislation the way it is interpreted by those who are affected by it?" "In the context of a charge that segregation *with equal facilities* is a denial of equality," he asked, "is there not a point in *Plessy* in the statement that if 'enforced separation stamps the colored race with a badge of inferiority' it is solely because its members choose 'to put that construction upon it'?" After all, few would conclude that "enforced separation of the sexes discriminate[s] against females merely because it may be the females who resent it and it is imposed by judgments predominantly male."[23]

Wechsler thought that a more promising rationale for the result in *Brown* would have characterized segregation, "not [as a problem] of discrimination at all," but as a "denial by the state of freedom to associate, a denial that impinges in the same way on any groups or races that may be involved." Yet, while he thought "that the Southern white also pays heavily for segregation, not only in the sense of guilt that he must carry but also in the benefits he is denied," he acknowledged that "integration forces an association upon those for whom it is unpleasant or repugnant." Sadly, he confessed that he could not discover "a basis in neutral principles for holding that the Constitution demands that the claims for association should prevail" over the desires of those who would avoid it. In the absence of a principled argument, Wechsler was prepared to affirm the illegitimacy of *Brown*. For he reiterated that "the courts ought to be cautious to impose a choice of values on the other branches or a state, based upon the Constitution, only when they are persuaded, on an adequate and principled analysis, that the choice is clear." Adherence to this norm of behavior, he believed, "is all that self-restraint can mean and in that sense it always is essential, whatever issue may be posed."[24]

Persons less sympathetic to the result in *Brown* were content to take Wechsler at his word that there existed no alternative basis for the decision. They set about, instead, to demonstrate the vulnerability of the Court's empirical claims regarding segregation. Ernest van den Haag challenged the validity of the social science evidence to which the Court referred. Confessing that he was "doubtful . . . about the wisdom of the decision in the desegregation cases" as well as the sufficiency of the Court's evidence, van den Haag went well beyond Wechsler's abstract musings regarding the effects of segregation. As John W. Davis had done on behalf of certain of the defendants during oral argument, van den Haag took direct aim at Kenneth Clark, who had been the chief witness for the petitioners, and whose research the Court placed first among the social science studies listed in the eleventh footnote of the *Brown* decision. He found Clark's conclusions disturbingly lacking in empirical support. Indeed, like Davis, van den Haag argued that Clark's doll study—in which the researcher offered black children a choice between a black and a white doll—did more to harm than help the cause of the petitioners in *Brown*. A comparison between the responses of black children in segregated and non-segregated schools "shows that 'they do not differ' except that *Negro children in segregated schools 'are less pronounced in their preference for the white doll' and more often think of the colored dolls as 'nice' or identify with them.*" Van den Haag concluded: "[I]f Professor Clark's tests do demonstrate damage to Negro children, then they demonstrate that the damage is *less* with segregation and *greater* with congregation."[25]

A. James Gregor agreed with van den Haag's contention and offered his support in the form of a review of relevant social science literature. Sharply critical of the empirical case for the petitioners in *Brown*, Gregor characterized the evidence presented to the Court as a collection of "suppositions" that "traffic on the promissory notes of vague hypotheticals and surmise." Focusing on a weakness that had concerned the NAACP's lawyers, he suggested that "[l]ittle if any direct evidence of the impairments attributable to school segregation *per se* is tendered. . . . The closest approximation to the real issue before the Court is in the discussion of 'segregation' [in the petitioners' social science appendix to their brief], which in itself covers a host of ill-defined situations: housing, recreational facilities, public conveniences, transportation, and eating places as well as nursery, grammar, secondary schools, colleges, and universities."[26] "The evident disposition to avoid any discussion of the available evidence with respect to school segregation *per se*," he surmised, "is conceivably the result of an awareness that whatever evidence *is* available *tends* to support racial separation in the schools at least throughout childhood and adolescence." For Gregor drew attention to studies which indicated that "racial separation may materially enhance the formation of a coherent self-system on the part of the Negro by reducing the psychological pressure to which the child is subjected." In an ironic paraphrase of Warren's language in *Brown,* he said: "[*I*]*ntegration* gives every evidence of creating insurmountable tensions for the individual Negro child and impairing his personality in a manner never likely to be undone."[27]

Scholarly Defenses of *Brown*

Early Apologias

Efforts to defend the empirical basis of the *Brown* decision actually began several years before Wechsler, van den Haag, and Gregor—among others—questioned the validity of the social science evidence to which the Court referred. Indeed, in the year following the decision, Edmond Cahn anticipated and sought to answer such criticism. Rather than stand by the social scientists and their work, however, Cahn sought to de-emphasize their significance for the ruling. He regarded as a "genuine danger" the mistaken belief that the outcome of the desegregation decisions, "either entirely or in major part, was caused by the testimony and opinions of the scientists." For he "would not have the constitutional rights of Negroes—or of other Americans—rest on any such flimsy foundations as some of the scientific demonstrations in these records." Cahn contended that some of Clark's interpretations of his data seemed to be "predetermined." And, heralding Gregor's critique, he observed that Clark's doll test did not reveal the effects of *school* segregation. "If it disclosed anything about the effects of segregation on the children," he said, "their experiences at school were not differentiated from other causes." But Cahn maintained that, "Fortunately, the outcome of the *Brown* and *Bolling* cases did not depend on the psychological experts' [*sic*] facing and answering the objections, queries, and doubts I have presented." "The cruelty [of segregation to black children] is obvious and evident," he explained. In fact, "it is so very obvious that the Justices of the Supreme Court could see it and act on it even after reading the labored attempts by plaintiffs' experts to demonstrate it 'scientifically.' " Cahn characterized Warren's decision to make reference to the studies as a mere "gesture" of "courtesy" from a "magnanimous judge" to the "devoted efforts [of the plaintiffs] to defeat segregation."[28] As Monroe Berger suggested in an article that paralleled Cahn's conclusions, the Court could "simply have stated, quite baldly, that it took 'judicial notice' of the fact that segregation means inequality"; "it could have ignored [the social science materials] completely without changing its decision in the slightest."[29]

Responses to Cahn from several scholars who defended the petitioners' and the Court's use of social science evidence reveal that van den Haag and Gregor had ample reason to believe that they were not wasting their efforts when attempting to discredit *Brown* by attacking the studies contained in the decision's eleventh footnote. Had the Court not made reference to social science evidence, William Ball wondered, "could it have counter[ed] the objection of the state attorneys general, who said . . . that they agreed that Negroes and whites should enjoy equality, but that the separate facilities furnished provided such 'equality'?"[30] In other words, judges may take judicial notice only of facts that are not properly the subject of testimony, or which are universally recognized as common knowledge. Neither circumstance applied in *Brown,* at least as far as a substantial portion of the American population in 1954 was concerned. Indeed, as Herbert Garfinkel noted (using the words of Thurgood Marshall, the NAACP's lead attorney in *Brown,* to make his point): " 'Acceptance of the [sic] segregation under the "separate but equal" doctrine ha[d] become so ingrained that overwhelming proof was sorely needed to demonstrate that equal educational opportunities for Negroes could not be provided in a segregated system.' "[31] Clark added that "[t]his was not the first time that the lawyers of the NAACP had sought to convince the Supreme Court of the United States that segregation in and of itself was unconstitutional." He thought it more than mere coincidence that "the lawyers of the NAACP succeeded in overruling the *Plessy* doctrine only after they enlisted an impressive array of social science testimony and talent and attacked the problem with this approach."[32]

Although these proved compelling responses to Cahn, an effective defense of the Court required of Clark and his colleagues equally effective rejoinders to van den Haag and Gregor. Garfinkel, however, provided a critique of Clark's research that rivaled that of van den Haag.[33] And Clark defended his integrity and that of the social scientists rather than the usefulness of their findings. He took umbrage at Cahn's implication "that the primary motive of the social psychologists who participated in these cases was not 'strict fidelity to objective truth.' " And, with regard to his failure to control for the effect of public school segregation on the personalities of black children, he insisted he had been well aware of the limitations of his research and had pointed out to the NAACP's lawyers "that the available studies had so far not isolated this single variable from the total social complexity of racial prejudice, discrimination, and segregation."[34]

While Garfinkel was unwilling to maintain the validity of the social-science evidence relating to the harms of segregation, he alluded to a seemingly more promising strategy to defend the *Brown* decision when he suggested that *Plessy v. Ferguson* was no less dependent upon controversial empirical assumptions. "[T]he opinion in *Plessy* might well have cited the social science 'modern authority' of its day to support some aspects of its position," he contended. For "[a]t that time psychologists did believe in the inherent intellectual inferiority of the Negro, and most sociologists and political scientists did believe that 'stateways do not make folkways.' That the 1896 Court did not choose to cite expert authorities does not alter the nature of these questions or the relevancy of the evidence."[35] Garfinkel, however, relegated these observations to the conclusion of his essay and thus left their meaning and force undeveloped.

Barton Bernstein illuminated Garfinkel's point with a more elaborate rendering and critique of the empirical basis of the *Plessy* decision. In maintaining the reasonableness, and thus the constitutionality, of Louisiana's segregation statute, Bernstein claimed, Justice Henry Billings Brown "wrote conservative theory and the prevailing social science 'truths' into law." More specifically, "[t]he court explained that the standard of reasonableness is determined 'with reference to the established usages, customs, and traditions of the people.'" While Brown thought that the segregation statute was reasonable because it observed custom with a view to preserving public peace and good order, he regarded the petitioner's argument as plainly contrary to reason because it reflected the mistaken belief "that 'social prejudices may be overcome by legislation.'" In concluding "that 'legislation is powerless to eradicate racial instincts,'" Bernstein noted, Brown drew upon the tenets of "the popular sociology which emerged after the Civil War." For "most sociologists" at the time were "good Spencerians," who believed "that society, the organism of evolution, could not be refashioned by legislation." As "William Graham Sumner explained[,] . . . 'legislation cannot make mores' and stateways cannot change folkways." More than this, "Franklin Henry Giddings . . . had emphasized 'consciousness of kind,' a new guise for the 'racial instincts' concept, to explain segregation. The implication in *Plessy* was that this social custom, the desire for racially segregated facilities, was grounded in 'race instincts.' These instincts were unchangeable before man-made law."[36]

Bernstein took issue with Justice Brown's "questionable factual allegations" and "dubious legal and scientific theories." Without elaborating, he characterized as "poor history" Brown's suggestion that social attitudes cannot be shaped by law. But, even if it were the case that legislation is powerless to eradicate prejudice, Bernstein noted, a declaration of unconstitutionality in *Plessy* would not have been equivalent to legislation forcing racial commingling. Rather, a ruling in favor of the petitioners would have done no more than preclude laws enforcing racial separation in transportation. "The practices of railroads and the social habits of passengers would not have been immediately affected. The prevailing policy would have been maintained: where informal segregation existed, it would have remained; where commingling occurred, it would have continued." As for Brown's belief that segregation statutes were reflective of racial instincts—were part of a long-standing effort to avoid the baleful effects of racial prejudice through the curtailment of interracial contact—Bernstein insisted, first, that such laws were inconsistent with custom or tradition. Drawing upon the research of C. Vann Woodward, among other historians, he said: "When the *Plessy* court judged it custom, Jim Crow transportation was but a recent Southern creation. By 1896 only eight Southern states had such laws, and seven of the statutes were less than eight years old." Next, he suggested that southern states did not need these laws to stem racial conflict, for historical investigations of the post-bellum era reveal that "Negroes and whites frequently shared the same coaches" without incident. As "[a] South Carolinian remarked in 1877[,] . . . Negroes in his state 'were permitted to, and frequently do ride in first-class railway and street cars.' At first this had caused trouble, but it was then 'so common as hardly to provoke remark.' "[37]

Unlike Bernstein, Garfinkel recognized the obvious problem with efforts to shift scholarly and legal attention from the controversial nature of the holding in *Brown* to the vulnerability of the empirical basis of *Plessy.* Unfortunately, Garfinkel's attempt to meet the conventional view that the Court had always extended a presumption of constitutionality to segregation legislation was as cursory as his discussion of Justice Brown's reliance upon the sociological assumptions of his day. Garfinkel simply declared that a presumption of constitutionality (which, in placing the burden of proof upon challengers to legislation, liberated southern states from having to do anything more than demonstrate a basis in reason for segregation laws) "is of questionable materiality to the school segregation cases. The burden of proof is placed on the legislatures in these cases, requiring that they demonstrate that their statutory restrictions on the relations of Negroes and whites do not violate the equal protection and due process requirements of the Constitution."[38]

Garfinkel might have defended this view by noting, as did Louis Pollak, that, in the federal desegregation case *Bolling v. Sharpe*,[39] the Court invoked the Japanese curfew and exclusion cases of 1943 and 1944, respectively, to identify racial classifications as constitutionally suspect.[40] In so doing, to use Pollak's words, the Court "could not . . . sustain the reasonableness of these racial distinctions and the absence of harm said to flow from them, unless [the Justices] were prepared to say that no factual case can be made the other way."[41] But, in view of the fact that the Court failed to provide an explanation for its placement of the burden of proof in the curfew and exclusion cases, as well as in the desegregation cases, Pollak could not have expected that his observation would help to quell criticism of the Justices. Persons sympathetic to the results in the desegregation cases, as well as persons alarmed by the decisions, would have been justified in demanding such an explanation from the Court, because *Brown* and *Bolling*, unlike the Japanese curfew and exclusion cases, involved the *invalidation* of governmental action.

Brown Recast

Charles Black provided the earliest and most compelling scholarly defense of the view that the Court had ample reason to expect the defenders of racial segregation to assume the burden of justifying the constitutionality of the practice. Although Black expressed his indebtedness to Pollak, he noted rightly that his rationale for *Brown* differed from that of his colleague. Where Pollak said that he "[did] not think it incumbent upon [him], at least for present purposes, to resolve controversies as to the justification for and impact of Jim Crow legislation,"[42] Black took it upon himself to demonstrate that "segregation is a massive intentional disadvantaging of the Negro race, as such, by state law." In arguing that segregation "[is] a system which is set up and continued for the very purpose of keeping [a whole race] in an inferior station," he scorned Wechsler's refusal to assess the motives of southern legislators. While Black acknowledged "the entirely sincere protestations of many southerners that segregation is 'better' for the Negroes . . . [and] is not intended to hurt them," he believed that "a little probing would demonstrate that what is meant is that it is better for the Negroes to accept a position of inferiority at least for the indefinite future."[43]

Turning first to history, Black contended that "[s]egregation in the South comes down in apostolic succession from slavery and the *Dred Scott* case. The South fought to keep slavery, and lost. Then it tried the Black Codes, and lost. Then it looked around for something else and found segregation." To support his impressionistic view that "[t]he movement for segregation was an integral part of the movement to maintain and further 'white supremacy,' " he, like Bernstein, made reference to the work of C. Vann Woodward. "Professor Woodward has shown," he maintained, that "[segregation's] triumph . . . represented a triumph of extreme racialist over moderate sentiment about the Negro." But even without resorting to the scholarship of such a respected academic figure, Black believed, "[h]istory . . . tells us that segregation was imposed on one race by the other race; consent was not invited or required. Segregation in the South grew up and is kept going because and only because the white race has wanted it that way— an incontrovertible fact which in itself hardly consorts with equality." An accurate picture of southern race relations, in short, is "not [one] of mutual separation of whites and Negroes, but of one in-group enjoying full normal communal life and one out-group that is barred from this life and forced into an inferior life of its own."[44]

Black defended the view that the non-involvement of blacks in the construction of southern society secured the group's inferior status therein by noting that "[s]egregation is historically and contemporaneously associated in a functioning complex with practices which are indisputably and grossly discriminatory." He drew his reader's attention to "the long-continued and still largely effective exclusion of Negroes from voting." One could not believe seriously that "segregation [was] not intended to harm the segregated race, or to stamp it with the mark of inferiority," he said, when, "at about the same time [that segregation occurred], the very same group of people . . . [was] barred . . . from the common political life of the community—from all political power."

Black also noted that, "generally speaking, segregation is the pattern of law in communities where the extralegal patterns of discrimination against Negroes are the tightest, where Negroes are subjected to the strictest codes of 'unwritten law' as to job opportunities, social intercourse, patterns of housing, going to the back door, being called by the first name, saying 'Sir,' and all the rest of the whole sorry business." While not state action, these oppressive cultural norms "assist us in understanding the meaning and assessing the impact of [contemporaneous] state action." Finally, the fact that " '[s]eparate but equal' facilities are almost never really equal" provides clear "evidence of what segregation means to the people who impose it and to the people who are subjected to it." Black asked rhetorically, "Can a system which, in all that can be measured, has practiced the grossest inequality, actually have been 'equal' in intent, in total social meaning and impact?" His answer was a direct response to Wechsler's stated incertitude about the nature of apartheid: "[S]egregation, in all visible things, speaks only haltingly any dialect but that of inequality."[45]

Indeed, Black believed that to suggest otherwise—or even to express uncertainty about the nature of segregation—is not to take a reasonable, alternative position on a contested issue but to engage in "self-induced blindness" and to perpetuate a "flagrant contradiction of known fact." While he "[did] not maintain that the evidence is all one way" ("it never is on issues of burning, fighting concern"), he thought the case "so onesided" that he could not appreciate Wechsler's concerns over judicial fact-finding. Even if one accepts "the good faith of those who assert that segregation represents no more than an attempt to furnish a wholesome opportunity for parallel development of the races," and one acknowledges "the few scattered instances [segregationists] can bring forward to support their view of the matter," there could be no doubt, Black thought, about "which balance-pan flies upward" in any objective weighing of the competing claims at issue. Going beyond a mere summary of his earlier observations, he said:

> The society that has just lost the Negro as a slave, that has just lost out in an attempt to put him under quasi-servile 'Codes,' the society that views his blood as a contamination and his name as an insult, the society that extralegally imposes on him every humiliating mark of low caste and that until yesterday kept him in line by lynching—this society,

> careless of his consent, moves by law, first to exclude him from voting,
> and secondly to cut him off from mixing in the general public life of
> the community. . . . .
>
> [In view of these "matters of common notoriety,"] it would be the
> most unneutral of principles, improvised *ad hoc,* to require that a court
> faced with the present problem refuse to note a plain fact about the soci-
> ety of the United States—the fact that the social meaning of segregation is
> the putting of the Negro in a position of walled-off inferiority—or the
> other equally plain fact that such treatment is hurtful to human beings.[46]

Convinced of the force of this argument, Black speculated that
Wechsler possessed "no actual doubt . . . as to what segregation is for and
what kind of societal pattern it supports and implements." Rather, his
colleague seemed concerned that "there is no ritually sanctioned way in
which the Court, as a Court, can permissibly learn what is obvious to
everybody else and to the Justices as individuals."[47] Black also thought
(as did Wechsler)[48] that the Justices likewise regarded segregation as
oppressive, and that this belief (as opposed to "the formally 'scientific'
authorities, which are relegated to a footnote and treated as merely cor-
roboratory of common sense") formed the true basis of *Brown.* Black
suspected that the Court's failure to "[spell] out that segregation . . . is
perceptibly a means of ghettoizing the imputedly inferior race" was
caused by a "reluctance to go into the distasteful details of the southern
caste system." This "venial fault" of the opinion aside, he reiterated that
the Justices "had the soundest reasons for judging that segregation violates the fourteenth amendment." The Court could acknowledge the
oppressive nature of segregation, just "as it advises itself of the facts that
we are a 'religious people,' [or] that the country is more industrialized
than in Jefferson's day. . . ."[49]

Perhaps aware that many (including Wechsler) would challenge the
fairness of these analogies, and that his argument (like Cahn's) would
thus not square with the doctrine of judicial notice, he called upon the
legal community to "[develop] ways to make it permissible for the Court
to use what it knows." The absence of a formal mechanism for resolv-
ing disputes over abstract social facts, however, did not dampen his faith
in the accuracy of the Court's assessment of social reality in the segregation decisions. "[S]urely," he declared, "the fact that the Court has
assumed as true a matter of common [if not universal] knowledge in
regard to broad societal patterns, is (to say the very least) pretty far down

the list of things to protest against." Black expressed confidence "that in the end the decisions will be accepted by the profession" on the basis that "the segregation system is actually conceived and does actually function as a means of keeping the Negro in a status of inferiority."[50]

In the same way that the Little Rock integration crisis of 1957–1958 must have confirmed for Black (if it did not inspire his assessment of) the oppressive nature of segregation, events in the years immediately following the publication of Black's essay would make it almost impossible for others to accept alternative interpretations of the practice. Specifically, the mistreatment and violence that black children endured when attempting to enter formerly white schools, and the hostility that young civil rights workers experienced during non-violent protests at segregated lunch counters, restaurants, libraries, theaters, beaches, motels, and swimming pools, did much to illuminate the brutality of apartheid. The events in Birmingham, Alabama during the spring of 1963, perhaps more than any other occurrence, solidified this understanding of segregation in the nation's collective conscience and, in so doing, helped to establish an exalted status for *Brown*. News viewers witnessed club-wielding patrolmen, vicious police dogs, and high-pressure water hoses which the city's police commissioner, Eugene "Bull" Connor, unleashed upon Martin Luther King, Jr. and the peaceful protesters he led. Tragically, thousands of black children were among those who experienced the fury of Connor's forces. Henceforth, Americans would have great difficulty accepting southern protestations that segregation reflected consideration for the welfare of blacks.[51]

Within the legal community, Wechsler's concern over the difficulties involved in ascertaining the legislative motives behind segregation lost considerable force. Indeed, Bickel's restatement of Wechsler's argument, compelling though it may have seemed in 1962, served the ironic function the following year of illuminating the hollowness of that concern. To demonstrate the "inscrutable" nature of such motives, he asked:

> Who is to say that the majority of a legislature which enacts a statute segregating the schools is actuated by a conscious desire to suppress and humiliate the Negro? Who is to say that for many members more decent feelings are not decisive—the feeling, for example, that under existing circumstances Negro children are better off and can be more effectively educated in schools reserved exclusively for them, and that this is the most hopeful road to the goal of equality of the races under law?[52]

As events demonstrated, black children may well have been in less danger in separate schools. But the ferocity that state governments directed toward peaceful protest groups comprised, in part, of children, and the fact that state troopers acted to intimidate rather than to protect black students, enabled scholars and jurists to assume that negative effects stemming from the illicit motives behind segregation outweighed any benefits that legislative and executive officials may have anticipated for black children.

In diminishing the basis for concern over the ascertainment of the legislative motives behind segregation, the events of the early 1960s lent credence to Black's belief that the oppressive nature of segregation was a social fact capable of judicial notice. In Bickel's words: "To determine that segregation establishes a relationship of the inferior to the superior race is to take objective notice of a fact of our national life and of experience elsewhere in the world, now and in other times. . . . It is no different from a similarly experiential judgment that official inquiries into private associations inhibit the freedom to join, or that hearsay evidence . . . has a tendency to become distorted." Having said this in the same work in which he expressed concern over the difficulty of discovering the intentions of southern legislators, however, Bickel added that one could make such an observation about segregation "quite without reference to legislative motives and without reliance on [the] subjective and perhaps idiosyncratic feelings [of blacks]."[53] But, like Black, Bickel could not expect near-universal agreement over the oppressive nature of segregation until circumstances deprived southerners of self-serving rationales for the practice. In short, as Joseph Tussman and Jacobus tenBroek observed in an article published five years before *Brown,* it "is indeed difficult to see that anything else is involved in . . . discriminatory legislative cases than questions of motivation" . . . "[l]aws are invalidated by the Court as discriminatory because they are expressions of hostility or antagonism to certain groups of individuals." In a passage that anticipated Black's recasting of the basis of *Brown,* they added: "Should the temper of the Court change, it could, no doubt, find that segregation laws aim at white supremacy or are spawned of the great anti-Negro virus and thus make belated amends for the shameful history of the 'separate but equal' evasion."[54]

Transposed Reputations

The upshot of developments following the publication of Black's defense of *Brown* was the vindication of his predictions regarding the legal profession's eventual acceptance of the decision and the basis upon which this outcome would take place. Indeed, opponents as well as proponents of the view that the "living Constitution" concept extends to individual rights as well as governmental powers have accepted not only the legitimacy of *Brown* but the greatness of the decision as well. As Michael Perry suggests, "*Brown* . . . is generally thought to represent the Court at its best."[55] And, while few contemporary scholars would dispute Perry's view or Gerald Gunther's claim that *Brown* "was an entirely legitimate decision,"[56] most do not believe that Warren's opinion reflected the Court's true rationale for the ruling. In the words of Philip Kurland: "It would take an extraordinarily sophisticated, or perhaps an extraordinarily naïve, approach to judicial behavior to believe that the cited [social science] literature was the cause of the Court's judgment rather than the result of it."[57] Or, as Robert Bork suggests, "nobody who read *Brown* believed for a moment that the decision turned on social science studies about such matters as the preference of black children for white or black dolls. . . ."[58] The certitude with which Bork made this historically inaccurate statement reflects just how far the legal profession has moved from the arguments of van den Haag, Gregor, Ball, and Garfinkel.

With regard to the conventional understanding of the actual basis of *Brown*, J. Harvie Wilkinson reveals how contemporary legal scholars exhibit none of Wechsler's reluctance to question the nature of segregation, or to characterize *Brown* as an attack upon the motives that most now agree informed the practice. According to Wilkinson, *Brown* was "one of the last, great actions whose moral logic seemed so uncomplex and irrefutable," because the "opposition [to the decision] seemed so thoroughly extreme, rooted as it was in notions of racial hegemony and the constitutional premises of John C. Calhoun."[59] Surely, Black felt a certain satisfaction when Mark Yudof, seconding Wilkinson's point, invoked Black's essay as support for the proposition that "*Brown* was premised on the notion that state statutes and constitutions that require the separation of white and black children in the public schools are designed to and have the effect of stigmatizing black Americans as inferior beings."[60]

Brown's ascendance in status occasioned a corresponding decline in the reputation of the *Plessy* decision. As David Strauss contends, the decision in which the Court placed its imprimatur upon the "separate but equal" doctrine "is now universally condemned."[61] Few scholars would regard as excessive Perry's statement that *Plessy* was a "ridiculous and shameful opinion."[62] *Plessy,* Richard Posner explains, "had come to seem, in the fullness of time, bad ethics and bad politics."[63] Indeed, Wilkinson characterizes the opinion in that case as "a warehouse of segregationist 'truths' that echo through our history."[64] Similarly, and in sharp contrast to Wechsler's refusal to criticize the logic of *Plessy,* Bruce Ackerman states: "Whatever Justice Brown . . . might have thought, it is now absurd to dismiss the 'badge of inferiority' imposed by state officials as they shunt black children to segregated schools as if it were 'solely' the product of a 'choice' by the 'colored race' . . . to put [a degrading] construction upon it."[65]

Scholars now contrast the abstract nature of Justice Brown's majority opinion in *Plessy* with the striking candor of John Marshall Harlan's dissent in that case. Perry, for example, notes that, unlike the *Plessy* majority, Harlan was willing to face the "undeniable fact" that segregation was "rooted in white-supremacist ideology." For, "in one of the most prophetic dissents ever penned by a Supreme Court Justice, [Harlan] protested: "We boast of the freedom enjoyed by our people above all other peoples. But it is difficult to reconcile that boast with a state of the law which, practically, puts the brand of servitude and degradation upon a large class of our fellow-citizens, our equals before the law."[66] H. N. Hirsch expresses a similar admiration for Harlan's dissent, which, he says, "makes clear . . . [that] 'separate but equal' can be interpreted as constitutional only by the most stubborn refusal to face social facts."[67]

While the transposed reputations of *Plessy* and *Brown* served to vindicate Charles Black, this shift made a controversial figure of Herbert Wechsler, the most visible of *Brown's* more credible critics. As events in the 1960s began to give substance to Black's discussion of the oppressive nature of segregation, Wechsler became a lightning rod for the invective of *Brown's* defenders. Indeed, a number of scholars went so far as to charge him with jurisprudential naiveté. Arthur Miller and Ronald Howell declared that Wechsler's counsel of "[a]dherence to neutral principles . . . [was a call for the discovery of] principles which do not refer to value choices."[68] And Martin Shapiro characterized his constitutional jurisprudence as little more than an echo of "the traditional myth of the impersonal, nonpolitical, law-finding judge whose decisions are the results of the inexorable logic of the law and not of his own preferences and discretion."[69]

In response, Wechsler reiterated that he "[did] not deny that constitutional provisions are directed to protecting certain special values or that the principled development of a particular provision is concerned with the value or the values thus involved."[70] And he claimed that he "never thought the principle of neutral principles offers a court a guide to exercising its authority, in the sense of a formula that indicates how cases ought to be decided."[71]

Wechsler would require the aid of others to respond to the somewhat more mannerly criticism that he was "more misleading than enlightening" regarding what the doctrine of neutral principles implies, and was thus irresponsible in challenging a decision that "struck a tremendous blow for the Declaration of Independence, the Gettysburg Address, and the fourteenth amendment, not to mention our position in a world in which a majority of the people are not white."[72] To clarify Wechsler's position, M. P. Golding suggested that "[n]eutrality and generality are to be found not in the *content* of the law but in its *application* or *administration*."[73] Adhering to the same view, Louis Henkin elaborated: "[A] court should not announce a principle if it is . . . not intended to be applicable in a general area in which no legitimate distinctions are apparent."[74] In short, the basic elements of Wechsler's doctrine of neutrality include uniformity of application (a decision ought to rest only on a principle that judges are willing to apply in other, similar contexts) and adequate generality (judges must articulate a principle broadly enough to make its scope of application fairly clear.)

Wechsler apparently accepted this formulation of his argument. He commented that courts should not "judge the instant case in terms that are quite plainly unacceptable in light of other cases that it is now clear are covered by the principle affirmed in reaching judgment and indistinguishable upon valid grounds." Returning, once again, to *Brown,* he elaborated upon the Court's failure to adhere to the formal requirement of neutrality in its opinion. Assuming the need to find a basis for the holding other than the vulnerable empirical argument that the Court offered, Wechsler argued that one "could not responsibly declare the principle that race is outlawed as a basis of official action." For, to provide adequate generality, the Justices "were required to anticipate the problem of benevolent [racial] quotas, which would be outlawed by the principle . . . [mentioned], and indicate if they considered them distinguishable."[75] The Court's failure to discuss the impact of the ruling "upon measures that take race into account to equalize job opportunity or to reduce *de facto* segregation" thus rendered the opinion in *Brown* unprincipled.[76]

While these observations may have saved Wechsler from the charge of incoherence, other comments he made subsequent to his initial criticism of *Brown* prompted vehement criticism from contemporary scholars who conclude that his constitutional jurisprudence is incompatible with judicial recognition of racial oppression. As one who *rejects* the view that Wechsler's neutral principles requirement precludes judicial acknowledgment of racial domination, Kent Greenawalt offers the following as a "principle [that] would satisfy Wechsler's demand [for neutrality]": "Racial classifications that disadvantage or stigmatize members of minority racial groups are unconstitutional unless they are necessitated by a very grave public need or, perhaps, unless they promote integration and the long-term advantage of those groups."[77] As Barbara Flagg points out, however, Wechsler indicated that Charles Black's justification of *Brown*, which is implicit in Greenawalt's principle, "would not allay his concerns."[78] Specifically, Wechsler confessed that he was "[unable] to accept [Black's and Pollak's] rationales as an answer to the difficulties [he had] raised." The principle in *Brown*, or any constitutional decision for that matter, he said, should have "a scope that is acceptable *whatever interest, group, or person may assert the claim.*"[79] Flagg concludes that Wechsler believed neutrality requires judges to avoid making "analytic outcomes turn on the identity of affected individuals" or the actual social status of groups.[80] Or, as Cass Sunstein observes, Wechsler thought that "[t]he existing distribution of power and resources as between blacks and whites should be taken by courts as simply 'there': neutrality lies in inaction; it is threatened when the Court 'takes sides' by preferring those disadvantaged."[81]

Echoing Black,[82] Gary Peller is willing to entertain the possibility that "Wechsler was not asserting that broad-scale racial domination did not exist." Rather, in spite of his defense of the "living Constitution" concept and the attendant belief that the meaning of constitutional provisions (including constitutional rights) is relative to time and circumstance, Wechsler was concerned about "the contingent and subjective nature of any evaluation of power in society." He thought that "[t]he determination whether broad scale social domination of blacks existed—so that the segregation in *Brown* would be seen as part of a larger social inequality—was a [subjective] value question," as opposed to an objective determination of fact. In spite of his protestations against his early critics, then, Wechsler apparently imposed a substantive, and not merely a formal, constraint upon judicial decision-making when he forbade judges to make this value choice. In Peller's view, however, "the actual distribution of wealth, jobs, political power, intellectual prestige, educational opportunity, housing, and social status between whites and blacks in fifties America" (to say nothing of the racial violence during the early 1960s) was more than sufficient to "prove the inequality that Wechsler could not find from the fact of segregated schools in *Brown*." Since Wechsler never wavered from his earlier position, Peller concludes, in a statement at odds with the measured tone of his initial assessment, that Wechsler "assumed that social domination of blacks either did not exist or that such a racial regime did not impugn the legitimacy of the legislature."[83]

Peller's criticism of Wechsler's "apologetic vision of American society,"[84] however, pales in contrast to that of David Richards. Borrowing from Black's analysis of *Brown,* Richards characterizes the decision "as an attempt to assure special protection to groups systematically denied the moral consideration due them." *Brown,* he believes, "reflects serious consideration of social facts of group prejudice and its unfair force in majoritarian politics." Wechsler's "summary dismissal of any kind of inquiry into legislative motives," by contrast, "evidences his refusal to take seriously familiar facts of social life, in this case, the force of the separate-but-equal doctrine as a formal mask of racial hatred." Wechsler's resulting conclusion that *Brown* is unprincipled and, therefore, illegitimate, Richards contends, reveals not only "the excessively formal character of his notion of 'neutral principles' " but a "striking failure of moral imagination" on his part as well.[85]

Conclusion

The near-universal agreement regarding *Brown's* greatness, and the invective visited upon those few individuals who would question the legitimacy of the decision, should not lead one to conclude that *Brown* is no longer the subject of scholarly controversy. Ironically, one contemporary debate focuses upon an issue that even the members of the Supreme Court in 1954 had conceded to defenders of segregation— *Brown's* apparent inconsistency with the intentions of the framers of the Fourteenth Amendment. The urgency that certain scholars exhibit in defending the view that *Brown* can be reconciled with traditional legal materials[86] stems, in part, from the fact that the decision has been a particularly effective weapon in the arsenal of defenders of the "living Constitution" concept.[87] As Michael McConnell notes: "[W]hat was once seen as a weakness in the Supreme Court's decision in *Brown*"—namely, the decision's nonconformity to the framers' intentions—"is now a mighty weapon against the proposition that the Constitution should be interpreted as it was understood by the people who framed and ratified it." Indeed, "[s]uch is the moral authority of *Brown* that if any particular theory [of judicial review] does not produce the conclusion that *Brown* was correctly decided, the theory is seriously discredited."[88]

A more pertinent line of inquiry from the perspective of the majority of scholars who accept *Brown's* irreconcilability with traditional materials of constitutional interpretation is the decision's import for current constitutional controversies involving race. While Wechsler was wrong about the legitimacy of *Brown,* he observed correctly that the decision did not provide clear guidance for controversies over "benevolent" racial classifications. Even the scholarly recasting of *Brown* in the 1960s did not afford such guidance, since a judicial attack upon institutions of white supremacy can be justified through resort to principles that legitimize such classifications as well as through reference to principles that are hostile to them. Not surprisingly, scholars who are convinced of the dangerousness of and the lack of the need for remedial racial classifications seek to enlist the moral authority of *Brown* by reconciling the decision with the color-blindness concept.[89] Similarly, scholars who are persuaded of the need for and the benign nature of affirmative action are equally intent to link *Brown* to the racial subordination concept, or the idea that government may not act to reinforce the subordinate status of a racial group but may employ racial classifications to aid the victims of discrimination.[90] This debate over *Brown's* legacy reinforces an important lesson of the battle over the legitimacy of the decision: that Supreme Court Justices are limited in their ability to give permanence to the meaning of their decisions. As the history of *Brown* demonstrates, the meaning of the Court's decisions is, at times, the result of a contest among political forces—forces that would use those decisions as symbols for political purposes.[91]

Endnotes

1. *Brown v. Board of Education of Topeka, Kansas,* 347 U.S. 483 (1954). *Brown* was one of four consolidated state cases involving racial segregation in public schools at the elementary and secondary school levels. The other three cases came from South Carolina (*Briggs v. Elliott*), Virginia (*Davis v. County School Board of Prince Edward County, Virginia*), and Delaware (*Gebhart v. Belton*). *Bolling v. Sharpe,* 347 U.S. 497 (1954), a companion case to *Brown,* involved the public schools of the District of Columbia, which were under the control of the national government.

2. *See, e.g.,* "A.F.L. Chief Hails Court," *The New York Times,* 18 May 1954, Late City edition; "Experts Approve Timetable on Bias," *The New York Times,* 18 May 1954, Late City edition; "Historians Laud Court's Decision," *The New York Times,* 18 May 1954, Late City edition; "Editorial Excerpts From the Nation's Press on Segregation Ruling," *The New York Times,* 18 May 1954, Late City edition.

3. *Plessy v. Ferguson,* 163 U.S. 537 (1896). In *Plessy,* the Supreme Court sustained the constitutionality of a Louisiana statute that required railroads to provide equal but separate accommodations to whites and blacks and forbade persons from occupying rail cars other than those to which their race had been assigned. The Court held that the law, like similar laws that established separate schools for white and black children, did not violate the equal protection clause of the Fourteenth Amendment. Rather than imply the inferiority of blacks, the Court argued, the law was simply a reasonable exercise of the state's police power to preserve public peace and good order.

4. Howard Gillman, "The Collapse of Constitutional Originalism and the Rise of the Notion of the 'Living Constitution' in the Course of American State-Building," *Studies in American Political Development* 11 (1997): 191–247.

5. Given the differences among the Justices after the 1952 deliberations on *Brown,* the Court ordered reargument of the segregation cases. In its reargument order,

the Court asked the parties to respond to a series of questions (which Justice Frankfurter formulated) that focused upon the history of the Fourteenth Amendment and the matter of enforcing a desegregation decree (Richard Kluger, **Simple Justice: The History of *Brown v. Board of Education* and Black America's Struggle for Equality,** 2 vols. (New York: Alfred A. Knopf, 1975), 2: 777–79; Felix Frankfurter, Memorandum for the Conference, Re: The Segregation Cases, 27 May 1953, Papers of Felix Frankfurter—Harvard Collection, Library of Congress, Manuscript Division, Part II, Reel 4. The questions relating to constitutional history and precedent in the Court's reargument order read:

1. What evidence is there that the Congress which submitted and the State legislatures and conventions which ratified the Fourteenth Amendment contemplated or did not contemplate, understood or did not understand, that it would abolish segregation in public schools?

2. If neither the Congress in submitting nor the States in ratifying the Fourteenth Amendment understood that compliance with it would require the immediate abolition of segregation in public schools, was it nevertheless the understanding of the framers of the Amendment (a) that future Congresses might, in the exercise of their power under Sec. 5 of the Amendment, abolish such segregation, or (b) that it would be within the judicial power, in light of future conditions, to construe the Amendment as abolishing such segregation of its own force?

3. On the assumption that the answers to questions 2 (a) and (b) do not dispose of the issue, is it within the judicial power, in construing the Amendment, to abolish segregation in public schools? (*Brown v. Board of Education of Topeka, Kansas,* 345 U.S. 972, 972–73 [1953]).

6. *Brown v. Board of Education of Topeka, Kansas,* 347 U.S. 483, 489 (1954) (emphasis added).

7. Congressional Record, House, vol. 102, Part 4, p.4515, March 12, 1956. *See also* Charles Fairman, "Foreword: The Attack on the Segregation Cases," *Harvard Law Review* 70 (1956): 83–94; Michael W. McConnell, "Originalism and the Desegregation Decisions," *Virginia Law Review* 81 (1995): 949, 1133–1134. For the arguments of the lawyers for the defendant school boards regarding the intentions informing the equal protection clause of the Fourteenth Amendment, *see* Leon Friedman, ed., **Argument: the Oral Argument Before the Supreme Court in *Brown v. Board of Education of Topeka,* 1952–55** (New York: Chelsea House, 1969), 207–213.

8. *Brown v. Board of Education of Topeka, Kansas,* 347 U.S. 483, 494 (1954). To demonstrate the inherent inequality of educational segregation, the NAACP's lawyers referred to social science studies that purportedly revealed the psychological harm that segregation inflicted upon black children. And, to demonstrate that educational segregation had no basis in reason, the Association referred to social science studies that attributed differences in the

educational performances of racial groups to environmental causes and that documented peaceable integration efforts in a number of social contexts. Appellants' Statement as to Jurisdiction, *Brown v. Board of Education of Topeka, Kansas,* 1951, 12–13, Papers of the National Association for the Advancement of Colored People, Library of Congress, Manuscript Division (hereafter cited as NAACP Papers), Box II-B-138; Brief for Appellants, *Brown v. Board of Education of Topeka, Kansas,* 1952, 6–10, NAACP Papers, Box II-B-138; Appendix to Appellants' Briefs, *Brown v. Board of Education of Topeka, Kansas, Briggs v. Elliott, and Davis v. County School Board of Prince Edward County, Virginia,* 1952, 3–10, 12–16, NAACP Papers, Box II-B-138.)

9. James Reston, "A Sociological Decision," *The New York Times,* 18 May 1954, Late City edition.

10. As quoted in Paul L. Rosen, **The Supreme Court and Social Science** (Urbana: University of Illinois Press, 1972), 174–75.

11. *See* Brief for Appellants in *Brown v. Board of Education of Topeka, Kansas, Briggs v. Elliott, and Davis v. County School Board of Prince Edward County, Virginia,* and for Respondents in *Gebhart v. Belton,* 1953, 18, 118–20, NAACP Papers, Box II-B-142.

12. One can find a copy of Bickel's memorandum for Justice Frankfurter (entitled, "Legislative History of the Fourteenth Amendment") in Papers of Robert H. Jackson, Library of Congress, Manuscript Division, Box 184.

13. Alexander M. Bickel, "The Original Understanding and the Segregation Decision," *Harvard Law Review* 69 (1955): 59, 58, 60, 62, 61. *See also* Alfred H. Kelly, "The Fourteenth Amendment Reconsidered," *Michigan Law Review* 54 (1956): 1049–86; Louis H. Pollak, "The Supreme Court Under Fire," *Journal of Public Law* 6 (1957): 439–443.

14. Bickel, "The Original Understanding and the Segregation Decision," 63.

15. *Brown v. Board of Education,* 347 U.S. 483, 489 (1954). *See also* Michael Klarman, "An Interpretive History of Modern Equal Protection," *Michigan Law Review* 90 (1991): 252 n.180.

16. For criticism of the view that the framers and ratifiers of the Fourteenth Amendment contemplated that the meaning of the amendment's abstract provisions would change as social circumstances changed, *see* Raoul Berger, **Government by Judiciary: The Transformation of the Fourteenth Amendment** (Cambridge: Harvard University Press, 1977), 99–116.

17. Learned Hand, **The Bill of Rights** (Cambridge: Harvard University Press, 1958), 29–30, 55.

18. Herbert Wechsler, "Toward Neutral Principles of Constitutional Law," *Harvard Law Review* 73 (1959): 12, 16–17, 19, 16, 15.

19. *Ibid.,* 15–16, 19, 11, 19.

20. *Ibid.,* 31–33. *See also* Kenneth Karst, "Legislative Facts in Constitutional Litigation," in *The Supreme Court Review,* ed. Philip B. Kurland (Chicago: University of Chicago Press, 1960), 103–105.

21. Wechsler, "Toward Neutral Principles of Constitutional Law," 32–33. The relevant per curiam rulings are *Muir v. Louisville Park Theatrical Association,* 347 U.S. 971 (1954); *Mayor of Baltimore v. Dawson,* 350 U.S. 877 (1955); *Holmes v. City of Atlanta,* 350 U.S. 877 (1955); *Gayle v. Browder,* 352 U.S. 903 (1956).

22. *See* text accompanying notes 42–50 below.

23. Wechsler, "Toward Neutral Principles of Constitutional Law," 33 (emphasis in original).

24. *Ibid.,* 34, 25.

25. Ernest van den Haag, "Social Science Testimony in the Desegregation Cases—A Reply to Professor Kenneth Clark," *Villanova Law Review* 6 (1960): 70, 77 (emphasis in original). *See also* Rosen, **The Supreme Court and Social Science,** 173–96; I. A. Newby, **Challenge to the Court: Social Scientists and the Defense of Segregation, 1954–1966** (Baton Rouge: Louisiana State University Press, 1967), 185–212. For John Davis's attack during oral argument upon Kenneth Clark's research into the effects of segregation, *see* Friedman, ed., **Argument,** 58–59.

26. A. James Gregor, "The Law, Social Science, and School Segregation: An Assessment," *Western Reserve Law Review* 14 (1963): 626. For evidence of the NAACP's lawyers' concerns regarding the weaknesses of their empirical argument regarding the effects of segregation in public schools, *see* Appendix to Appellants' Briefs, *Brown v. Board of Education of Topeka, Kansas, Briggs v. Elliott, and Davis v. County School Board of Prince Edward County, Virginia,* 1952, 8–9, NAACP Papers, Box II-B-138.

27. Gregor, "The Law, Social Science, and School Segregation," 626 (emphasis in original), 628, 629 (emphasis added).

28. Edmond Cahn, "Jurisprudence," *New York University Law Review* 30 (1955): 157–58, 163–65, 159–60. Ernest van den Haag "concur[red]" with Cahn's finding that the Court did not base the *Brown* decision on the social science evidence to which it made reference. Nevertheless, he believed that "the Court's reasoning . . . [has] something in common with Professor Clark's conclusions even though not relying on his evidence" (Van den Haag, "Social Science Testimony in the Desegregation Cases," 69–70). Van den Haag thus felt compelled to critique Clark's research (*see* article text accompanying note 25 above).

29. Monroe Berger, "Desegregation, Law, and Social Science: What was the Basis of the Supreme Court's Decision?" *Commentary* 23 (1957): 475. *See also* Pollak, "The Supreme Court Under Fire," 436–438.

30. William B. Ball, "Lawyers and Social Scientists–Guiding the Guides," *Villanova Law Review* 5 (1959): 221.

31. Herbert Garfinkel, "Social Science Evidence and the School Segregation Cases," *Journal of Politics* 21 (1959): 43.

32. Kenneth B. Clark, "The Desegregation Cases: Criticism of the Social Scientist's Role," *Villanova Law Review* 5 (1959): 234–235. For a discussion of

the NAACP's non-social science based attack upon segregation *see* Mark V. Tushnet, **The NAACP's Legal Strategy Against Segregated Education, 1925–1950** (Chapel Hill: University Of North Carolina Press, 1987).

33. Garfinkel, "Social Science Evidence and the School Segregation Cases," 46–58.

34. Clark, "The Desegregation Cases," 230–31. Clark defended himself against van den Haag's criticisms in a similar manner, i.e., by emphasizing that he had been aware and was candid about the limitations of his research (*ibid.,* 236–240).

35. Garfinkel, "Social Science Evidence and the School Segregation Cases," 58.

36. Barton J. Bernstein, "*Plessy v. Ferguson:* Conservative Sociological Jurisprudence," *Journal of Negro History* 48 (1963): 198–99, 201–202. *See also* Herbert Hovenkamp, "Social Science and Segregation Before *Brown*," *Duke Law Journal* (1985): 624–672.

37. Bernstein, "*Plessy v. Ferguson*," 199, 201, 200. *See* C. Vann Woodward, **The Strange Career of Jim Crow** (New York: Oxford University Press, 1957).

38. Garfinkel, "Social Science Evidence and the School Segregation Cases," 41–42.

39. *Bolling v. Sharpe,* 347 U.S. 497 (1954).

40. *Hirabayashi v. United States,* 320 U.S. 81 (1943), and *Korematsu v. United States,* 323 U.S. 214 (1944). In *Hirabayashi,* the Court, despite noting that racial distinctions are "odious to a free people," upheld wartime curfews restricting the movement of Japanese Americans on the West Coast. In *Korematsu,* the Court, despite noting that racial restrictions are "immediately suspect," upheld the federal government's wartime relocation of West Coast Japanese Americans to inland detention centers.

41. Louis H. Pollak, "Racial Discrimination and Judicial Integrity: A Reply to Professor Wechsler," *University of Pennsylvania Law Review* 108 (1959): 27. *See also* Ira Michael Heyman, "The Chief Justice, Racial Segregation, and The Friendly Critics," *California Law Review* 49 (1961): 121–24.

42. Pollak, "Racial Discrimination and Judicial Integrity," 27.

43. Charles L. Black, Jr., "The Lawfulness of the Segregation Decisions," *Yale Law Journal* 69 (1960): 421, 424.

44. *Ibid.,* 424–25.

45. *Ibid.,* 425–26 (emphasis omitted).

46. *Ibid.,* 426–27.

47. *Ibid.,* 427.

48. *See* text accompanying notes 21–23 above.

49. Black, "The Lawfulness of the Segregation Decisions," 430n 25, 428, 426.

50. *Ibid.,* 428, 430. Cf. Heyman, "The Chief Justice, Racial Segregation, and The Friendly Critics."

51. For general discussions of this period of the history of the civil rights movement, *see* Donald G. Nieman, **Promises to Keep: African-Americans and the**

Constitutional Order, 1776 to the Present (New York: Oxford University Press, 1991), 148–188; and John Hope Franklin and Alfred A. Moss, Jr., **From Slavery to Freedom: A History of African Americans,** 7th ed. (New York: Alfred A. Knopf, 1994), 492–531.

52. Alexander M. Bickel, **The Least Dangerous Branch: The Supreme Court at the Bar of Politics,** 2d ed. (1962; reprint, New Haven: Yale University Press, 1976) 61–62. *See also* Alexander M. Bickel, "Foreword: The Passive Virtues," *Harvard Law Review* 75 (1961): 70.

53. Bickel, **Least Dangerous Branch,** 57.

54. Joseph Tussman and Jacobus tenBroek, "The Equal Protection of the Laws," *California Law Review* 37 (1949): 358–359.

55. Michael J. Perry, **The Constitution, the Courts, and Human Rights: An Inquiry into the Legitimacy of Constitutional Policymaking by the Judiciary** (New Haven: Yale University Press, 1982), 1.

56. Gerald Gunther, "Some Reflections on the Judicial Role: Distinctions, Roots, and Prospects," *Washington University Law Quarterly* (1979): 819.

57. Philip B. Kurland, " '*Brown v. Board of Education* was the Beginning': The School Desegregation Cases in the United States Supreme Court–1954–1979," *Washington University Law Quarterly* (1979): 318.

58. Robert H. Bork, **The Tempting of America: The Political Seduction of the Law** (New York: Touchstone Press, 1990), 76.

59. J. Harvie Wilkinson III, **Serving Justice: A Supreme Court Clerk's View** (New York: Charterhouse, 1974), 133.

60. Mark G. Yudof, "School Desegregation: Legal Realism, Reasoned Elaboration, and Social Science Research in the Supreme Court," *Law and Contemporary Problems* 42 (Autumn,1978): 1. *See also* McConnell, "Originalism and the Desegregation Decisions," 1138–1139. Cf. Richard A. Posner, **The Problems of Jurisprudence** (Cambridge: Harvard University Press, 1990), 302–309.

61. David A. Strauss, "Discriminatory Intent and the Taming of *Brown,*" *University of Chicago Law Review* 56 (1989): 954.

62. Michael J. Perry, **The Constitution in the Courts: Law or Politics?** (New York: Oxford University Press, 1994), 145.

63. Posner, **The Problems of Jurisprudence,** 307.

64. J. Harvie Wilkinson III, **From *Brown* to *Bakke:* The Supreme Court and School Integration: 1954–1978** (New York: Oxford University Press, 1979), 18–19.

65. Bruce Ackerman, **We the People: Foundations** (Cambridge: Harvard University Press, Belknap Press, 1991), 150.

66. Perry, **The Constitution in the Courts,** 145–46.

67. H. N. Hirsch, **A Theory of Liberty: The Constitution and Minorities** (New York: Routledge, 1992), 92n 64.

68. Arthur S. Miller and Ronald F. Howell, "The Myth of Neutrality in Constitutional Adjudication," *University of Chicago Law Review* 27 (1960): 664.

69. Martin Shapiro, **Law and Politics in the Supreme Court: New Approaches to Political Jurisprudence** (New York: Free Press, 1964), 26. *See also* Martin Shapiro, "The Supreme Court and Constitutional Adjudication: Of Politics and Neutral Principles," *George Washington Law Review* 31 (1963): 593.

70. Herbert Wechsler, **Principles, Politics, and Fundamental Law: Selected Essays** (Cambridge: Harvard University Press, 1961), xiii.

71. Herbert Wechsler, "The Nature of Judicial Reasoning," in **Law and Philosophy: A Symposium,** ed. Sidney Hook (New York: New York University Press, 1964), 299. *See also* Kent Greenawalt, "The Enduring Significance of Neutral Principles," *Columbia Law Review* 78 (1978): 990–94.

72. Benjamin F. Wright, "The Supreme Court Cannot Be Neutral," *Texas Law Review* 40 (1962): 600, 605. *See also* M. P. Golding, "Principled Decision-Making and the Supreme Court," *Columbia Law Review* 63 (1963): 46, 48–49; Addison Mueller and Murray L. Schwartz, "The Principle of Neutral Principles," *UCLA Law Review* 7 (1960): 577–80.

73. Golding, "Principled Decision-Making and the Supreme Court," 42 (emphasis added).

74. Louis Henkin, "Neutral Principles' and Future Cases," in Hook, ed., **Law and Philosophy: A Symposium,** 304. *See also* Louis Henkin, "Some Reflections on Current Constitutional Controversy," *University of Pennsylvania Law Review* 109 (1961): 652–55; Jan G. Deutsch, "Neutrality, Legitimacy, and the Supreme Court: Some Intersections Between Law and Political Science," *Stanford Law Review* 20 (1968): 188; Greenawalt, "The Enduring Significance of Neutral Principles," 985–90; Barbara J. Flagg, "Enduring Principle: On Race, Process, and Constitutional Law," *California Law Review* 82 (1994): 961.

75. Wechsler, "The Nature of Judicial Reasoning," 297–98.

76. Wechsler, **Principles, Politics, and Fundamental Law,** xiv.

77. Greenawalt, "The Enduring Significance of Neutral Principles," 1003.

78. Flagg, "Enduring Principle," 962.

79. Wechsler, **Principles, Politics, and Fundamental Law,** xv, xiii–xiv (emphasis added).

80. Flagg, "Enduring Principle," 962.

81. Cass R. Sunstein, "*Lochner*'s Legacy," *Columbia Law Review* 87 (1987): 895.

82. See text accompanying note 47 above.

83. Gary Peller, "Neutral Principles in the 1950's," *Journal of Law Reform* 21 (1988): 608–09, 612. *See also* Sunstein, "*Lochner*'s Legacy," 895 n111.

84. Peller, "Neutral Principles in the 1950s," 620.

85. David A. J. Richards, "Rules, Policies, and Neutral Principles: The Search for Legitimacy in Common Law and Constitutional Adjudication," *Georgia Law Review* 11 (1977): 1104, 1103. See also Mark V. Tushnet, "Following the Rules Laid Down: A Critique of Interpretivism and Neutral Principles," *Harvard Law Review* 96 (1983): 804–824.

86. *See* McConnell, "Originalism and the Desegregation Decisions," 947–1140; and Bork, **The Tempting of America,** 74–84, 144.

87. *See, e.g.,* Ronald Dworkin, **Law's Empire** (Cambridge: Harvard University Press, Belknap Press, 1986), 359–363.

88. McConnell, "Originalism and the Desegregation Decisions," 952–953. *See also* Bork, **The Tempting of America,** 77.

89. *See, e.g.,* Kurland, *"Brown v. Board of Education* was the Beginning," 316–36, 403; William Van Alstyne, "Rites of Passage: Race, the Supreme Court, and the Constitution," *University of Chicago Law Review* 46 (1979): 783–84, 803–10; William Bradford Reynolds, "Individualism vs. Group Rights: The Legacy of *Brown,*" *Yale Law Journal* 93 (1984): 995–1005.

90. *See, e.g.,* Laurence H. Tribe, "In What Vision of the Constitution Must the Law be Color-Blind?" *John Marshall Law Review* 20 (1986): 204–05; Dworkin, *Law's Empire,* 393–96; Strauss, "Discriminatory Intent and the Taming Of *Brown,*" 942–943, 946–951.

91. The battle over *Brown's* legacy is the subject of another article that I am writing.

NOTE: *This article is reprinted from 2003* **Journal of Supreme Court History,** *vol. 28, no. 1.*

&c; D I A N A E. H E S S

Brown as a Classroom Icon

These are challenging days for the *Brown* decision. There is an academic assault on *Brown*. Some are asking difficult and troubling questions about precisely how much impact *Brown* really had on American life.

Law professor Burt Neuborne, 1996

I teach *Brown* because it is such a clear example of how a democracy, when it works the way it is supposed to, can make progress. It is obvious to my students that segregation was wrong and that the Court was right—few things in our history are just so manifestly good.

High School Social Studies teacher, 2003

The same day the Supreme Court of the United States handed down its decisions in the two Michigan affirmative action cases, Justice Ruth Bader Ginsburg spoke to middle and high school social studies teachers attending the summer institute about the Supreme Court.[1] After a short speech, she entertained questions. I asked her which Supreme Court cases she thought students in secondary schools should learn and why. She paused for a few seconds and gave this response: "Well, *Marbury* (*v. Madison*, 1803) and, of course, *Brown* (*v. Board of Education*, 1954), also the Virginia Military Institute (VMI) case (*United States v. Virginia*, 1996), because it was the culmination of many years of developing doctrine about gender discrimination. And they should learn some of our mistakes too—*Dred Scott* (*v. Sandford*, 1857) and *Korematsu* (*v. United States*, 1944)."[2]

I found Ginsburg's list interesting for several reasons. First, she foregrounds cases about conflicts over equality. With the exception of *Marbury* (the watershed case in which the Court ruled that it had the power of judicial review), all of the cases focus on discrimination, based on race (*Dred Scott*, *Brown*, and *Korematsu*) or gender (VMI). It seems likely that Ginsburg's selection of the VMI case emerged from her long-standing commitment to reducing gender discrimination. Ginsburg spent many years as a lawyer arguing equal protection cases, six of them before the Supreme Court. Second, Ginsburg finds it important for young people to learn that the Court makes mistakes. Implicitly and laudably, Ginsburg is emphasizing the importance of teaching students to critique the Supreme Court and its decisions. But another aspect of Ginsburg's list struck me as well. Only in her choice of *Brown* did Ginsburg preface the selection with the words, "of course," signifying that there can be no dispute that *Brown* is a case that all secondary students should learn. Although why she thought *Brown* was a seminal case for students to learn is unclear from her reply to my question, what is clear is that to Ginsburg, *Brown* unquestionably deserves inclusion in the curriculum. Her use of the phrase, "of course," was an indication, perhaps, of the self-evidence of *Brown*'s significance.

I was not surprised that Justice Ginsburg included *Brown* on her list. Over the years I have asked many legal and educational experts the same question I posed to her: Which Supreme Court cases should students learn and why? Law professors, high school teachers, judges, and another Supreme Court Justice (Sandra Day O'Connor) have answered, and without exception, all include *Brown* on their lists. This seemingly universal view—that *Brown* is a case of such import that all students need to learn it in schools—is reflected in many states' official educational policies. In 1999, I worked with Anand Marri to analyze the state social studies standards from the 48 states which had standards at the time. We found that, of the 20 state standards which included Supreme Court cases, *Brown* was the most frequently mentioned case. *Marbury* ranked a close second. While most states included mention of only five or fewer Supreme Court cases, some included substantially larger numbers: California, for example, included 11, while Indiana had an astonishing 39. *Brown* appeared in 15 of the 20 standards documents. The privileged position that *Brown* holds in state social studies standards can be found in other social markers of what Michael Apple and James Beane call "official knowledge"[3] (i.e., high status knowledge produced or endorsed by the dominant culture). The case receives prominent attention in virtually all government, law, and history textbooks, shows up on many state tests, and is included in web-based curricular resources about the Supreme Court.[4]

The ubiquity of *Brown* in the curriculum is not difficult to explain. The significance of the case within the school curriculum is clearly linked to its status as one of, or perhaps even the, most important Supreme Court case in the history of the United States. As Michael Klarman points out, "Constitutional lawyers and historians generally deem *Brown v. Board of Education* to be the most important U.S. Supreme Court decision of the twentieth century, and possibly of all time." Roger Wilkins goes further, writing that *Brown* "may have been the seminal civil rights event of the twentieth century."[5]

There are other reasons why *Brown* is an integral part of the historical canon of cases taught in the secondary school curriculum. According to my analysis of the cases that appear in state standards documents, the cases deemed most important for young people to learn were those that generate little contemporary social controversy, those that the Supreme Court "got right."[6] As illustration, *Roe v. Wade* (1973) is clearly one of the most important Supreme Court decisions of the twentieth century, yet it is only listed in four states' social studies standards. Likewise, the famous affirmative action case, *Bakke v. California* (1976), appears only in three states' standards. Because both of these cases continue to generate tremendous social debate, they tend not to appear in state social studies standards.

Brown, on the other hand, is apt to be conceived of by teachers as a democratic achievement of such magnitude that it deserves iconic status. An object of uncritical devotion, *Brown* is most likely to be taught not simply as a correctly decided court case, but as an important symbol that continues to shape contemporary ideas about justice, equality, and the power of the Supreme Court. High school teacher Jennifer

Brandsberg-Engelmann writes, "*Brown* is not just a decision of our high court, but is also an integral part of our social consciousness. It represents the power of our legal system to spur social changes of great magnitude and the strength of the rule of law in the face of popular opposition."[7] Erik Shager, also a high school teacher, considers the case the "slam dunk of all Supreme Court decisions."[8]

While there are many reasons that could account for the iconic status of *Brown*, one that stands out is how the normative quality of the decision compares to other events in history. The teacher whose remark forms the epigraph to this article was making just that point when she said, "few things in our history are just so manifestly good." This teacher's explanation typifies what I have heard other teachers say about their approaches to the case.

In June, 2002, I asked the sixty teachers from across the country who attended the Supreme Court Institutes whether they taught *Brown* and its legacy as a matter of current controversy or as a historical conflict that was correctly decided. Many seemed flabbergasted by the question, as if the very suggestion that *Brown* could be viewed as controversial was unthinkable. One teacher responded, "treating *Brown* as a controversy would be like letting a Holocaust denier into my classroom." Another remarked that to do so would violate her dedication to serving as an "anti-racist role model" for her students. A third teacher said she would likely be thought of as racist if she presented *Brown* or its legacy as controversial. These views were not universally shared. A fourth teacher was the first to inject into the discussion the possibility of *Brown's* moral and practical complexities. She remarked, "It's not that I teach *Brown* as a mistake, but we do talk about whether integration was the right approach to improving educational opportunity. We analyze how much progress has really been made."

The fourth teacher's point resonates with critiques of *Brown* that have been simmering for well over a decade, especially within academic circles. Although I will describe the nature of the controversies in more detail below, a brief preview is necessary to lay the groundwork for my claim that there exists a gulf between the "world outside of school" and what is taught in schools *vis à vis Brown* and its legacies.

A particularly provocative critique by Derrick Bell and others raises questions about whether the fundamental integrationist premise of *Brown* was the surest and most moral path to equal educational opportunity. Bell argues that racial integration of the schools only occurs when it is in the interest of whites. Thus, a surer path to equal educational opportunity for blacks would have been a ruling that the racially separate schools violated the Constitution because they were unequal, not because they were segregated.[9] Other critiques focus less on the Court's decision, and more on the legacies of the decision. Critics point out that even if the integration of the schools was the right remedy for the problem of race-based inequality of educational opportunity, its promise is unfulfilled as evidenced by the number of school children who attend schools that are not racially integrated. Forty years after the decision, Robert Carter (Thurgood Marshall's one-time aide and now a federal judge) wrote, "For most black children, *Brown*'s constitutional guarantee of equal education opportunity has been an arid abstraction, having no effect whatever on the educational offerings black children are given or the deteriorating schools they attend."[10]

As the fiftieth anniversary of *Brown* approaches, there appears to be a startling contradiction between how the case and its legacy are taught to school children (as a grand democratic achievement) and how it is viewed in the academy (as controversial). This contradiction, of course, is not unique to *Brown*. Many scholars have noted the differences between "school" and "academic" knowledge.[11] School knowledge is often presented as "static" and "settled," while academic knowledge is, almost by definition, a cauldron of competing perspectives and ideologies. Notwithstanding this general tendency, the differences I have described *vis à vis Brown* seem particularly sharp, which raises a number of questions: Given that *Brown* and its legacy are matters of increasing controversy in the academy and elsewhere, why is there so little evidence that these controversies have impacted the school curriculum? That is, what accounts for why *Brown* and its legacy are taught solely as great achievements? While there are forces that work to keep controversy out of the curriculum generally, are there factors, specific to *Brown*, that account for why it is so often approached as a democratic icon? Moreover, should more teachers engage secondary school students in analyzing these controversies? That is, should the iconic status of *Brown* and its legacy become matters that students deliberate? Or are there sound educational reasons for transmitting *Brown* to students in a celebratory and triumphalist fashion? In particular, since *Brown* is so often promoted as an achievement of democracy, what consequences for democratic education are embodied in the distinction between transmitting *Brown* and opening it up for deliberation?

Perspectives on *Brown*

The controversies about *Brown* may be organized into categories of representation that, while distinct, are not mutually exclusive. These categories include *Brown* as rightful icon, *Brown* as liberation referent, *Brown* as unfulfilled promise, *Brown* as well-intentioned error, and *Brown* as irrelevant.

Brown as Rightful Icon

This first category solidifies agreement that the Court did the right thing, at the right time, and for the right reasons. In other words the primary reason the *Brown* decision has been iconicized is that it deserves its laudatory label. The fact that *Brown* dealt with schools, which are powerful sites of cultural formation, clearly enhances its import. A decision that stated—in a clear and forceful manner—that what James T. Patterson calls "the very heart of constitutionally sanctioned Jim Crow" was legally and morally wrong sent a powerful democratic message that American apartheid had to end.[12] If schools, one pillar of society, could not be segregated, then it was obvious that the other institutional supports of an immoral system would be felled as well. One of the 20,000 mourners who paid tribute to Supreme Court Justice Thurgood Marshall in 1993 remarked that her grandchildren would not suffer the harsh de jure segregation that existed in Washington, D.C. when she was younger. As she put it, they "won't see colored fountains, colored restaurants. No sir, Justice Marshall saw to that."[13] Though not likely a teacher, this grandmother subscribed to the school of thought in which *Brown* is a rightful icon.

Brown as Liberation Referent

Much of the glowing language used to describe *Brown* focuses not so much on what changes it caused at the time, but how it has become a symbol for other rights movements—a liberation referent of sorts. As Ellen Condliffe Lagemann points out, *Brown* "set the stage for the civil rights movement, Martin Luther King, the women's movement, the Lau decision, and Hispanics, Asian groups, the American Association of Retired Persons, and other groups concerned about equality in this country."[14] Symbolically, though, *Brown* also reinforced the idea that one event can catalyze change. The Supreme Court's 2003 decision in *Lawrence v. Texas* that struck state laws banning homosexual sodomy has been hailed by some as the *Brown v. Board of Education* for gay Americans.[15] What happened after *Brown* is not always interpreted in such a positive light.

Brown as Unfulfilled Promise

To many, the legacy of *Brown* diminishes its status as a rightful icon or liberation referent, positioning it instead as an example of an unfulfilled promise. If the goal of *Brown* was to create equal educational opportunities for students of color through desegregation, then even a cursory analysis of the current educational landscape in the United States provides evidence that the goal remains unmet. Gloria Ladson-Billings and William Tate wrote in 1995 that students of color were more segregated than ever, and the same holds true nearly ten years later. Moreover, they argued that when school desegregation has occurred, its benefits have not gone to children of color, but to whites. Similarly, Jamin Raskin argues that the refusal of the Burger and Rehnquist Courts to stay the course that began in *Brown* has resulted in the ironic and pernicious reality that "in many parts of America, there are 100-percent white suburban schools and 100-percent black or minority schools, and they are all perfectly lawful because the segregation is not commanded by the state."[16] In 1980, 63 percent of African-American students attended predominantly minority schools. By 1998, the figure was 70 percent.[17] As Raskin aptly elaborates, whether the government has segregated by law or allowed it to happen in practice is a distinction that "surely escapes most elementary children."[18] Recall that *Brown* was based on the idea that the very experience of segregation was harmful to African-American children and, as Chief Justice Warren wrote in the opinion, "may affect their hearts and minds in a way unlikely ever to be undone."

Brown as Well-Intentioned Error

Frustration with the difference between the progress many civil rights advocates hoped *Brown* would spark and the persistence of race-based unequal educational opportunities and outcomes has caused some to question the fundamental premises of *Brown*. As mentioned previously, Derrick Bell now believes that instead of ordering the desegregation of schools, a better path for improving the educational opportunities for African-American students would have been to equalize the resources going into segregated schools. In response to the question, "What should *Brown* have said?" Bell advocates, instead of the more ambiguous order to desegregate "with all deliberate speed," the following:

> Effective immediately on receipt of this Court's mandate, school officials of the respondent school districts must: 1) ascertain through standardized tests and other appropriate measures the academic standing of each school district as compared to nationwide norms for school systems of comparable size and financial resources. This data will be published and made available to all patrons of the district. 2) All schools within the district must be equalized in physical facilities, teacher training, experience, and salary with the goal of each district, as a whole, measuring up to national norms within three years.[19]

Implicit in Bell's alternative is the view that improving educational opportunities did not have to be achieved via desegregation. Instead, improving the quality of education offered to African-American students could occur through an outpouring of resources. It is interesting to note that this solution might have prevented what is widely considered a particularly harmful consequence of the *Brown* decision—the loss of teaching and school administrative positions for African-American educators.

There are other ways in which *Brown* is characterized by critics as an error, if a well-intentioned one. The ponderous phrase, "with all deliberate speed" is viewed by many as an open invitation to resistance (which, of course, is what occurred in much of the nation). By not setting a firm deadline, the Court compromised the overall impact of *Brown*. Civil rights lawyer Oliver Hill argues that "there's no question about" whether "all deliberate speed" was a mistake; Chief Justice Earl Warren admitted as much to him on two separate occasions.[20] While Bell is arguing that desegregation per se was the wrong strategy, Hill finds fault not with ordering the integration of the schools, but with the slow pace implicit in the Court's language. What both share, however, is the view that the Court's decision was fundamentally flawed.

Brown as Irrelevant

Another aspect of the controversy over *Brown* focuses on the role it played in causing change. Unlike the claims I have described above, some legal scholars believe *Brown* simply did not matter very much. That is, rather than serving as a catalyst for change, *Brown* was irrelevant. Gerald Rosenberg advances this position by questioning whether litigation was the right mechanism for furthering civil rights goals. In doing so, he explicitly challenges the conventional wisdom about the power of courts in the United States, especially of the Supreme Court. Rosenberg marshals an array of evidence to support his argument that "given the praise accorded to the *Brown* decision, examining its actual effects produces quite a surprise . . . A decade after *Brown* virtually nothing had changed for the African-American students living in the former Confederacy that required race-based segregation by law. . . For nearly ninety-nine of every 100 African-American children in the south a decade after *Brown*, the finding of a constitutional right changed nothing."[21] According to Rosenberg, *Brown* failed to cause significant change because there was too little political pressure to enforce the decision—and quite a bit of pressure to resist it. Thus, it is misguided to expect the courts to act as the great engine of reform, and to claim that *Brown* is an example of the judiciary at its majestic best is a "naïve and romantic belief in the triumph of rights over politics."[22]

While this review of the many controversies that revolve around *Brown* and its legacy is not comprehensive, the differences of opinion on central and important questions exhibited by these five "takes" illustrate my central premise. In the world outside of school, perhaps especially in the academy, but not only there, real controversy punctuates discussions of *Brown* and the extent to which it has shaped contemporary society.

Teaching *Brown*

Given these controversies in the academy, why is it they have not entered the school curriculum? In other words, what accounts for the curricular iconization of *Brown* and its legacy? And relatedly, to what extent does the iconization of *Brown* advance or detract from important educational goals? Finally, what are some alternatives to teaching about the case in such a fashion?

Lack of Controversy Generally

One reason why *Brown* and its legacy are not treated as topics of controversy that students should deliberate is that there is little controversy in the curriculum generally. Scholars who have investigated the content of history textbooks (even when the scholars come from dramatically different ideological positions), agree that textbooks present history as questions for which there are clear answers, instead of as controversies for which there could be multiple and competing answers.[23] James Loewen explained, "The stories that history textbooks tell are predictable; every problem has already been solved or is about to be solved. Textbooks exclude conflict or real suspense."[24] While there are multiple reasons why textbooks present history as a series of answered questions, one is the fear that adding controversy to the curriculum creates controversy, as opposed to simply reflecting it. And there is little support in the public at large, and even within schools, for the idea that controversy, even when dealt with well, is inherently educational. As one of Jonathan Zimmerman's students remarked, "You'll never see a parents' group called 'Americans in Favor of Debating the Other Side' in Our Schools."[25] This is not to suggest controversy is always avoided. Catherine Cornbleth's year-long study of history classes provides especially compelling evidence that teachers often present students with multiple perspectives and divergent views. But she did not find many instances where students were engaged in deliberations about controversial issues.[26] Similarly, Katherine Simon's study of moral and existential issues in high school classes showed clearly that although authentic issues do arise, discussions of them are "alarmingly truncated." The teachers she studied "seemed reluctant to organize their courses or class time in ways that would invite students to delve into these issues on a regular basis or in a sustained way."[27]

Reasons Specific to Brown

Alongside the general resistance to controversial issues in schools, there are factors specific to *Brown* which account for why so few teachers engage their students in the controversies. One is teachers' lack of awareness of just how controversial *Brown* and its legacy have become in the world outside of school. The controversies are not in most textbooks, are rarely aired at professional development activities, and are most prominent in law and political science journals that teachers do not commonly read. Moreover, because most teachers in the United States are white, they are less apt to know that within the African-American community *Brown* and its legacy have been controversial for quite some time. This may account for why virtually all of the teachers I know who do challenge the iconization of *Brown* are African American.[28]

What critical race theorists have identified as "interest convergence" may also explain why *Brown* is likely to be presented as an icon. Bell discussed interest convergence as it relates to *Brown v. Board of Education* as follows:

> The interests of blacks in achieving racial equality will be accommodated only when it converges with the interests of whites. However, the Fourteenth Amendment, standing alone, will not authorize a judicial remedy providing effective racial equality for blacks where the remedy sought threatens the superior societal status of middle- and upper-class whites.[29]

Bell is arguing that the *Brown* decision had particular economic and political advantages that whites in policymaking positions recognized. These include the widely held view that the abolition of *de jure* school segregation would enhance America's reputation in the world, that African Americans would be unwilling to serve in the military unless the formal segregationist policies were eradicated, and that economic growth in the South was being held back by racist policies. Thus, *Brown* is an example of what happens when interests of African Americans (for equal treatment under the law) and whites converge.

In a similar fashion, it is important to ask whose interests are served by how *Brown* is currently taught. Celebrating *Brown* serves the interests of people who want to believe that racial discrimination was largely a problem of the past. This claim overstates the efficacy of *Brown*, but de-emphasizes contemporary racial inequalities. And for many students, even if they are attending a segregated school, *Brown* is viewed as a grand achievement because it outlawed segregation.

I learned how this seemingly incongruous belief could be constructed from a high school history teacher who told me that his students could barely believe there was a time in the United States when the law was used to segregate schools. As a consequence, this teacher said that there was nothing controversial about *Brown* or its legacy to his students. I asked him to describe the student population in his school. He responded that virtually all the students were white. Knowing that he lived near a racially diverse city, I asked where the students of color went to school. He told me that there was another high school—less than five miles away—where virtually all of the students were African American. How, I asked the teacher, can your students believe that segregation was a thing of the past, when they went to a segregated school? He responded that the students made a distinction between *de jure* and *de facto* segregation (even though they might not use those labels). That is, his students could simultaneously believe that *Brown* was a grand achievement because it mandated integration (thus, ridding the nation of a constitutional and moral blight) and that the school they attended was fulfilling the mandates of *Brown* because it was not segregated by law. To these students, the idea that *Brown* forced the desegregation of schools was such a powerful myth that it shrouded the reality of segregation, arguably perpetuating the same inequalities, but now without legal recourse. Thus, the interests of these white students were catered to by not problematizing *Brown* and its legacy. They did not have to confront continuing (and in many places, worsening) inequalities in educational opportunities that are parsed based on race.

Up to this point I have concentrated on reasons for the iconization of *Brown* that are largely negative. But other, more laudable reasons, also account for why *Brown* is more likely to be celebrated than problematized. Teachers may focus on the majesty of *Brown* as a moral exemplar they hope will shape their students' views. As William McNeill writes, sometimes what is needed is "an appropriately idealized version of the past that may allow a group of human beings to come close to living up to its noblest ideas."[30] *Brown* can deliver a number of moral messages, but the most critical focuses on the nature of U.S. equality: what it is, why it is so important, and why individuals should be committed to advancing a more equal society. Thus, teachers may see the controversies about *Brown* in the world outside of school as quibbles in the academy that, if given air time, may serve to undermine the very moral commitments they are trying to build in students. Moreover, this argument continues, *Brown* is a part of United States history that young people can easily feel proud of because it serves as such a powerful example that wrongs can be righted. Thus, the iconization of *Brown* is a perfect example of a redemptive narrative. The story of *Brown*, with its powerful heroes, its injustices overcome, and its unanimous decision, is employed to do much more than simply teach young people about a court case. Instead, its primacy rests with its utility as a moral example.

The Harms of Iconization

Although taking a non-controversial approach to *Brown* and its legacy could help students build moral understandings and commitments that are valuable, the arguments against teaching *Brown* as a triumphalist tale are more compelling. These reasons include the problems associated with intellectual dishonesty, with downplaying the importance of race, and with reifying the Supreme Court.

The controversies that exist in the world outside of school about *Brown* and what it means for people today are powerful and growing. While much of the debate exists within the academy, there also is evidence to support the claim that these controversies are not simply academic concerns. Consider that civil rights organizations, such as the NAACP, have held conferences about whether school desegregation is a failed policy, and the continuing debate that revolves around affirmative action. Both are evidence that the legacy of *Brown* is being fought on a terrain that is rife with conflict. For teachers (and textbooks) to present *Brown* and its legacy as non-controversial is intellectually dishonest and arguably a form of indoctrination. Noam Chomsky supported this position when he wrote that "It is the intellectual responsibility of teachers—or any honest person, for that matter—to try to tell the truth. That is surely uncontroversial."[31] And while the meaning of "truth" is contested and notoriously slippery, the fundamental premise that *Brown* and its legacy are controversial is supported by an array of evidence. What the truth is about *Brown* and its legacy is unclear. But that is just the point. It is the differing interpretations of the "truth" of *Brown* that make it controversial.

In addition to the intellectual dishonesty of presenting *Brown* and its legacy as non-controversial, the case and its legacy could provide especially compelling vehicles for infusing authentic issues related to race into the school curriculum. We know that issues related to race present pedagogical challenges. Gloria Ladson-Billings writes, "Issues of race are avoided in U.S. classrooms for the same reasons that they are avoided in everyday life. We have not found ways to talk about them without feelings of rancor and guilt."[32] However, ignoring issues does not solve them, and ignoring those related to race signals to students of color that the issues of particular concern to them are not important enough for the curriculum.[33] Given the prominence of *Brown* in the curriculum, denying its controversies sends the especially strong "official" message that racial inequalities are a past problem now solved, instead of part and parcel of the contemporary reality of the world in which we live. Moreover, issues related to race may be more productively discussed in schools than in other venues. As Amy Gutmann writes, "Schools have a much greater capacity than most parents and voluntary associations for teaching children to reason out loud about disagreements that arise in democratic politics."[34] Public schools' greater capacity lies in the fact that they contain more ideological diversity than one would expect to find in many families or associations. This diversity of views (and, by extension, diversity about which issues matter the most) provides a good setting to promote "rational deliberations of competing conceptions of the good life and the good society."[35]

A third harmful consequence of the iconization of *Brown* focuses more generally on the misconceptions it may promote about the Supreme Court and its role in American life. Because of *Brown*'s prominence in the curriculum, it is likely that young people form ideas about the Court from learning this case that become part of their conceptual framework for thinking about the Court generally. And if that occurs, it is especially problematic because generalizations typically drawn from this case are contested at best and, at worst, outright myths.

One such generalization is that the Court's primary and more frequently enacted function in United States democracy is to liberate people who are suffering under the heavy hand of a discriminatory majority. Michael Klarman traced this misconception to *Brown* when he wrote, "The conventional assessment of the Court's countermajoritarian capacity has been distorted, I believe, by a single decision—*Brown*. Because that ruling rescued us from our racist past, the conventional story line runs, the Court plainly can and does play the role of heroic defender of minority rights from majoritarian oppression."[36] Thus, the conventional presentation of *Brown* reinforces a particular view of the Supreme Court as an agent of social justice that, itself, is a matter of controversy.

I learned about the relationship between *Brown* and the formation of the "liberation generalization" when a very skillful and experienced teacher told me how learning about the contemporary Supreme Court worked to diminish her interest in teaching a course in American Government. She had attended a professional development program where she was taught that the primary function of the Supreme Court is to ensure uniformity in the federal judiciary. Consequently, most of the cases the Court chooses to decide revolve around legal issues for which there was disagreement among the lower federal courts. This information was profoundly disturbing to this teacher. She exclaimed, "I grew up at the time of *Brown*—we revered the Court." By iconicizing *Brown*, the Supreme Court is represented in ways that are inaccurate and potentially damaging to democracy.

How *Brown* Could Be Taught

I have argued here that the way *Brown* is typically presented in the school curriculum deserves re-thinking. While detailed explanations of lesson plans are beyond the scope of this article, a brief summary of three alternatives may clarify the distinction I am drawing between celebrating *Brown* and its legacy and educating about them.

The first approach is to infuse directly the controversies about *Brown* that exist in the academy into the school curriculum. This would entail teaching students the different ways in which *Brown* and its legacy are viewed and have them deliberate core questions about them. For example, what accounts for the differing interpretations of *Brown*? Whose interests are advanced by each interpretation? Which interpretations do students think have the most merit? And are there other interpretations they can create? The main point here is to engage students directly in learning the controversies—not to suggest that there is one right answer that students should build and believe.

A second approach that could complement the first is to use *Brown* as a launching pad for investigating contemporary issues related to race in the United States. For example, students could examine what accounts for the resegregation that Gary Orfield and John Yun have so thoroughly documented, and deliberate an array of policy options that have been advanced to address the persistent educational inequalities in the United States, *Brown* being only one of these.[37]

Another approach to treating *Brown* and its legacy as controversies is to have students focus on what happened in their own schools and communities as a consequence of *Brown* and what contemporary issues that history has created. As an example, a group of students in an experimental civics course at Northwestern High School in Maryland spent the spring of 2003 creating an oral history project on school integration and resegregation in their county from 1955 to 2000. The class, composed entirely of students of color, learned the techniques of oral history and then interviewed people who had first-hand knowledge about what transpired during this time. The students interviewed an African American who had been the first to integrate a white school in 1956, a civil rights lawyer who had sued the county to institute busing, and teachers. The students heard a wide range of sharply competing opinions about how *Brown* and its legacy played out in their county. One of the course teachers, Peter Levine, explained that "A major goal [of the project] is to help our students see history not only as the record of state actions, powerful people, and downtrodden victims, but also as a story of communities making difficult decisions." Students discussed possible answers to the question, "What should have been done to address school segregation in 1955?" The students generated a long list ranging from "leave it alone" to "integrating the teaching staff first," to busing to achieve equal racial distribution in all schools."[38]

The fact that this project captured the controversies about *Brown* and its legacy speaks volumes about why iconicizing *Brown* is inauthentic to the world beyond school—is the larger political world that we need to teach students how to negotiate and shape. Pretending an issue is uncontroversial does not make it so, and depriving students of the opportunity to genuinely deliberate competing points of view on issues as significant as the relationship between race and educational opportunity does not turn that fiction into fact. When teachers teach controversial questions as if there were one best answer, they deprive their students of the opportunity to do the necessary work of democracy and make them dangerously susceptible to the blind acceptance of the political conclusions of others. Even if the decision to deny a controversy is made with the best of intentions (and I believe that is often the case when *Brown* is celebrated in the curriculum), I fear the result because orthodoxy is, by definition, the enemy of inquiry. That is, redemptive narratives, such as presenting *Brown* and its effects as unequivocally positive, may become historical "comfort foods." While soothing an immediate need perhaps, ultimately they will lull us away from teaching young people how to deal with the important and thorny issues that are part and parcel of the world in which we live.

References

Apple, Michael & Beane, James, **Democratic Schools** (Alexandria, VA: Association for Supervision and Curriculum Development 1995).

Banks, James, **Multicultural Education, Transformative Knowledge, and Action: Historical and Contemporary Perspectives** (New York: Teachers College Press 1996).

Bell, Derrick A., "Revised Decisions: Dissenting," in J. Balkin, ed., **What *Brown v. Board of Education* Should Have Said; The Nation's Top Legal Experts Rewrite America's Landmark Civil Rights Decision,** 185–200 (New York: New York University Press 2001).

Bell, Derrick A., "*Brown v. Board of Education* and the Interest Convergence Dilemma," in K. Crenshaw, N, Gotanda, G. Peller, & K. Thomas, eds., **Critical Race Theory: The Key Writings that Formed the Movement** at 20–29 (New York: New York Press 1995).

Chomsky, Noam, **Chomsky on Mideducation** (Boulder, CO: Rowman & Littlefield Publishers, Inc. 2000).

Cornbleth, Catherine, "Images of America: What Youth Do Know About The United States," 2002 *American Educational Research Journal,* 39, (2), 519–552.

Epstein, Terrie, "Sociocultural Approaches to Young People's Historical Understanding" 1997 *Social Education,* 61 (1), 28–32.

Graff, E.J., "The High Court Finally Gets it Right" June 29, 2003 *Boston Globe* (On-line), Available: http://www.sodomulaws.org/lawrence/lweditionals20.htm

Gutmann, Amy, **Democratic Education** (Princeton: Princeton University Press 1987/1999).

Hess, Diana & Marri, Anand, "Which Cases Should We Teach?" 2002 *Social Education,* 66 (1), 53–59.

Hill, Oliver, "Transcript of a Symposium on *Brown v. Board of Education*: An Exercise in Advocacy" in 2001 *Mercer Law Review*, 52 (2), 581–630.

Klarman, Michael J., "How *Brown* Changed Race Relations: The Backlash Thesis," 1994 *Journal of American History*, 81 (1), 81–118.

Ladson-Billings, Gloria, "Multicultural Issues in the Classroom: Race, Class, and Gender" in Evans, R.W. & Saxe, D.W., eds., **Handbook on Teaching Social Issues**, at 10–110 (NCSS Bulletin 93, Washington, DC: National Council for the Social Studies 1996).

Ladson-Billings, Gloria & Tate, William F., "Toward a Critical Race Theory of Education" 1995 *Teachers College Record*, 97 (1), 47–68.

Loewen, James W., **Lies My Teacher Told Me: Everything Your American History Textbook Got Wrong** (New York: Touchstone 2005).

Lagemann, Ellen Condliffe, "An American Dilemma Still" in E.C. Lagemann and L.P Miller, eds., ***Brown v. Board of Education*: The Challenge for Today's Schools** at 1–8 (New York: Teachers College Press, Columbia University 1996).

Neuborne, Burt, "*Brown* at Forty: Six Visions," in E.C. Lagemann and L.P Miller, eds., ***Brown v. Board of Education*: The Challenge for Today's Schools** at 198–205 (New York: Teachers College Press, Columbia University 1996).

Orfield, Gary, & Yun, John T., **Resegregation in American Schools** (Cambridge, MA: Civil Rights Project, Harvard University 1999).

Patterson, James T., ***Brown v. Board of Education*: A Civil Rights Milestone and Its Troubled Legacy** (New York: Oxford University Press 2001).

Raskin, Jamin B., **Overruling Democracy: The Supreme Court vs. the American People** (New York: Routledge 2003).

Rosenberg, Gerald N., "African-American Rights after *Brown*" 1999 *Journal of Supreme Court History*, 24 (2), at 201–225.

Simon, Katherine G., **Moral Questions in the Classroom: How to Get Kids to Think Deeply about Real Life and Their Schoolwork** (New Haven: Yale University Press 2001).

Wilkins, Roger, "Dream Deferred But Not Defeated" in E.C. Lagemann and L.P Miller, eds., ***Brown v. Board of Education*: The Challenge for Today's Schools** at 14–18 (New York: Teachers College Press, Columbia University 1996).

Zimmerman, Jonathan, **Whose America: Culture Wars in the Public Schools** (Cambridge MA: Harvard University Press 2002).

Endnotes

1. *Grutter v. Bollinger* (2003), and *Gratz v. Bollinger* (2003). The institute is sponsored by Street Law, Inc. and the Supreme Court Historical Society. Lee Arbetman, deputy director of the domestic programs at Street Law, Inc. is

the director of the institute, and I have co-taught with him for seven years. For information about the institute, go to www.streetlaw.org.

2. In *Dred Scott*, the Court ruled that slaves were not and could not become citizens; the *Korematsu* ruling held that it was constitutional to force persons of Japanese ancestry into internment camps during World War II. In the *Virginia* decision, Justice Ginsburg wrote for the majority that the public Virginia Military Institute violated the Constitution's Equal Protection Clause when it barred women from admission.

3. Apple, Michael & Beane, James, **Democratic Schools**. (Alexandria, VA: Association for Supervision and Curriculum Development 1995).

4. Hess, Diana & Marri, Anand, "Which Cases Should We Teach?" 2002 *Social Education*, 66 (1), at 53–59. Justice Ginsburg might be disappointed to learn that two of the cases she mentioned, VMI and *Korematsu* did not fare well in the standards. Only California lists *Korematsu*, and no states included VMI. For an example of the prominence given to *Brown* in web-based resources, *see* www.landmarkcases.org, and in text-based materials, *see* **We The People: The Citizen and the Constitution** Calabasas, CA: Center for Civic Education (1996).

5. Klarman, Michael J., "How *Brown* Changed Race Relations: The Backlash Thesis," 1994 *Journal of American History*, 81 (1), at 81–118; Wilkins, Roger, "Dream Deferred But Not Defeated" in Ellen C. Lagemann and L.P Miller, eds., ***Brown v. Board of Education*: The Challenge for Today's Schools**, New York: Teachers College Press, Columbia University (1996) at 14–18.

6. Hess & Marri *supra* note 4 at 53–59. There are some exceptions to this blanket characterization, specifically the inclusion of *Plessy v. Ferguson* (1896) and *Dred Scott v. Sandford* (1857) listed respectively in 11 and 8 of the 20 states that include specific cases. However, both of these cases have been overturned and consequently are often used to illustrate how wrongs can be righted.

7. *Ibid.*, at 66.

8. *Id.* at 71.

9. Bell, Derrick A., "*Brown v. Board of Education* and the Interest Convergence Dilemma," in K. Crenshaw, N, Gotanda, G. Peller, & K. Thomas, eds., **Critical Race Theory: The Key Writings that Formed the Movement**, New York: New York Press (1995) at 20–29.

10. Patterson, James T., ***Brown v. Board of Education*: A Civil Rights Milestone and its Troubled Legacy**, New York: Oxford University Press (2001) at 210.

11. Banks, James A., **Multicultural Education, Transformative Knowledge, and Action: Historical and Contemporary Perspectives**, New York: Teachers College Press (1996).

12. Patterson *supra* note 10 at 221.

13. *Id.* at 204.

14. Lagemann, Ellen Condliffe, "An American Dilemma Still" in Ellen C. Lagemann and L.P Miller, eds., ***Brown v. Board of Education*: The Challenge for Today's Schools**, New York: Teachers College Press, Columbia University (1996) at 11.
15. Graff, E.J., "The High Court Finally Gets it Right" *Boston Globe* (On-line) June 29, 2003. Available at http://www.sodomulaws.org/lawrence/lweditionals20.html
16. Raskin, Jamin B., **Overruling Democracy: The Supreme Court vs. the American People**, New York: Routledge (2003) at 159.
17. Orfield, Gary, & Yun, John T., **Resegregation in American Schools**, Cambridge, MA: Civil Rights Project, Harvard University (1999).
18. Raskin *supra* note 16 at 159.
19. Bell *supra* note 9 at 22.
20. Hill, Oliver, "Transcript of a *Symposium on Brown v. Board of Education*: An Exercise in Advocacy" 2001 *Mercer Law Review*, 52 (2), at 623.
21. Rosenberg, Gerald N., "African-American Rights After *Brown*," 1999 *Journal of Supreme Court History*, 24 (2), at 204.
22. *Id.* at 221.
23. *See generally*, Loewen, James W., **Lies My Teacher Told Me: Everything Your American History Textbook Got Wrong**, New York: Touchstone (1995), and Zimmerman, Jonathan, **Whose America: Culture Wars in the Public Schools**, Cambridge MA: Harvard University Press (2002).
24. Loewen *supra* note 23 at 13.
25. Zimmerman *supra* note 23 at 197.
26. Cornbleth, Catherine, "Images of America: What Youth Do Know About The United States," *American Educational Research Journal*, Summer 2002, vol. 39, No. 2, at 519–552.
27. Simon, Katherine G., **Moral Questions in the Classroom: How to Get Kids to Think Deeply About Real Life and Their Schoolwork**, New Haven: Yale University Press (2001).
28. I wish to thank Paulette Dilworth, at Indiana University, and Mary Curd Larkin of Street Law, Inc. for helping me understand the nature and history of the controversies related to *Brown* and its legacy in the African-American community.
29. Bell, *supra* note 9 at 22.
30. Quoted in Zimmerman, *supra* note 23, at 222.
31. Chomsky, Noam, **Chomsky on Mideducation** Boulder, CO: Rowman & Littlefield Publishers, Inc. (2000) at 20.
32. Ladson-Billings, Gloria, "Multicultural Issues in the Classroom: Race, Class, and Gender" in Evans, R.W. & Saxe, D.W., eds., **Handbook on Teaching Social Issues**, NCSS Bulletin 93, Washington, DC: National Council for the Social Studies (1996) at 101.

33. Epstein, Terrie "Sociocultural Approaches to Young People's Historical Under-standing" 1997 *Social Education*, 61 (1) at 28–32.

34. Gutmann, Amy, **Democratic Education**, Princeton: Princeton University Press (1987/1999) at 58.

35. *Id.* at 44.

36. Klarman, *supra* note 5 at 82.

37. *See* Orfield & Yun, *supra* note 17.

38. I learned about this project from Peter Levine. For an explanation of the activities the students engaged in and the content of their discussions, go to http://www.peterlevine.ws/hsclassthread.htm. The students created an on-line historical exhibit, which includes the oral histories, a slide show, and a delib-erative poll, which can be found at: http://www.princegeorges.org/history.htm

℘ J A M E S T. P A T T E R S O N

Legacies and Lessons

Anyone who reads this far will be aware of the many disappointments and triumphs surrounding *Brown*. A few examples still stand out in the twenty-first century.

One involves race and legal education. Thurgood Marshall had celebrated in 1950 when the Supreme Court ordered the all-white Texas Law School to admit Heman Sweatt, a black mail carrier. By the 1980s, the University of Texas (UT) was educating more minorities than any law school in the United States. In March 1996, however, the Fifth Circuit Court of Appeals prohibited the UT Law School from enforcing affirmative action guidelines that had reserved places for African Americans and other minorities. Enrollment of blacks plummeted from thirty-one in 1996 to four in 1997.[1]

Ted Shaw, associate director of the still combative Legal Defense Fund, complained that the court's decision was "disturbing" and "troubling." Like other advocates of desegregation, he feared that it would harm the quest for racial diversity in higher education that Justice Blackmun had espoused in the *Bakke* case of 1978. But conservatives applauded. Clint Bolick, director of the Institute for Justice in Washington, exulted that the court had "banged another nail in the coffin of racial preferences." Bolick insisted that *Brown* had established color-blindness as a constitutional principle. This was inaccurate but ironic: *Brown,* which many conservatives had deplored in the 1950s, had become a guiding light for some on the right by the 1990s.[2]

The situation in Summerton, South Carolina, where Marshall had begun a struggle against racial discrimination in the late 1940s, revealed other legacies discouraging to desegregationists in the 1990s. School District No. 1 of Summerton still had an overwhelmingly black population. Its schools received more funding per pupil than the state average. Yet student achievement scores lagged badly, and only a few white students went there in the mid-1990s. Other whites still attended all-white private academies or predominantly white public schools in nearby Manning, where parents with money had bought land so that their children might enroll. Race relations at Manning High were said to be calm. But academic tracking was common, with few African Americans in college prep courses. Reporters observed that white and black students rarely socialized. Self-segregation seemed to be the norm.[3]

Summerton's high level of segregation was not typical of towns in South Carolina, which like many southern states continued in the 1990s to have a larger percentage of black students attending schools with white majority enrollments than most states in the union. Who would have expected in 1954 that the South would climb out of the abyss of Jim Crow to stand tall in this way? Yet it was surely discouraging to proponents of desegregation that some of Summerton's schools, like many others in heavily black areas of the South, were just about as segregated in the 1990s, though not *de jure,* as they had been in 1954.

The legacy of *Brown* in Topeka also remained unsettling. In 1994 a federal district court finally approved a new city plan to desegregate the schools. The plan featured magnet schools, voluntary transfers of white and black students, and the closing of some heavily black schools. The courts, however, continued to oversee the plan. And Linda Brown-Thompson, whose children had gone to segregated schools in Topeka, remained pessimistic. She said, "Sometimes I wonder if we really did the children and the nation a favor by taking this case to the Supreme Court. I know it was the right thing for my father and others to do then. But after nearly forty years we find the Court's ruling unfulfilled."[4]

A happier legacy of *Brown* could be found at the University of Alabama, from which Autherine Lucy had been expelled in 1956. Federal muscle had finally forced token integration of 'Bama in 1963, and desegregation inched ahead there—as at other white universities in the South—in the next two decades. Lucy reenrolled at Alabama in 1989 and graduated in 1992 with a master's degree in elementary education. Her daughter received an undergraduate degree at the same time. She was one of 1,755 African Americans at a campus of 18,096 students. George Wallace, who had tried to bar black students in 1963, had been crippled by a would-be assassin's bullet in 1972 but lived until 1998. By then he had long since claimed to rue his racist past. Recognizing the power of blacks at the polls, he had wooed African Americans in political campaigns.[5]

In Little Rock, where troops had patrolled Central High School for all of the 1957–58 school year, the legacy of *Brown* was mixed in the 1990s. By then the school was approximately 60 percent black. Some 50 percent of whites of school age in the district fled to academies outside the city. Although some students at Central—blacks as well as whites—thrived academically (twenty-three students became National Merit Scholarship semifinalists in 1997), 70 percent of the black students and 30 percent of the whites read below grade level. Whites and blacks did not socialize much at Central, but advocates of racial diversity remembered the bad old days when *de jure* segregation had prevented black and white students from associating at all.

Central High's only African-American senior in 1958—of the nine who had dared to desegregate the school—had been Ernest Green. He had gone on to earn a master's degree at Michigan State and to become a managing director of Lehman Brothers, a major investments firm. He had contributed to the Democratic party and become acquainted with President Bill Clinton, who flew to Little Rock in 1997 for ceremonies commemorating the forty years since Governor Faubus had tried to stop desegregation. Green rode with Clinton on *Air Force One*.

Green's eight black schoolmates had also attended colleges and universities. All but one had left Little Rock and said in 1997 that they were glad they had challenged racial segregation. Their experiences, while bruising, had not left scars. Elizabeth Eckford appeared to be an exception. In 1997, she was unemployed and lived in Little Rock. When asked if she felt good about what she had done, she said, "Absolutely not. Positively not." She complained that her oldest child had had to be bused ten miles so as to promote better racial balance in the district. She added, "There was a time when I thought integration was one of the most desired things. . . . I appreciate blackness more than I did then."[6]

In New Orleans, where Ruby Bridges had braved abusive crowds in 1960 in order to attend a white school, race relations were calmer in the 1990s. Bridges had graduated from the city's increasingly black public schools and gone on to take business courses and work as a travel agent. By 1992, as Ruby Bridges-Hall, she was the mother of four children. Using royalties from a book about her experience, she set up the Ruby Bridges Educational Foundation, which gave grants to inner-city schools for art education. She also returned to her old elementary school—all-black by 1992—as a volunteer. Bridges-Hall, too, seemed proud of her efforts and unscarred by her travails. The city's school board, meanwhile, decided to rechristen any school that had been named after a slaveowner or after someone who had not supported equal opportunity for all. Two dozen schools were to receive new names, including one that had been called George Washington.[7]

༄

Anecdotal examples such as these highlight a few legacies of judicial decisions concerning race and schools in the decades since *Brown* in 1954. Some of these outcomes suggested progress toward desegregation in public education; others obviously did not.

A number of scholars kept the faith in court action that optimists had expressed immediately after *Brown* and had reiterated following decisions such as *Green* in 1968 and *Swann* in 1971. In 1975, for instance, Richard Kluger, who wrote a magisterial book about *Brown,* said that the decision "represented nothing short of a reconsecration of American ideals." It showed, he said, that the United States stood for more than anticommunism or material abundance. Four years later, J. Harvie Wilkinson, author of another thoughtful book on the subject, wrote that *Brown* had been the "catalyst that shook up Congress and culminated in the two major Civil Rights acts of the century." Glowing appraisals such as these were harder to find in the more dispirited 1990s, but Aldon Morris, a historian of civil rights, concluded in 1993 that with *Brown* "a significant chunk of the symbolic pillar of white supremacy crumbled." The decision, he said, enabled blacks to believe that it was possible to bring down the "entire edifice of Jim Crow."[8]

Many Americans in the 1990s, however, shared the gloom of Linda Brown-Thompson and Elizabeth Eckford. Robert Carter, Marshall's one-time aide, wrote in 1994 that "for most black children, *Brown*'s constitutional guarantee of equal educational opportunity has been an arid abstraction, having no effect whatever on the educational offerings black children are given or the deteriorating schools they attend." A still bitter Kenneth Clark, when asked in 1995, "what is the best thing for blacks to call themselves?" answered, "white." Four years later Gary Orfield, a prominent scholar concerned with segregation in schools, lamented, "We are clearly in a period when many policy makers, courts, and opinion makers assume that desegregation is no longer necessary, or that it will be accomplished somehow without need of any deliberate planning."[9]

As earlier, there was ample reason for liberal laments like these. The civil rights movement continued to be weak and fragmented in the 1990s. In 1996 California voters approved Proposition 209, which barred affirmative action in state university admissions, hiring, or public contracting. Voters in the state of Washington favored a similar referendum in 1998. Then and later, race-based admissions procedures faced serious court challenges in many other states. Most liberals, of course, still asserted the virtues of affirmative action. Undaunted, they managed to pass laws and devise procedures that minimized the impact, at least in the short run, of these conservative court decisions and referenda. Their moves in turn, unsettled many whites and Asian Americans whose academic test scores were generally superior to those of blacks and Hispanics. Overall, however, proponents of affirmative action remained on the defensive at the turn of the century.[10]

Robert Carter's pessimism about the education of blacks was also understandable, in part because the resources of America's schools still differed greatly across districts. As in the past, wealthy suburban areas—most of them overwhelmingly white in makeup—tended to offer far more in the way of facilities and quality instruction than did poorer districts, many of which were heavily populated by minorities. The persistence of such inequality, rooted in class as well as racial cleavages, revealed the chasm that often separated the rhetoric of equality of educational opportunity in America from the reality of it.[11]

America's inability to desegregate many of its neighborhoods and schools, moreover, stood out in the early twenty-first century as the largest failure among efforts—most of them more successful—to move toward greater interracial mixing. Classrooms in many big cities, notably in the Northeast and Midwest, were still overwhelmingly black and Hispanic. In 1998–99, 90 percent of public school students in Chicago were African American or Latino; 83 percent lived in poverty-stricken households. In Detroit, 90 percent of public school students were black and 70 percent were poor enough to qualify for free school lunches; more than one-half of the city's students did not graduate from high school. Mayors in both cities despaired of their school boards, which seemed unable to promote academic progress (or in some schools, to ensure discipline or safety), and assumed control of public education. Many other cities considered the same therapy, even though there was little strong evidence to suggest that mayoral doctoring would cure the ills of their schools.

By the beginning of the new century there was special reason for civil rights activists to worry about resegregation. The trend encouraged by decisions such as *Dowell* (1991) and *Jenkins* (1995) seemed to accelerate in the late 1990s, to affect Latinos as well as blacks, and to involve southern as well as northern areas. Some of the larger school districts—including Cleveland, Dallas, Denver, Minneapolis, Buffalo, Nashville, Grand Rapids, Jacksonville, Mobile as well as Prince Georges County, Virginia, and Wilmington, Delaware—were allowed by judges in the late 1990s to phase out or terminate court supervision.

For this and other reasons, notably white flight and segregation of housing, racial mixing in schools was showing an overall national decline by the late 1990s. In 1999 Gary Orfield and his colleagues estimated that in 1972–73 (following the encouraging burst of desegregation after *Swann*), 63.6 percent of black public school pupils had gone to schools where less than half the student body was white. Similar percentages had persisted until the late 1980s. By 1996–97, however, this percentage had increased to 68.8. Many suburbs, among the fastest growing areas in the nation, also seemed to be breaking apart along racial lines: in 1996–97 the typical African-American child residing in the suburbs of a large metropolitan region went to a school in which 60 percent of students were nonwhite. The luminous star of racial mixing in schools had dimmed.[12]

Lawsuits in the late 1990s further troubled proponents of desegregation. In San Francisco, a Chinese-American parent threatened legal action when his fourteen-year-old son was denied admission to Lowell High, an academically well-regarded school. His lawyers turned the tables on Marshall's arguments in *Brown* by maintaining that the use of racial classifications in assignment of students to public schools violated the Equal Protection Clause of the Fourteenth Amendment. The city's school board managed to avoid the suit in 1999 when it agreed to drop race-based admissions procedures. Though the board said that it would seek racial diversity through other means, it seemed clear that efforts by liberals to achieve considerable racial balance had a dim future in the city.[13]

Litigation also exposed racial divisions in Boston, which was still trying to recover from the battles over busing that had bruised the city twenty-five years earlier. A white parent accused the school board of racial discrimination when the prestigious Boston Latin School did not admit his daughter. Her test scores were higher than those of many minority students who were accepted. A host of people—not all of them conservatives—rallied to her side, asking in effect whether Earl Warren and his colleagues had intended a legacy such as this. In November 1998 a federal court agreed with them and struck down the Latin School's affirmative action procedures. City school officials, fearing to invite an adverse Supreme Court ruling that would be binding nationwide, decided not to appeal. In July 1999 the school board voted to drop racial considerations in pupil placements. The mayor, meanwhile, said that he would try to build more schools in heavily minority neighborhoods. No one imagined that nonsegregated education had much promise in the Hub, an increasingly nonwhite city.[14]

Integrationists found litigation in Charlotte particularly disturbing. The Charlotte-Mecklenburg district, after all, had complied with the *Swann* decision in 1971, which had sanctioned busing to achieve better racial balance. To many people, the city thereafter seemed to be a model community. As in San Francisco and Boston, however, a white parent complained that the city had discriminated against his daughter by denying her admittance (via lottery) to a magnet school. Other white parents joined him. In September 1999 a federal judge concluded that local school officials had done all they could to abolish the vestiges of *de jure* segregation and ordered an end to race-based busing in the city.

Integrationists, maintaining that discrimination persisted, lamented that the court was dismantling nearly thirty years of effort.[15]

What especially troubled advocates of desegregated education at the turn of the century was their sense that federal court decisions, including those from the Supreme Court, were closing the door to virtually all strategies aimed at elevating the value of racial balance in the schools. What quest for racial diversity, if any, might pass constitutional muster? Feeling vulnerable, desegregationists often feared to go to court or to appeal when they lost.

Widely noted litigation involving Montgomery County, Maryland greatly intensified these feelings of vulnerability in 2000. Hoping to preserve racial balance at an elementary school where white enrollment was declining, county officials adopted a policy in 1998 that no student could transfer out of a school if the transfer would adversely affect racial diversity, unless the student could prove some sort of unique "personal hardship." A white parent who sought to send his kindergartner to a magnet school complained, whereupon the federal court of appeals for the fourth circuit in Virginia struck down the county's policy. The Constitution, said the court, prohibited "racial balancing" from being used as the decisive factor in school assignments.

The county then appealed to the Supreme Court, which in March 2000 let the decision stand. The National School Boards Association (which had filed a brief supporting the county) said it was "profoundly disappointed" that the Justices would not hear the case. It added that "education attorneys advising the 15,000 school districts across the country still remain in the dark as to what constitutional standard applies when dealing with this issue."[16]

The dismay of desegregationists was fully understandable. For the Court's refusal to intervene indicated that it tended to value parental choice over strategies that seriously tried to ensure racial diversity. As in *Dowell* (1991) and *Jenkins* (1995), its most recent statements on the subject, the Rehnquist Court remained cool indeed toward tougher enforcement of desegregation of America's schools.

၁၇

Results of various standardized educational test scores further discouraged proponents of educational desegregation in the new century.[17] As was well known by then, scores for blacks had risen slowly between 1970 and the late 1980s, and gaps in scores that separated blacks and whites had narrowed. These were heartening results. But the gaps remained huge. And they widened again in the 1990s, when scores for whites grew faster than those for blacks.[18] The gaps, moreover, seemed mystifyingly intractable as of the new century. They did not seem to be narrowing within districts where compensatory education programs (still receiving $7.7 billion in 1999–2000) were important to funding. Nor did they appear to stem from differences in the physical resources available to predominantly black and predominantly white schools within given districts: as James Coleman had discovered as early as 1966, intradistrict funding per pupil, white or black, did not differ significantly in most places. Even the extent of racial mixing within schools also did not seem to affect the gaps—blacks in schools with fairly well-mixed student populations tended to read a little better at age nine than blacks in more segregated schools, but to do no better in math, and they lost the small gains they had made in reading by the time they reached junior high school.[19]

Social class and parental educational levels also did not do much to explain the gaps in scores. Most black students from relatively well-off families, like blacks from poorer families, continued (*vis-à-vis* whites from families with comparable incomes and educational backgrounds) to score poorly on many of these tests. Black children from families in the top income bracket ($70,000 and up) actually did a little worse on Scholastic Aptitude Test (SAT) verbals, and considerably worse on SAT mathematics tests, in 1994 than white students from the poorest income brackets. And family structures did not seem to matter: black children from single-parent homes scored no lower on the average than black children in two-parent families of comparable class standing.

The conclusions from data like these were sobering indeed. As of the new century it seemed depressingly clear that the considerable increases in educational levels and income among blacks since World War II and *Brown* had not brought about the degree of relative improvement in black academic achievement that many optimists had expected would occur among younger generations of African Americans.[20]

Why, then, do these gaps persist? Some observers think that they stem in part from flaws in the tests. They say accurately that many of the widely used standardized tests measure a relatively narrow range of talents, rewarding students who are quick readers and problem solvers.[21] Critics of these tests further maintain (although unconvincingly) that questions measuring verbal skills tend to be greatly biased against minorities. Critics, finally, point out that many wealthy students pay for prep courses that help them do better on SATs, thereby widening the gap between their scores and those of poorer students, including African Americans. SATs continue to be used, many critics lament, mainly because admissions officers at many of the most selective colleges and universities—a small minority of higher education institutions in the United States—seek additional guidance to help them choose among the hordes of applicants who appear qualified.[22]

Other people who try to account for test score gaps take a historical view that emphasizes the power of racist oppression. Some blame the dark shadow of slavery, when most blacks were forbidden to learn to read, as well as racial and social class isolation stemming from longstanding discrimination and residential segregation.[23] The poverty rate for blacks, continues to be three times as high as that for whites. Average black incomes still hover at around two-thirds of white incomes.[24] Anticipating dim futures such as these, why would black students, especially lower-class students, strive hard for academic excellence? Many observers also deplore the persistence (though in somewhat weakened form) of a historically powerful racist preconception among many whites—that blacks are fit for brawn work, whites for brain work. This stereotype, it is plausibly believed, continues to appeal to a number of whites, including teachers, who expect too little academic achievement from blacks, and to damage blacks, some of whom are said to absorb these low expectations and give up trying.

Students of the gaps suggest a range of specific remedies. One rests on the obvious fact that a number of predominantly black schools, while generally equal in financial resources to predominantly white schools within a given district, are far from equal to many wealthy schools in middle-class, white-dominated towns and suburbs. Because relatively few black students go to these white schools, they are at a competitive disadvantage. Stuck in unequal schools, they are likely to score less well, on the average, on standardized tests. A remedy, therefore, would be to reconfigure state and federal aid to education formulas so as to provide still more compensatory education and other forms of academic assistance to schools in low-income towns and cities. Such an effort would lessen the cross-district inequality of educational resources that the decision in *Rodriguez* (1973) had refused to challenge.

Other proposed remedies also stem from this same assumption: that the key to narrowing gaps in academic achievement is to upgrade schools that are heavily attended by minorities. One calls for considerable reassignment of teachers within districts: predominantly black schools, critics point out, are still less likely than largely white schools to have teachers with strong educational backgrounds and high test scores. Another recommendation is to fight for still smaller classes for black students; learning in small groups is generally thought to make a considerable difference.[25] Reformers also urge other efforts to improve the schools: battling against peer pressures, which have led some black students to accuse their academically ambitious black classmates of "acting white;" expanding mentoring groups, in which bright high schoolers tutor minority junior high school students; developing test preparation courses for minorities; "clustering" minorities in advanced courses so as to reduce their feelings of racial isolation; offering greater support for after-school and summer programs that focus on cognitive development; and—a key—doing everything possible to raise academic standards.[26]

Helpful though some of these school-based reforms would be, scholars are surely correct to emphasize that the gaps start when children are very young—before they get to school. Black children, for instance, are more likely than white children to bring severe academic and behavioral problems with them to the first grade. They have far smaller vocabularies, on the average, than white children do at that age. It follows, these reformers maintain, that schools with pupils such as these need more than equality of resources. They require considerably greater support per child than do other schools.

It also follows, however—as Coleman had emphasized in 1966— that better financed schools alone may not go far to close the gaps, which stem from deeper social and cultural forces that badly affect the cognitive development of very young black children. For this reason, America would very probably do well to strengthen the cognitive content of programs such as Head Start and to invest heavily in day-long, year-long child care and preschool programs that would concentrate on stimulating the cognitive development of all children—or at least of all poor children—beginning at age three.[27]

None of these explanations for test score gaps, however, fully satisfies scholars who have studied the question. Stephan and Abigail Thernstrom, who explored the issue, speculated in 1997 that rising levels of urban violence associated with the spread of crack cocaine in central cities may have depressed black scores in the early 1990s. They also thought that many educators of black children, especially those of an Afrocentric persuasion, were guilty of "dumbing down" the curriculum. But the Thernstroms did not really know what was happening to scores in the 1990s. They conceded, "We're stumped."[28]

A year later, Christopher Jencks and Meredith Phillips edited a book of essays on the problem, in which they argued that the gaps—environmental, not genetic in origin—could be narrowed, perhaps significantly. More desegregation of schools, they speculated, might help a little to close the gulf. They also called for smaller classes and for assignment to minority schools of teachers with high test scores. Like Coleman three decades earlier, they looked primarily to parental and community efforts, not to better financed school resources, for improvement in the cognitive skills of black children. But they, too, conceded that they did not fully understand the reasons for the gaps. In 1999 they confessed that they had "hardly more than hunches about the causes of the black/white test gap."[29]

Why dwell on these gaps? One answer is that they have large and long-range social and economic consequences, because academic achievement and credentials have become vitally important in modern American society. So long as these gaps persist they will slow the mobility of African Americans who yearn to do well in school, go to college, and advance in life. Jencks and Phillips argue cogently that "reducing the black-white test score gap would do more to move America toward racial equality than any politically plausible alternative."[30]

A second answer is that parents are deeply aware of the gaps. Until the gaps close, a number of white people will continue to believe that blacks are less intelligent. Many people (including some African Americans) will remain cool to school desegregation, let alone of strategies like busing, if these approaches do not seem to have beneficial academic effects. Like Thurgood Marshall, like the parents who embarked on "bright flight" from Montclair, New Jersey, they will send their kids to schools—that is, heavily white schools—that promise to give their children a competitive edge in life.

Deeply concerned about these problems, proponents of school desegregation continue to fight their good fight. The gaps, they predict, will narrow as more and educated parents come to emphasize the value of imparting strong cognitive skills to their very young children. Significant academic progress among marginalized groups, they remind us, takes time. They insist also that desegregation involves more than *academic* issues. Americans, they declare, have a moral obligation to fight against racial segregation and inequality in public education. These advocates especially celebrate the *social* virtues of racial mixing and diversity. As Thurgood Marshall had done, they argue that desegregation, especially of such formative influences as schools, can help to break down ugly stereotypes, to promote interracial understanding, and—in time—to nudge the nation toward integration. Backsliding from the goal of racial mixing in schools would therefore be catastrophic. As Jencks wrote in 1998, segregation and resegregation "lead to the general erosion of social ties in society. The more you let society pull itself apart, the less commitment the haves have to the have-nots."[31]

Advocates such as these accurately emphasize that racial discrimination in housing, which reflects class as well as racial divisions, still feeds the roots of school segregation. It is vital, therefore, to combat such discrimination, which as in the past stems from public policies as well as from private actions. Orfield, for instance, has applauded activists who take minority families on trips to suburbs so as to encourage them to move out of the inner city. Like others, he has praised the Gautreaux experiment in the Chicago area, which has subsidized interracial public housing in white suburbs. The key to advancing desegregation in schools, he points out, is to promote and preserve stable, desegregated communities. Once parents and children feel secure in such surroundings, they will rally—as some have done in Montclair, and other places—behind their neighborhoods and their schools. Proposals such as these assert two important truths: school desegregation requires vigilant, unending community commitment from whites as well as blacks, and it depends on larger structural reforms, especially in housing arrangements.[32]

But how to implement these various ideas for reform? In what ways, for instance, can well-meaning "outsiders" get parents, especially those who are poor and over-burdened, to engage more consistently in those key activities—reading regularly to their children, seriously encouraging their creative tendencies, taking them on intellectually liberating excursions—that are vital to early cognitive development? How many white people can be mobilized to storm the barricades of housing segregation? How can school superintendents move their teachers to demand more of students? What would induce white taxpayers to support a vast and expensive preschool and summer school network that would primarily benefit minorities?[33] And why would taxpayers agree to reconfigured formulas of school aid that would direct more of their money to controversial federal programs such as compensatory education? Many Americans, indeed, continue to believe strongly that education must be a local matter. Like Justice Powell in his *Rodriguez* decision, they are convinced that faraway federal and state bureaucrats cannot understand the needs of communities.

Since the 1960s, moreover, no substantial lead for change in race relations has come from the federal government. In the 1990s neither Congress nor the Clinton administration did much to combat segregation in schools or housing. And a majority of the American people, as skeptical as ever since the late 1960s about the capacity of government to do good things, still seem content with the "benign neglect" of the civil rights agenda that President Nixon had agreed to in the early 1970s. They have not applied strong pressure on public officials.[34]

So it is that many African Americans, resenting these attitudes, understandably blame whites for the persistence of racially segregated and unequal schools. They feel no guilt—no great responsibility—for the barriers that since the 1960s have blocked their once grand expectations. Many therefore conclude that further fights for desegregated schools, especially those that depend on complicated, expensive, and slow-moving litigation, are no longer worth the effort. With varying degrees of resignation, resentment, and rage, they live with a good deal of separate-but-equal within districts, so long as it is truly equal and not *de jure,* especially if they can have a major hand in running their own schools.[35]

For blacks like these—and many others—the "wonderful world of possibilities" that Ralph Ellison had dared to anticipate in 1954 has seemed to become an all-too-distant dream by the onset of the twenty-first century.

࿎

These, then, were some of the reasons that advocates of racial justice such as Carter and Clark had grown pessimistic. They were valid reasons, for stalemates that had developed since the brighter years of the 1960s still stymied the lengthy agendas of most civil rights leaders at the turn of the century.[36] But Clark and others like him, their expectations dashed, tended to downplay the extent of changes in race relations since *Brown.* These, to repeat, have been large. The many developments promoting progress for blacks since the 1950s—mass migrations out of the poverty-stricken rural South, the inspiring civil rights movement, strong and well-enforced federal civil rights laws, significant economic growth, wide expansion of public education, more liberal white attitudes, memorable court decisions—vastly improved the legal and socioeconomic status of black people, including millions who by the 1960s were moving into the middle classes and sending their children to colleges and universities. Many of these impressive gains remained real—apparently permanent—at the turn of the twenty-first century.[37] Moreover, few people in this new century would abandon the goals of *Brown,* let alone endorse the return of state-sponsored racial segregation.[38] As if rooted in sand, the ugly institutions of Jim Crow had finally collapsed.

Robert Carter and others nonetheless ask: to what extent was *Brown* responsible for these considerable improvements? The answer to this question remains impossible to pin down. On the one hand, we can agree that the decision did not quickly transform race relations in public education. For many years, *Brown* promoted little change in schools outside some of the border regions. Only in the late 1960s, when the Civil Rights Act of 1964; court decisions like *Jefferson, Green,* and *Alexander;* and firm federal enforcement attacked evasion that had persisted under the guise of "all deliberate speed," did white southerners begin to comply. Potentially explosive racial tensions nonetheless simmered thereafter in cities like Selma, and highly segregated schools persisted in heavily black areas such as Summerton. *De facto* segregation thrived in many cities, especially large metropolitan areas with substantial African-American populations. It survived also in thousands of towns and suburbs, in the North as well as in the South. Court decisions and other governmental efforts finally did destroy *de jure* segregation—a huge achievement—but *de facto* segregation was, and is, another story.

We also need to qualify claims, such as Wilkinson's, that *Brown* touched off the spark that ignited the more militant civil rights movement of the 1960s. To be sure, the decision aroused feelings of guilt and responsibility among many liberally inclined whites. The ruling also spurred a number of activists to demonstrate—activists such as the four students who launched the electrifying sit-ins in Greensboro. Blacks who accelerated the movement took heart from knowing that the High Court, at last, was bravely on their side. But the expanding civil rights movement of the 1960s also depended on the many other powerful social and economic sources noted above, most of which had helped to inspire *Brown* itself. A more militant civil rights movement, even in the absence of a decision such as *Brown,* seems in retrospect to have been highly likely by the 1960s.

Yet *Brown* is far more than a footnote to the history of race relations in the postwar era. After all, the decision took aim at the heart of constitutionally sanctioned Jim Crow—segregated public education. Once enforced at last, Warren's ruling did help to desegregate many American schools, especially in the border states and the South. And it greatly stimulated the transformation of the Court. Energized by their boldness in 1954, the Justices pursued a liberal, activist course, especially in the 1960s, that profoundly affected American jurisprudence. The Burger Court, too, briefly felt obliged to protect and to extend the Warren Court's rulings regarding race and schools. And passionately committed liberal bureaucrats and judges, inspired by the civil rights revolution and the Court, ensured that these rulings would continue to make a difference. Even in the 1980s and 1990s, when conservative Court rulings began to proliferate, the liberal jurisprudence set in motion by the Warren Court—especially by the example of *Brown*—still mattered to many of these judges and officials. Their responses sustained a larger rights-consciousness that deeply influenced American law and life throughout much of the late twentieth century.[39]

Some of these responses, of course, called for major reforms—not only of race relations, but also of criminal justice, welfare administration, and management of civil liberties, among many other matters—that majorities of democratically elected congressmen and state legislators normally opposed. Court-ordered busing, never popular, often aroused furious controversy. Was it appropriate that nonelected, life-tenured Justices and judges—or appointed federal bureaucrats—should so greatly affect the lives of a democratic people? Apostles of judicial restraint generally thought not. From Felix Frankfurter and John Marshall Harlan in the 1950s to Potter Stewart and Byron White in the 1970s and 1980s, and to the conservatives on the Rehnquist Court at the turn of the century, they often assailed the "judge-made law" of Earl Warren, William Brennan, Thurgood Marshall, and their interventionist ilk on the lower courts. But advocates of judicial restraint, too, sometimes concluded that the courts—comparatively isolated as they are from popular attitudes— had to challenge oppressive racial practices. Thus it was in 1954 that the Supreme Court, acting alone, unanimously took the bold and fateful step of assailing *de jure* segregation in the public schools.

Richard Kluger, finally, was on target when he wrote that *Brown* enabled a "reconsecration of American ideals"—ideals of justice and equality that outshone contemporary goals such as anticommunism and material prosperity. This reconsecration by the highest court in the land had considerable, though incalculable, symbolic value, for liberal whites as well as for many hopeful blacks. To be sure, *Brown* called for changes that the Court by itself could not enforce. In time, however, some of these changes came to pass, even in schools, those most highly sensitive of institutions. And it was the courts, aided powerfully by civil rights activists, civil rights acts, and federal officials, that stepped forward to give these changes constitutional standing.

Jack Greenberg, a thoughtful observer of the role of law in American life, has come as close as anyone to assessing the influence of *Brown,* and by extension the capacity of the Court to affect American society. It is a cautiously positive appraisal that credits the role of the judiciary but that also recognizes the necessity of greater popular and governmental engagement on behalf of racial justice if the grand expectations of 1954 and the 1960s are ever to be realized. In 1994 he wrote, "Altogether, school desegregation has been a story of conspicuous achievements, flawed by marked failures, the causes of which lie beyond the capacity of lawyers to correct. Lawyers can do right, they can do good, but they have their limits. The rest of the job is up to society."[40]

NOTE: *This chapter is from James T. Patterson,* **Brown v. Board of Education:** **A Civil Rights Milestone and Its Troubled Legacy (Oxford University Press 2001)** *and is reprinted with permission.*

Endnotes

1. *Hopwood v. Texas*, 78 F. 3d 932 (1996); *The New York Times* 20–25, 1996, Sept. 1, 1997.
2. *The New York Times*, March 21, 1996; *Washington Post*, March 20, 1996. Texas quickly devised new procedures—requiring the university to admit the top 10 percent of graduates of every high school in the state—in order to circumvent *Hopwood*.
3. *Atlanta Constitution,* May 17, 1994; *Newsweek,* May 16, 1994, 26–31.
4. *Washington Post*, May 18, 1994; Brown-Thompson quoted in *Newsday*, May 15, 1994. For the long history of litigation in Topeka, *see* Paul Wilson, **A Time to Lose** (Lawrence, 1995), esp. 224–230. In 1998 the all-black Monroe School, where Linda Brown had gone to school in the early 1950s, became a national park. It is called the *Brown v. Board of Education* National Historic Site.
5. Jack Greenberg, **Crusaders in the Courts** (New York, 1994), 225–226.
6. Damon Freeman, "Reexamining Central High," *Organization of American Historians Newsletter*, Feb. 2000, 3ff; *The New York Times*, Sept. 21, 1997; *Newsday,* Sept. 22, 1997; *St. Louis Post Dispatch*, Sept. 28, 1997. *See also* Melba Pattillo Beals, **Warriors Don't Cry** (New York, 1994), xix–xxii, passim; and Elizabeth Huckaby, **Crisis in Central High** (Baton Rouge, 1980), 220–221.
7. Liva Baker, **The Second Battle of New Orleans** (New York, 1996), 478–480; *People*, Dec. 4, 1995, 104.
8. Kluger, **Simple Justice** (New York, 1975), 710; Wilkinson, **From *Brown* to *Bakke*** (New York, 1979), 49; Morris, "Centuries of Black Protest: Its Significance for America and the World," in **Race and America**, ed. Herbert Hill and James Jones, Jr., (Madison, 1993).
9. Carter in *Washington Post*, May 28, 1994; Clark cited in William Bowen and Derek Bok, **The Shape of the River: Long-Term Consequences of Considering Race in College and University Admissions** (Princeton, 1998), xxiii; Orfield in *New York Times*, June 13, 1999.
10. For ambivalent public attitudes concerning affirmative action *see* Paul Sniderman and Edward Carmines, **Reaching Beyond Race** (Cambridge, Mass.), 143-144. For liberal views, *see* Bowen and Bock, **Shape of the River**, 276–285; and Ronald Dworkin, "Affirming Affirmative Action," *New York Review of Books*, Oct. 22, 1998, 91–102. For a more conservative view, *see* Stephan and Abigail Thernstrom, "Reflections on The Shape of the River," *UCLA Law Review,* 46 (June, 1999), 1583ff. For an informative debate *see*

Nathan Glazer and Abigail Thernstrom, "Should the SAT Account for Race?" *New Republic*, 22 (Sept. 27, 1999), 26–29.

11. Especially large per student differences in school funding characterized New York City and suburban areas in Long Island. Some inner-city school districts heavily populated buy blacks, however, offered higher per student financial backing than did surrounding suburban districts that were predominantly white. Newark, New Jersey, whose students scored poorly on academic achievement tests, was one prominent example. Money, in short, was not a panacea. *See* James Traub, "What No School Can Do," *New York Times Magazine*, Jan. 16, 2000, 52ff.

12. Gary Orfield and John Yun, **Resegregation in American Schools** (Cambridge, Mass., 1999), 14, 24; Orlando Patterson "What to Do When Busing Becomes Irrelevant," *The New York Times*, July 18, 1999. *See also* Megan Twohey, "Desegregation is Dead," *National Journal*, Sept. 17, 1998. In April 2000 the *The New York Times* estimated that one-third of black students attended schools in which 90 percent of the students were non-white. Section IV, April 2, 2000. *See* Appendix II, Table 5 in James T. Patterson, ***Brown v. Board of Education:* A Civil Rights Milestone and Its Troubled Legacy** (Oxford University Press, 2001).

13. *The New York Times*, Feb. 18, 1999; April 2, 2000.

14. *Boston Globe*, April 14, 1998; *The New York Times*, Nov. 20, 1998, March 14, 1999; *Providence Journal*, July 15, 1999. In 1999 15 percent of public school students in Boston were white (as opposed to 60 percent in the early 1970s), 49 percent were Latino, and 9 percent were Asian American.

15. Alison Morantz, "Desegregation at Risk: Threat and Reaffirmation in Charlotte," in **Dismantling Desegregation**, ed., Gary Orfield and Susan Eaton, (New York, 1996), 179–206; *Charlotte Observer*, April 5, Sept. 11, 1997; *The New York Times*, April 25, Sept. 11, 1999.

16. *The New York Times*, March 21 and April 2, 2000.

17. Achievement tests focused on in these pages are the federally sponsored National Assessment of Educational Progress (NAEP) test, given to millions of American students at various ages in reading, mathematics, science, and other subjects. They measure cognitive skills. SATs, which until the late 1990s were misleadingly called "aptitude" tests, in fact reflect levels of cognitive development that depend on a host of social and environmental forces, not on innate "intelligence." *See* Stephan and Abigail Thernstrom, **America in Black and White** (New York, 1997), 348–385, 397–405.

18. Christopher Jencks and Meredith Philipps, "The Black-White Test Score Gap: An Introduction," in **The Black-White Test Score Gap**, ed., Jencks and Phillips, (Washington, 1998), 1–51. They note, 1, that the "typical American black still scores below 75 percent of American whites on most standardized test." Data released in 2000, showed in the average black seventeen-year-old reads about as well as the average white thirteen-year-old

on National Assessment of Educational Progress tests. *The New York Times*, Aug. 25, 2000.

19. Much of the following discussion of test score gaps, including these observations, rests on conclusions in Jencks and Philipps, eds., "The Black-White Test Score Gap"; and on Taub, "What No School Can Do."

20. Thernstroms, **America in Black and White**, 402–405; *The New York Times*, Aug. 25, 2000.

21. Nonetheless, the tests do all right as predictors of performance by students in college.

22. For discussion of these many critiques, *see* Nicholas Lemann, **The Big Test: The Secret History of the American Meritocracy** (New York, 1999), passim.

23. *See* Brent Staples, "How the Racial Literacy Gap First Opened," *The New York Times,* July 23, 1999; Patterson, "What to Do."

24. For a description of inner-city black life that emphasizes economic problems associated with instability of employment *see* William J. Wilson, **When Work Disappears; The World of the New Urban Poor** (New York, 1996).

25. Average class sizes had declined since 1960. Indeed, spending per capita on public schools rose considerably faster than inflation every year between 1945 and 1997 (except during the recession years between 1978 and 1982). *See* National Center for Educational Statistics, U.S. Dept. of Education, *Digest of Education Statistics,* 1997 (Washington, 1998), 172.

26. *USA Today*, Nov. 12, 1999.

27. *See* Traub, "What No School Can Do," France, he argues, supports such a system. Head Start programs, he adds, have normally given relatively little emphasis to cognitive development and have had no lasting impact on the gaps.

28. Thernstroms, **America in Black and White**, 359.

29. Jencks and Philipps, "The Black-White Test Score Gap"; *The New York Times*, July 4, 1999.

30. Jencks and Philipps, "The Black-White Test Score Gap," 43.

31. Cited in Twohey, "Desegregation is Dead."

32. Orfield and Eaton, **Dismantling Segregation**, 90–93; 297–345; and Orfield and Yun, **Resegregation**. For other solutions *see* James Comer, **Waiting for a Miracle: Why Schools Can't Solve Our Problem** (New York, 1998); Orlando Patterson, **The Ordeal of Integration** (New York, 1997), esp. 185–190; and Diane Ravitch, "Our Pluralistic Common Culture," in **Civil Rights and Social Wrongs**, ed., John Higham, (University Park, Pa., 1997), 134–148.

33. Traub, "What No School Can Do" estimates the cost of such a program as at least $25 to $30 billion per year, three times the amount spent on Head Start in 2000. A program of this sort that would also give substantial benefits to middle-class preschoolers would cost three times that much.

34. A study emphasizing the deep historical roots of these urban problems is Jean Anyon, **Ghetto Schooling: A Political Economy of Urban Educational Reform** (New York, 1997).

35. Blacks who dominated school boards in Yonkers, Seattle, and Prince George's County, Maryland, among other places, opted in the late 1990s to dismantle desegregation plans in favor of supporting better-financed neighborhood schools. Twohey, "Desegregation is Dead."

36. These agendas varied, but many leaders continued to support an essentially integrationist set of goals, demanding that federal and state governments act firmly against segregated housing and schools. Most black leaders continued to be Democratic and to call for well-funded social legislation that would attack widespread black poverty, especially in central cities.

37. *See*, for example, Appendix II Table 3 in Patterson, ***Brown v. Board of Education: A Civil Rights Milestone and Its Troubled Legacy*** (Oxford University Press, 2001).

38. Orfield and Eaton, **Dismantling Desegregation**, 108–109, cites a Gallup poll in 1994 revealing that 87 percent of Americans believed *Brown* to be appropriate.

39. For two of many studies that emphasize the staying power of liberal jurisprudence, especially as it encouraged the efforts of an activist federal bureaucracy, *see* R. Shep Melnick, **Between the Lines: Interpreting Welfare Rights** (Washington, 1994); and Jeremy Rabkin, "The Judiciary in the Administrative State," *Public Interest*, 71 (Spring, 1983), 62–84.

40. Greenberg, **Crusaders in the Courts**, 401.

⁖ M E L V I N   I .   U R O F S K Y

Selected Bibliography

In terms of segregation, the key work is C. Vann
Woodward's classic, **The Strange Career of Jim
Crow** (3rd rev. ed., 1974), which argues that segregation need not have become the dominant pattern in
Southern racial relations. A case study testing and
supporting this thesis is Joseph H. Cartwright, **The
Triumph of Jim Crow: Tennessee Race Relations
in the 1880s** (1976). A variation on the Woodward
thesis is Howard N. Rabinowitz, **Race Relations
in the Urban South, 1865–1890** (1978), while
questions of black interest in separation as well as the
timing of segregation laws are explored in two books
by Joel Williamson, **After Slavery: The Negro in
South Carolina during Reconstruction, 1861–1877**
(1965) and **The Crucible of Race: Black/White
Relations in the American South since Emancipation** (1984). Specifics on various states are found
in Pauli Murray, **State's Laws on Race and Color**
(1951), which documents the adoption of Jim Crow
laws. Other works dealing with the treatment of
blacks after the Civil War include William Gillette,
Retreat from Reconstruction, 1869–1879 (1979),
and Daniel A. Novak, **The Wheel of Servitude:
Black Forced Labor After Slavery** (1978). The

standard work on *Plessy* is Charles A. Lofgren, **The *Plessy* Case: A Legal-Historical Interpretation** (1987).

For the beginnings of the civil rights movement after World War II, *see* Louis Ruchames, **Race, Jobs, & Politics** (1953), and Samuel Krislov, **The Negro in Federal Employment: The Quest for Equal Opportunity** (1967). Integration of the armed services is examined in Richard M. Dalfiume, **Desegregation of the U.S. Armed Forces: Fighting on Two Fronts, 1939–1953** (1969). For the Truman administration in general, see Donald R. McCoy and Richard T. Ruetten, **Quest and Response: Minority Rights and the Truman Administration** (1973), and William C. Berman, **The Politics of Civil Rights in the Truman Administration** (1970). The spread of antibias laws into the states is detailed in Duane Lockard, **Toward Equal Opportunity: A Study of State and Local Anti-Discrimination Laws** (1968). The relationship of civil rights to the Cold War and American foreign policy is detailed in Mary L. Dudziak, **Cold War Civil Rights: Race and the Image of American Democracy** (2000).

For the *Shelley* case, *see* Clement E. Vose, **Caucasians Only: The Supreme Court, the N.A.A.C.P. and the Restrictive Covenant Cases** (1959), and Mark V. Tushnet, "*Shelley v. Kraemer* and Theories of Equality," 33 *New York Law School Law Review* 383 (1988). For other pre-*Brown* decisions, *see* Daniel T. Kelleher, "The Case of Lloyd Lionel Gaines: The Demise of the Separate but Equal Doctrine," 56 *Journal of Negro History* 262 (1971); Loren Miller, **The Petitioners: The Story of the Supreme Court of the United States and the Negro** (1966); Darlene Clark Hine, **Black Victory: The Rise and Fall of the White Primary in Texas** (1979); Irving F. Lefberg, "Chief Justice Vinson and the Politics of Desegregation," 24 *Emory Law Journal* 243 (1975); and Catherine A. Barnes, **Journey from Jim Crow: The Desegregation of Southern Transit** (1983).

The NAACP strategy is explicated in two books by Mark V. Tushnet, **The NAACP's Legal Strategy Against Segregated Education, 1925–1950** (1987), and **Making Civil Rights Law: Thurgood Marshall and the Supreme Court, 1936–1961** (1994). See also Jack Greenberg, **Crusaders in the Courts** (1994), the story of the NAACP legal challenge to segregation by one of the then-young legal staff. For more on Marshall, *see* Juan Williams, **Thurgood Marshall: American Revolutionary** (1998).

For civil rights and black status in general during the 1940s and 1950s, *see* Donald G. Nieman, **Promises to Keep: African-Americans and the Constitutional Order, 1776 to the Present** (1991), Harvard Sitkoff, **The Struggle for Black Equality, 1954–1992** (1993), and Taylor Branch, **Parting the Waters: America in the King Years, 1954–1963** (1988). A good overview of the period in general is James T. Patterson, **Grand Expectations: The United States, 1945–1974** (1996).

The literature on *Brown* is massive, but the definitive analysis is Richard Kluger, **Simple Justice: The History of *Brown v. Board of Education* and Black America's Struggle for Equality** (1975, rev. ed. 2004). Kluger covers all the cases leading up to *Brown,* the divisions on the Court, as well as the litigation strategies on both sides. Other useful works on the case include Daniel M. Berman, **It Is So Ordered: The Supreme Court Rules on School Segregation** (1966); Alfred H. Kelly, "The School Desegregation Case," in John A. Garraty, ed., **Quarrels That Have Shaped the Constitution** (1964); Charles L. Black, Jr., "The Lawfulness of the Segregation Decisions," 69 *Yale Law Journal* 421 (1960); and Ira M. Heyman, "The Chief Justice, Racial Segregation, and the Friendly Critics," 49 *California Law Review* 104 (1961). The question of how the Justices divided before the opinion is discussed in Mark V. Tushnet and Katya Lezin, "What Really Happened in *Brown v. Board of Education,*" 91 *Columbia Law Review* 1867 (1991), while the unanimity matter is examined in Dennis J. Hutchinson, "Unanimity and Desegregation: Decision-making in the Supreme Court, 1948–1958," 68 *Georgetown Law Journal* 1 (1979).

The relevance of the Fourteenth Amendment to the case is discussed in Alfred H. Kelly, "The Fourteenth Amendment Reconsidered: The Segregation Question," 54 *Michigan Law Review* 1049 (1956), and Alexander M. Bickel, "The Original Understanding and the Segregation Decision," 69 *Harvard Law Review* 1 (1955), originally prepared as a research memorandum when Bickel clerked for Justice Frankfurter. The problem of social science data is touched on in I. A. Newby, **Challenge to the Court: Social Scientists and the Defense of Segregation, 1954–1966** (1967), most of which is an attack on scientific racism.

Works dealing with southern resistance to desegregation include Benjamin Muse, **Virginia's Massive Resistance** (1961); Bob Smith,

They Closed Their Schools: Prince Edward County, Virginia, 1951–1964 (1965); Numan V. Bartley, **The Rise of Massive Resistance: Race and Politics in the South During the 1950s** (1969); Neil R. McMillen, **The Citizens' Council: Organized Resistance to the Second Reconstruction, 1954–1964** (1971); and Charles Fairman, "The Attack on the Segregation Cases," 70 *Harvard Law Review* 83 (1956). Southern constitutional theory is presented in James J. Kilpatrick, **The Southern Case for School Segregation** (1962). A good overview is Benjamin Muse, **Ten Years of Prelude: The Story of Integration Since the Supreme Court's 1954 Decision** (1964). A unique study is J. W. Peltason, **Fifty-eight Lonely Men** (1961), a sympathetic examination of federal judges in the South who enforced the desegregation decisions. On Arkansas, *see* the excellent case study by Tony Freyer, **The Little Rock Crisis: A Constitutional Interpretation** (1984).

The literature on the Warren Court is growing rapidly. An excellent book placing the Court and its decisions within the larger political context of the times is Lucas A. Powe, Jr., **The Warren Court and American Politics** (2000). A short introduction is Morton J. Horwitz, **The Warren Court and the Pursuit of Justice** (1998). Two useful collections of essays are Mark V. Tushnet, ed., **The Warren Court in Historical and Political Perspective** (1993), and Bernard Schwartz, ed., **The Warren Court: A Retrospective** (1996). The older Alexander M. Bickel, **Politics and the Warren Court** (1965) is still pertinent.

A better understanding of what the legal battles were all about requires knowledge of the civil rights struggle itself. Some well-balanced accounts include Taylor Branch, **Parting the Waters: America in the King Years, 1954–1963** (1988); Hugh Davis Graham, **The Civil Rights Era: Origins and Development of National Policy, 1960–1972** (1990); Harvard Sitkoff, **The Struggle for Black Equality, 1954–1992** (1993); and John Higham, ed., **Civil Rights and Social Wrongs: Black-White Relations since World War II** (1997). For a look at how the movement played out in local areas, *see* William H. Chafe, **Civilities and Civil Rights: Greensboro, North Carolina, and the Black Struggle for Freedom** (1980); John Dittmer, **Local People: The Struggle for Civil Rights in Mississippi** (1994); and the dramatic story that Russell H. Barrett tells in **Integration at Ole Miss** (1965).

The Court's growing annoyance with Southern delay is covered in J. Harvie Wilkinson, III, **From *Brown* to *Bakke:* The Supreme Court and School Integration, 1954–1978** (1979). For case studies on the attack on segregated schools, *see* Liva Baker, **The Second Battle of New Orleans: The Hundred-Year Struggle to Integrate the Schools** (1996); Frye Gaillard, **The Dream Long Deferred** (1988), which deals with Charlotte, North Carolina; and Bob Smith, **They Closed Their Schools: Prince Edward County, Virginia, 1951–1964** (1965).

The expansion of the attack on racial segregation is looked at in Catherine A. Barnes, **Journey from Jim Crow: The Desegregation of Southern Transit** (1983), and Thomas P. Lewis, "*Burton v. Wilmington Parking Authority*—A Case Without Precedent," 61 *Columbia Law Review* 1458 (1961). For the miscegenation cases, *see* Harvey M. Applebaum, "Miscegenation Statutes: A Constitutional and Social Problem," 53 *Georgetown Law Journal* 49 (1964), and Peter Wallenstein, "Race, Marriage, and the Supreme Court: From *Pace v. Alabama* (1883) to *Loving v. Virginia* (1967)," 1998 *Journal of Supreme Court History* 25, no. 2.

There is a growing body of material on the long-term effects of *Brown* and its progeny on education and race relations. A good synthesis is James T. Patterson, ***Brown v. Board of Education:* A Civil Rights Milestone and Its Troubled Legacy** (2001). *See* the even more discouraging view in Peter Irons, **Jim Crow's Children: The Broken Promise of the *Brown* Decision** (2002). Other analyses of the half-century following *Brown* include David J. Armor, **Forced Justice: School Desegregation and the Law** (1995); Lino A. Graglia, **Disaster by Decree: The Supreme Court Decisions on Race and the Schools** (1976); Andrew Kull, **The Color-Blind Constitution** (1992); and Gerald N. Rosenberg, **The Hollow Hope: Can Courts Bring About Social Change?** (1991). The long-term debate can be examined in such books as Orlando Patterson, **The Ordeal of Integration: Progress and Resentment in America's "Racial" Crisis** (1998) and Andrew Hacker, **Two Nations: Black and White, Separate, Hostile, Unequal** (1992); a contrary and more upbeat view can be found in Abigail and Stephan Thernstrom, **America in Black and White: One Nation Indivisible** (1997).

Contributors

Herbert Brownell (1904-1996) served as Attorney General from 1953 to 1957.

Clare Cushman is Director of Publications at the Supreme Court Historical Society.

John D. Fassett clerked for Justice Stanley F. Reed during the 1953–54 Term. He is the author of **New Deal Justice: The Life of Stanley Reed of Kentucky** (1994).

Bradley D. Hayes is a doctoral candidate in the Government and Politics Department at the University of Maryland, College Park.

Diana E. Hess is a professor of education at the University of Wisconsin-Madison.

Jeffrey D. Hockett is an assistant professor of political science at the University of Tulsa and the author of **New Deal Justice: The Constitutional Jurisprudence of Hugo L. Black, Felix Frankfurter, and Robert H. Jackson** (1996).

Andrew Kull is a professor at Emory University School of Law and the author of **The Color-Blind Constitution** (1998).

David W. Levy is the Sam K. Viersen Presidential Professor of American History at the University of Oklahoma.

James T. Patterson is the Ford Foundation Professor of History at Brown University. "Legacies and Lessons" is excerpted from ***Brown v. Board of Education*: A Civil Rights Milestone and Its Troubled Legacy** (Oxford University Press 2001).

Gerald N. Rosenberg is associate professor in the Department of Political Science at the University of Chicago and a lecturer at the University of Chicago Law School. He is the author of **The Hollow Hope: Can Courts Bring About Social Change?** (1991)

Melvin I. Urofsky, Chairman of the Board of Editors of the *Journal of Supreme Court History*, is professor of public policy at Virginia Commonwealth University. He is now at work on a study of campaign finance reform and the courts.

Paul E. Wilson was the assistant attorney general who argued the *Brown* case for Kansas. He was a Distinguished Professor at the School of Law at the University of Kansas before his death in 2001.

Index

ABA Journal, 212, 213
Abernathy, Ralph David, 224, 225, 237, 239
Academic achievement, 304–311
Academic knowledge, 279–280
Acheson, Dean, 9
Ackerman, Bruce, 262, 272
Adair v. United States (1980), 29, 44
Adkins v. Children's Hospital (1923), 29, 44
"Affected with a public interest," 4–5
Affirmative action, 275, 277, 287, 297–298, 301, 303
African-American rights, *Brown* contributions to, 203–240
African independence, 228
Alabama, 27, 35, 37
Alexander v. Holmes, 197, 311
"All deliberate speed," 34, 38, 56–58, 62, 183, 196–197, 200, 282–283, 311
American Bar Association (ABA), 212
American Civil Liberties Union (ACLU), 154
American Dilemma, An (Myrdal), 28, 68
Amicus briefs, 17, 34, 182, 194, 195, 201
Anderson, J. W., 236
Anderson, Marian, 83
Anyon, Jean, 317
Apologias, 251–255
Apple, M., 277, 293

Arguments
  first argument, 20–24, 153, 163–167
  reargument, 24–25, 142, 153, 163–169, 172, 175, 194–195, 242–243
Arkansas, 9, 27, 35, 181
Little Rock, 190, 197, 201, 209–210, 211, 259, 299–300
Asian Americans, 301
Atlanta, Georgia, 226
Atlanta Constitution, 27, 217
Atwell, William, 35–36

Baker, Leonard, 42
Baker, Liva, 124, 145, 314
Bakke v. California (1976), 277, 297
Ball, Howard, 42, 135–136, 148
Ball, William B., 112, 252, 270
Baltimore, Maryland, 32, 70–71
Banks, J. A., 293
Barnes, Catherine A., 40, 234
Barrows v. Jackson (1953), 41
Bartley, Numan V., 85
Baton Rouge, Louisiana, 225
Beals, Melba Pattillo, 314
Beane, J., 277, 293
Beiser, Edward, 31
Bell, Derrick A., 278–279, 282, 285, 293, 294
Bell v. Maryland (1964), 65

Bender, Paul, 31
Berea College v. Commonwealth [of Kentucky] (1906), 65
Berea College v. Kentucky (1908), 39, 58–59, 65, 178
Berger, Monroe, 112, 113, 251, 270
Berger, Raoul, 109, 111, 269
Berman, Daniel M., 236
Berman, William C., 40
Bernstein, Barton J., 253–254, 271
Berry, Mary Frances, 125, 146
Bickel, Alexander M., 22, 39, 63, 65, 98, 103, 109, 114, 128, 146, 204, 233, 244–245, 259–260, 269, 272
Birmingham, Alabama, 38, 259
Black, Charles L., Jr., 44, 112, 113, 255–260, 261, 262, 271
Black, Earl, 234
Black, Hugo L., 19–20, 21, 111, 114, 123, 124, 197
Black boycotts, 226–227
Black Codes, 2, 256
Black colleges, 68–70
Black groups, 228–230
Black middle class, 84, 311
Black revolution, 223
Blacks
    Brown contributions to black rights, 203–240
    economic power of, 225, 226–227
    effect of *Brown* on, 223–224
    inferiority of, 96, 101, 103, 105, 143
    migration to North, 83
Blaustein, Albert P., 145
Bob-Lo Excursion Co. v. Michigan (1938), 10–11
Bois-Blanc Island, 10–11
Bok, Derek, 314
Bolick, Clint, 297–298
Bolling, Spottswood, 189
Bolling v. Sharpe (1954), 43, 117, 170, 179, 255, 271
Bombings, 211
Bond, Horace Mann, 85
Bork, Robert H., 261, 272, 274
Boston Latin School, 303
Bowen, William, 314

Bradlee, Ben, 206–207
Bradley, Joseph P., 4, 5, 49
Branch, Taylor, 235, 237, 238, 239
Brandeis brief, 25, 28–29
Brands, H. W., 40
Brandsberg-Engelmann, Jennifer, 277–278
Brennan, William, 313
Bridges-Hall, Ruby, 300
Briggs, Harry, Jr., 189
Briggs v. Elliott, 170, 176
Brink, William, 235
Brotherhood of Railway Trainmen v. Howard (1952), 41
Brown, Cheryl, 154, 155
Brown, Ethel Louis Belton, 189
Brown, Henry Billings, 5, 253–254, 262
Brown, John R., 35, 198–199
Brown, Linda, 151–156, 159, 188, 189, 298, 314
Brown, Oliver and Leola, 151–152, 159
Brown v. Board of Education (Patterson), 140
Brown v. Board of Education 50th Anniversary Presidential Commission, 155
Brown v. Board of Education National Historic Site, 155, 314
Brown v. Board of Education of Topeka (1954)
    as classroom icon, 275–295
    conference discussions, 124, 129, 130, 139–140, 141–143
    criticism of, 28–31, 89–90, 99–103, 242–250
    decision handed down, 25–27, 153, 171–179
    defense of opinion, 31–32
    delays in, 22–23
    effects of, 54–58, 283
    empirical critique, 246–250
    first argument (1952), 20–24
    historical critique, 242–245
    historical perspective, 1–45
    initial reactions, 27–28
    as irrelevant, 283
    lessons and legacies, 297–317

as liberation referent, 280–281
narrow scope of, 27
reargument (1953), 24–25, 142, 153,
    163–169, 172, 175, 194–195,
    242–243
recasting of basis, 255–260
reversal attempts, 101–102
as rightful icon, 280
"rightness of," 31–32
transposed reputations of *Plessy* and
    Brown, 261–265
as unfulfilled promise, 281
voting, 123–124, 129
as well-intentioned error, 282–283
Brown v. Board of Education of Topeka
    (1955), 34–35, 169, 196–197. See
    also Implementation
decision handed down, 181–183
legal theories for enforcement,
    200–201
reaction to, 153
*Brown et al. v. Board of Education of
    Topeka, Shawnee County, Kansas et
    al.* (1994), 156
Brown Foundation for Educational
    Equity, Excellence and Research,
    155
Brown II. *See Brown v. Board of Education
    of Topeka* (1955)
Brown-Thompson, Linda, 151–156, 159,
    188, 298, 314
Brownell, Herbert, 190, 193–201, 229
Buchanan v. Warley (1917), 40, 61–63
Bullock, Charles S., III, 234
Burger, Warren E., 194, 281, 312
Burk, Robert Fredrick, 236
Burton, Harold H., 10, 20–21, 106, 123,
    125
Burton v. Wilmington Parking Authority
    (1961), 41
Bus boycotts, 224–225, 227, 228–229
Bush v. Orleans Parish School Board
    (1956), 44
Busing, 303–304
Bus segregation, 10, 211, 224–225
Butler (1936), 44
Butler, Pierce, 72

Byrd, Harry F., 36–37
Byrnes, James F., 28

Cahn, Edmond, 29, 44, 112, 113,
    251–252, 270
Calhoun, John C., 36–37, 261
California, 277, 301, 303
Canada, 10–11
Canon, Bradley C., 107, 109, 115
Cardozo, Benjamin N., 243
Carmines, Edward, 314
Carolene Products Co.; United States v.
    (1939), 50, 64
Carson, Clayborne, 238, 239
Carter, Robert, 165, 166, 168, 279, 301,
    311
Carter, Roy E., Jr., 235
Casper, Gerhard, 43
Causation, 207–208, 215–217
Central High School (Little Rock, Ark.),
    190, 209–210, 299–300
Chafe, William H., 239
Charlotte, North Carolina, 303–304
Cheney, Dick, 206–207
Cherokee Indians, 56
Chesapeake & O. Ry. v. Kentucky (1900),
    65
Chicago, Illinois, 302
Chicago Defender, 27
Chief Justice (Cray), 139, 140
Child care, 307–308
Chiles v. Chesapeake & O. Ry. (1910), 65
Chinese Americans, 303
Chomsky, Noam, 287, 294
Cincinnati Enquirer, 27
Citizens Councils, 32, 36, 197, 200,
    210–211
Citizenship rights, 3, 4
Civil rights, 8
    acts and bills, 219–220
    American sensitivity to, 222–223
    Brown contributions to, 203–240
    cultural barriers to, 210–211
    demonstrations, 223–224, 225–227
Civil Rights Act of 1866, 12, 57, 244
Civil Rights Act of 1875, 2, 3–4, 49
Civil Rights Act of 1957, 221, 229

Civil Rights Act of 1960, 221
Civil Rights Act of 1964, 216, 220, 221,
    232, 311
  Title VI, 215
  Title VII, 57, 220
Civil Rights Act of 1968, 57, 65
Civil Rights Cases (1883), 4–5, 6, 49
Civil Rights Commission, 220
"Civil-rights era," 49–50, 52
Civil rights jurisprudence, 4
Civil rights movement, 54, 84, 220,
    228–230, 301, 312
Civil War Amendments, 6, 23
Clark, Kenneth B., 28, 43–44, 112, 179,
    188, 249–252, 270–271, 301
Clark, Tom C., 17, 19, 20–21, 114, 120,
    124
Cleghorn, Reese, 235
Clinton, Bill, 299, 310
Cold War, 8, 12, 83–84
Coleman, James, 305, 307
Coleman, William T., Jr., 22, 42
Color-blindness concept, 6, 47, 63,
    266–267, 298
Columbia Law Review, 129
Columbia University, 120
Comer, James, 316
Commerce, 11–12
Commerce Act, 9
Commerce Clause, 10, 53
Common carriers, 5–6, 9–12, 15, 211
Common Law, The (Holmes), 83
Communism, 28
Compliance, 32–33, 35–38, 96,
    102–103, 182–183
Confederate states, reinstatement of,
    92–93
Conference discussions, 124, 129, 130,
    139–140, 141–143
Conference of Chief Justices of State
    Courts, 212–213
Confidentiality, 124, 126, 130, 134, 139
Congress
  civil rights legislation, 8, 97–98,
    219–221
  drafting 14th Amendment, 49
  employment discrimination, 57

enforcement of *Brown,* 215
  power to implement decisions, 93–94
  powers under 14th Amendment, 4
  reaction to *Brown,* 36–37, 215–217,
    220
  state action and, 5
Congress of Racial Equality (CORE), 228
Connor, Eugene "Bull," 259
Consciousness of kind, 253
Constitution, U.S. *See also* Fourteenth
    Amendment
  color-blindness concept, 47, 63,
    266–267
  Commerce Clause, 10, 53
  Fifteenth Amendment, 19–20, 52, 56,
    92
  "living Constitution," 30, 241–242,
    245–246, 261, 266
  Thirteenth Amendment, 4
Constitutional adjudication, 56–57
Constitutional interpretation, 29–30, 266
Constitutional law, 54–55, 58–63
Cooke, Jack Kent, 206–207
Cooper, John Milton, Jr., 39
Cooper, Phillip J., 42
Cooper v. Aaron, 211
Cornbleth, Catherine, 284, 294
Court-ordered school admissions, 18
Court-packing crisis, 49, 50
Courts. *See also* Supreme Court
  enforcement and, 196–199
  implementation and, 94
  local courts, 213–215
  social change by, 204, 231
  state courts, 214
Covenants, 12, 53, 57
Cox, Archibald, 113
Cray, Ed, 139, 148
Crenshaw, K., 293
Criticism, 28–31, 89–90, 99–103,
    242–250
Cross, George Lynn, 74–75, 76, 79, 86,
    87
Cross burnings, 199–200
Cultural barriers to civil rights, 210–211
Cumming v. County Board of Education,
    173, 178
Cushman, Clare, 131, 147

Dallas, Texas, 35–36, 214
Daniels, William J., 233
Davidson, T. Whitfield, 36
Davis, John W., 20, 24, 29, 165–167, 186, 249–250
Davis v. County School Bd. of Prince Edward County, Virginia (1951), 170, 176–177
Day, William Rufus, 61–62
De facto segregation, 3, 286, 311–312
De jure segregation, 286, 310, 311, 313
Decision day, 131, 134–135
"Declaration of Constitutional Principles." *See* Southern Manifesto
Defense contracts, 7
Delaware, 19, 32, 172, 177, 179, 183
Demonstrations, 223–224, 225–227
Dent, Francis, 12
Dental colleges, 69
Department of Health, Education, and Welfare, 215
Department of Justice, 8, 17, 193–196, 199–201
Derrington v. Plummer (1957), 41
Desegregation
    costs of, 14, 78
    immediate, 196
    progress of, 97–98, 208–209, 214–215, 279, 281, 298
Desegregation and the Law (Blaustein & Ferguson), 119
Desegregation plans, 196, 200–201
Detroit, Michigan, 302
Deutsch, Jan G., 273
Devins, Neal, 233
Dickson, Del, 139–140, 142, 146, 148, 149
Dilworth, Paulette, 294
Discrimination, 220
    employment, 8, 57, 220
    gender, 275–276
    housing, 12–13, 57, 61–62, 309
    private, 4, 57
    segregation as, 6
District of Columbia, 12, 19, 21, 32, 43, 92, 195–197
Diversity, 84

Dixon, Robert G., Jr., 235
Dolbeare, Kenneth M., 234
Doll study, 188, 250, 251
Douglas, Dave, 233
Douglas, William O., 11, 20–21, 120, 123, 126, 146
Dowell v. Board of Ed. of Oklahoma City (1991), 302, 304
Drafting the opinion, 26, 130, 140
Dred Scott v. Sandford (1857), 48, 256, 276, 293
DuBois, W. E. B., 28
Dudziak, Mary L., 40
Due Process Clause, 12, 175, 246
Dunne, Gerald T., 124–125, 145
Dworkin, Ronald, 111, 274, 314

Eaton, Susan, 315, 316, 317
Eckford, Elizabeth, 299–300
Economic coercion, 211
Economic forces, 54–55
Economic power of blacks, 225, 226–227
Education standards, 276–277
Eisenhower, Dwight D., 24, 94, 98, 190, 193–199, 201, 209, 220–221
Electoral success, 209–210
Elementary & Secondary Education Act (1965), 215
Elites, 218, 219
Ellison, Ralph, 310–311
Elman, Philip, 42
Ely, John Hart, 44, 113, 114
Empirical basis of *Plessy*, 101, 252–254
Empirical critique of *Brown*, 101, 246–250
Employment discrimination, 8, 57, 220
Enforcement, 56–57, 58–63, 93, 193–201
    Congress and, 215
    courts and, 196–199
    of equal rights, 50–54, 61
    legal theories for, 200–201
    timetable for, 196–197
Enforcement Clause, 3–4
Engineering schools, 69
Epstein, Lee, 233, 234
Epstein, Terrie, 295

Equal facilities, 9, 14, 248–249, 257
Equal protection, 51
Equal Protection Clause, 1–2, 11, 12–13, 48, 75, 246, 303
Equal rights
    enforcement of, 50–54, 61
    logical exactness and, 61
    tests of, 61
Erskine, Hazel Gaudet, 236
Evans, R. W., 294
Evers, Medgar, 211
Ex Parte Virginia (1880), 110, 178
Executive authority, 8
Executive orders, 7, 8
Extra-judicial path of causal influence, 208, 215–217
Extra-legal materials. *See* Social science evidence

F. S. Royster Guano Co. v. Virginia (1920), 110
Fair Employment Practices Commission (FEPC), 7–8
Fairclough, Adam, 237, 239
Fairman, Charles, 268
Farmer, James, 228, 238, 239
Fassett, John D., 117–145, 147, 149
Faubus, Orval, 201, 209–210, 222, 299
Fayer, Steve, 239
Federal funding for schools, 215
Federalism, 10, 50, 52–53, 56
Federalist Papers, 205
Ferguson, Clarence Clyde, Jr., 145
Fifteenth Amendment, 19–20, 52, 56, 92
Fifties, The (Halberstam), 131
Finch, Minnie, 239
Finkelman, Paul, 45
Fisher, Ada Lois Sipuel, 13–14, 41, 74–76, 84–85, 86, 87
Fisher v. Hurst (1948), 110
Fitzwater, Marlin, 206–207
Flagg, Barbara J., 264, 273
Florida, 33, 35, 37, 181
Fly-paper court, 230–233
Folsom, "Big Jim," 27
Footnote 11, 28–29, 36, 43, 243–244, 249–250. *See also* Social science evidence

Foreign commerce, 11
Forman, James, 228–229
Forman, Thomas, 238, 239
Fourteenth Amendment
    in *Brown* opinion, 172–173
    congressional powers under, 4
    Court dismissal of, 28
    drafting of, 49
    Due Process Clause, 12; 175, 246
    Enforcement Clause, 3–4
    Equal Protection Clause, 1–2, 11, 12–13, 48, 75, 246, 303
    framers' intentions, 22, 98, 266
    history of, 25, 242–245
    housing discrimination and, 61–62
    Jackson memorandum and, 90–96
    Plessy and, 5
    restrictive covenants and, 57
    rule of reason and, 61
    state action and, 4–5, 51–52
    white primaries and, 52
Frankfurter, Felix, 56
    legal profession's support of *Brown,* 212
    mootness of case, 168
    and Reed, 120, 126–129, 141, 144
    reservations on Court's power, 11, 17, 20–24, 313
    Wilson, Paul, and, 166, 168
Franklin, John Hope, 272
Freedom of association, 249
Freedom riders, 211, 228, 231
Freeman, Damon, 314
Freund, Paul, 22
Friedman, Leon, 214, 235, 239, 268, 270
Fugitive slave laws, 4
Future mandates promise, 62–63

Gaines (1938), 7, 9, 17, 40, 50–51, 72–73, 86, 110, 144, 173
Gaines, Lloyd, 51, 72–73, 86
Gaither, Thomas, 238
Gallen, David, 135, 147
Gallup poll, 222
Garfinkel, Herbert, 112, 252–253, 254–255, 270, 271
Garrow, David J., 227, 234, 237, 238, 239

Gatell, Frank Otto, 236
Gayle v. Browder (1956), 64, 237, 270
Gaylord, Helen, 132, 134–135, 143
Gebhart v. Belton (1952), 170, 177
Gellhorn, Walter, 14–15
Gender discrimination, 275–276
Georgetown Law Journal, 126
Georgia, 27, 35, 37, 56, 210, 226
Giddings, Franklin Henry, 253
Giles v. Harris, (1903) 55–56
Gillette, William, 39
Gillman, Howard, 267
Ginsburg, Ruth Bader, 275–276, 293
Glazer, Nathan, 315
Golding, M. P., 263, 273
Goldman, Roger, 135, 147
Goldman, Sheldon, 233
Gong Lum v. Rice (1927), 65, 173, 178
Good, Paul, 238
Gotanda, N., 293
Graduate education, 17, 69–70
*Graduate Instruction for Negroes in the
    United States* (McCuistion), 69–70
Grantham, Dewey W., 27–28, 43
Gratz v. Bollinger (2003), 292
Graves, John Temple, 37
*Green v. County School Board of New Kent
    County* (1968), 300, 311
Green, Ernest, 299
Greenawalt, Kent, 264, 273
Greenberg, Jack, 187, 204, 208, 223,
    231, 236, 313–314, 317
Greensboro, North Carolina, 226–227,
    312
Gregor, A. James, 102, 113, 250,
    251–252, 270
Grooms, Harlen H., 199
Grovey v. Townsend (1935), 52, 64
Grutter v. Bollinger (2003), 292
Gubernatorial candidates, 209–210
Gugin, Linda C., 138, 141–142, 148,
    149
Gunther, Gerald, 64, 261, 272
Gutmann, Amy, 288, 295

Halberstam, David, 131, 147
Hall v. DeCuir (1878), 5, 10
Hamilton, Alexander, 205

Hamm v. City of Rock Hill (1964), 65
Hampton, Henry, 239
Hand, Learned, 245, 246, 269
Harlan, John Marshall, 4, 5–7, 26,
    47–48, 184, 262, 313
Harris poll, 206
Harvard Law Review, 213
Hastie, William H., 8, 9–10
Hayes, George E. C., 187
Head Start, 307–308
Health, Education, and Welfare Depart-
    ment, 215
Henderson, Cheryl Brown, 154, 155
Henderson v. United States (1950), 15, 17
Henkin, Louis, 263, 273
Hess, Diana E., 293
Heyman, Ira Michael, 271
Higham, John, 316
Higher education, 67–88
Hill, Herbert, 314
Hill, Oliver, 282–283
Hinckley, Barbara, 109
Hine, Darlene Clark, 42
Hirabayashi v. United States (1943), 65,
    271
Hirsch, H. N., 128, 147, 262, 272
Hispanics, 301, 302
Historical critique, 242–245
Historical perspective, 1–45
Hochschild, Jennifer L., 85
Hocutt v. Wilson (1933), 86
Holmes, Oliver Wendell, Jr., 55–56, 58,
    61, 83, 88
Holmes v. City of Atlanta (1955), 64, 270
Homosexual sodomy case, 281
Hook, Sidney, 273
Hopwood v. Texas (1996), 314
Horwitz, Morton J., 44, 240
Hospitals, 6
Housing discrimination, 12–13, 57,
    61–62, 309
Housing segregation, 302
Houston, Charles H., 71, 72
Hovenkamp, Herbert, 271
Howell, Ronald F., 262–263, 272
Huckaby, Elizabeth, 314
Hughes, Charles Evans, 7, 60–61, 72
Hurd v. Hodge (1948), 41

Hutchinson, Dennis J., 42, 108, 133, 146
Hyman, Herbert H., 222, 236

Iconization of *Brown,* 280, 287–289
Implementation, 32–35, 93–94, 169,
    181–183, 230. *See also* Brown v.
    Board of Education of Topeka (1955)
Indiana, 277
Indiana Historical Society, 138
Indirect effects, 215–217
Individual rights, 60
Inferiority of blacks, 96, 101, 103, 105,
    143
Institutional legitimacy, 213
Interbreeding, 96
Interest convergence, 285–286
Interstate carriers, 15
Interstate commerce, 10
Interstate Commerce Commission, 9
Irrelevancy, 283

Jackson, Andrew, 56, 205
Jackson, Robert H., 89–115
    Bob-Lo dissent, 11
    comment on *Brown,* 230
    limitations of memorandum, 103–106
    memorandum, 96–103
    Plessy and, 20–22
    Reed myth and, 120, 124, 127,
        133–134
    segregation and Fourteenth Amend-
        ment, 90–96
    Youngstown and, 197
Jacob, Herbert, 234
Jahnige, Thomas P., 233
Japanese curfew and exclusion cases, 255
Japanese Relocation cases, 62
Jaybird Democratic Association, 19–20
Jemison, T. J., 225
Jencks, Christopher, 308, 309, 315, 316
Jenkins (1995), 302, 304
Jim Crow laws, 2, 3, 6, 10
Job discrimination, 8, 57, 220
Johnson, Charles A., 107, 109, 115
Johnson, Frank, 35, 198, 214
Johnson, Lyndon B., 197, 209, 220–221
Jones, James, Jr., 314
Jones, Richard, 154

Jones, Walter B., 214
Jones v. Alfred H. Mayer Co. (1968), 65
Journal of Negro Education, The, 69, 70, 86
Judges, 8, 35–36
Judicial action, 89–115
Judicial activism, 29, 204
Judicial appointments, 198–199
Judicial enforcement, 196–199
Judicial notice doctrine, 258–260
Judicial path of causal influence, 207–208
Judicial power, 50–54
Judicial reaction, 35–36
Judicial restraint, 22
Judiciary, and implementation, 94
Juries, 2, 62
Justice Department, 8, 17, 193–196,
    199–201

Kansas, 19, 158–160, 162, 167–169,
    176, 178
Kansas Museum of History, 161
Karst, Kenneth L., 31–32, 44, 269
Kasper, John, 199
Kastner, Daniel L., 233
Kelley, Alfred H., 43, 269
Kennedy, John F., 197, 209, 214,
    220–221, 222
Kennedy, Robert, 220
Kentucky, 32, 58–59, 61–62, 122, 132,
    136
Kilpatrick, James J., 45
King, Martin Luther, Jr., 224–225,
    227–229, 231, 237, 239, 259
King, Mary, 238
Klarman, Michael J., 63–64, 65, 233,
    269, 293, 295
    cause and effect of *Brown,* 54–55
    importance of *Brown,* 203, 277
    minority rights and Supreme Court,
        288–289
Kluger, Richard, 20, 33, 40, 41, 42, 43,
    44, 79–80, 85, 86, 87, 88, 107, 108,
    109, 110, 111, 112, 113, 114, 115,
    117, 119–122, 126, 128–129,
    132–133, 138, 139, 145, 157, 166,
    170, 236, 239, 268, 300, 313, 314
Korematsu v. United States (1944), 114,
    271, 276, 293

Krull, Andrew, 64
Krytocracy, 120, 132, 142
Ku Klux Klan, 38, 210
Kurland, Philip B., 23, 43, 261, 269, 272, 274

Ladies Home Journal, 218
Ladson-Billings, Gloria, 281, 288, 294
Lagemann, Ellen Condliffe, 281, 293, 294
Langston University, 73, 76, 85
Larkin, Mary Curd, 294
Lash, Joseph P., 146
Latinos, 301, 302
Law, and social change, 83–84
Law clerks, 22, 97, 117–149, 244
Law schools, 69
Lawrence v. Texas (2003) 281
Lawson, Steven F., 236
Lawsuits, 36, 37, 70, 303–304. *See also* Litigation
Lawyers, 205, 212–213
Legacies of *Brown,* 297–317
Legal education, 297–298
Legal profession, 212–213, 258–260
Legislation, 8, 97–98, 219–221
Legitimacy
    adding to issues, 204
    of *Brown,* 241–274
    institutional legitimacy, 213
    moral legitimacy, 204
Lemann, Nicholas, 316
Lesher, Stephan, 146
Lessons of *Brown,* 297–317
Letter From Birmingham Jail, 228
Leuchtenburg, William E., 45
Leventhal, Harold, 120
Levin, Henry M., 235, 236
Levine, Peter, 290, 295
Levy, David W., 41
Lewis, David Levering, 237
Lewis, John, 228
Lezin, Katya, 21, 42, 43, 145
Liberation referent, 280–281
Life, 218
Lincoln University, 51, 72
Lindsley v. Natural Carbonid Gas Co. (1911), 110

Litigation, 227, 228, 230–232, 283, 303–304
Little Rock, Arkansas, 190, 197, 201, 209–210, 211, 259, 299–300
Litwack, Leon F., 39
"Living Constitution," 30, 241–242, 245–246, 261, 266
Livingston, J. Edwin, 214
Local courts, 213–215
Local governments, 211
Local school districts, 35
Lochner v. New York (1905), 29, 44
Loewen, James W., 284, 294
Lofgren, Charles A., 39, 48, 64, 109
Logical exactness, 61
Louis, Joe, 83
Louisiana, 2, 35, 37, 210, 225, 253, 300
Louisville, Kentucky, 32, 61–62
Louisville, New Orleans & Texas Railway v. Mississippi (1890), 5
Louisville Courier-Journal, 27
Lowell High (San Francisco), 303
Lucy, Autherine, 298–299
Lynching, 2

Magazine coverage, 218
Mansfield, Texas, 200
Marbury v. Madison (1803), 275, 276
Margold, Nathan, 40
Marri, Anand, 276, 293
Marshall, Burke, 222
Marshall, John, 30, 56, 205
Marshall, Thurgood, 17, 19, 63, 204, 252, 308–309, 313
    enforcement and, 209
    funding request, 231
    Gaines, 9
    as Justice, 279, 280
    McLaurin, 15, 77
    Morgan v. Virginia, 9–10
    Pearson v. Murray, 71
    photos of, 187, 189
    reargument, 24–25
    Reed myth, 135
    Sipuel, 74
    strategy change, 79–80
    Wilson, Paul E., and, 165, 166, 167
Maryland, 32, 70–71, 84, 181, 290, 304

Mason, Alpheus T., 243–244
Mathews, Tom, 234
Mayor & City Council of Baltimore v. Dawson (1955), 64, 270
McAdam, Doug, 234, 239
McCabe v. Atchison, Topeka & Santa Fe Railway (1914), 59–61, 62
McConnell, Michael W., 266, 268, 272, 274
McCuistion, Fred, 69–70, 86
McGill, Ralph, 217
McGovney, D. O., 40–41
McKnight, C. A., 217
McLaurin, George W., 15–16, 18–19, 76–79, 82, 87, 185
McLaurin v. Oklahoma State Regents, 15–16, 17–19, 76–82, 87, 110, 173, 174
McNeill, William, 286
McReynolds, James C., 72
Media coverage, 153, 184, 217–219
Medical schools, 69
Meier, August, 239
Melnick, R. Shep, 317
Memoirs (Warren), 123–124, 140
Meredith, James, 82
Michigan Civil Rights Act, 11
Mickum, George, 117, 121–122, 126, 128, 132–138, 140
Militancy, 84, 312
Military integration, 8
Miller, Arthur M., 262–263, 272
Miller, L. P., 293, 294
Miller, Loren, 40, 236
Milliken v. Bradley (1974), 64
Minton, Sherman, 17, 20–21, 138–139
Miscegenation, 105
Mississippi, 5, 6, 32, 37, 38, 210, 211
Missouri, 32, 50–51, 53, 71–73, 84, 110
Missouri ex rel. Gaines v. Canada (1938). *See* Gaines
"Mr. Justice Reed and *Brown v. Board of Education*" (Fassett), 127–128
Mitchell, Arthur W., 9
Mitchell v. United States (1941), 40
Mixed blood, 95
Monroe Elementary School (Topeka), 152, 155

Montgomery Advertiser, 214
Montgomery bus boycott, 224–225, 227, 228–229
Montgomery County, Maryland, 304
Moore, T. Justin, 24
Mootness, 167–168
Moral legitimacy, 204
Morantz, Alison, 315
Morgan, Irene, 9–10
Morgan v. Virginia (1946), 9–10, 149
Morris, Aldon D., 237, 238, 300–301, 314
Mosbacher, Georgette, 206–207
Mosbacher, Robert, 206–207
Moss, Alfred A., Jr., 272
Most-admired-men poll, 222
Mueller, Addison, 273
Muir v. Louisiana Park Theatrical Assn. (1954), 41, 270
Munn v. Illinois (1877), 4
Murders, 211
Murphy, Frank, 14, 17
Murphy, Walter F., 97, 99, 109, 110, 113, 233
Murray, Donald, 70–71
Muse, Benjamin, 45
Myrdal, Gunnar, 28, 68, 85, 86
Myth of Reed's dissent, 117–149

NAACP (National Association for the Advancement of Colored People), 152–153, 227
    Brandeis brief, 25, 28
    Brown II, 200
    conventions, 227
    funding, 231
    Gaines, 7, 72
    Henderson v. United States, 15
    implementation, 33, 196
    litigation against, in Alabama, 214
    McLaurin, 15–16, 80–81
    Montgomery bus boycott, 225
    Morgan v. Virginia, 10
    Pearson v. Murray, 71
    petitions for desegregation, 35–36
    public relations, 231
    Sipuel, 13–14, 74
    Smith v. Allwright, 9

social science evidence, 25, 28–29,
243, 252
strategy, 7, 9, 17, 19, 80–81
Sweatt, 16–17, 80–81
NAACP Legal Defense and Educational
Fund, Inc., 36, 63, 187, 232, 297
NAACP v. Alabama ex rel. Patterson
(1958), 64
Nabrit, James M., Jr., 187
Naim v. Naim, 64
Namorato, Michael V., 235, 236, 240
National Association for the Advance-
ment of Colored People. *See*
NAACP
National Guard, 199, 200
National School Boards Association, 304
*National Survey of Higher Education of
Negroes,* 69
Navasky, Victor S., 234
Neier, Aryeh, 208, 217, 221, 233, 234,
235, 236
Neuborne, Burt, 275
Neutral principles doctrine, 30–31, 249,
263–265
New Deal, 29, 44
New Deal Justice (Fassett), 136, 138, 142
New Orleans, Louisiana, 2, 300
New Republic, 218
New York state, 8
New York Times, 48, 75, 218, 243
New York Times Magazine, 218
Newby, I. A., 107, 111, 113, 270
Newman, Roger K., 149
Newspaper coverage, 217–218
Newsweek, 218
Nieman, Donald G., 271–272
Nixon, Richard M., 310
Nixon v. Condon (1932), 64
Nixon v. Herndon (1927), 64
NLRB v. Jones & Laughlin Steel Corp.
(1937), 53–54, 57, 65
Nonjudicial factors, 54–55
Norman, Oklahoma, 74
North, Oliver, 207
North Carolina
Brown II, 181
Greensboro sit-in, 226–227, 312
Reconstruction, 2

response to *Brown,* 37
Swann, 303–304
University of North Carolina, 70
North Central Association, 69
Northwestern High School (Maryland),
290
Novak, John, 111, 114

O'Brien, David M., 107, 115
O'Connor, Sandra Day, 276
"Official knowledge," 277
Oklahoma, 73–74
Brown II, 181
*McCabe v. Atchison, Topeka & Santa Fe
Railway,* 59–60
McLaurin, 15–16, 17–19, 76–82, 87,
110, 173, 174
Sipuel, 13–15, 16, 18, 41, 74–76,
84–85, 87, 110, 173
*Oliver Brown et al. v. Board of Education
of Topeka, Shawnee County, et al.*
(1987), 156
101st Airborne Division, 201
Opinion, 25–27, 153, 171–179
defense of, 31–32
drafting, 26, 130, 140
Fourteenth Amendment in, 172–173
Oppenheimer, Martin, 239
Oral arguments. *See* Arguments
Orfield, Gary, 234, 236, 290, 294, 295,
301–302, 309, 315, 316, 317
Out-of-state scholarships, 71–72, 73–74
Owens, Jesse, 83
Oxford University Press, 139

Painter, Theophilus Schickel, 16
Parks, Rosa, 224–225
Patterson, James T., 140, 148, 280, 293,
297–317
Patterson, Orlando, 316
Pearson v. Murray (1936), 71, 86
Peck, Jim, 238, 239
Peller, Gary, 235, 265, 273, 293
Peltason, Jack W., 44, 209, 234, 235
"People's Court, The," 206
Perry, Michael J., 107, 111, 261, 272
Pharmacy schools, 70
Philadelphia, Mississippi, 211

Philipps, Meredith, 308, 315, 316
Phone booths, 73
Plessy v. Ferguson (1896), 15, 20–23, 25–26, 153, 267
  as authority, 59
  Berea and, 58–59
  Court discomfort with, 59–61
  dissent, 5–6, 48
  empirical basis of, 101, 252–254
  equal facilities and, 160
  Fourteenth Amendment and, 5
  graduate education and, 17, 18–19
  Jackson, Robert H., and, 20–22
  origin of "separate but equal" doctrine, 173
  post-*Plessy,* pre-*Brown* period, 47–65
  press coverage, 184
  Reed and, 126
  transposed reputations of *Plessy* and *Brown,* 261–265
Police power, 47, 51, 125
Political agenda, 216, 217, 218
Political decisions, 216
Political forces, 54–55
Political means, and equal rights enforcement, 50–54
Pollack, Jack Harrison, 125, 146
Pollak, Louis H., 44, 255, 269, 270, 271
Posner, Richard A., 262, 272
Post-*Plessy,* pre-*Brown* period, 47–65
Post-secondary education, 67–88
Poverty rate, 306
Powe, Lucas A., Jr., 44, 139, 148
Powell, Adam Clayton, 225
Powell, H. Jefferson, 111
Powell, Lewis F., 310
Prairie View University, 16
Preschool programs, 307–308
Presidential reaction, 215–217, 219, 220–221
President's Committee on Civil Rights, 8
Press coverage, 153, 184, 217–219
Prettyman, E. Barrett, Jr., 97, 108
Primaries, 9, 19–20, 52, 55–56
Prince Edward County, Virginia, 170, 176–177, 191
Pritchett, C. Herman, 11, 40, 113, 216, 235

Private discrimination, 4, 57
Private groups, 210–211
Private schools, 7, 37, 210
Pro-segregation laws, 210
Professional education, 69–70
Progressive movement, 7
Property rights, 12, 53, 57, 61–62
Public accommodations, 3–4
Public carriers, 5–6, 9–12, 15, 211
Public education, 105, 172–174
Public knowledge of court decisions, 205–206
Public opinion, 27–28, 89–90, 205–207, 221–223
Public relations, 231

Rabinowitz, Howard N., 3, 39
Rabkin, Jeremy, 317
Racial classification, 10, 47–48, 51, 61, 94–96, 255, 266–267, 303
Racial instincts, 253–254
Racial zoning, 53
Railroads, 2, 5–6, 9, 15, 47–48, 59–60, 61
Railway Express Agency v. New York (1949), 110
Railway Mail Association v. Corsi (1945), 149
Raines, Howell, 239
Rainey, Homer, 16
Raleigh Standard, 2
Randolph, A. Philip, 7
Raskin, Jamin B., 281, 294
Ravitch, Diane, 316
Ray, Sarah Elizabeth, 11
Reader's Digest, 218
Reader's Guide to Periodical Literature, 218
Reargument, 24–25, 142, 153, 167–169, 172, 175, 194–195, 242–243
Reasonableness standard, 51, 60–61, 253–255
Reconstruction, 2–6, 91, 197
Reconstruction Act of March 1867, 2
Redding, Louis, 187
Reed, Stanley F., 10, 20–21, 114, 117–149
Reeves, Frank D., 187
Rehnquist, William H., 207, 281, 304, 313

Reiser, Bob, 239
Remedy, 26, 27, 32–33
Resegregation, 290, 302–304
Reston, James, 29, 44, 243
Restrictive covenants, 12, 53, 57
Reversal attempts, 101–102
Reynolds, William Bradford, 274
Reynolds v. Sims (1964), 111
Richards, David A. J., 265, 273
Richmond News-Leader, 36
Rights of African Americans, *Brown* contributions to, 203–240
Rioting, 199
Rives, Richard, 35
Roberts, Owen J., 52
Roberts v. City of Boston (1880), 178
Robeson, Paul, 83
Robinson, Jackie, 83
Robinson, Jo Ann Gibson, 237
Robinson, Spottswood W., III, 187, 189
Rodgers, Harrell R., Jr., 234
Rodriguez (1973), 307, 310
Roe v. Wade (1973), 204, 277
Rogers, Richard, 154–155
Roosevelt, Franklin D., 7
Roosevelt, Theodore, 7
Rosen, Paul L., 111, 112, 113, 115, 269, 270
Rosenberg, Gerald N., 45, 283, 294
Rostow, Eugene V., 204, 233
Rotunda, Ronald D., 42, 111, 114
Rowan, Carl T., 135, 148
Ruby Bridges Educational Foundation, 300
Rudko, Frances Howell, 40
Rudwick, Elliott, 239
Rutledge, Wiley, 11, 14, 17

St. Clair, James E., 138, 141–142, 148, 149
St. Louis, Missouri, 32, 53, 110
Salience, 217
San Antonio Independent School District v. Rodriguez (1973), 307, 310
San Francisco, California, 303
Sarratt, Reed, 234, 235, 239
Saturday Evening Post, 218
Saxe, D. W., 294

Schechter v. United States (1935), 44
Scheingold, Stuart A., 240
Schmidt, Benno C., Jr., 39, 63, 65
Scholarly controversy, 241–274
    criticism, 28–29, 242–250
    defenses, 251–255
Scholastic Aptitude Test (SAT), 305–306
School knowledge, 279–280
School Segregation Cases, 63
Schwartz, Bernard, 42, 127, 130–131, 138–139, 146, 147, 148
Schwartz, Murray L., 273
Scientific racism, 102
SCLC (Southern Christian Leadership Conference), 228
Scott, John, 187
Secondary schools, teaching *Brown* in. *See* Teaching *Brown* in secondary schools
Secrecy, 124, 126, 130, 134, 139
Seeger, Pete, 239
Segal, Jeffrey A., 234
Segregation, 90–96
    de facto, 3, 286, 311–312
    de jure, 286, 310, 311, 313
    as discrimination, 6
    economics of, 14–15
    effects on public education, 173–174
    harms of, 247–248
    in housing, 302
    lawsuits, 36, 37, 70, 303–304
    private schools and, 7, 37, 210
    pro-segregation laws, 210
    Reconstruction period, 2–6
    resegregation, 290, 302–304
    unconstitutionality of, 80–82
    versus total exclusion, 3
Sellers, Cleveland, 238, 239
"Separate but equal" doctrine
    in *Brown* opinion, 1, 25–26, 123–124
    costs of, 14–15
    equal facilities, 9, 14, 248–249, 257
    legitimacy of *Brown* and, 247–248
    NAACP strategy and, 9, 19
    origin of, 173
    out-of-state scholarships and, 71
    Plessy and, 5, 153, 173
    post-*Plessy,* pre-*Brown* period, 47–65

Separation of powers doctrine, 197
Separatism, 91
Shager, Erik, 278
Shapiro, Martin, 263, 273
Shaw, Ted, 297–298
Sheatsley, Paul B., 222
Shelley v. Kraemer (1948), 12–13, 39,
    53–54, 57, 64
Simon, James F., 42, 126, 146
Simon, Katherine G., 284, 294
Simple Justice (Kluger), 20, 117–118, 121,
    123, 125–128, 131–132, 136,
    138–140, 142, 157
Simpson, Bryan, 214
Sipuel, Ada Lois, 13–14, 41, 74–76,
    84–85, 86, 87
*Sipuel v. Oklahoma State Board of Regents
    of the University of Oklahoma, et al.*
    (1948), 13–15, 16, 18, 41, 74–76,
    84–85, 87, 110, 173
Sit-ins, 225–227, 228, 259, 299, 312
Slaughter-House Cases (1873), 178
Slavery, 4, 10–11, 256, 306
Smith, Charles, 154
Smith, Linda Brown, 151–156, 159, 188,
    189, 298, 314
Smith v. Allwright (1944), 9, 19, 52, 53,
    55–56, 144
SNCC (Student Non-Violent Coordinat-
    ing Committee), 228
Sniderman, Paul, 314
Sobeloff, Simon, 199
Social change
    by the courts, 204, 231
    law and, 83–84
Social forces, 54–55
Social science evidence
    Brandeis brief, 25, 28–29
    in *Brown* opinion, 174–175
    criticism of *Brown*, 28–29, 153
    doll study, 188, 250, 251
    footnote 11, 28–29, 36, 43, 243–244,
        249–250
    Jackson memorandum and, 100–102
    in *McLaurin* and *Sweatt*, 80
    NAACP and, 25, 28–29, 243, 252

scholarly criticism and, 243–244,
    247–250, 261
scholarly defense and, 251–253
Sorensen, Ted, 119
South Carolina
    Briggs v. Elliott, 176
    Brown, 19, 24, 163
    Jim Crow laws, 6
    response to *Brown*, 33, 37, 178–179,
        298
    response to *Sipuel, McLaurin,* and
        Sweatt, 18
South Carolina State College, 18
Southern Christian Leadership Confer-
    ence (SCLC), 228
Southern Education Reporting Service,
    217
Southern Manifesto, 36, 196, 197–198,
    209, 243
Spaeth, Harold J., 234
Spears, Earnestine Beatrice, 87
Spy Magazine, 206–207
Standardized educational test scores,
    304–311
Stanley, Thomas, 27, 32
State action doctrine, 4–5, 13, 41, 49–54,
    57–58
State Commission Against Discrimina-
    tion, 8
State constitutions, 37
State courts, 214
State education standards, 276–277
State legislatures, 210
Stewart, Potter, 313
Stone, Harlan Fiske, 50, 62
Strauder v. West Virginia (1880), 62, 110,
    178
Strauss, David A., 262, 272
Student Non-Violent Coordinating Com-
    mittee (SNCC), 228
"Substantially equal," 79
Substantive due process, 50, 62
Sullivan, Kathleen M., 64
Summerton, South Carolina, 298
Sumner, William Graham, 253
Sumner Elementary School (Topeka),
    152, 154

Sunstein, Cass R., 264, 273
Super Chief (Schwartz), 127, 140
Supreme Court
    acting in interest of minorities, 204,
        288–289
    adding legitimacy to issues, 204
    "civil-rights era," 49–50
    clerks, 22
    constrained view of, 205
    as fly-paper court, 230–233
    judicial versus legislative function, 58
    political and social change caused by,
        204
    political influence of, 54–55
    public knowledge of decisions,
        205–206
    public's ability to name justices, 206
    ruling only on case before it, 32–33, 81
    teaching about, 288–289
    transformation in doctrine, 48–52
Supreme Court Historical Society,
    127–128, 131–132
Supreme Court Practice (Stern & Gress-
    man), 161
Sutherland, Elizabeth, 239
*Swann v. the Charlotte-Mecklenburg Board
    of Education* (1971), 300, 302,
    303–304
Sweatt, Heman Marion, 16–17, 18, 79,
    81, 297
Sweatt v. Painter et al. (1950), 16–18, 41,
    79–81, 87, 88, 110, 112, 173–174,
    297
Swisher, Carl Brent, 244

Taft, William Howard, 7
Tanenhaus, Joseph, 233
Tate, U. Simpson, 187
Tate, William, 281
Teacher pay, 9
Teaching *Brown* in secondary schools,
    275–295
    harms of iconization, 287–289
    how *Brown* could be taught, 289–291
    as irrelevant, 283
    lack of controversy generally, 284
    as liberation referent, 280–281

perspectives on *Brown,* 280–283
reasons specific to *Brown,* 284–287
as rightful icon, 280
as unfulfilled promise, 281
as well-intentioned error, 282–283
tenBroek, Jacobus, 260, 272
Tennessee, 35, 199
Terry v. Adams (1953), 19–20, 55–56
Test scores, 304–311
Texas
    Brown II, 181, 200
    Dallas desegregation case, 214
    Hopwood v. Texas, 314
    Jaybird primary, 19–20, 55
    Lawrence v. Texas, 281
    Reconstruction, 2
    response to *Brown,* 32, 35–36
    Sweatt, 16–17, 18, 79, 81, 84, 297
    white primary cases, 52, 55
Texas Democratic Party, 55
Texas State University for Negroes, 16
Textbooks, 284
Thernstrom, Stephan and Abigail, 308,
    314, 315, 316
Thirteenth Amendment, 4
Thomas, K., 293
Thompson, Charles H., 69, 86
Thornton, J. Mills, III, 237
Time, 217, 218
Times Index, 218
Timetable for acceptance, 34–35
Title VI (Civil Rights Act of 1964), 215
Title VII (Civil Rights Act of 1964), 57,
    220
"To Secure These Rights," 8
Topeka, Kansas, 152, 154, 155, 298
Topeka [Kansas] Board of Education,
    152, 154–155, 157–170, 176
Tribe, Laurence H., 274
Truman, Harry S., 7–9
Tushnet, Mark V., 21, 40, 41, 42, 43, 86,
    87, 129–130, 142–143, 145, 147,
    149, 271, 273
Tussman, Joseph, 260, 272
Tuttle, Albert, 35, 198
TV Guide, 218
Twohey, Megan, 315, 316, 317

Ulmer, S. Sidney, 106, 108, 110, 115
Unanimity
    in *Brown* opinion, 26
    division on the bench, 20–21, 194
    Jackson memorandum and, 90, 106
    Reed myth and, 118–119, 121,
        123–126, 129, 131–132, 138–142
Underground railroad, 10–11
United States v. Butler (1936), 44
United States v. Carolene Products Co.
    (1939), 50, 64
United States v. Virginia (1996), 275–276,
    293
United States Court of Appeals, 8, 35
Universal News-reels, 218
University of Alabama, 82, 298–299
University of Kentucky, 122, 132, 136
University of Maryland, 70–71, 84
University of Missouri, 50–51, 84
University of North Carolina, 70
University of Oklahoma, 13–18, 73–79,
    81–82, 84–85
University of South Carolina, 18
University of Texas, 16–17, 18, 79, 81,
    84, 297
Unpublished Opinions of the Warren Court
    (Schwartz), 127
Urofsky, Melvin I., 45, 128–129, 147

Value choices, 247–249, 263
Van Alstyne, William, 274
van den Haag, Ernest, 44, 249, 250,
    251–252, 270
Vandiver, Ernest, 35
Vinson, Fred
    death of, 23–24, 167
    Henderson, 17–18
    McLaurin, 17–18, 80–81
    Morgan v. Virginia, 149
    photo of, 190
    Reed myth and, 122, 126, 141–142
    Shelley v. Kraemer, 12
    Sipuel, 14
    Sweatt, 17–18, 80–81
    unanimity and, 20–21, 23–24,
        193–194

Violence, 2, 38, 197, 199–200, 211, 259
Virginia
    Brown, 19, 24, 163, 170, 176–177
    Davis v. County School Bd., 170,
        176–177
    Ex Parte Virginia, 110, 178
    F. S. Royster Guano Co., 110
    Morgan v. Virginia, 9–10, 149
    Reconstruction, 2
    response to *Brown,* 27, 32, 33, 36–37,
        179, 210
    United States v. Virginia, 275–276, 293
    Virginia v. Rives, 110, 178
Virginia (1996), 275–276, 293
Virginia v. Rives (1880), 110, 178
Virginia Military Institute (VMI),
    275–276, 293
Voice of America, 27, 218
Vose, Clement E., 41
Voter registration, 55–56
Votes on *Brown,* 123–124, 129
Voting rights, 55–56, 92, 229, 256
Voting Rights Act of 1965, 56, 221, 232

Waite, Morrison R., 5
Walker, Thomas G., 234
Wallace, George, 82, 299
Walters, David, 85
Walters v. City of St. Louis, 110
Ware, Gilbert, 240
Warren, Charles, 65
Warren, Earl
    "all deliberate speed" as mistake, 282
    appointment, 25, 167
    Brown opinion, 1, 25–27, 48, 82, 153,
        171–179
    Brown II, 34, 181–183
    constitutional interpretation, 29–30
    footnote 11, 28–29
    Fourteenth Amendment, 98, 100
    implementation, 33
    "judge-made law," 313
    reargument, 24
    Reed myth, 117, 120, 122–125, 127,
        134, 139, 145

scholarly criticism of *Brown,* 242–245
unanimity, 25
Washington, Booker T., 7
Washington, D.C., 12, 19, 21, 32, 43,
    92, 195–197
Washington Post Magazine, 135
Washington state, 301
Washington v. Davis (1976), 64
Watters, Pat, 235
Wechsler, Herbert, 107, 235, 269, 273
    Black criticism of, 255–256, 257–259
    as controversial figure, 262–265
    empirical critique of *Brown,* 246–250
    neutral principals theory, 30, 44, 213,
        266, 270
Weinstein, Allen, 236
Weiss, Nancy J., 239
Welles, Gideon, 3
West Virginia, 32, 62, 110, 115, 178
West Virginia State Bd. of Educ. v. Barnette
    (1943), 115
Whalen, Charles and Barbara, 236
"What Really Happened in *Brown v.
    Board of Education*" (Tushnet), 129
White, Byron, 313
White, G. Edward, 43, 126–127, 146
White, Walter, 231
White Citizens Councils, 32, 36, 197,
    200, 210–211
White flight, 302
White groups, 210–211
White primary cases, 52, 55–56
White supremacy, 3, 242, 256, 262
Whites, effects of *Brown* on, 221
Wilkins, Roger, 277, 293
Wilkins, Roy, 209, 228, 234, 236
Wilkinson, J. Harvie, III, 44, 107, 109,
    111, 114, 115, 236, 237, 272
    civil rights opinion, 312

comments on *Brown,* 31, 219, 223,
    261–262, 300
social science evidence, 31, 113
Williams, Juan, 135, 147, 238, 239
Williams, Nat, 27
Williams, Robin M., Jr., 239
Williamson, Mac Q., 14–15
Wilmington, Delaware, 32
Wilson, Paul E., 157–170, 186, 314
Wilson, William J., 316
Wilson, Woodrow, 7
Wisdom, John Minor, 35, 198, 213–214,
    235
"With all deliberate speed," 34, 38,
    56–58, 62, 183, 196–197, 200,
    282 283, 311
Wolff, Miles, 226, 238, 239
Wolters, Raymond, 85
Women's Political Council (WPC),
    224–225
Woodward, C. Vann, 38, 39, 44, 45, 109,
    114, 239, 254, 256, 271
Woolworth's, 226
Worcester v. George (1832), 205
World War II, 7, 73, 83
Wright, Benjamin F., 273
Wright, J. Skelly, 35, 213

Yearbook, Supreme Court Historical
    Society, 127–128, 142
Young, J. Nelson, 111, 114
Youngstown Sheet & Tube v. Sawyer
    (1952), 197
Yudof, Mark G., 235, 261, 272
Yun, John T., 290, 294, 295, 315, 316

Zanden, James W. Vander, 238, 239
Zimmerman, Jonathan, 284, 294
Zinn, Howard, 238, 239